Faith in Bikinis

MW00331672

POLITICS AND CULTURE IN THE TWENTIETH–CENTURY SOUTH

SERIES EDITORS

Bryant Simon, Temple University
Jane Dailey, University of Chicago

ADVISORY BOARD

Lisa Dorr, University of Alabama
Grace Elizabeth Hale, University of Virginia
Randal Jelks, University of Kansas
Kevin Kruse, Princeton University
Robert Norrell, University of Tennessee
Bruce Schulman, Boston University
Marjorie Spruill, University of South Carolina
J. Mills Thornton, University of Michigan
Allen Tullos, Emory University
Brian Ward, University of Manchester

FAITH IN BIKINIS

*Politics and Leisure in the Coastal South
since the Civil War*

ANTHONY J. STANONIS

The University of Georgia Press   *Athens and London*

© 2014 by the University of Georgia Press
Athens, Georgia 30602
www.ugapress.org
All rights reserved
Set in Minion Pro by Graphic Composition, Inc. Bogart, GA.
Printed and bound by Thomson-Shore, Inc.

The paper in this book meets the guidelines for
permanence and durability of the Committee on
Production Guidelines for Book Longevity of the
Council on Library Resources.

Most University of Georgia Press titles are
available from popular e-book vendors.

Printed in the United States of America
18 17 16 15 14 P 5 4 3 2 1

Library of Congress Cataloging-in-Publication Data

Stanonis, Anthony J. (Anthony Joseph)
    Faith in bikinis : politics and leisure in the coastal South since the Civil War / Anthony J. Stanonis.
        pages cm — (Politics and culture in the twentieth-century South)
    Includes bibliographical references and index.
    ISBN 978-0-8203-3384-7 (hardcover : alkaline paper) — ISBN 0-8203-3384-0 (hardcover : alkaline
paper) — ISBN 978-0-8203-4733-2 (paperback : alkaline paper) — ISBN 0-8203-4733-7 (paperback
: alkaline paper) 1. Leisure—Political aspects—Southern States—History. 2. Tourism—Political
aspects—Southern States—History. 3. Seaside resorts—Southern States—History. 4. Seaside
resorts—Atlantic Coast (South Atlantic States)—History. 5. Seaside resorts—Gulf Coast (U.S.)—
History. 6. Social change—Southern States—History. 7. Southern States—Social conditions—
1865–1945. 8. Southern States—Politics and government—1865–1950. 9. Southern States—Race
relations. 10. Southern States—Economic conditions. I. Title.
    GV54.A13S73 2014
    306.4'8120975—dc23   2014011858

British Library Cataloging-in-Publication Data available

TO BENEDICT ANTHONY STANONIS (1933–2008)

FOR BEACH VACATIONS PAST

AND

TO OTTORINO BENEDICT MORRIS STANONIS (2009–)

FOR BEACH VACATIONS TO COME

CONTENTS

ACKNOWLEDGMENTS

If the pages that follow have any sand in them, it's because of my father. He joined the Air Force ROTC program at the University of Kentucky back in the 1940s. After he graduated, he served as an officer for more than twenty years. He went to places such as Labrador, Venice, Wiesbaden. His orders took him to Léopoldville in 1960 as the Belgian Congo moved toward independence. In 1967–1968, he witnessed the carnage of the Tet Offensive while stationed in Saigon.

During his long career, he also found himself on many southern beaches. He spent a year at Keesler Air Force Base in Biloxi in 1965 and another year at Eglin Air Force Base in Fort Walton before being shipped off to Vietnam. In 1972 he was in Miami setting up communication systems for the Democratic National Convention. Soon after, he retired. He settled in New Orleans with my mother, a German whose family owned the moving company that handled my father's belongings while stationed in Wiesbaden. If a mover had not forgotten to get my father's signature on a form, I wouldn't be here.

My father loved to tell stories. And I loved to listen to them. He talked about the tawdry nightlife along the Mississippi Gulf Coast in the 1960s. Strip clubs and bars were filled with illegal whiskey and slot machines. He spoke of the ravages of Hurricane Betsy, which turned at the last second to land a direct hit on New Orleans. Harrison County's coastal boulevard disappeared under sand. Poisonous snakes washed in from the swamps, making any trek outdoors dangerous. He told of the massive military exercises along the Florida Panhandle as servicemen prepared for their tour in Vietnam. He joked about sneaking off to Hialeah Park to bet on horses instead of going to supervise the personnel setting up the antennas in Miami. As I grew up in the 1970s, 1980s, and 1990s, we regularly made daytrips to Gulfport and Biloxi. Every year before the start of school, we would plan a family vacation to the Florida Panhandle—the early years at Fort Walton Beach, the middle years at Destin, then onward toward Panama City in the later years. My dad liked to escape the rising condos for the less developed parts of the Emerald Coast. So we continuously drifted like flotsam eastward until there was no more underdeveloped coast.

I miss those days.

The travails of the academic job market made this book an anchor as I journeyed from one university to the next after Vanderbilt University graduated me in 2003.

I'd like to thank my friends at Loyola University New Orleans, where I attended as an undergraduate. They hired me as a part-timer, giving me a means of keeping my head above water. On afternoons after I finished teaching, I'd wander into the library to flip through hard copies of *Life* and other magazines to begin my research for this book. I cannot say enough about the faith Mark Fernandez, David Moore, Bernard Cook, and the rest of the faculty have maintained in me from the first days I stepped on campus.

I am especially grateful to Tad Brown of the Watson-Brown Foundation for funding a postdoctoral fellowship at the Institute for Southern Studies at the University of South Carolina. In 2004–2005, Walter Edgar, Tom Brown, and Bob Ellis graciously hosted me as a fellow. I would also like to thank Aaron Marrs, Adam Hark, Adam Piper, Adrienne Murray, and Lee Crawford for telling me about Myrtle Beach and life in the Palmetto State.

My next stop, from 2005 to 2007, was at Texas A & M University. I thank Walter Buenger, Joseph Dawson, Harold Livesay, Carlos Blanton, and the rest of the faculty for shepherding me through Aggie traditions. My teaching assistants Tara Scamardo and Ervin James III were lifesavers. My fellow visiting assistant professors Chuck Grear and Gerald Betty convinced me to buy real cowboy boots. I'm still awed by Krissy Vogel's menagerie of glass and plastic squirrels in all colors and forms. And I have no idea how I would have survived without Eleanor Dahlin's Thai curry. My students also kept me on my toes and taught me what it means to be an Aggie: Meredith Paddon, Crystal Vinal, Becca Stahlman, Terry Dike, Jason Fite, and Sarah Fite. To all of you and the many more who made life in College Station worth whooping about, "gig 'em!"

Since 2007 my academic home has been Queen's University Belfast. I thank my fellow American historians Brian Kelly and Catherine Clinton for bringing me into the program. I also thank Marie Coleman, James Davis, Elaine Farrell, Peter Gray, David Hayton, Andrew Holmes, Keith Jeffrey, Danny Kowalsky, and everyone else on the faculty. I also thank the numerous postgrads who have made teaching American history abroad fun: Fran Abbs, Aurelia Aubert, Victoria Black, Lewis Eliot, Caroline Fenning, Ronan Hart, Matt Haynes, Blake

Hill, Stephanie Jordan, Laura Kilpatrick, Conleth Mullan, Patrick Pollock, Conor Salters, Ashleigh Simpson, Emma Swan, Rachel Wallace, James Wilkey, and many others who have participated in the program. I thank the PhD students who kept me focused on this project by sharing the enthusiasm for their own work: Daniel Brown, Jen Davison, Aoife Laughlin, and Conall MacMichael. I thank my undergraduate students for listening to my tales of southern tourism, including Catherine McCaffrey, James McAlister, Joe McKee, Andrew Carruthers, and many others. Lastly, I thank John Nathan for occasionally cleaning my office—it was his job after all—despite his commitment to conducting guerrilla warfare against capitalist exploitation.

I'd like to thank all the organizations that helped fund my research. The Virginia Historical Society provided a Mellon Research Fellowship. I thank particularly Nelson Lankford, Paul Levengood, and the staff for making me feel at home in Richmond and a part of the Society. The Forest History Society awarded an Alfred D. Bell Fellowship. I am grateful to Steven Anderson, Cheryl Oakes, and other staff for the warm welcome to Durham. A Fellowship for the Study of the Global South from Tulane University funded essential research trips to archives across the Gulf Coast.

I'd like to thank the many colleagues and friends who provided insight and feedback about this study, whether by reading drafts, discussing papers at conferences, or sharing tales of beach vacations. Many thanks to Aaron Astor, Bruce Baker, Julia Brock, Fitz Brundage, Karen Cox, Mike Crane, Tycho DeBoer, Don Doyle, Glenn Eskew, John Giggie, Georgina Hickey, Randy Hourigan, Patrick Huber, Alison Isenberg, Harvey Jackson III, Andrew Kahrl, Nicole King, Rob Lawson, Andrew McMichael, Marko Maunula, Ted Ownby, John Shelton Reed, LeeAnn Reynolds, Blain Roberts, Chanelle Rose, Marjorie Spruill, Barbara Stokes, Lynnell Thomas, Frank Towers, John Quist, and the dozens of other friends within the profession. Also, thanks to the anonymous reviewers and everyone at the University of Georgia Press, past and present, who towed this manuscript into safe harbor. Any leaks are my own fault.

Lastly, I thank my son Otto, for keeping me focused on the things that are important.

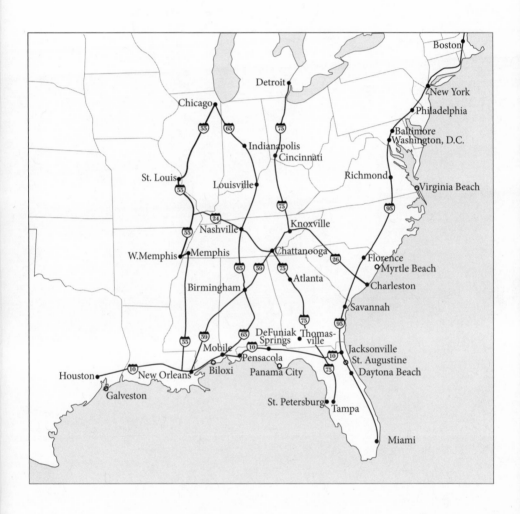

Faith in Bikinis

Introduction
Heading South

When the war of rebellion ended he was yet a young man. He had been a soldier in the Northern army. War and wounds had told somewhat on his chances of life. A milder clime was commended to him. He hailed the dawn of peace and the opening to quiet occupancy of the region over which war had swept as a godsend.
—Albion Tourgée, *An Appeal to Caesar* (1884)

For southerners such as Edgar Allan Poe, the seashore was a mysterious place. The sandy soil too poor to farm sheltered lore of ghosts, pirates, and buried riches. Sullivan's Island outside of Charleston, South Carolina, was ideal for one of Poe's early experiments with tales of ratiocination, or detective fiction. Three miles long and a quarter mile wide, the oceanfront island was "separated from the main land by a scarcely perceptible creek, oozing its way through a wilderness of reeds and slime." The "vegetation, as might be supposed, is scant, or at least dwarfish." On the western end of the island near Fort Moultrie stood "some miserable frame buildings, tenanted, during summer, by the fugitives from Charleston dust and fever." In this setting, Poe described William Legrand and his slave Jupiter, who hunt for the buried treasure of the pirate Captain Kidd. Published in 1843, "The Gold-Bug" brought Poe acclaim. He recognized the ominousness of the seashore and the potential treasure hidden in its sands.[1]

Even as the nineteenth century waned, the southern coast offered little to interest visitors. Writers depicted overgrown swamps along the shore. The gothic imagery suggested the collapse of a flawed southern civilization once based on slavery and still marginalized within the industrializing United States. Even towns looked far from appealing. John Edwards ventured to Florida from Liverpool in pursuit of wild game in December 1889. As his train from Washington,

D.C., passed southward, he noted that the "climate in many parts—from the great heat & numerous swamps, is very bad & only fit for blacks to work in." He eventually reached his destination. Edwards was not impressed: "The streets of 'Pensacola' are ankle deep in sand—not one is paved, so that on a windy day one's clothes are covered, & eyes, ears & mouth filled with it. The drainage is all surface & the stench in places arising from the heat of the sun reminds me of my visit to Tangiers." American towns remained burdened by filth and stench until Progressive Era reformers and City Beautiful movement promoters introduced more efficient sewer, lighting, sanitation, and park systems, among other improvements, in the early twentieth century.[2]

The development of Florida and the rise of local-color literature in the late nineteenth century spurred a revolution in American travel patterns and concepts of leisure. Railroad magnates Henry Plant and Henry Flagler turned the Sunshine State into a haven for the wealthy. Flagler's Ponce de Leon Hotel captivated travelers after it opened in 1888. "Jacksonville and St. Augustine are in winter what Saratoga, Newport, and Long Beach are in summer: the *rendezvous* of all who have any pretensions to a place in the fashionable world," declared a visitor from France a year after the grand opening. In 1904 J. E. Rawlings pursued a career in Florida after graduating in medicine from the University of Maryland. A brief stay in Daytona Beach allowed Rawlings to rub elbows with some of the richest Americans. He started 1905 with a letter to his girlfriend: "Tourists are arriving in great numbers and the next 10 wks. will be very busy around. Autos. and fine teams are very much in evidence and yours truly has several Millionaire speaking acquaintances." Local-color writers romanticized coastal areas from Texas to Virginia. The readership, largely residing in the urban North, was stirred with longings to visit Galveston, Biloxi, Saint Augustine, and other locales where traces of colonial architecture and lush scenery beckoned. Readers imagined escapes to warmer climes in a region seemingly more tranquil and closer to nature. In many instances, the stories turned readers into tourists as they sought to walk in the footsteps of their favorite authors or characters.[3]

Where the rich went, others followed. "Just think what advantages people with money enough to always be in pleasant climate have," pondered Rawlings, "North in summer South in winter." But more and more Americans gained the time and wealth for leisure travel. British commentator James Muirhead expressed awe at the sheer volume of leisure travel by all Americans at the start of the twentieth century: "The enormous extent of the summer exodus to the mountains and the seas in America is overwhelming; and a population of sixty-five million does not seem a bit too much to account for it." He noted the "oceans of summer and winter visitors" venturing to California, Florida, and other havens scattered across the United States. Some retiring Union veterans of the Civil War viewed the warm climate of the former Confederacy ideal for their golden years. So many moved to Saint Cloud, Florida, that the community gained the nickname "G.A.R. town," one of the few southern communities with a chapter of the Grand Army of the Republic. The pensions received for their military service—considerably larger allotments than what southern states could provide Confederate veterans—aided their decision. Although the working class of urban America rarely escaped beyond day trips to Coney Island, Atlantic City, or other nearby destinations, by 1900, the coming decades provided the resources and technology to facilitate even their participation in leisure travel. Furthermore, urban boosters, corporate executives, and government officials increasingly encouraged vacationing.[4]

The healthful benefits of the coast remained a common selling point. During the antebellum period, invalids from the North often trekked southward, mainly to the area around Jacksonville, Florida, for sea breezes and salubrious climes during the winter. White southern elites frequently escaped to Louisiana's barrier islands, the Mississippi Gulf Coast, North Carolina's Outer Banks, or the Virginia shore, creating summer enclaves only the very wealthy could afford. Lodging for tourists eclipsed sanitariums for the ailing by the twentieth century, but healthful nature remained a selling point. For instance, boosters along Pensacola Beach, Florida, and nearby Santa Rosa Island beckoned hay fever sufferers in 1954 with a "Sneeze Map of the U.S.A." The coast of the Florida Panhandle "afforded complete relief."[5]

Reaching the southern coast was daunting, even into the 1960s. Roads were poor, and poverty was rampant. Across the inland South, where family ties were strong and fears of labor or racial unrest simmered, suspicion often fell on strangers. In Kingston, North Carolina, a Boston family driving to Florida in 1924 met an unwelcoming town. The family "hoped to buy supplies but were met at the curb by a man who informed us that there was a ten minutes parking law." The Bostonians recorded, "We remarked that there was no sign to that effect but he said of course townspeople could park longer but if strangers did they were fined and he seemed quite pleased over it." The predominantly rural South also lacked an infrastructure capable of meeting the needs of motorists. Anna Kelly, driving with her husband and son in 1927, noticed a sharp distinction on their trip southward from Massachusetts: "Evidently people south of N.J. are not keen about accommodating tourists as in N.E. & N.Y. State & places where one can camp are simply not to be found about here. The darkies might let you camp in their door yards but it would not be appropriate to say the least." Only the rise of chain restaurants, motels, and gas stations after the Second World War eased motorists' minds. Worse, fear of racist whites suspicious of outsiders discouraged vacationers, especially as violence erupted against civil rights activists in the postwar era. Richard Schweid, a white Tennessean who grew up during the 1960s, planned trips to the Gulf Coast so that the journey through the Deep South, rife with racial violence, could be completed before sunset: "Don't let the sun set on you in Mississippi if you're in a car with out-of-state plates, is what I used to think."[6]

Travelers regularly noted the peculiar racial customs of the South. A white Pennsylvanian passing through Virginia in 1902 expressed aggravation at being removed from the smoking car because it was for "colored people." At the next stop, he recorded, "While standing in the Southern R.R. depot at Charlotte N.C. noticed a great many niggers and among them were some wenches a couple of young wenches were talking about a nigger getting arrested and one remarked that 'you got arrested now days if you only looked crooked.'" Edith Miller, a Massachusettsian, headed by train to Florida in March 1913. At Richmond, Virginia, Miller encountered racial segregation: "What struck me, particularly, was the fact, that although there were so many negroes, we never seemed to come in contact with them. The railroad stations, instead of being labelled 'Men' and 'Women,' as in the North, were labelled 'White' and 'Colored,' and even in the trains, the negroes had to travel in cars by themselves."[7]

Certainly the Jim Crow South, where laws into the mid-1960s reinforced racial customs, was not exceptional on matters of race, as recent studies of segregation outside the South by Matt Lassiter and Victoria Wolcott have demonstrated. De facto segregation, what Lassiter defines as the legal doctrine by which "spatial landscapes and racial arrangements exist beyond the scope of judicial remedy, attributable solely to private market forces in the absence of any historical or contemporary government responsibility," ensured that the color line divided whites from persons of color throughout the United States, a condition that persists in many respects despite the civil rights triumphs of the 1960s. In the Jim Crow South, however, the prominent black presence and the signs separating white from colored confronted white northerners with a seemingly exotic landscape that reinforced the mythology of southern exceptionalism on race.[8]

Tourists remarked on the racial topography of the Jim Crow South. Jeanelle Landstrom and her family from Tuscola, Illinois, drove to Florida in 1931. The Deep South proved an unsettling experience. Of Arkansas, Landstrom wrote that in one town she "only saw 8 white men and hundreds of niggers." Mississippi was equally strange. She recorded, "Plenty of niggers—we got lunch at Hernando walked two blocks before we saw a white man to ask where we could get lunch. he directed us to a little hole in the wall—hold about a dozen people, but they were white. this sure is a dark town." Indeed, the presence of so many blacks defined a trip to Dixie. Maude Lierch of Kansas City, Missouri, toured the Gulf Coast in 1945. She expressed frustration when African Americans—a female cotton picker in Georgia and a female sugarcane worker in Texas—hid rather than have their photographs taken.[9]

Tourists also noted the extreme poverty of the region—a poverty that crossed racial lines. Pearl Noegel, driving through Arkansas on her way home to Florida in 1921, recorded an encounter in Forest City: "There met a rounder who advised us to stay out of the South if we work for a living." New Jersey tourists driving through coastal Georgia on their way to Florida on Independence Day 1938 remarked upon "some terrible sights with the black and white shacks." Their travel diary recorded, "Sleep on floors 10 or 15 in one room, no windows or doors, almost falling down, no sanitary conditions but with every 6 houses they have a church or a shack called a church." Few wore shoes. The state of white southerners was particularly shocking: "They call them white trash, well I guess that is the right name because they live like the negros [sic] or worse. You can see the dirt on the white but not the black." Driving to Florida in May 1956, Hazel Timms of Mohall, North Dakota, observed the poverty of African American farmworkers in South Carolina and Georgia. She penned, "Seeing more negroes. many small farm shacks—no screens (some had no glass) no paint." Nearer to Florida, Timms wrote, "Highway lined with trees—rather swampy territory. Negro road gangs, evidently from prison as there were armed guards. They were cutting weeds in ditches with hand scythes." A New Yorker likewise noted the chain gangs as she passed through North Carolina in the 1950s: "Up to now we have seen only one road gang. It was just a bunch of young kids, but the guns held by the guards give you the feeling that they're not fooling." On entering Wilson, North Carolina, the same chronicler was "amazed to realize how black 'black' can be."[10]

After emancipation, freedmen who accumulated enough wealth frequently pursued landownership as a means of fostering their independence. Coastal property, typically hardscrabble land, provided an affordable refuge in the late nineteenth and early twentieth centuries, with Princess Anne County in Virginia demonstrating some of the highest rates of black landownership in the country. Numerous entrepreneurial black landowners converted portions of their beachfront into resorts for fellow African Americans denied equal accommodation within the white supremacist nation, especially after the First World War. The development of white resorts, however, confronted black landowners with rising tax rates, unscrupulous lawyers, con artists, and hostile local governments seeking to profit from the increasingly valuable beachfront. Black landowners thus faced efforts to pry them off coastal property beginning in the mid-twentieth century, a process that is still occurring. As Andrew Kahrl, in his study of African American landownership along the southern coast, explains, "Steadily pushing blacks back from the sea became fundamental to the region's growing reputation as a fashionable vacation destination."[11]

Whereas the relationship between African American leisure and civil rights activism has recently gained attention, scholarship about the white beachfront communities that undermined black landownership remains sparse. Most studies of southern tourism concentrate on natural springs, mountain retreats, or urban centers. A growing number of historical studies since the late 1990s argue that southern coastal communities contrasted sharply from the inland South in their religious, economic, and ethnic diversity. Yet the impact of these coastal counties on the politics, finances, and culture of southern states has yet to be fully appreciated. This study is a foray into exploring coastal areas' broader influence on the American South. Though books exist on Galveston and Myrtle Beach, cities such as Gulfport, Biloxi, Panama City, and Virginia Beach have yet to receive extensive examination of their histories. Most work on southern beaches focuses on Florida. Many scholars make the distinction that Florida, at least from Orlando southward, is not the South. As sociological studies have shown, residents of South Florida less frequently identify with "Dixie" or "Southern" culture. However, the Sunshine State, particularly South Florida, spurred travel through Dixie and inspired boosters along the southern shore to mimic their Florida-based competitors. The prosperity of Florida tourism set the standard by which promoters elsewhere constructed vacation meccas.[12]

This study nuances scholars' treatment of the New South. The rhetoric of Henry Grady, editor of the *Atlanta Constitution* in the late nineteenth century and booster of an industrial New South, has long focused attention on enterprises such as steel and textile mills. Consequently, economic analysis of the region has largely overlooked the importance of tourism within Dixie after the Civil War. Calvin Hoover and R. U. Ratchford only mentioned tourism once—that in relation to Florida—in their 1951 classic *Economic Resources and Policies of the South*. Their study (which surpassed four hundred pages) upheld the view that agriculture and manufacturing stood as the "primal base upon which incomes earned in the supplementary 'industries'" depended. C. Vann Woodward's *Origins of the New South, 1877–1913*, also published in 1951, influenced generations of historians to concentrate on timber, railroad, mining, or textile industries, with a focus on labor rather than leisure. In Ed Ayers's influential *The Promise of the New South* from 1992, for instance, the discussion of South Carolinian John T. Woodside, whom Ayers uses as the embodiment of "how the South created an indigenous business class," never veers from the discussion of Woodside's rise as a textile magnate despite his prominent role in crafting Myrtle Beach. Clearly interest in tourism marched arm in arm with other New South pursuits as industrialists, such as Woodside and others to be discussed shortly, diversified their holdings by investing in coastal havens. Tourism may have been in its infancy in the late nineteenth and early twentieth centuries, but the potential profits from the vacation trade were very much on the minds of industrialists.[13]

Furthermore, this study seeks to refine understanding of the Sunbelt. The term is often linked to political analyst Kevin Phillips's *The Emerging Republican Majority* from 1969. Phillips used the term to describe a growing bloc of conservative white voters who occupied the southern third of the United States stretching from California to Virginia. Within this geographical band, military installations and the energy industry proliferated. Retirees and tourists flocked to the warmer climate. The hostility of state legislatures to labor unions encouraged factory owners from the Rust Belt, stretching from the Midwest to the Northeast, to relocate. A probusiness, antilabor, religiously conservative, small-government ethos predominated among white residents. De facto segregationist policies and economic inequality persisted through white suburbanization and hostility to welfare rights. Scholarship on the Sunbelt, with a focus largely on suburbanization or the changes affecting labor, often suggests but never fully examines how tourism was a quintessential Sunbelt industry that influenced state politics, economics, and public perceptions.

Furthermore, studies generally consider the Sunbelt a post-1945 phenomenon. Urban historian David Goldfield cites the term as "journalistic shorthand for metropolitan prosperity below the thirty-seventh parallel—the demarcation of the 'Sunshine Belt' in an early 1940s Army/Air Force report." He elaborates, "Sunbelt cities have grown up with the automobile, during a time when planners and politicians expressed revulsion to density and congestion, and a strong attraction to numerous federal incentives to build outward and build new." For Goldfield, 1965 stands as the "watershed year in the Sunbelt's emergence as a phenomenon." Yet shrewd urban developers, as the history of Los Angeles reveals, understood since the dawn of the twentieth century the real-estate profits to be gained by fostering a low-density urban environment. And the impact of the automobile was immediate as suburbs and parking lots, the latter often sparking historic preservation movements, altered urban spaces after 1920. Elizabeth Tandy Shermer has recently argued in her study of Phoenix, Arizona, that the business and political elite of this Sunbelt city forged their philosophy of hypergrowth and probusiness politics while undertaking municipal reforms during the interwar period. Similarly, white southerners' commitment to growth and free-market capitalism were imbedded in New South boosterism, though obviously mitigated by self-interested protectionism for agricultural goods such as sugar and continued control of African American laborers. Like the revisions undertaken over the last decade in regard to the "long" civil rights movement, the Sunbelt—both as a term and as an emerging region—dates to well before the Second World War as the tourism industry and urban growth fostered by California and Florida boosters inspired copycat efforts from Santa Fe to San Antonio and Galveston to Virginia Beach.[14]

Though studies of tourism have largely focused on the post-1945 boom when a matured tourist industry rivaled the value of the agricultural and industrial sectors of southern states, tourism had already long captivated southern businessmen. The era of modern mass tourism—what I define as a "tourist trade inclusive of the middle- and lower-class members of both sexes"—dates to the First World War as a growing number of Americans seized the freedom afforded by the automobile. Urban boosters in New Orleans and elsewhere obsessed about crafting tourist havens. A competitive market for vacationers quickly emerged in the interwar period, shifting focus from the wealthy tourists that dominated the industry before the First World War.[15]

Southern communities tied to tourism often promoted very different images from places dependent on agriculture, industry, or Lost Cause yarns. Many beach resorts in the region were born after the Civil War and thereby lacked the revered plantations or Confederate history popularized in Charleston or Natchez. Some residents along the Gulf Coast, moreover, traced their lineage back to colonial settlement under the French or Spanish. Others descended from a mix of ethnic groups drawn to the fishing trade. Southern beach resorts—even those restricted to whites—embodied a coastal culture distinct from inland communities and often more malleable in regard to race.

The beach is a liminal space. The towns dependent on beaches for their livelihoods are castles literally built on sand. The land erodes, rebuilds, and shifts according to the winds and waves. Beaches retreat and barrier islands migrate as each absorbs the wave action. "The nature of sand is to move," explain marine geologists Wallace Kaufman and Orrin Pilkey. They elaborate, "Beach erosion, geologically speaking, is not usually a permanent loss, but a strategic retreat. As any war-game player knows, fewer troops are lost in strategic retreat than in unending battle." Nevertheless, coastal residents have tended to ignore natural patterns by entrenching along the shoreline only to witness breaches of the obstacles meant to hold the sand in place and repel the relentless seas. Even determining something as simple as the divide between land and sea proves no easy task. Geographer Mark Monmonier shows that land drift, storm surges, and tides make the process a constant—losing—battle for mastery. Mapping the coastline is thus a complex process of determining high-water lines, low-water lines, flood lines, and, with the growing risk of climate change, inundation lines. For settlements along the shore, the constant struggle with the sea is one of life or death.[16]

Beach Towns

The book draws heavily from events in Virginia Beach, Myrtle Beach, Panama City, Biloxi-Gulfport, and Galveston. These five communities expose attitudes toward tourism in a range of southern states while also offering comparisons across time and space. Boosters in coastal resorts shared strong historical, economic, social, ecological, and cultural interests that oftentimes set them apart from fellow southerners merely a few miles inland, where agriculture dominated community life. Furthermore, as emerging urban centers, these resorts serve, to quote historian Frank Freidel, as "the dynamisms for the spread of culture and capital."[17]

To capture the story of these resorts, this study depends heavily on local newspapers. A meticulous reading of newspapers was essential given the scarcity of scholarship about these communities. In most cases, resort towns sustained only one newspaper, a publication that typically served as the voice of local businessmen—a soapbox for the chamber of commerce. These organizations have long maintained, in the words of historian N. D. B. Connolly, a "general culture of corporate secrecy," making access to chamber of commerce minutes difficult. Nevertheless, the local newspaper offers a window into the thinking of the business elite. Although these accounts often depict a rosy image of their town, newspapers also identified blighted areas and problems that hindered tourism. Editors generally insisted on accuracy of information and achievable urban improvements. Urban historian Carl Abbott explains that booster rhetoric reflected businessmen's need for "realistic and often precise knowledge about the economic bases" of their communities. Moreover, newspapers in other resorts maintained a close eye on their competition, giving insight into flaws in rival communities. Myrtle Beach and Virginia Beach claimed a particularly sharp rivalry as they competed for the same pool of tourists, northerners headed to Florida and Canadians seeking warm Atlantic waters. To provide greater balance, oral histories are consulted. Chamber of commerce records from Galveston, state investigative reports from Florida, journalistic exposés in national publications such as *Life*, as well as diaries and letters from archival collections provide greater depth and interrogate the accounts found in the press. Finally, I have personally gathered a collection of more than forty travel diaries and scrapbooks from vacationers dating from the late nineteenth century into the late twentieth century. These accounts supply an often difficult-to-obtain glimpse of how travelers themselves perceived resorts, exposing how the tourism industry described in newspaper accounts did not always reflect vacationers' experiences.[18]

Many southern beach towns first gained prominence after the Civil War as railroad and timber interests cut their way through virgin longleaf pine forests. Although historians have closely examined these industries, they have neglected tourism despite its importance in supplementing the profits of lumber and railway companies. Tourism was a New South industry. The successful efforts of Henry Flagler to lay tracks down Florida's rugged Atlantic Coast and of Henry Plant to bring a link to Tampa inspired copycat efforts across the South. The Spanish-American War, during which Tampa served as a staging area for troops destined to Cuba and Puerto Rico, further bolstered Florida's fame and fortune. Railway mileage in the Sunshine State increased from a mere 408 miles in 1880 to 3,878 miles in 1907; Flagler controlled more than 16 percent of the state's railroad tracks, particularly trunk lines. Writing in the early twentieth century, James Ingraham, one of Flagler's lieutenants, remarked that Flagler's example had a "tremendous influence in development all over the State and indeed on much of the southern States." He elaborated, "The Pullman Car lines from west and north that were originally established for the benefit of his hotel guests, have been made permanent all year around lines, thus giving a strong impetus to travel to 'way places' that could not alone have secured such business facilities." The luxurious cars allowed rich Yankees to travel in comfort.[19]

The early twentieth century brought ever more American vacationers to southern shores, a trend explored in the first two chapters of this study. Even the Florida Panhandle, far from major resorts, witnessed a dramatic shift in population. One local observer in Walton County commented in August 1913 that within the "last decade or so there has been a strong influx of people from the northern states." Tourists were converting southern towns into more cosmopolitan places. In 1925 the *Atlanta Constitution* reported the impact across Dixie: "Due especially to the remarkable growth of the tourist traffic to the extreme south, which last winter was so heavy as to completely overwhelm most of the tourist centers and tax every available guest room to capacity, an extensive building program is especially noticeable along the South Atlantic and Gulf coasts."[20]

Galveston, devastated by the hurricane of 1900, gained national publicity for municipal efforts to restore the city and protect it from future storms. The railroad first linked the port to the mainland in 1860. The twentieth century brought the first significant boom in Galveston tourism, peaking during the summers. With the newly completed seawall standing as a modern marvel, boosters in 1906 opened "Electric Park" with a pavilion illuminated by a thousand electric lights. The Seawall Amusement Company offered a Ferris wheel, carousel, and photograph gallery. The majestic 250-room Galvez Hotel, built by Isaac Kempner at a cost of $750,000, opened in 1911. Eager to augment the surge in guests, Galvestonians launched the Cotton Carnival in 1909, which drew more than sixty thousand visitors for the annual two-week affair before the First World War. In 1916, to highlight the start of the summer tourist season, they organized Splash Day, a festival that remained on the calendar until 1965. Boosters heralded the city as the playground of the Southwest. By 1930 some million bathers flocked to the island during the summer.[21]

Along the Gulf Coast, railroads elbowed for position in capturing trade passing through the Panama Canal. After French engineers failed in the 1880s,

Americans fixated on acquiring the isthmus. The gunboat diplomacy of President Theodore Roosevelt brought the project under U.S. control in 1904; the canal was completed in 1914. Well before American takeover of the project, railroad firms laid track to the Gulf shore in anticipation. These businessmen revealed a stunning vista. A Pennsylvanian aboard a train passing from Florida to New Orleans in 1902 remarked how the ride "was a most beautiful one. through large swamps over large Rivers, bays etc. once the train was so far out on a bay that I couldn't see land. Once I saw a large body of water and couldnt see the other side and it appeared as if the tracks had been laid to the ocean and that the train would plunge in."[22]

Mississippians since the mid-1800s had contemplated a port that would allow cotton, timber, and other resources to bypass New Orleans and thereby keep business within the state. The Panama project convinced investors and allied politicians to fund a shipping channel with railroad connections. William Harris Hardy had already assisted the New Orleans and Northeastern Railroad in connecting Meridian, Mississippi, to the Crescent City. He established Hattiesburg and oversaw the construction of a twenty-one-mile bridge across Lake Pontchartrain—the longest railroad bridge in the world when completed in 1883. As president of the Gulf and Ship Island Railroad, Hardy bought five thousand acres along Mississippi Sound. The centerpiece of this holding was to be Gulfport. The name suggested a grand vision of the municipality as the main American port along the Gulf. Here, the railroad, stretching to Jackson and cutting through vast tracts of virgin longleaf pine forests, would connect to a shipping channel to be dredged a dozen miles to deep Gulf water.[23]

Outlined in 1884, Hardy's blueprint for a port along Mississippi's coast floundered until 1890 when he convinced lenders to fund the first twenty miles of track, thus preventing the forfeiture of the company's 63,000-acre land grant. Unable to meet its expenses, the railroad fell into the hands of oilman Captain J. T. Jones of New York who moved to the coast to complete Hardy's grand vision. When the federal government refused to dredge the channel from Gulfport to Ship Island, Jones spent more than $2 million of his own money to finish the project. Gulfport, established in 1898, opened its docks in 1902. Over the next five years, a billion feet of lumber passed through the port. Cooper Darby, a native of the area, recalled, "You see, back in those days there was a sawmill about every mile on the G&SI Railroad." To complete his town, Jones funded banks and an electricity plant. The "pride and delight of Captain Jones's heart," according to a 1905 sketch in the *American Lumberman*, was the

250-room "great Southern hotel." The government agreed to maintain the vital channel in 1906. Gulfport boosters celebrated the massive cargoes of timber passing through the docks, yet they still saw cotton from the Delta travel down the Mississippi River while railroads siphoned other freight to northeastern ports. The railroad, however, would prove a boon to tourism and real estate.[24]

Entrepreneurs along the Florida Panhandle also prepared to capture trade from the Panama Canal. The town of Florapolis floundered after being established in 1882. Real-estate developers renamed the town Park Resort and, later, Harrison. Prosperity still eluded them despite erecting a hotel, a store, and a short-lived college to lure investors. Then, in 1905, Chicago railroad executive George West, who had owned a vacation home in the area since 1887, established the Gulf Coast Development Company to hawk real estate. He also founded the community's first bank and a telephone company. The town soon received a new name—Panama City—to reflect its proximity to the canal in Central America. West also started the weekly *Panama City Pilot* to publicize the port and resort, as well as his belief in "old time religion." A railroad arrived in 1908. By the 1920s, more than twelve thousand residents occupied the town.[25]

Panama City's driving forces came via two other businessmen. A Spanish-American War veteran from Georgia named Walter Colquitt Sherman arrived in 1913. He soon built a timber, shipbuilding, and railroad empire that stretched throughout Florida. He completed the Dixie Sherman Hotel, Panama City's first skyscraper, in 1926. Sherman also played a significant role in attracting a paper mill operated by the International Paper Company. His extensive land-holdings and involvement in the hotel industry made tourism an increasingly important aspect of Sherman's business by the time he died in 1967. The press facilitated Sherman's efforts. Population growth in and around Panama City led to the establishment of the first daily newspaper, the *Panama City Herald*, by John Perry in 1935. The native Kentuckian championed the construction of a coastal highway between Pensacola and Panama City and the Atlantic-Gulf Ship Canal across the Florida peninsula. He also owned a network of newspapers throughout Florida and Pennsylvania with news services based in New York City. Perry used his publications for the task of "everlastingly hammering away" at projects meant to promote the Sunshine State.[26]

Like Gulfport, Myrtle Beach began as a by-product of the timber industry. Franklin Burroughs and Benjamin Collins of Conway, South Carolina, established the Burroughs and Collins Company in 1895 to manage a diverse empire of real estate, milling, naval stores, farming, and transportation operations. Burroughs's sons, Frank and Donald, directed the company after his death in 1897. The company completed the Conway and Seashore Railroad in May 1900. The last stop, known as New Town, was rebranded Myrtle Beach that November. Little more than a few family farms populated the area. By May 1901 the company had opened the Sea Side Inn and began marketing lots, though sales were slow for the next decade. Then Simeon Chapin, a native of Milwaukee who had earned a fortune as a Chicago banker and broker, arrived. The financier had honeymooned in Daytona Beach in 1892 and visited Myrtle Beach in 1911 on a hunting trip. Seeing the economic potential, Chapin partnered with the Burroughs brothers, who managed the 65,000-acre tract operated by their company. In October 1912 the land was transferred to the new Myrtle Beach Farms Company. By 1928 Chapin and the Burroughses formed the Chapin Company, which operated a department store in the growing coastal community. Textile tycoon John T. Woodside of Greenville, South Carolina, also invested heavily along the Grand Strand, buying 64,488 acres from the Myrtle Beach Farms Company—basically everything but coastal residences and the downtown area—for $950,000 in 1926. With this land purchase coinciding with the peak of the real-estate bubble, Woodside's development, called Arcady, failed. However, his impressive Ocean Forest Hotel, opened in 1930, became a fixture of Myrtle Beach.[27]

Virginia Beach contained little more than United States Life Saving Station No. 2 in 1878—a facility built to protect not swimmers but shipwreck survivors. Edward Drinkwater, who arrived as a toddler after his father became keeper of the station, described the area: "Why Virginia Beach was just a wilderness in those days." He continued, "There were no houses. The only activity here were the two men who fished along the beach and took their catches back to Norfolk in a horse and cart." Since Norfolk elites often traveled to Nags Head, North Carolina, for the summer, a closer site promised profits. Norfolk businessman Marshall Parks, leader of the Norfolk and Virginia Beach Railroad and Improvement Company, pushed the completion of a narrow-gauge track to the coast in 1883. Four years later the Princess Anne Hotel opened. Virginia Beach became an accessible recreational haven. A hunting club opened its doors, attracting millionaires and, in time, Presidents Benjamin Harrison and Howard Taft. The popularity of the club led to improved transportation links. Vacation cottages sprouted. Families from eastern Virginia and North Carolina took excursion trains to Virginia Beach for a day on the sands, particularly as part of Sunday school picnics. The elite of Norfolk especially crowded the shores as they spent a day or weekend at the beach. Sarah Blackford noted in a diary entry from June 1895: "A great many people came to spend the afternoon from Norfolk and eat dinner at the Princess Anne. There were so many people that we had to wait nearly an hour for our dinner."[28]

A Journey South

This book explores how diverse southern beach resorts carved their niche in a burgeoning but cutthroat tourism market. The early portion of this study explains how beach resorts mastered the terrain. The first chapter focuses on infrastructure. Highways and airports became vital transportation links. Cities accommodated seasonal fluctuations in population requiring large police departments and massive water systems, among other services, by passing tax burdens onto vacationers. Beach resorts developed attractions to stretch the tourist season as well as courted military installations and colleges to foster a year-round economy. The second chapter analyzes the escalating struggle between beachfront developers and the environment. The plagues of malaria and yellow fever needed containment, birthing mosquito eradication campaigns. Beach towns simultaneously addressed the dangers of hurricanes. Massive seawalls, inspired by Galveston, and renourished beaches, stirred by the example of Harrison County, Mississippi, became commonplace along American shores. Rapid development, however, carried consequences as resorts struggled with the effects of DDT and the pollution caused by tourists.

The book then turns to a cultural analysis of southern beach towns and their relationship to the inland South. The third chapter examines ethnicity, race, tanning, and the civil rights struggle. Coastal settlements and port cities harbored diverse, activist populations that challenged Jim Crow. Tourism, a publicity-sensitive industry, made southern economies vulnerable to racial violence, a factor exploited by civil rights advocates. Chapter 4 turns to the role of gender, religion, and the marketing of sexuality. As swimwear became scantier, resorts mediated the display of vacationers' bodies in a conservative region. Bathing beauties were celebrated, but forums such as beauty pageants placed the display of bodies in a morally palatable format. More generally, resorts emphasized religion, particularly nondenominational Christianity, to restrain visitors' behavior. The final chapter considers the underground economy of moonshining and illegal gambling, which thrived in the South until the

1970s. Resorts were rife with corruption as boosters resisted state laws to satisfy tourists. The rights revolution of the 1960s finally encouraged legalization of gambling and the end of prohibition of alcohol.

Beach tourism in the American South is the story of the region's transition from an agricultural to a service economy. As tourists started arriving in the late nineteenth century, coastal southerners coined a "saying that one yankee was worth two bales of cotton, and a lot easier to pick." White southerners confronted contradictions between a stultifying Jim Crow social structure and a dynamic, diverse global economy. As social theorist David Harvey explains, "Under capitalism there is, then, a perpetual struggle in which capital builds a physical landscape appropriate to its own condition at a particular moment in time, only to have to destroy it, usually in the course of a crisis, at a subsequent point in time."[29] Tourism promised sectional reconciliation and wealth in a region mired in poverty. And the industry assuaged unease about racism by depicting seemingly happy black waiters and bellhops, as well as picturesque fieldworkers. However, the increasing dependence on outsiders fostered corruption. Tourism-oriented communities regularly bent cultural mores and laws to meet vacationers' needs. In an industry sensitive to public perceptions, instances of racial injustice severely damaged visitation numbers and, in turn, local and state budgets. The wages offered by the service sector provided some black southerners escape from the cotton fields, though not from poverty. For those African Americans whose families had purchased coastal lands in the decades after the Civil War, beachfront tourism was Janus faced—raising property values but also property taxes, not to mention making their coveted lands the target of deceitful speculators. Putting faith in bikinis bore the Jim Crow South to scrutiny and, ultimately, led to a dramatic cultural, political, and racial revolution during the 1960s and 1970s. This was the moment of crisis when the South's tourism landscape manufactured over the previous hundred years finally bulldozed the agricultural landscape. Here is a study of how a once minor industry slowly but radically transformed a region.

CHAPTER ONE

Coastal Empires

Southern Beach Resorts and the Rise of the Sunbelt

J. Lewis Brown, writing for *Outlook* in 1924, wanted to learn why roughly two million Americans from the Northeast and Midwest found "it absolutely necessary to go South every winter to round out their realm of happiness—something most of their forebears never thought of." He identified three factors, of which climate proved most important. Brown quipped that "during the last ten years, and particularly since the [First World] war, the nouveau riche, the social world, and those who aspire to both of these circles have found that no longer are their good red corpuscles able to turn aside the intimate touches of Jack Frost." A boom occurred throughout what would become known as the Sunbelt "from Florida to California." Next, Brown pointed to the "publicity agent." Advertisers transformed the South into a haven for the wealthy and middle class. Yet something was still missing.[1]

The last catalyst was the creation of attractions. Access to nature was a lifeline to the vacation industry, but man-made playgrounds enhanced the landscape. Brown identified the South's first "indispensable something—golf." Socially popular among men and women and increasingly affordable, golf courses at posh hotels acted as magnets for vacationers. Southerners first built links in the 1890s, but only after 1910 did sand traps, water hazards, and manicured greens dot the countryside. Florida, with fewer than a dozen courses before 1910, claimed more than ninety by the mid-1920s. Hotels and real-estate developments maintained 90 percent of these. "What is true of Florida was duplicated in California, with Texas, Louisiana, Georgia, the Carolinas, Bermuda, Cuba, and even Mexico, following in their wake," observed Brown. Railroad and steamship companies facilitated such travel by vying for quicker and cheaper transportation methods. The real-estate boom and burgeoning tourist trade was "making the South." Cotton fields and textile mills gave way to resorts and an increasingly vital service economy.[2]

Without attractions appealing to a broad range of tastes, tourism across the South would have floundered. Boosters encouraged vacationers with new transportation links, particularly concrete highways. Boosters then turned to the task of fostering year-round prosperity. Their success depended on technologies, mainly air-conditioning, and the construction of military bases and universities after the Second World War.[3]

Breaching Barriers

The First World War solidified the American tourism industry. With German U-boats sinking freighters and passenger liners, most famously the *Lusitania* in May 1915, wealthy Americans looked for recreation closer to home. Southern boosters seized the opportunity. George Grayson, president of the Biloxi Commercial Club, noted that advertising campaigns had begun "considerably earlier" in 1914 as domestic resorts courted travelers while Europe slid into war. Like many other vacation spots, Biloxi enjoyed the largest influx of vacationers yet experienced during the winter of 1914–1915. By October 1915, Grayson urged advertising Biloxi as a winter haven in "newspapers published in the north." American entry into the conflict in 1917 further strengthened domestic tourism. For those contemplating sea travel, the sinking of the Diamond Shoal Lightship No. 71 in August 1918 just twelve miles off the North Carolina coast— residents of Hatteras heard the German submarine's deck gun—gave cause for reconsideration. After the war, the transfer of 25,000 heavy trucks and 1,500 tractors from the federal military to state highway departments, along with the Federal Highway Act of 1921 providing states matching funds for road construction, encouraged automobile travel.[4]

American car ownership jumped over the next decade. By 1927 more than half of the 27.5 million American families owned cars. A startling 5.3 million vehicles were manufactured in 1929 alone, saturating the market. Sociologist James West observed how the automobile virtually ended "geographical isolation." Prominent editor Charles Merz wrote of the Jazz Age: "America is cruising. It is bumper to bumper."[5]

Automobiles exposed the need for paved roads. Beirne Brues and her family typified the new motoring tourist. These Bostonians saw their vehicle as a convenient means of escape and adventure. "When the East Wind sweeping across the Bay piled our doorways high with snow and intense cold came down from the North to chill our bones we began to feel the insidious spell of Wanderlust," she recorded in her 1924 diary. She cheered, "We were going South, as far south as our Dodge could pull us, into that strip of tropical America at the tip of Florida." When they diverted toward Virginia Beach, the "road became more sandy, some stretches very rough and hard pulling, much worse than mountain grades." The family quickly returned to the main highway. An Illinois family declared the "roads pretty rough today" as they approached Gulfport, Mississippi, in February 1931. A Horry County resident remembered the difficulty of reaching Myrtle Beach during the interwar years. The road was "virtually impassable; if you tried to drive a Model-T from Conway to Myrtle Beach you'd usually run your axle in two." As late as 1949, motorists from Baltimore reported, "South Carolina has rough roads until after Myrtle Beach."[6]

Emphasis on road and bridge construction increased as railway patronage declined after the First World War. Southern rail lines had long been inferior to northern counterparts. One Yankee tourist in 1913 complained, "Trains are never on time in the South. They have a time table just to let you know that trains go some time in the morning or afternoon." Travel writer Terry Pindell concurred after riding the last commercial service line, Southern Railroad's *Crescent*, terminated in the 1970s: "Southern custom and habit could never adopt the 'bustle' or 'scurry' so characteristic of railroads in the north. Southern conductors proved themselves downright insubordinate on issues such as punctuality pulling out of a station and leaving tardy ladies on the platform or interrupting the romantic farewells of parting lovers."[7]

By the mid-twentieth century, railroads eager to escape the unprofitable commercial market sabotaged their service. Although locals protested cuts to rail service and received the staunch support of state railroad commissions, railroad companies stymied their efforts. Myrtle Beach boosters in the late 1940s fruitlessly pressed railroads to maintain service to the coast. Mississippi coast promoters spent a decade fighting to restore twice-a-day service between Jackson and Gulfport, which had been halted by the Illinois Central Railroad in 1950. The Missouri Pacific Railroad announced the end of passenger service to Galveston in 1954. By the early 1960s, the Louisville and Nashville Railroad halted commuter service between New Orleans and Pass Christian—a link that had buoyed coastal tourism since the late nineteenth century. To justify such cuts, railroad executives pointed to a steady decline in passengers. Yet they also adopted tactics that repelled riders. Ronnie Caire, a resident of the Mississippi Gulf Coast who used the commuter train to New Orleans until service discontinued, recalled, "The cars were so damn bad that nobody that ever had any sense would ride the thing. The car we rode in was built in 1895; when it rained the roof leaked. It had no screens, and only the fact that we either drank or played cards kept us from being totally smoked out, you know. The smoke was terrible."[8]

Despite local and state efforts to improve roads during the interwar years, boosters soon realized the need for greater federal involvement. Myrtle Beach businessmen regularly complained that North Carolina failed to invest in coastal roads. Floridians chafed at the reluctance of Georgia, with little seafront tourism, to improve coastal highways. Faced with such disparities, tourism interests rallied for an improved federal highway system. In 1949 the Atlantic-Gulf and Pacific Safeway Association, with Florida politicians in the lead, lobbied Congress to fund a project linking the Sunshine State to the Golden State. Oil interests and automobile companies also eyed a major highway system. For President Dwight Eisenhower, a four-lane grid promised economic dividends and a bolstered national defense. The National Interstate and Defense Highways Act passed in 1956.[9]

Increased highway travel led states to create welcome centers. In November 1949 Florida pioneered its first "welcome station" outside Yulee on U.S. Highway 17. By 1968 the state operated nine such facilities where "one or more attractive hostesses greet each visitor with a smile and a cup of orange juice." One welcome center sat on Fernandina Beach near Jacksonville, greeting boaters on the Intracoastal Waterway. Some four thousand visitors a day passed through each station during the peak of the tourism season. South Carolina constructed its first welcome center at Little River in 1967. The state government operated seven centers by 1970. Other southern states likewise followed Florida's lead, especially as businessmen sought to downplay the negative publicity spawned by racial tensions during the civil rights movement.[10]

Resort communities also became ardent supporters of the Intracoastal Waterway. Debated for much of the nineteenth century, the waterway gained traction in Congress at the same time the Panama Canal came under American control. President Theodore Roosevelt also championed improved waterways to increase competition with railroads. The River and Harbor Act of 1910 facilitated development of the channel in the Florida Panhandle. German submarine attacks during the First World War encouraged extension of the waterway. A subsequent act in 1925 funded a canal between New Orleans and Galveston. The need to bolster employment under the New Deal would help complete the Gulf and Atlantic waterways in the 1930s, setting off a heated debate over the construction of a connection across Florida. Efforts to build the Cross Florida

Barge Canal, however, ended in 1971 when President Richard Nixon canceled the project.[11]

The Atlantic portion of the waterway, though intended for barge shipments, became a popular avenue for yachts. Even before Florida greeted these boaters with a welcome center, Myrtle Beach and other communities provided anchorages to entice yachters to stop. In December 1946 New Yorkers boating through North Carolina described how "at times it was like traffic on the highway— even passing each other." Once in Florida, the diarist declared, "It seems everybody & his brother is spending the winter in Fla. by boat." Leisure traffic on the waterway grew over the postwar period. Richard Bissell, who made the journey in the mid-1960s, remarked upon "all the big yachts going south with us, and there were many (where in hell does all that money come from?)." The waterway not only encouraged yachting but also allowed resorts to add attractions expected by Yankees visiting Dixie. By the 1980s entrepreneurs along the Grand Strand enticed vacationers with dinner, dancing, or sightseeing cruises "down the historic Intracoastal Waterway aboard the Grand Strand's only true paddle-wheeler . . . surrounded by authentic Riverboat décor." Without the cut across Florida, the Gulf waterway drew few yachts. Heavily used by the oil industry, the commercial traffic proved more daunting. Worse, in the swamps of Louisiana, trappers regularly fired upon fast-moving vessels that scared away game.[12]

Born in the late 1920s, commercial air travel did not catch a strong tailwind until after the Second World War. A network of airports, many funded through New Deal programs, allowed airlines to expand, though planners largely thought in terms of metropolitan or regional air travel until the war demonstrated the long-distance capabilities of aircraft. Although Myrtle Beach opened its first airport in 1928, for instance, the facility catered to private fliers. Beginning in 1950, Piedmont Airlines became the first carrier to provide regular service to Myrtle Beach from nearby cities. In 1954 the Myrtle Beach airport recorded more than 7,500 landings, of which some 5,500 were single-engine planes. Overhead, some 75,000 aircraft passed Myrtle Beach each year on the route to Florida and other locations. By 1967 tourists arriving by air accounted for approximately $2 million spent along the Grand Strand. In 1956 Southern Airways inaugurated regular service between Panama City and cities in Alabama and Georgia. By linking to Atlanta, Southern boasted that they maintained flight connections via other airlines to "Anywhere in the World." The company also flew to the Mississippi Gulf Coast. By the mid-1950s Eastern Airlines alone operated 218 daily flights to and from Florida with a capacity for 14,544 passengers. A study in Miami revealed that 35 percent of all tourists in 1953 arrived by air, while 50 percent traveled by automobile and a mere 15 percent journeyed by rail. So significant was air travel by the 1950s that 26 percent of all car rentals in the world occurred in Miami. The introduction in 1958 of the Boeing 707, the first commercially successful jet, revolutionized air travel. By 1970 airlines carried 150 million passengers each year, triple the number from a decade earlier. By 1980 more than two-thirds of the American population had boarded a plane.[13]

Southern coastal communities largely modeled themselves on Florida. "So tightly are Florida's resorts tied to the economy of the industrial North and Midwest that bankers here say this state can act as a seismograph to record a shift in the nation's business sentiment," reported journalist Sam Dawson in 1954. Competitors watched closely. "In fact Galveston is to Texas what Miami is to Florida," boasted a Galvestonian. Sal Romano of Virginia Beach, after a vacation in Saint Petersburg, Florida, in September 1963, believed his hometown was in dire need of modernization: "In St. Petersburg you notice immediately the cleanliness of the streets and buildings, the dramatic lavishness of the lighting at night, the never-ending improvements and repairs of the streets, the constant mushrooming of new structures." Residents of Myrtle Beach were equally impressed with Saint Petersburg—so much so that the Myrtle Beach Chamber of Commerce hired Fred Burton, assistant manager of the Saint Petersburg chamber, to serve as their manager. A South Carolinian commented, "It seems that our favorite pastime here in Myrtle Beach is that of deliberately comparing our town with Miami and Atlantic City along lines in which we admittedly fare second-best."[14]

The burgeoning Florida tourism industry turned highways through the South into economic lifelines. The Packer Corporation, which placed billboard advertisements along highways, estimated Florida's tourism trade at $180 million in 1935. Nearly 1.4 million tourists drove to Florida in 515,000 automobiles. The average visit lasted 29.4 days. Each tourist spent an average of $2.25 per day. Motorists represented half of all tourists entering the Sunshine State in the 1930s. The company reported, "The great 'extra' circulation starts early in November and not only continues through March and April but right through the summer, when Florida becomes the resort state for southerners just as it is the winter play-ground for those from the north." In 1939 Lloyd Wickersham, vice president of the Norfolk Southern Bus Corporation, noted the "approximately 1,500 tourists' automobiles passing daily through Piedmont Virginia en route to and from the North and the South."[15]

The South proved the leading destination for the nation's travelers. By the late 1950s, one in fifteen American families vacationed along the Gulf Coast or Florida each winter. Even the once poverty-ridden southern populace began to enjoy costly and lengthy vacations. A survey conducted by the automaker Renault in 1960 found that 79 percent of southerners planned a holiday in their home region, with Florida and North Carolina as the most popular destinations. Southern families on vacation averaged 1,572 miles of driving and spent $380. Of all Americans, 36 percent intended to visit the region. Again, Florida led all states as a destination. The national average for spending on a family vacation stood at $462. Southern tourists, like their fellow Americans, preferred summer vacations. Some 70 percent of southerners took their holiday in July and August. The average vacation lasted two weeks and typically consisted of at least two persons. The result produced a national tourism industry valued by the American Automobile Association at $15 billion during the 1950s.[16]

By the mid-twentieth century, tourism rivaled traditional economic sectors. In 1950 the American Automobile Association valued the Florida tourism industry at $700 million a year, drawing more than four million travelers to the state.[17] In 1951 South Carolina tourism, valued at $67 million, ranked as the fifth largest industry within the Palmetto State's economy—behind textile products ($754 million), cotton ($92 million), tobacco ($82 million), and lumber ($78 million). Virginia harvested a tourism industry worth $400 million, while North Carolina reaped $300 million from travelers. By the mid-1950s the Virginia Travel Council estimated the state's tourism industry at $600 million distributed among more than twenty thousand firms licensed under the tourist establishment inspection laws. Among southern states, the Old Dominion stood second to Florida's $970 million tourism industry and ahead of Tennessee's $535 million tourism industry. The typical tourist in Virginia averaged 2.5 days in the state and spent $7.68 per day. In the mid-1950s the American Automobile Association estimated that, of every dollar, tourists spent 20 cents on lodging, 29 cents on food, 21 cents on transportation, 18 cents on retail merchandise, 7 cents on amusements, and 5 cents on incidentals. Practically each year during the Cold War brought more vacationers as Americans prospered, families grew larger, and beaches increased in popularity.[18]

Coastal resorts had grown considerably since the interwar period. In the late 1930s Virginia Beach and neighboring communities claimed 3,500 year-round residents while maintaining an infrastructure built to handle fifty thousand vacationers. A census of permanent residents in 1940 found 2,032 whites and 308 blacks living in Virginia Beach, with the main African American community of Seatack—home to many hotel workers, waiters, and other service workers— excluded from the city limits since Virginia Beach's incorporation in 1906. By the early 1950s, Virginia Beach claimed 5,000 residents but hosted a summertime population of 75,000. In 1962 voters agreed to merge the city with the rest of Princess Anne County in an effort to block annexation efforts pursued by Norfolk, thereby sustaining a low tax base tied to revenue from hotel and sales taxes while evading absorption into a city with a large African American population. The referendum passed by a five to one margin. Virginia Beach thus evolved from a town of just over two square miles to a sprawling urban center of more than 255 square miles with an additional fifty-five square miles of water, making the resort the ninth largest city by landmass in the United States. The city now included thirty-eight miles of beachfront. The city's population leapt from 8,091 to 85,318 residents. Boosters soon heralded Virginia Beach as the "World's Largest Resort City." Virginia Beach, despite repeated threats by Norfolk to curtail water service and thus its competitor's growth, pursued a vigorous economic diversification program over the next two decades that included construction of industrial parks and a larger convention center. Yet the city regularly reported more guests than could be handled by the motels. Conditions were so overcrowded that municipal officials often ignored ordinances banning vacationers from sleeping on the beach. "I walked down on the boardwalk shortly after daylight Sunday morning," remarked chamber of commerce president A. B. Crews in July 1965, "and people were lined up along the beach asleep. I don't have any idea how many there were, but they looked like railroad ties." Such conditions lingered into the 1970s despite a massive building boom that supplied more than three thousand rooms.[19]

Myrtle Beach grew from 1,597 residents in 1940 to 3,345 inhabitants in 1950, an increase of 109 percent. The growth was the largest in Horry County and among the largest in the two Carolinas. The town boasted a summer population of 60,000—with peak holidays such as the Fourth of July drawing 100,000 vacationers—and a winter tourist population several thousand above the permanent figure. A federal survey in 1955 revealed that Myrtle Beach possessed a permanent population of 5,824 residents. With the opening of Myrtle Beach Air Force Base in 1956, the population skyrocketed to an estimated 13,000 inhabitants as nearly 6,000 military and civilian personnel arrived. Henrietta Abeles, who operated a boardinghouse, described the construction boom in the early 1960s: "Here in Myrtle Beach the town is growing physically at an enormous rate, down on the waterfront motels going up that are fantastic dwarfing anything that was before." By the early 1970s Myrtle Beach claimed nearly 17,000 residents and military personnel.[20]

Communities along the Gulf witnessed similar growth. In 1955 the Mississippi Gulf Coast claimed 3,717 rooms in 122 hotels and motels, accommodating 2,553,515 guests who spent $6.8 million on lodging. These travelers spent an estimated $19.7 million on food, $7.6 million in miscellaneous stores, and $3.5 million on amusements. Tourism thus brought more than $37.8 million to the Mississippi beachfront. The tourists, according to the Mississippi Economic Council, equated to "millions of 'free' money." By 1968 Biloxi alone claimed four hotels and twenty-eight motels, providing a capacity of 2,500 rooms.[21] Panama City witnessed a steady rise in population. From 422 residents in 1910, Panama City grew to 1,722 inhabitants in 1920 and 5,502 inhabitants in 1930. By 1935 Panama City bulged with a population of 10,826 after the opening of a massive $6 million paper mill operated by the International Paper Company— the only paper mill in Florida.[22] John Rainey, manager of the Panama City Chamber of Commerce, valued the city's tourism industry at $10 million by 1950. In contrast, the local paper mill employed 1,200 workers with a payroll of $3 million, while newly established Tyndall Air Force Base maintained a payroll of $12 million. Growth in tourism grew steadily over the decades. Even in the midst of the oil crises of the 1970s, the number of tourists venturing to Florida continued to rise, exceeding 30 million annually by 1977.[23]

The electorate began sanctioning the consolidation of shoreline hamlets during the 1960s as population growth and continued expansion of the tourism industry severely stretched community resources. Mergers of small beach towns promised greater efficiency and, thus, savings. The Grand Strand's Ocean Drive Beach, Cherry Grove Beach, Windy Hill Beach, and Crescent Beach voted to merge in December 1967. Although some in Atlantic Beach, an African American community, also sought to join the new city, too few freeholders signed the petition to hold the required referendum—at least according to white officials. A subsequent referendum named the sprawling creation North Myrtle Beach. Fred Burton, manager of the Myrtle Beach Chamber of Commerce, was pleased since the name maintained the local brand, giving "the area an immediate identification." Not all voters agreed. More than a dozen possibilities received more than one vote, including the names Petticoat Junction Beach, Peyton Place Beach, and Grandest Grand Strand Beach. One voter suggested a "name so vulgar that election officials were ashamed to mention it."[24] Those along the shores near Panama City failed to convince the state legislature to sanction consolidation until 1970. In August 1970 Panama City Beach was born as a municipality uniting Long Beach Resort, Edgewater Gulf Beach, West Panama City Beach, and Panama City Beach. The move meant a greater efficiency in resources, more political muscle in the county and state, and a shared infrastructure. Business leaders and politicians especially eyed an improved sewage system, uniform street lighting, and better police and fire protection. A challenge to the consolidation on the grounds that only property owners could vote in the referendum reached the Florida Supreme Court in 1972. Citing a 1935 decision, the judges ruled that restricting such a decision to "freeholders" rather than all qualified voters was legal.[25]

The travails of fostering tourism in states supportive of an agricultural economy chafed coastal boosters. Growth economically or in population meant little when state legislatures failed to adjust representation to reflect demographic shifts. Worse, representation in state senates was often based on counties rather than population. Residents of resort towns thought of themselves as southern yet also culturally and economically distinct. The Galveston Chamber of Commerce in 1955 explained, "Over the years, a situation has developed whereby a general feeling seems to have been born that Galveston is separated from the Mainland, and therefore is a law unto itself." Boosters elsewhere along the seashore shared such sentiment. Stephanie Pace of Myrtle Beach described her hometown in the early 1970s: "In Myrtle Beach we may have an industrial mask displaying pretentious motels and 'fine, citylike restaurants.' We may talk a worldly game, but we still remain a small Southern town." Yet Pace's comments noted a pretense of sophistication seen lacking further inland. Myrtle Beach residents, frustrated at the lack of state support for promoting tourism, considered themselves "divorced" from South Carolina.[26]

Even Florida tourism interests regularly battled agricultural political kingpins, known as the Pork Chop Gang, based in the northern and central parts of the state. From the earliest days, tensions existed. Hotelier Karl Abbott recalled, "The cattlemen resented the influx of Northerners, and the citrus growers and native Floridians resented the Johnny-come-lately real estate operators." Cash-rich south Floridians believed that cash-poor north Floridians, who dominated the legislature, wasted tax revenue on nontourism projects. Twenty districts with 13 percent of the state population claimed the majority of seats in the Florida house and senate. Judge S. D. Clarke, longtime leader of the state senate, retired in 1965. He represented Jefferson County with almost ten thousand constituents, while the more than one million residents of Dade County also claimed only one senator.[27]

The tension between beach communities and inland areas of southern states even led to secession debates. In 1923, as the Miami area boomed, author Clara Stillman reported "talk sometimes of a separation into two States—North and South Florida—and even into three—part of northwestern Florida to become part of Alabama so that Alabama may have a larger access to the sea and the north gulf coast a better representation." Such proposals remained alive through the twentieth century. In March 1982 state representative Tommy Sandusky of Mobile drafted a resolution calling for a meeting between counties of southern Alabama and the Florida Panhandle to consider the creation of a new state. "If we were part of the same ballgame," Sandusky explained with a clear reference to tourism, "we could really go somewhere." Tom Tobiassen, a state senator representing Pensacola, agreed. He argued that Floridians of the Panhandle had more in common with Alabama than with the transplanted Yankees of South Florida. Furthermore, the prominence of South Florida tourism overshadowed the Panhandle. Few politicians in either state supported this kind of secession, although Governor Fob James offered Florida $500 million for the Panhandle.[28]

Sun Spots

The tourist season varied for each coastal town depending on its proximity to population centers and the climate. Since the mid-1800s wealthy New Orleanians as well as Mississippi and Alabama planters maintained vacation homes and patronized rooming houses along the Mississippi Gulf Coast during the summers. An 1875 guide to vacation spots elaborated, "Biloxi, Pascagoula, Pass Christian, and Bay Saint Louis, are resorted to more or less by the people of both cities [New Orleans and Mobile] during the season, though neither of them can be properly classed under the head of popular resorts." This changed by the early twentieth century. Julius Lopez, a native of Biloxi, noted that the area's proximity to the Louisiana port fostered year-round tourism: "Biloxi was a combined summer and winter resort. Now, in the summer it hit its peak and you had the people from the Delta upstate, you had a lot of New Orleans people." Former Confederate president Jefferson Davis retired to the beachfront in 1876. Many facilities along the Mississippi Sound also welcomed wintering northerners, especially after a visit by President Woodrow Wilson in 1913.[29]

Excluding South Florida, southern resorts catered primarily to summertime vacationers. For Galveston, Myrtle Beach, Panama City, and Virginia Beach, the tourist season stretched from May to September as nearby southerners escaped the broiling sun, although the rise of affordable air-conditioning units in the 1950s radically altered other aspects of southern life. Marion Holmes and her family stopped in Long Beach one early spring in the 1950s only to find cottages with freshly painted interiors and stacked furniture. "We were told that Long Beach was a *summer* resort, but that signified nothing to people from Maine," explained Holmes. "Florida, any part of it, meant warmth to us." A landlord fearful of losing these Yankees called a "happy-go-lucky negro, armed with brooms and dusters, bedding and towels" to prepare a cottage. Many northerners opted to spend the winter closer to Miami. "February is always the biggest month of the year in South Florida," remarked James Wingfield, president of the Hotel and Motel Industry Association of Palm Beach County in 1982. Yet a change had occurred. Since the 1950s more tourists arrived in Florida for the summer season than for the winter season.[30]

Seashore resorts materialized rapidly during the land boom of the 1910s and 1920s. A boating trip along the Panhandle convinced Chicago industrialist John Perrine to become a land developer. In 1918 he bought fifteen thousand acres and created the Valparaiso Realty Company. Perrine founded Valparaiso, Florida, in 1921. Three years later a promotional booklet titled "The End of the Rainbow"—a sly reference to tranquility, beauty, and the supposed pot of gold that was Florida real estate—revealed the rapid growth born of the land craze: "Houses sprang up almost over night, fourteen miles of hard roads have been constructed, several miles of cement sidewalks have been laid, the sewage problem has been solved, a power plant furnishes ice and electric lights, an artesian well furnishes water in abundance for the entire city." Valparaiso was an instant town with homeowners from New Orleans, Chicago, Cleveland, Wichita Falls, Washington, D.C., and other cities.[31]

The architecture of the boom reflected the celebration of year-round warmth. Boosters either used exotic names, as at Valparaiso, or names such as Palm Springs or Coconut Grove that advertised the subtropical climate. Promoting leisure and luxury, developers mimicked Mediterranean styles. This reinforced the message about the climate while suggesting the permanence of newly created communities. "A new world arose in Florida—a world of fronds and palms and palaces, of Moorish shops, Italian streets, Castilian clubs and Neapolitan ice cream," wrote editorialist Charles Merz in 1928. Although "Florida may lead the way," the Sunshine State's land craze meant that "no important city in the country" lacked new "suburbs with a Continental flavor." Spanish and Italian references in name and architectural style flourished.[32]

Events along the Mississippi Sound exemplified the euphoric boosterism of the 1910s and 1920s. In 1922 the Mississippi Coast Super Chamber of Commerce formed to galvanize the 35,000 residents of the state's three coastal counties. Eager to accrue wealth and demographic growth, the Mississippians pondered, "Why should Florida and California have these things and we not?"[33] Refashioned as the Mississippi Coast Club in November 1925, organizers launched a $100,000 membership drive to facilitate advertising campaigns and infrastructural improvements. Biloxi residents oversubscribed their quota of $25,000 in an hour.[34] Over the next two years, combined national advertising of Mississippi's beachfront by the Mississippi Coast Club, Louisville and Nashville Railroad, Illinois Central Railroad (which had bought the Gulfport and Ship Island line in 1925), local chambers of commerce, and individual hotels and other businesses amounted to $500,000. The Illinois Central Station in Chicago bore a forty-foot electric sign promoting the "BEAUTIFUL MISSISSIPPI GULF COAST." A similar sign on Michigan Boulevard tempted Chicagoans: "BE AT YOUR DESK TODAY AND PLAY GOLF ON THE MISSISSIPPI GULF COAST TOMORROW." The same two-year period witnessed an investment of $56 million in infrastructural improvements. These included a massive seawall and boulevard project stretching nearly thirty miles; bridges across Bay Saint Louis, Back Bay, and the Pascagoula River; and grand resorts such as the Edgewater Gulf Hotel, the Markham, and the Tivoli.[35]

Whereas southern Florida drew heavily from Americans in the northeastern United States, especially New York City, resorts along the Gulf targeted Midwesterners, especially Chicagoans. When a motorcade of Chicagoans arrived at the Mississippi coast in 1925, locals promised that these visitors would see "what has been advertised more extensively in Illinois, perhaps, than in any other state." The visitors left impressed. *Chicago Tribune* reporter Arthur Evans wrote, "The Mississippi gulf coast is having a boom all its own and is fast developing its advantage as the nearest of the great winter playgrounds to Chicago and the middle west." With southerners vacationing in the summer and northerners visiting in the winter, the state's three coastal counties offered a valuable refuge. Between April and November 1925, beach frontage real-estate values jumped from $75 a foot to $400. One businessman who purchased an office building in downtown Gulfport for $35,000 early in the year received an offer of $175,000 seven months later. Acreage several blocks from the shore increased in value from $5 or $6 at the start of 1925 to $15 to $18 by year's end. Conservative estimates for 1925 held that land value in Mississippi's three coastal counties had increased by $50 million. That said, Evans noted that these prices were "still at a low level compared with Florida."[36]

Evidence from the Harrison County Advertising Advisory Commission, created in 1954, reveals the Mississippi coast's key markets and the seasonal shifts within their tourist population. During the spring and fall seasons, advertising concentrated on the Midwest and nearby southern states. Illinois, Wisconsin, Missouri, Ohio, Iowa, Michigan, and Indiana received particular attention. The Mississippians also concentrated on Texas and Louisiana. Ads appeared in magazines such as *Holiday* and *Better Homes and Gardens* as well as in nearly twenty midwestern and Texas metropolitan newspapers. During the late spring and summer months, however, the commission targeted Louisiana, Texas, Florida, Tennessee, Arkansas, Alabama, and Mississippi. The principal means of promotion during these campaigns was television, although ads were also placed in metropolitan newspapers and magazines such as *Southern Living* and *Southern Outdoors*. Only in the early 1970s did Mississippians begin targeting Canadians.[37]

More remote Panhandle communities focused on southerners within a day's drive of what would become known as the Redneck Riviera. During the 1920s, for example, R. E. L. McCaskill hawked lots in a development called Inlet Beach near Panama City: "It is the logical playground in summer for the good folks of southern Alabama and southeast Georgia." The *WPA Guide to Florida* described the Gulf shore between Panama City and Pensacola as "the popular weekend and summer vacation ground for many Alabamans who travel less than 100 miles to achieve a salt-water tan." The range would grow over coming decades, drawing from across the Deep South.[38]

Evidence from advertising campaigns shows the geographic market targeted by Panama City. The Panama City Chamber of Commerce in 1958 placed ads in fourteen southern newspapers; six midwestern newspapers in Illinois, Indiana, Ohio, and Wisconsin; and three national magazines, including *Holiday*, *Outdoors*, and *Life*. The businessmen also advertised on thirty-six billboards and in "special newspapers and magazines appealing to the retired clientele." Motels and resorts between Panama City and Fort Walton directed mail campaigns at Alabama, Georgia, Louisiana, Arkansas, Tennessee, and Kentucky.[39]

Tapping that market produced an obvious result. A survey assessing the success of promotional efforts in 1954 found that tourists drawn to Florida's Bay County came in groups of, on average, 3.5 persons who stayed four days along the shore. Each group averaged an expenditure of $143. Nearly thirteen thousand vacationers came to Panama City in the first half of 1954, spending more than $524,000. By 1968 Panama City ranked as the sixth most visited community in Florida. An estimated 750,000 tourists stayed in motel rooms lining the coast; the number of rooms surpassed six thousand, more rooms than in the other nine counties of the Panhandle combined. The local tourism industry was valued at $100 million annually. Yet this tourist migration remained largely dependent on residents of the Deep South. Local student Michael Fiorelli described the Panhandle in the 1980s: "For Panama City, the norm in appearance is jeans, a flannel shirt and cowboy boots. If a guy doesn't wear a hat that says 'Hank Jr.' on it, then he's subject to being called a freak." He concluded, "Redneck is the norm for our town."[40]

Resorts along the Atlantic coast largely focused on northeasterners. "Hundreds of automobiles are seen daily at and near Myrtle Beach and up and down the great north-south boulevard, the Ocean Highway, U.S. 17. The majority of the States of the Union are represented with New York and New Jersey in the lead," commented the *Myrtle Beach News* in 1937. A 1952 study found a daily average of 1,144 out-of-state automobiles passing along U.S. Highway 17 near Myrtle Beach. The chamber's Travel Development Department analyzed the more than two hundred thousand vacationers who flocked to the Grand Strand for Easter in the early 1970s. The research revealed that approximately 70 percent of vacationers came as a family from the Carolinas, eastern states of the United States, or Canada. Golfers and students accounted for 13 percent each. Based on inquiries received by the chamber in 1972, travelers from Virginia (9.5 percent), North Carolina (9.2 percent), New York (7.9 percent), Pennsylvania (7.9 percent), and New Jersey (6.9 percent) dominated Grand Strand tourism. Virginia Beach, via billboards, newspaper ads, posters, and promotional pamphlets, targeted a similar geographical market. Indeed, Virginia Beach boosters directly competed with Myrtle Beach for tourists traveling between New York and Florida.[41]

Boosters in the early twentieth century realized that tourists turned into real-estate investors and bolstered communities' "city" status by increasing the municipal population. Such growth—and promises of further development— raised real-estate prices. A land broker in Myrtle Beach during the 1920s emphasized the rising population: "This is a good talking point in making

sales." Another directive from the Myrtle Beach Sales Company to its salesmen emphasized the importance of guaranteeing profits to prospective buyers. S. D. Cox, a native of Myrtle Beach, recalled the land boom of the 1920s:
"Those lots down there [near the beach] were $25.00 each to begin with. Now
they went up pretty quick. They got up to way, [sic] up to $200.00." Others
stoked the frenzy. Meyer Eiseman, a realtor in Biloxi, included a warning in
his December 1925 advertisement for Bay Terrace subdivision: "Do not wait for
the advance in price that is soon to come." Promoters of Clifton-by-the-Sea on
Galveston Bay declared, "Greatest Investment Ever Offered." The developers
promised that lots running $75 to $200 "will be selling for several thousand
each" in only a "few short years." Some realtors turned land sales into entertain-
ing events. Harry Fitzpatrick and Company enticed customers to an auction of
"splendid, high, sandy beach" near Mobile by offering a free train ride, $300 in
cash prizes, and concerts. If that was not enough, the realtor promised, "FITZ-
PATRICK BUYERS ALWAYS MAKE MONEY—BUY IN MOBILE NOW." So outlandish
were the gimmicks that the Marx Brothers used the bubble as fodder for their
first film, *Cocoanuts* (1929).[42]

High-pressure tactics complemented promises of instant profits. The Myrtle
Beach Sales Company purchased four seven-passenger sedans in 1926 to provide free rides to prospective buyers and their families. The vehicles were "luxu-
riously furnished with velour upholstering and other requisites that go to make
them comfortable for the prospects." The chauffeur was a "driver-salesman."
Although potential buyers were responsible for their own hotel bills, company
managers arranged discounts. More importantly, as one manager informed
his sales force, the company's close relationship with hoteliers meant that the
realtors' guests were "assured of accommodations no matter how crowded the
place may be." As sales slumped by mid-decade, company executives launched
special arrangements with newspapers through which editors purchased lots
by paying half the price in cash and the other half in advertising for the Myrtle
Beach Sales Company. The tactic "struck a responsive cord [sic]," according to
John Conder, a district sales manager.[43]

Real-estate salesmen heralded the cultural acceptance of leisure after the
First World War. Recreation meant rejuvenation. Modern technologies from
radio to electric lights to the automobile had so detached humankind from
natural rhythms that Americans needed to reengage with nature. The promoters of a land development near Myrtle Beach during the 1920s captured this
sentiment in a booklet aptly titled "Arcady: A National Playground Where the

Leaders of Contemporary Life May Sustain Their Capacity for Work by Bringing to Its Utmost the Art of Rest and Recreation." A passage declared, "The pace of modern life had been so greatly accelerated during the past decade that both men and women have learned that the time allotted to work and play must be more equally divided, if the demands of present-day business and society are to be properly met." Modern life had eroded the serenity of natural rhythms. "Leave off for a season living in the city, eating canned foods, cooked on canned fuel of gas and gasoline, listening to canned music of phonographs, viewing dramas and scenery canned in the celluloid film, displayed with canned light of electricity," urged the editors of the *New Era*, a booster magazine for northwestern Florida, in July 1929. The writers waxed, "Turn off the canned breeze of your electric fan and hie yourself to Panama City's beaches for a little real life in God's out-of-doors."[44]

The collapse of the real-estate bubble by 1926 burdened beach towns for the next decade. Falling cotton prices further eroded southern consumers' buying power. "The continued downward trend of the cotton market has undoubtedly held up sales to a very great extent," noted a Myrtle Beach realtor in October 1926. Northerners wary of the speculative frenzy likewise avoided purchases. Coastal landowners faced even greater burdens as the onset of the Great Depression erased jobs, shrank savings, and eroded available credit. A property developer in South Florida described one "poor devil" who purchased a lot in 1926, paid three-fourths of the price, then fell on hard times. The developer decried the worsening situation in 1931: "For four years he has been unable to even pay the interest on the note remaining so I've been just rocking along telling him I wouldn't foreclose and would give him plenty of time, just so he kept up the taxes." Five other property owners in debt to the developer were in the same dire straits. Such horror stories left many Americans unnerved. The wife of one transplant to the Sunshine State confided to Eleanor Roosevelt in 1934: "To be personal, my husband and I came down here from Chicago a few years ago and suffered all the depressing things that Florida endured about five years longer than the general depression."[45]

Florida communities bore the brunt of the collapse. Coastal Texas, Mississippi, South Carolina, and Virginia did not carry the burden of negative publicity suffered by Florida, where boosters became the victims of their own success—and the victims of nature. The rapid population increase strangled Florida railroads. Railroads restricted building supplies so that freight cars carrying food could stave off shortages. Worse, devastating hurricanes in 1926 and 1928 put the lie to promoters' promises of a tranquil climate. Olive Clower recalled her honeymoon in the state during 1927: "Florida was supposed to be so thriving. But it was not thriving then—vacant rooms, houses half built, hotels half built, motels half built. It was just a big . . . well it was depression; it was a big mess."[46]

As dreams of prosperity turned into a nightmare in Florida, towns such as Galveston, Biloxi, Myrtle Beach, and Virginia Beach showed greater resilience. J. W. McCann, reporting conditions for a Myrtle Beach real-estate firm, described the typical vacationer in 1926: "Conservatively stated we have had at least 2,000 people at the Beach all summer. Most of them high class people on vacation with ample spending money." Several state conventions further buoyed the Grand Strand economy. The *Biloxi Daily Herald* recorded that land values as of 1928 remained higher than over the previous two decades when "there was no appreciable increase in the values on Coast property during the entire period from 1907 to 1925[,] although there was a substantial increase in population and progressive changes" in infrastructure. Even Panama City fared better than areas along the state's Atlantic coast, where prices for beachfront had skyrocketed farthest.[47]

The Great Depression did not squelch the dreams forged in the 1920s. The crisis encouraged a concentration of resources to more effectively advertise local attractions. In June 1935 some forty "hotel managers and businessmen" met in Virginia Beach's Cavalier Hotel to establish a chamber of commerce. The main concern was launching a successful publicity campaign. Businessmen in Myrtle Beach organized a chamber of commerce in 1938, the same year the town incorporated.[48] Rising land prices were sustained as more and more Americans traveled despite the Depression. The *Myrtle Beach News* reported on the revival of real estate in the mid-1930s: "Dirt is believed to be almost as liquid as bank notes." Coastal resorts again enjoyed an economic boom as those with jobs could better stretch their dollars given depressed prices. Moreover, a shaken public considered land titles safer than stocks or bank account deposits, despite reassurances from new federal agencies. "Many who purchased property at the peak of high prices are now able to re-sell at a profit," explained the newspaper. The dunes around Myrtle Beach literally hummed with activity: "More construction than ever before and the tune of the saw and hammer is refreshing and proof that 'good times are here again.'" Furthermore, with thinner pocketbooks and war clouds arising abroad, travelers eyed domestic destinations. Tour guide Edward Reser, who led vacationers through Europe in 1931, remarked, "There are very few Americans over here this year, and what few we *do* see are those who live here."[49]

Real-estate developers and growth-oriented public officials excluded blacks and Jews. The Hardie and Ellis Realty Company of Gulfport echoed others across the region as their salesmen reassured buyers that restrictive covenants kept blacks and Jews out. "Wise and reasonable restrictions," they promised. Jim Crow dictated resort life and property access, facilitated by bank and government policies.[50]

Grand hotels built in the 1920s buoyed tourism by drawing conventions. Structures similar to Galveston's Galvez Hotel and Saint Augustine's Ponce de Leon Hotel dotted the coast. In January 1927 residents of the Mississippi coast feted the opening of the Edgewater Gulf Hotel, a $2.5-million structure standing 165 feet tall. Chicagoans had invested heavily in the hotel equipped with a golf course, tennis courts, stables for twenty horses, a glass-enclosed heated swimming pool, and a parking garage. Chicago's Mayor Devers ceremoniously dug the first spade and hundreds from the Windy City attended the opening a year later, including the film censorship czar Will Hays.[51] The four-hundred-room facility hosted banquets of more than a thousand diners. Locals boasted that the figure was equivalent to "exactly one-fifth of the most optimistic estimate of the population of the entire Harrison county coast cities and their suburbs and environs. A fine percentage indeed." The nearby Buena Vista Hotel contained 250 rooms and supplied a payroll of $75,000 to white staff members alone. The hotel maintained nearly sixty employees. The prestigious Cavalier Hotel opened in Virginia Beach in 1927. Nearly fifteen years later, the *Virginia Beach News* remarked, "The Cavalier did not 'make' Virginia Beach. . . . But none can deny that the money spent for advertising this 'Dominion of Pleasure' greatly aided the marked upsurge of vacationist patronage which followed for the entire Beach." Myrtle Beach benefited from the Ocean Forest Hotel, opened in February 1930. With more than two hundred rooms and a central tower ten stories high, the facility anchored the Grand Strand's convention trade until demolished in 1974. Grand hotels were the castles of the American beachfront.[52]

Coastal municipalities developed an extensive infrastructure capable of managing water supply, sewage treatment, garbage disposal, street maintenance, municipal lighting, and other services, including fire and police protection, for a population that swelled from an annual influx of tourists during the summer. Pavilions, piers, and boardwalks, as well as a modern infrastructure of water systems, schools, hospitals, and highways, drew vacationers and permanent residents. Even isolated communities such as Saint Marks, Florida, just south of Tallahassee on Apalachee Bay, labored to meet tourists' needs by expanding the waterworks and paving highways. In late 1927 Thomas Turner, secretary for the Tallahassee Chamber of Commerce, noted that "resorts along the Gulf shore [near Saint Marks were] being developed so rapidly that even now, the week ends find the hotels and boarding houses over crowded." Few projects were as grand as Galveston's Pleasure Pier. Begun in 1940, the pier, which cost $1.3 million, was considered by boosters the centerpiece for maintaining the city's position "as the leading Southwestern tourist resort." Myrtle Beach civic leaders boasted of the Chapin Memorial Library, opened in June 1949. Through the twentieth century, the facility remained the only public library in the state funded by the town rather than the county. In 1963 librarian Shirley Boone explained the importance of the facility: "A lot of visitors, especially from northern states, express amazement at our selection. . . . They come under the illusion the South is still dirt-poor and a cultural desert."[53]

For vacationers eager for edifying adventures, coastal boosters, like their counterparts in New Orleans and Charleston, preserved historic sites. In the early 1930s the Gulfport Post of the American Legion purchased Ship Island, a 1,200-acre site twelve miles off Mississippi where white sand beaches and emerald water surrounded Civil War–era Fort Massachusetts. Croatian immigrant Pete Skrmetta, who had worked in Mississippi's fishing industry, saw promise in the Legion's effort to create an "immense national playground and amusement resort of the South."[54] Skrmetta won a contract from the Legion to ferry tourists to Ship Island in 1936. He not only ran the route twice daily during the summer season for more than twenty years but personally funded the rebuilding of recreational facilities destroyed in a 1947 hurricane. Skrmetta constructed a canteen, bathhouse, and even two overnight cabins. With Congress's creation of Gulf Islands National Seashore in 1971, Ship Island gained federal protection with private ferries run by the Skrmetta family still plying the waters.[55]

Resorts also rushed to turn mothballed military wares, especially warships, into tourist attractions. Businessmen in Mississippi dismissed efforts to park the battleship U.S.S. *Mississippi* on the coast, chuckling that the vessel would provide a "good concession stand" or a "mighty fine breakwater." The jokes subsided when, in January 1965, boosters in Mobile opened the U.S.S. *Alabama*, a similar decommissioned battleship from the Second World War, to the public. The vessel became one of the Gulf Coast's most popular attractions.[56]

Festivals to honor local culture or an area's natural wonders became a staple of resort calendars. Biloxi launched its first Mardi Gras parade in 1908. In 1916 the Biloxi Literary and Carnival Association formed to make a coastal parade an annual event. John McDermott, a Biloxi native and public official, explained the commitment to Mardi Gras in a 1978 interview: "Like here in Biloxi, Carnival always lands at a time when we don't have tourists. That brings fifty or sixty thousand additional people down from north Mississippi, west Alabama and east Louisiana." Other Biloxians favored the Annual Blessing of the Fleet and Shrimp Festival, started in 1929, as a distinctly local attraction that highlighted a major industry and the area's unique history. Biloxi also heralded Beauvoir, Confederate president Jefferson Davis's coastal retreat. The site became the centerpiece of the Mississippi Gulf Coast Pilgrimage, inaugurated in 1948, which mimicked the more famous home-tour festival in Natchez. Beauvoir alone drew forty thousand visitors annually by the 1970s. Galveston hosted the Oleander Fete each May from 1921 until 1977. In 1955 Virginia Beach launched the Lotus Festival, running for a week in mid-July. Myrtle Beach organized the Sun Fun Festival in June 1951. By the mid-1950s the event attracted crowds of more than sixty thousand vacationers. The local press in 1956 exhorted, "It is no wonder that Sun-Fun will soon become a rival to the famous Mardi-Gras." By the mid-1970s the celebration entertained three hundred thousand revelers through two parades, consisting of forty-five bands and thirty floats.[57]

Elsewhere, dramatic performances highlighted local history and attractions. During the late 1930s the Virginia Beach Historical Society raised funds for "Cavalcade of the Sea," an outdoor spectacular portraying in "song and story the tale of man's conquest of the turbulent deep." Professional directors, actors, and technicians oversaw the extravaganza. In 1958 Virginia Beach boosters launched an outdoor drama titled "The Confederacy" to exploit interest in the Civil War centennial. Felt Confederate officer hats were sold to raise funds and publicize the drama. Inside a new 1,750-seat amphitheater, the audience witnessed the story of the soldiers and, especially, Robert E. Lee. Despite a strong push by local tourism boosters, the drama folded after two seasons. South Carolina claimed its first outdoor drama in 1965 when Pirateland near Myrtle Beach staged a one-act play featuring the buccaneer Blackbeard.[58]

Resorts quickly capitalized on American trends. Boosters along the Grand Strand launched the Myrtle Beach Harley Davidson Biker Rally in 1952, drawing roughly five hundred bikers. The following year attracted 1,500 Harley devotees. One of the largest, most successful motorcycle rallies in the United

States had taken root.[59] The Virginia Beach municipal government embraced as its symbol the Mercury space capsule in the late 1950s as astronaut Alan Shepard brought fame to the resort he called home. By the mid-1960s city leaders replaced the "outdated" image used on official stationery, tie clasps, and other items. They opted for the Cape Henry Lighthouse built in 1790 on a site where the first English colonists landed in 1607 before establishing Jamestown. The image pointed to the rich history of the location as well as the lighthouse's association with water, honoring an edifying as well as a recreational location. By 1968 civic leaders had established a Virginia Beach tour directing motorists to historic sites via some fifty large road signs with "Virginia Beach Tour" emblazoned on a "distinctive, stylized gold sunburst on a blue field."[60]

The popularity of moving pictures proved a boon to tourism as images of crashing waves, bright sun, and coastal breezes promised warmth and tranquility. Throughout the 1920s film crews scoured the nation for events to show before features. Dudley Read, working for the Kinogram and Selznick Companies, added Biloxi to the "Visual News of the World" series. Read visited Mississippi in 1920 to cover ceremonies recognizing the 221st anniversary of Biloxi's founding. Images of oyster fishing, Beauvoir, and "other scenes along the water front" supplied free publicity. In 1950 the Myrtle Beach Chamber of Commerce produced *The Myrtle Beach Story*, a fifteen-minute black-and-white movie about the Grand Strand. Six residents played the role of honeymooners. Television stations in Baltimore, Washington, New York, Chicago, Cleveland, Memphis, Birmingham, Atlanta, and numerous other cities broadcast the film. In 1953 the Virginia Beach Chamber of Commerce, aided by the state, financed *Playtown, U.S.A.* More than two dozen copies of the thirty-minute color movie were distributed to television stations, primarily in the Midwest and Northeast, desperate to fill airtime given the newness of the technology.[61]

Professionalization also emerged. Following on the heels of Biloxi, the Gulfport Chamber of Commerce, in cooperation with state and city officials, established a free school for training restaurant employees and waitresses in May 1942. Such seminars were common. Galveston's National Hotel employees took a six-day course in 1949. The effort inspired businessmen to educate other hotel clerks, lifeguards, "and all those who actually had any dealings with the tourists" on how to be courteous. During the 1960s Virginia governor Albertis Harrison arranged for a series of nearly fifty travel conferences across the state to educate the public on local attractions and hospitality. Owners of tourism-related businesses such as restaurants, motels, and service stations were especially encouraged to send their employees along with policemen and other public servants. Harrison explained, "These people [tourists] will form their opinion of Virginia from the people they meet and the friendly courtesy of their reception. A great many of them might be influenced to stay another day or so in Virginia." By the late 1950s states such as Florida passed laws that required owners renting apartments and houses for short periods to obtain a license. The regulations set standards for lodging but also pushed many homeowners out of the business. In Bay County alone, an estimated six hundred apartments and houses catered to vacationers, thereby cutting into the profits of motels and hotels with the deeper pockets to push favorable legislation. State Hotel and Restaurant Commissioner Richard Egerton declared, "We especially intend to enforce this law."[62]

Continued investments in large hotels and, eventually, large civic halls capable of tapping the convention market paid considerable dividends. In June 1935 the Cavalier Hotel in Virginia Beach hosted nine conventions, bringing more than two thousand attendees. The Ocean Forest Hotel in Myrtle Beach booked forty-two conventions for 1950, attracting some ten thousand conventioneers. In May 1949 alone, eight conventions brought 4,700 visitors to Biloxi. By the 1950s Biloxi hosted more than a hundred conventions annually with attendees staying, on average, for three days. They spent approximately $30 a day on food, lodging, and entertainment. In 1952 Galveston hosted more than ninety conventions with a total of 29,357 attendees who stayed from two to four days. The Galveston Chamber of Commerce estimated that each conventioneer spent $100 in 1966. Of this, $30 went to hotels, $34 was spent at restaurants and on beverages, and roughly $15 went to retail stores. Theaters, sightseeing tours, and various nightclubs and sporting events accounted for more than $9. The remainder went toward transportation costs and miscellany.[63]

The convention trade proved particularly valuable in bolstering business during the off-season. Recognizing the promise of conventions, civic leaders focused on developing convention centers. Virginia Beach in 1957 invested $360,000 in an eye-catching, aluminum-roofed convention hall. The structure had a capacity of 2,500 plus parking for 400 cars.[64] The *Virginia Beach Sun-News* waxed, "Building of the convention hall should extend our normal season by months, both in the spring and fall. It should bring much publicity to our city because of these conventions." Completed before summer 1958, the facility quickly displayed its utility. In its first year, the hall hosted seven conventions, two exhibits, ten dances, twelve concerts, a wrestling match, and thirty-three meetings and events such as fashion shows and a Rotary Club auction. In May 1961 the Virginia Beach City Council named the space-age convention center after Alan Shepard.[65]

The success of Disneyland, opened in California in 1955, inspired the construction of copycat parks. By the 1960s tourists along the southern coast enjoyed a wide range of amusement parks, often with a slight educational bent. The Eight Flags complex in Mississippi opened in 1962. Inside, the Deer Ranch gathered deer from across the globe for tourists to feed and pet. Wild West–themed Six Gun Junction offered a town to explore and six daily shootouts. Visitors could also see several animal acts, including macaws and ducks playing poker. The park, one of the most popular along Mississippi beaches, drew a hundred thousand vacationers a year through the 1970s. Petticoat Junction near Panama City enticed visitors with smoke-spewing locomotives, taking crowds on a ride into history. Vincent "Val" Valentine arrived in Panama City in 1965. A noted illustrator for Popeye cartoons and other animations, he opened two popular Panhandle attractions. Jungle Land, built at a cost of $150,000, caught eyes along the beach as a pot of burning oil spewed black smoke from a faux volcano. A "version of Tarzan's 'Jane,' clad in a bikini jungle outfit" guided tourists through an artificial jungle. Valentine also operated the Old House, one in a chain of four haunted houses also in Indiana, Wisconsin, and Minnesota.[66] In the 1960s tourists flocked to Frontier City in Virginia Beach. Operated by Richard Helgren, the attraction, built at a cost of $250,000, consisted of an Indian village, a steam locomotive named General Sherman, a paddle wheeler, two stagecoaches, and twenty-three buildings, including a general store complete with cracker barrel. Such attractions concocted clever ways to boost attendance while bolstering travel to their community. Frank Luter, a Baptist minister from Virginia Beach, traveled to Ocala, Florida, in March 1964 in order to drive nine hundred miles back to Frontier City aboard a stagecoach in time for the Fourth of July celebration. Along the way, he stopped in seventy communities to promote the park while passersby read signs celebrating Virginia Beach. The Grand Strand possessed Pirateland and Charles Towne, both opened in 1964. Pirateland celebrated the history of piracy along the colonial Atlantic coast but also recreated the haunts of Revolutionary War hero Francis "Swamp Fox" Marion. Stagecoaches traversed the park. Nearby Charles Towne featured a pioneer village and a colonial outpost named Fort Caroline. Mock battles and folk singing entertained patrons. The opening of Disney World in Orlando in October 1971 bolstered tourism across the South but undermined the appeal of these older, smaller amusement parks.[67]

Holidays brought heavy traffic. Jimmy Daffin, who organized Panama City's Fourth of July festivities in 1936, estimated a crowd of 35,000 celebrants, mostly from western Florida, southern Alabama, and southern Georgia. The three-day weekend gave a $350,000 jolt to the city economy. In Myrtle Beach, a community with barely three thousand residents, estimates of July Fourth crowds from the 1930s through the 1960s ranged from seventy-five to a hundred thousand celebrants. July Fourth celebrations by the 1970s drew an estimated two hundred thousand vacationers to the Grand Strand. Celebrants from South Carolina, North Carolina, Tennessee, West Virginia, and Georgia were most prominent.[68]

To fund the infrastructure, residents of beach communities typically favored, in order, a general sales tax, special taxes on hotel rooms and restaurant meals, and utility taxes. Least popular were increases in the cost of business licenses or property taxes. Residents and businessmen adopted measures that best passed costs onto tourists. Eschewing income and inheritance taxes disliked by retirees, Florida legislators leaned heavily on vacationers. During the mid-1950s tourists annually spent $900 million in the state and, as one observer in *Harper's Magazine* noted, "therefore contribute heavily to the consumer levies—gasoline, sales, beverage, cigarette, and racing taxes—which together make up 84.5 cents of each tax dollar collected." In 1951, for instance, Virginia Beach levied a hotel room tax of 3 percent, a two-cent tax on each pack of cigarettes, and a one-cent tax on every twenty cents of admission tickets sold at local movie theaters. The new taxes supplied $50,000 for beach erosion programs, $63,000 for a convention hall, $26,000 for advertising, and $12,000 for improved garbage collection. Though he never held elective office, Sidney Kellam was the political boss of Princess Anne County. He reasoned with residents in 1963: "You will lighten your tax burden if you will help in your own way to make the tourists at home." Happy tourists produced longer stays and good word of mouth that attracted even more vacationers—and thus greater tax revenue.[69]

Instituting a tax on hotels became a favored way of raising revenue for tourism promotion campaigns. Galveston businessmen supported such a levy in 1967, after studying similar measures in San Antonio, El Paso, Hot Springs, New Orleans, Miami, and Boston. Plans for the measure coincided with a proposed "good public relations job" to offset negative publicity in which a "Houston newspaper said the hotel people expected the tourist to pay to get them to come back." A 3 percent hotel and motel tax went into effect at the start of July—just in time for Independence Day.[70]

Southern states grew dependent on tourism-related taxes. The South Carolina treasury, for example, depended increasingly on the taxes drawn from Myrtle Beach. In 1969 the state legislature debated raising a statewide motel tax from 3 percent to 5 percent. Allison Farlow, speaking for the Myrtle Beach City Council, complained, "Forty per cent of the tax will come from within the city limits of Myrtle Beach . . . and 60 per cent of the entire amount will come from the Grand Strand." In the end, state legislators compromised by setting the motel tax at 4 percent. By the 1960s the tourism economy rivaled the agricultural economy across the South. The power of tax revenue and profit slowly turned state legislators from barons of agricultural interests to dukes of coastal empires. By the mid-1970s the South Carolina tourism industry raised more than $70 million annually in state taxes. Each year nonresident travelers spent approximately $750 million within the state.[71]

Fly-by-night merchants and workers followed tourists' migration. Campers in New York in August 1927 noted, with some hyperbole, how the automobile facilitated new ways of earning a living from the tourist trade: "Just above us was a luxurious house on a Packard chassis, just below a Coca-Cola sign painter from Tennessee with an old tent and an old Essex car. Working in the north during the summer and in the south thru the winter." The seasonal tourism market trapped some migrants. Others fell victim to real-estate busts. Traveling in the mid-1920s, a Massachusettsian recorded the human flotsam brought to Florida by the building boom: "There is only work for a limited number and others are stranded in tourist camps. Sometimes they sell their cars in hopes of tiding over until work comes and are left homeless and helpless. Some take flight when their money is gone, but while they still have a car, and travel back to Indiana, Ohio, Maine or wherever they had lived before, begging, working or pawning their clothes on the way for expenses." Resorts fretted over the arrival of jobless Americans seeking opportunities. Police harassment of vagrants became a standard tactic. "The 'no trespassing' sign is up on nine arteries leading into Florida as a warning to the jobless and penniless wanderer that there is no place for him in the state," boasted the *Panama City Herald* in October 1935. Yet the desperate ignored the signs. This was far from a Depression-era phenomenon. Without year-round tourism, resort communities witnessed a labor force in constant flux. Many workers moved elsewhere after the summer. Other low-income employees of closed motels or restaurants stayed, burdening charities and social services. Joyce Pugh, reporting on labor conditions in Florida's Bay County in March 1982, noted that the unemployment rate "traditionally drops by half" at the start of summer. She remarked, "Bay County's unemployment rate continues to hover around 12.5 percent, with out-of-work residents marking the days until the summer boom of beach jobs."[72]

Extended Stays

"Despite all of the complaining I do about the hordes of annoying tourists that invade Bay County during the summer, I am usually sorry to see them go," remarked college student Janice Prendergast of Panama City in 1983. She elaborated, "The reason behind this is that their departure signals the onset of six long months during which even the most imaginative of minds find it difficult to think of anything interesting to do." Fellow student Daniel Day agreed: "Panama City is hardly known for its wide array of wintertime diversions, in fact, it's downright boring."[73]

Although resort cities such as Panama City enjoyed a thriving tourism economy, boosters desired a less seasonal economy with enough diversity to sustain, though not usurp, tourism-related businesses. Those in Panama City expressed particular relief that the International Paper Company opened a mill nearby in 1931, instantly doubling Panama City's population. Fostering further industrial growth, however, was far from businessmen's minds. Local booster W. T. Childs captured the mindset of tourism towns in 1939: "We are particularly fortunate in Panama City in that we have a large factory which forms a backlog to the business life of the community, so with that as a year-round source of income, every business man here can further increase his business as the tourist industry is increased." For Childs and others, landing industrial plants, military bases, or other institutions were key not for economic diversification per se but for the expansion of the tourism infrastructure. Year-round payrolls kept restaurants and hotels open, thus making year-round tourism more likely. The steady flow of income offset, to some extent, the seasonal surge of vacationers. Tourism, however, remained paramount. In 1962 Florida governor C. Farris Bryant declared, "I would say that perhaps as much as half of our new industry that comes from outside of Florida comes as a result of individuals having first visited here as tourists and become aware of the potential of this area for their industries." Roy La Mere of the Virginia Beach Chamber of Commerce echoed Bryant in 1964: "It's a known fact that industry follows tourists."[74]

Boosters emphasized the trickle-out effect of tourism dollars as money spent at hotels, motels, restaurants, and amusements filtered across the community.

Governor Bryant reiterated the familiar reasoning of tourism advocates in a statewide radio broadcast in 1962: "One thing about Florida's tourist business of which we are certain is that the benefits of it flood out into every avenue of economic life. It's like good red corpuscles in the artery of Florida's economic veins." Bryant stressed, "Tourism puts money in the government's tax coffers that helps us build roads with gasoline tax revenues. The sales tax provides the monies on which we operate schools and provide the essential services of government. And then, of course, it supports the wages of the people."[75] When asked in another radio program about the propriety of structuring taxes to tap tourists, Bryant defended, "Well, they do pay a premium, of course. They pay a 7-cent gasoline tax, a cigarette tax, a liquor tax, a gambling tax and a sales tax. . . . This is the way it ought to be." Such arguments nipped in the bud calls for economic diversification while reinforcing commitment to the travel industry.[76]

Although Galveston, with more than fifty thousand residents since the 1920s, and the Mississippi coast, as a winter and summer haven, avoided extensive closures, other resorts were not so lucky. The off-season left stores closed and houses empty. As the Virginia Beach press noted in the 1930s, the end of summer warmth left a high "number of residences . . . unoccupied eight months of the year." The contradiction between advertising year-round recreation while businesses shuttered their doors and windows irked many boosters. By the early 1950s the Virginia Travel Council launched an advertising campaign to "abolish winter," highlighting the smaller crowds and more affordable hotel rates. P. F. Murray, mayor of Virginia Beach, nevertheless recognized that reality clashed with rhetoric. In a September 1953 appeal, Murray asked proprietors closing for the winter to "avoid that 'abandoned look.'" The mayor urged businesses not to cover windows with soap, sheets, or newspaper. The months of neglect also led to cries for sprucing up businesses as the tourist season approached. "As the days become warmer and the sunshine brighter, it should behoove every property owner to take an appraisal of the appearance of his or her property and start early to remodel, repaint, re-landscape or do anything that will make this town a better showplace," commanded the Myrtle Beach newspaper in January 1956.[77]

Little changed during the 1960s and 1970s. Tourists regularly found shops closed in Virginia Beach. Local business leaders likewise complained about the "hastily vacated appearance" of storefronts during the off-season. Yet such was the annual life cycle of many coastal resorts.[78] A Myrtle Beach native described the end of the tourism season in the early 1970s: "Many restaurants will close, beach shops will board up their inviting fronts and beach services will hide away umbrellas and chairs for a well-deserved rest." The closure of businesses meant the departure not only of tourists but also of workers: "College students who have made Myrtle Beach their home for the summer are beginning to vacate their apartments. Many motel owners will soon evacuate their premises for the long season ahead."[79]

The struggle to promote year-round tourism took strange turns, with Myrtle Beach launching the most elaborate and, for some, terrifying campaign. The *Myrtle Beach Sun-News* announced the creation of a secretive group called the Pirate Band in October 1962. Formed by the chamber of commerce's advertising committee, the Pirate Band pursued a "weird individual." Jimmy Allen, chairman of the committee, explained that the "mysterious culprit" was harming the Grand Strand through "sly off-hand remarks and notes or printed materials that contain misleading information." The man was unarmed and did not steal or damage property. Nevertheless, the "saboteur" spread economically lethal word of mouth. The Pirate Band solicited law enforcement. In early November two policemen chased the "bandit," clad in hat and overcoat, across the gridiron during halftime of a Myrtle Beach High School football game, capturing the suspect. A trial held at Myrtle Beach City Hall uncovered the name of the offender—"Auf C. Zonn." The month-long manhunt personified the damaging topic often "innocently talked about for a long time by well-meaning citizens." The chamber encouraged "positive thinking." The gimmick captured public attention in the age of Cold War fears of subversives. However, organizers admitted that the pursuit of Auf C. Zonn "got out of hand." Many residents had taken the newspaper accounts as factual, thereby stirring paranoia of a traitor in their midst.[80]

Teenagers and young adults increasingly filled jobs once taken by transient laborers. The shift reflected a racial transition as well. As Myra Armstead has shown in her study of Newport, Rhode Island, and Saratoga Springs, New York, resort communities before the Second World War made "perennial use" of African Americans, particularly students and teachers from across the South, to fill summertime service jobs. The activism of blacks during the civil rights movement dispelled the popular image of the contented black servant, as discussed further in a later chapter. Business owners increasingly turned to young whites to fill summer jobs, though blacks remained vital given the shortage of laborers. As school terms ended, white youths flocked to the restaurants, amusement parks, and other businesses desperate for summertime workers. Stephanie Pace, a young native of Myrtle Beach writing in the early 1970s, observed the pattern: "Those over 14 years of age graduate to positions such as bag boys, bus boys, waitresses and amusement park barkers." They also gained positions as that "golden tanned, pearly-toothed renter of floats, cabanas and chairs—the lifeguard." Those past the age of twenty gained the "position of valor, the desk clerk."[81]

Resorts long recognized that their eggs lay in one basket. In 1939 the *Virginia Beach News* declared, "Virginia Beach is and in all probability will be strictly a resort town, depending almost entirely on its visitors for an existence." Newspapers along the Grand Strand echoed such sentiment in 1951: "This whole sprawling, energetic, growing, optimistic enterprise called Myrtle Beach is built around a single strip of sand." Calls to attract industry to Myrtle Beach in the early 1970s, for instance, faced strong resistance from tourism interests and companion industries such as construction. Civic leader Collin Hucks observed, "Everybody's just a little bit afraid of growing anyway—the tourist businesses and industry. They figure, if it happens, somebody else will get their employes [*sic*] and they'll be worse off than they are now." Diversifying the economy threatened restaurant, lodging, and amusement establishments.[82]

A growing military infrastructure supplied economic balance. The First World War enlarged military camps in the South, giving resort communities with installations both revenue and an attraction. Marching soldiers, maneuvering naval vessels, and soaring planes created eye-catching entertainment. In June 1915 George Veitt of Virginia Beach heralded such "spectacle" as a "tremendous asset" given the numerous army and navy posts nearby. Virginia Beach celebrated the establishment of Fort Story on its outskirts in 1914, which brought welcomed dollars from the army. The strengthening of other coastal fortifications proved a boon to southern resorts. For instance, Indiana native Claire Cook, visiting Virginia Beach in July 1940, could not resist photographing soldiers on drill at Fort Story.[83]

Yet the experience of the Great War paled in comparison to the industrial and military mobilization associated with the Second World War. Again soldiers and sailors were positioned to fend off potential attacks and to practice firing or bombing runs over the water. Florida governor Millard Caldwell noted several factors that also drew the armed services to southern towns, especially those along the shore. The tranquil climate proved ideal for training aviators. The beaches supplied terrain to practice amphibious landings. And the large number of grand hotels at coastal resorts met the housing needs of a rapidly mobilizing military. Galveston mayor Brantly Harris, for example, boasted that within "easy commuting range there are upwards of 40,000 service men and approximately 100,000 war industry workers." This included Galveston, Texas City, and Houston.[84]

Residents of Virginia Beach witnessed a major transformation. More than 2,500 soldiers, federalized troops from the New York and Pennsylvania National Guard, crammed nearby Fort Story and the State Rifle Range in late September 1940. The men spent a year practicing on anti-aircraft and artillery guns. "The streets of Virginia Beach have almost over night assumed the atmosphere of a military center," declared the *Virginia Beach News*. The newspaper continued, "Army trucks and other equipment are constantly moving back and forth through the Town. Soldiers are to right and left of you during off duty hours. Military police are patrolling up and down the streets with their night sticks assisting the civilian police in preserving order." The Little Creek Naval Amphibious Base held a permanent staff of two thousand. During the Second World War, the base trained more than 180,000 men. The Navy's Fleet Anti-Air Warfare Training Center at Dam Neck contained a permanent staff of a thousand with an additional thousand in trainees. The Oceana Naval Air Station, established in 1942, housed up to 4,500 enlistees. Fort Story, transformed into a coastal artillery fort in 1917, maintained two thousand personnel.[85]

Other communities enjoyed similar mobilization. By March 1941 coastal Mississippians had landed a $6 million Army Air Corps mechanical training center that would host twelve thousand personnel. Keesler Air Force Base was born. The facility occupied a third of Biloxi and instantly doubled the city's population. Panama City also thrived as the federal government spent more than $3.7 million to construct a gunnery school, which opened the day before the attack on Pearl Harbor. The facility, eventually known as Tyndall Air Force Base, housed twenty officers and 1,450 enlisted men in December 1941, ballooning to more than four thousand troops during the Second World War and Cold War.[86]

The large troop presence as well as the influx of workers to provide services for the soldiers and to forge war materiel brought a booming business. Military posts enticed parents, siblings, friends, and partners to vacation near the GIs, although the summer of 1941 marked a high-water mark in tourism until after the conflict. War industries flourished in ports such as Galveston, New Orleans, Mobile, Panama City, Charleston, and Norfolk. Well-paid workers patronized nearby leisure spots. On a visit in 1943, John Dos Passos witnessed the influx of rural southerners into a cramped but thriving Mobile: "They can make more spot cash in a month than they saw before in half a year. They can buy radios, they can go to the pictures, they can go to beerparlors, bowl, shoot craps, bet on the ponies. Everywhere they rub elbows with foreigners from every state in the Union." They also ventured to nearby beaches.[87]

American entrance into the war brought a significant decline in leisure travelers. Rationing of tires and gasoline hindered travel. Whereas Virginia Beach hotels and cottages enjoyed a peak year for tourism in 1941, the same establishments witnessed an approximately 25 percent decline in business during summer 1942. Close proximity to population centers and shorter transportation routes buoyed numbers. Other resorts along the Gulf and Atlantic coasts suffered a nearly 50 percent drop in business. Customers for motels along main inland highways had "dropped almost to the vanishing point." For example, the popular Skyline Drive operated by the National Park Service endured a 95 percent decline in traffic.[88]

Coastal communities literally went dark during the Second World War. To reduce the silhouette of Allied ships threatened by German submarines, the military ordered a dim-out of lighting ten miles inland from the Gulf of Mexico; cities with a 5,000+ population within twenty-five miles of the coast were also subject to dim-outs. Similar regulations affected the Atlantic coast. Although dim-out restrictions eased in late 1943, orders rescinding all restrictions did not come until the defeat of Germany in May 1945.[89]

Federal officials commandeered many hotels, set lodging rates, and policed activities dangerous to the war effort. The navy, for instance, used the Cavalier Hotel in Virginia Beach as a radar training school. The army seized the nearby Hotel Warner to house civilian support staff. Rent controls hampered the ability of rooming houses and hotels to adjust rates during the peak tourist season—or to raise rates on military personnel and war workers already faced with a housing shortage. Security concerns also restricted camera use along the shore.[90]

The war left bolstered populations and valuable military bases that grew as the Cold War escalated. Built in 1937, the Myrtle Beach Municipal Airport fell under the jurisdiction of the Army Air Corps in June 1940. The airstrip became a training ground for bombardiers who flew practice missions over the Atlantic. Although the facility returned to public use in 1947, the U.S. Air Force claimed the site in 1956 as Myrtle Beach Air Force Base. Boosters rejoiced, noting that "seldom, if ever, has a $25 million plus installation failed to exert a positive and stimulating effect on the economy of the area in which it's located." Gulfport, near Keesler, added 2,102 family homes, 19 duplexes, 18 fourplexes, and 32 garage apartments to its neighborhoods during the 1940s. Biloxi claimed an additional 1,918 family homes as well as a number of apartment complexes and other dwellings. The Virginia Beach Chamber of Commerce even placed a bid to make the coastal resort headquarters for the newly formed United Nations. Certain of failure, chamber manager Joseph Spruill nevertheless understood the incalculable value of free worldwide publicity.[91]

Military installations thrived through the Cold War. Eglin Air Force Base, established in 1935 as Valparaiso Bombing and Gunnery Base, brought an economic boom to Fort Walton, Florida. Eglin became the largest air base in the world during the Vietnam War. Journalist Mike Darley observed in 1967: "Tourism once was the big thing in the Playground [as Okaloosa County was nicknamed] and only a few years ago the area had more tourists than Panama City. Eglin, however, long ago overshadowed tourism as the mainstay of the economy and this important industry has gone by the wayside." So crowded was the installation that a "big percentage" of motel rooms in the Fort Walton area were rented by the air force for year-round housing of temporary duty personnel. The severe shortage of motel rooms stirred a construction boom in the late 1960s as Okaloosa County sought to restore the tourism industry. The "pint-sized Army Transportation Corps" at Fort Story, as described by one reporter in 1957, deposited a monthly payroll of $258,000 into the Virginia Beach area. Nearly 850 military and civilian personnel—around two thousand persons when including spouses and children—paid more than $40,000 a month in rent in Virginia Beach. When including expenditures by the government, Fort Story's yearly financial impact stood nearly four times greater than Virginia Beach's municipal budget.[92]

The military bases provided year-round payrolls, entertainment, and visitors. Tourism promoters near Keesler Air Force Base noted during the 1950s that "visiting families are combining vacation time with a visit to their sons," adding to the roughly "20,000 vehicles . . . many of them tourists" passing along the coast daily.[93] The monthly payroll exceeded $5 million by 1960 as the facility supported 37,613 officers, airmen, civilian employees, and military dependents. To bolster American pride and confidence during the Cold War, the military launched Armed Forces Day in 1949. Installations across the country opened to the public for displays of marching soldiers and the latest armaments. Keesler Air Force Base in 1954 attracted 60,000 spectators who watched

12,000 airmen parading in review while more than 250 aircraft performed drills overhead. The celebration at the Norfolk Naval Base typically attracted twenty thousand spectators during the early 1950s.[94]

Such open houses gained importance during the Vietnam War, as the military struggled to uphold support for the conflict. For Armed Forces Day in May 1968, Eglin Air Force Base hosted a ninety-minute airshow. The performance featured "front line jet fighters, various bomber aircraft, the latest techniques and tactics of counterinsurgency aerial operations, and a demonstration of the variable sweep wing F-111A." Visitors also witnessed aerial refueling and a high-altitude–low-opening jump by commandos. Training exercises, which simulated wartime conditions, frequently entertained thousands of spectators. At other times, the air force's Thunderbirds and other daredevil units of the armed services traveled from installation to installation performing for the public. Military bands, marching units, and flyovers likewise played a "big role" in celebrations such as the Sun Fun Festival in Myrtle Beach.[95]

Military bases, however, were not a panacea. Harassment of local women by military personnel was common. In 1942, for example, a soldier assaulted a woman in a Gulfport tourist cabin. Paul Stults, an airman training along the Grand Strand in 1942, warned his girlfriend: "I know soldiers fairly well and there are *a few* good ones." Hunter Thompson, stationed at Eglin Air Force Base in 1957, recounted a drunken beach party in which he ran along a public strand in nothing more than flippers and goggles, all the while shouting, "Let's have an orgy!" One chronicler recounted an incident along the King's Highway in Myrtle Beach in the 1950s. As two young ladies drove along the road, a car driven by "young army men" pulled behind them and honked their horn. Ignored, the soldiers next pulled alongside the women, again honking. The women responded by reaching for a small baby, holding it "high enough for the soldiers to see," and the soldiers quickly sped away. "Commented one of the young housewives, 'it works better than trying to show your wedding ring.'"[96]

Other events were less threatening but equally troubling. Those in Virginia Beach in April 1958 expressed worry after hearing a massive nighttime explosion that caused "widespread damage in the area." An underwater demolition team had detonated a four-hundred-pound TNT charge during a training exercise. Less forceful explosions from the naval training grounds at Dam Neck frequently shook windows throughout the town.[97]

The presence of so much military hardware carried potentially deadly consequences. In 1954 a pilot based at Tyndall Air Force Base parachuted from his exploding fighter jet. Burning debris crashed in a wooded area less than two miles from the shore, sparking a forest fire. Other crashes were far more lethal. In 1958 an air force training jet smashed through the concession stand and several rows of parked cars near the pier in Myrtle Beach State Park. A father and his two young sons from New Albany, Indiana, were killed instantly as they sat in their vehicle. A recreational fisherman from Lancaster, South Carolina, also died.[98]

Sometimes ordnance made disconcerting appearances along the shore. Donald Spinell of Fort Walton Beach encountered a secret weapon designed for Vietnam when he strolled the beach in July 1967. Seeing a small, brown, plastic disk the size of a quarter with knobs protruding from each side, Spinell reached down to study the item. The object exploded, leaving him with hand and eye injuries. The beachcomber had discovered one of six thousand "mini-mines" accidentally dropped by a pilot into Choctawhatchee Bay and the Gulf of Mexico. Designed to burst with the sound of a large firecracker so as to alert troops of incoming enemy, the dangerous mini-mines drifted onto 120 miles of beachfront. Several hundred sailors, airmen, and soldiers scoured the shore for two days to recover the tiny explosives. An airplane equipped with a loudspeaker circled the beaches to warn tourists of the hazard. During the retrieval effort, serviceman also discovered a 260-pound fragmentation bomb buried in the sand.[99]

The economic and foreign policy of the United States during the Cold War also expanded the American tourism market. New technologies popularized distant locations. Cultural observer Betty Lou Points wrote in 1957: "In this air age of television, automobiles, and war-time mobility, concepts of distances have shortened in 50 years until your next-door neighbor may have lived in the farthest reaches of the United States or its territories, bringing national-mindedness into focus as essential to being up-to-date." She could well have added international-mindedness given the impact of the Cold War. With Europe focused on rebuilding after the Second World War, few Europeans traveled to the United States until the 1960s. In contrast, the federal government encouraged American travel abroad as a means of solidifying foreign economies and discouraging communism. Juan Trippe, president of Pan American World Airways, declared, "For we Americans, foreign travel is a cultural, political and economic necessity if our country is to fulfill its responsibility of world leadership."[100]

The resulting travel gap troubled federal officials by the 1960s. As the United States struggled with the costs of the War on Poverty and the war in Southeast Asia, the Commerce Department courted foreign travelers to offset the outflow of dollars to overseas destinations. In 1960 only 491,359 foreign tourists entered the United States. Congress passed the International Travel Act in 1961, providing matching funds of up to 50 percent—with a cap of $4 million—for advertising campaigns in foreign nations. The travel gap soon narrowed, although an imbalance persisted. Nearly three million Americans traveled abroad in 1967, spending $1.4 billion. In contrast, more than 1.1 million foreigners visited the United States, contributing $551 million to the domestic economy. President Johnson, confronting the burgeoning federal budget, proposed either a daily tax on Americans venturing to other countries or a two-year ban on nonessential American travel abroad. While tourism boosters certainly preferred Americans to vacation at home, they also feared foreign retaliation. Editors for the *Myrtle Beach Sun News* agreed with "South Carolina tourism officials that one point—curbing travel abroad—might upset Horry County's apple cart." Congress rejected both ideas. Yet the "travel gap" targeted by the president was worrying. As reported by *Life* in August 1968, the gap had exceeded $2 billion between what the 3.4 million American travelers disbursed in foreign nations and what the 1.5 million foreign tourists spent in the United States. Southern beach resorts now found themselves competing in an increasingly diverse, international market facilitated by the federal government's campaign to bolster the domestic tourism industry by increasing arrivals from Europe and elsewhere. In 1971 Congress raised the limit of matching funds to $15 million. The Virginia Beach city council became one of the first to apply for the funding.[101]

Jet travel facilitated the rapid internationalization of the American tourism industry. By the late 1960s ten foreign tourists arrived by air for every one who arrived by sea. Speaking in 1977, Florida governor Reubin Askew noted that 5 percent of tourists to the Sunshine State came from Canada while Latin America provided an "increasing source of tourism." Yet Europe possessed "abundant potential." In 1976 Florida led all other states as a destination for European travelers. Some 138,000 came to the Sunshine State, a 20 percent increase over the previous year. Estimates by boosters proposed that almost a million Europeans could be lured to Florida alone by the end of the decade through increased advertising and promotional campaigns. Askew spoke with optimism: "Even with the cost of airfare, a trip to Florida is a good deal in terms of dollars for a European. As the cost of air travel decreases with increased competition, this good deal will begin to look even better in European eyes."[102]

Of foreign nations, Canada became a prime target. By the 1960s about nine hundred thousand Canadians traveled to the United States each year. A "goodly portion of these travelers," explained tourist development coordinator

Samuel Scott of Virginia Beach, ventured to Atlantic resorts closest to Canada. "For a few days we have another investigative body visiting us which is paying its own way and helping us pay our taxes," rejoiced a Myrtle Beach resident. He continued, "It is a bunch of nice Canadians and they are investigating our golf courses, our restaurants and motels plus some of our natural wonders." To entice these foreigners, Virginia Beach businessmen sent representatives such as Julia Nelms to work the city's booth at the Canadian National Exposition, which drew roughly three million Canadians annually during the 1950s and 1960s.[103] Clad in southern belle garb complete with hoop skirt and sun hat, Nelms distributed "hundreds of pounds of promotional material (including salt water taffy)." The city's efforts made Canadians the largest segment of tourists during the fall. Further south, an estimated thirty-five thousand Canadians visited the Grand Strand each March during the early 1970s. Their arrival brought vital business during an otherwise quiet part of the year.[104]

Canadians formed such a significant portion of the tourism market for Myrtle Beach and Virginia Beach that both developed festivities to convert each resort into Canadian outposts. By the early 1960s Myrtle Beach businesses had launched Canada Days, a weeklong event held in early April. Retail stores and motels flew Canadian flags. Canadian shoppers received special discounts. Awards were given to the oldest Canadian couple and largest Canadian family vacationing in Myrtle Beach. In the 1970s the rebranded Can-Am Festival drew forty thousand Canadians and forty thousand Americans. "They're treated to 10 days of parades, beauty contests, tours, fish fries, pancake breakfasts, golf and fishing tournaments, sand castle building contests—they even try to catch a greased pig," described one guidebook. By the late 1960s Virginia Beach launched the weeklong Canadian Holiday by the Sea. Held at the end of April, the event transformed the resort. "Canadian flags will be flown, Canadians will receive free Canadian newspapers and Canadian currency will be accepted at most accommodations at even exchange on direct advance notice," announced the *Virginia Beach Sun*. Civic leaders planned a golf tournament, nature walk, square dance, and other festivities to entertain their foreign guests.[105]

Southern beach communities also welcomed a growing number of retirees. Yankees entering their golden years had come to the South since the late nineteenth century to escape cold winters, crowded cities, and industrial pollution. They often voiced more liberal political views. Some possessed a spirit of entrepreneurship. A retiree who farmed satsumas in Mississippi's Pearl River County told a WPA interviewer in the 1930s his reason for settling in Dixie: "I had been coming South for nine years for the International Harvester Company, and had watched the development of land in Oranges and Tung oil. I thought raising Oranges would be a delightful pastime after I retired as I had no desire to go to seed, and then too, the months of February, March and April are lovely here and on the gulf coast." With pensions fattened under the New Deal, retirees looked for sites where their budgets could stretch. Norman Ford's *Where to Retire on a Small Income*, first published in 1935 and in its nineteenth edition by the 1970s, urged those in northern cities to escape to "where prices were so much lower and the demands made by winter cold on the domestic budget so much less." The South's depressed wages—a by-product of Jim Crow—was thus "where living costs were way below average." Besides saving on housing and heating costs, Ford argued that the warmer climate encouraged "lighter and consequently less costly food" and made expensive winter clothing "superfluous." Skilled retirees could also find temporary work if needed in the booming construction industry.[106]

By the mid-twentieth century, retired veterans with military pensions started settling in the region. A Biloxi resident observed, "But since I have been here, you have had a lot of people from Keesler retiring here—a lot of them that were down here during their hitch in service liked it and came back." Bill Goodman, a former air force colonel, spent twenty-one years at more than a dozen bases around the globe. In 1973 Goodman and his wife settled in Enterprise, Alabama, but also purchased a vacation home in Panama City. According to an interviewer, the Goodmans were "among a growing number of people from Alabama, Georgia, Kentucky, Tennessee, Louisiana, Mississippi, and Florida who are acting on a 'someday' dream of owning a place on the beach."[107] Other Gulf communities likewise witnessed a wave of new settlers during the 1970s. Retired "ex-military and Midwestern couples" streamed into Fort Walton Beach; at Destin, "many ex-military officers and executives" dramatically altered the once sleepy fishing village. Similar increases affected Myrtle Beach and Virginia Beach.[108]

Boosters also looked to universities to balance the fiscal year. The academic year complemented the economic cycle by supplying young customers during the off-season and potential employees during holidays and summer. Virginia Beach enjoyed the benefits of an expanding Old Dominion University in Norfolk. Established as a division of William and Mary College in 1930, the institution became an independent college in 1962 and a university in 1969. Outside of Gulfport, Mississippi, Colonel James Chappel Hardy founded Gulf Coast Military Academy in 1912 and Gulf Park College for Women in 1919. The women's college emerged, according to the WPA guidebook for Mississippi, as "the center of the Coast activities in music, painting, and drama." The finishing school for girls closed in 1971, unable to recover from damage caused by Hurricane Camille. A year later, the facility reopened as the Gulf Park Campus of the University of Southern Mississippi. Gulf Coast Military Academy closed in 1976, and William Carey University of Hattiesburg purchased the facility. Panama City opened Gulf Coast Community College in September 1957 in the abandoned Wainwright Shipyard. The Grand Strand welcomed the groundbreaking in October 1962 of what would become Coastal Carolina University. Texas A&M University at Galveston opened in 1962 with a focus on maritime studies.[109]

Angry Tidings

The growth of tourist resorts threatened nearby small farmers. Throughout the early twentieth century, homeowners, vacationers, and resort managers complained about the encroachment of farm animals on their landscaped lawns and shrubs. Building a coastal empire for vacationers meant manufacturing a landscape of tranquility divorced from inland farms and open-range customs.

The Mississippi coast was representative of such tensions. "Almost daily reports come to the Herald office of damage done to yards and gardens by live stock in different parts of the city," declared the Biloxi newspaper in 1920. A Gulfport city ordinance banning livestock between the beach and the Louisville and Nashville Railroad tracks several miles inland failed. Roaming animals still encroached despite the hiring of two horseback officers to patrol the line during the day. Many of the hungry culprits drifted into town at night to munch on blossoms, expensive shrubs, and manicured lawns while depositing odorous piles. A. C. Purple awoke to see that cows had ravaged the garden around his beachfront home. The financial loss amounted to more than $100. Only forcing farmers to enclose their animals would remove the headache, yet doing so by law in a state legislature and court system controlled by agricultural interests proved daunting. In 1927 the Mississippi Coast Club and others expressed outrage when cattle ravaged Edgewater Park, adjacent to the Edgewater Gulf Hotel. The $25,000 spent on landscaping and beautification of the park seemed wasted after cows chewed on palms, lawns, and other plants. Finding the owners of the roving bovines proved difficult given the damages they might suffer. Again in 1934, efforts to restrict livestock south of the Louisville and Nashville Railroad tracks floundered as provisions of the 1890 Mississippi constitution prohibited the legislature from authorizing "local, private or special laws relating to the stock law" or granting authority to county officials to do so.[110]

Frustration mounted until 1954 when a Continental Trailways bus overturned on Highway 49, killing three passengers and injuring eighteen. The driver veered off the highway to avoid roaming cattle. After the accident, which occurred just nineteen miles north of Gulfport, coastal communities rallied to change the state's livestock laws. The legislature did so in 1956, authorizing counties to hold elections on the closed or open range question as well as allowing counties to use a gasoline tax to fence highways. Harrison County supervisors immediately fenced Highways 49 and 55 while retaining the open range. The legislature also authorized coastal counties to restrict livestock a mile from the shoreline. The provision permitted county supervisors to penalize violators and to accept donations for fencing.[111]

Tourism boosters in other southern states shared the frustration over roaming livestock. In 1939 state representative Fuller Warren of Duval County—who would become governor of Florida in 1949—proposed a bill that restricted livestock near highways. Proponents tried to maneuver the bill through the Forestry Committee rather than the Livestock Committee, which Warren recognized as "loaded against us." He argued that fencing laws fell under the Forestry Committee because such laws were "designed to stop the malicious practice of woods-burning which, it is suspected, is carried on by the owners of range cattle." Warren cleverly packaged a favored bill of tourism interests as a means to safeguard not only highways (and the landscape seen by motorists) but also valuable timber stands. Yet the powerful livestock industry mustered strong support, effectively killing such bills until the mid-twentieth century. In the meantime, tourists worried about roaming livestock. A Baltimore family remarked about their drive through the Panhandle in 1949: "Well here we have to watch out for cows and pigs that cross the roads." Tourists from Maine driving to Miami in March 1954 encountered an "oddity when along the heavily traveled highway we saw hundreds of cows and pigs that roamed uncontrolled along the sides of the road" in South Carolina and Georgia.[112]

During the 1950s, as tourism rivaled agriculture, Alabama, Georgia, Florida, and other states joined Mississippi legislators in eliminating the last vestiges of the open range in the South. But before hogs and cattle could be penned, however, officials needed to repel mosquitos and storm surges.

CHAPTER TWO

Sand Storms
Mosquitoes, Hurricanes, and the Environmental Movement

Though the adventurer wandered southward from Ohio "by the wildest, leafiest, and least trodden way," he soon confronted the scars made by civil war.[1] Trails led past "broken fields, burnt fences, mills, and woods ruthlessly slaughtered."[2] Homes were abandoned. Both blacks and whites pieced together new lives in the aftermath of emancipation. Southerners spoke largely of the war, slavery, and reconstruction. Conversations about botany seemed an odd topic. In late 1867 the young John Muir needed to exercise caution on his walk to the Gulf of Mexico. Farmers eyed him with suspicion when he stopped to ask for food or lodging. Dumbfounded Tennesseans and Georgians repeatedly warned Muir to tread carefully through the countryside where camps of "wild, runaway negroes" and "guerrilla bands . . . long accustom to plunder" threatened to waylay the nature lover.[3] Despite tense encounters with both, Muir persisted. He reached Savannah, spending days sleeping in Bonaventure Cemetery as he waited for his brother to mail him money. With his wallet replenished, Muir ferried to Fernandina, Florida, then crossed the swampy peninsula to Cedar Key. He had reached the Gulf of Mexico. But, within days, he lay near death—a victim of malaria.

John Muir, the pioneering environmentalist who would found the Sierra Club, reveled both in his journey and in his ability to survive the disease that left him unconscious for days. But his travelogue offered little to entice tourists. He remarked on his walk through Florida: "Vegetable cats of many species will rob him of his clothes and claw his flesh, while dwarf palmettos will saw his bones, and the bayonets will glide to his joints and marrow without the smallest consideration for Lord Man." Worse, Muir believed that "no portion of this coast, nor of the flat border which sweeps from Maryland to Texas, is quite free from malaria. All the inhabitants of this region, whether black or white, are liable to be prostrated by the ever-present fever and ague, to say nothing of the plagues of cholera and yellow fever that come and go suddenly like storms, prostrating the population and cutting gaps in it like hurricanes in woods." Inhospitable Florida confirmed a tenet often repeated by Muir. Man should seek harmony with nature, not domination of nature. Muir spat, "But when man betakes himself to sickly part of the tropics and perishes, he cannot see that he was never intended for such deadly climates."[4] John Muir was no booster.

Muir's analysis of the southern environment carried within it the cultural baggage shared by many white Americans regarding race and the tropics. Long-held beliefs that Africans were better suited to the southern climate had underpinned arguments for slavery. The presence of the sickle cell within some persons of African descent granted resistance to malaria, though the disease certainly crossed the color line. As the United States emerged as an imperial power in the late nineteenth century, debate raged over whether tropical climates belonged to colored peoples. In 1916 racial theorist Madison Grant warned in *The Passing of the Great Race* that "continuous sunlight affects adversely the delicate nervous organization" of whites, especially the Nordics of northern Europe who he claimed formed the pinnacle of human evolution. The "increasing proportion of 'poor whites' and 'crackers'" across the former Confederacy stood as "symptoms of lack of climatic adjustment." The arguments resonated; the book sold more than 1.5 million copies during the next two decades. Grant prophesied, "It is quite evident that the West Indies, the coast region of our Gulf States, perhaps, also the black belt of the lower Mississippi Valley must be abandoned to Negroes."[5]

Rather than fleeing, whites flocked to southern shores. Railroad, timber, and real-estate companies celebrated the scenery and supposedly salubrious climate of the coastal South. But American expansion into Hawaii, the Philippines, Cuba, Puerto Rico, Panama, and other tropical areas at the turn of the century and the military occupation of Haiti (1915–1934) and the Dominican Republic (1916–1924) increased concerns about exposure to tropical climates. Robert Ward, in the *New England Journal of Medicine*, wrote in 1929, "The acclimatization of the white race in the tropics is a question of vast importance. Upon it depend the future settlement, control, government and utilization of the tropics." Converting winter retreats into year-round tourism industries required taming the environment. Only by conquering disease, suppressing mosquitoes, and guarding against hurricanes could southern tourism flourish. Tourists needed to feel safe; investors demanded assurances that their beachfront property would not disappear under storm surges or piles of vacationers' litter.[6]

Beach Fever

The death of Sherry Seymour at Ocean Springs, Mississippi, in September 1897 alarmed the Gulf Coast. An autopsy by Dr. Juan Guiteras, one of the world's foremost experts on yellow fever, confirmed the worst. Yellow Jack had arrived. Officials along the coast scattered tons of disinfectant onto the streets. Factories closed, eventually leading Biloxi mayor Harry Howard to beg for donations of food and medicine, neither of which many laborers could afford. New Orleanians flushed gutters. Some towns, including the Crescent City, quarantined neighborhoods with infected residents. The Louisville and Nashville Railroad carried evacuees to Atlanta, minus any baggage since germs were thought to cause the disease.[7]

Beach resorts in the late nineteenth century rested precariously between seasons of life and death. During the winters, roughly from October through March, the southern coast offered a refuge for the sickly. Places such as Biloxi and Fernandina provided salubrious warmth for a few wealthy northerners fleeing bone-chilling winters, rank and overcrowded cities, and a countryside where steel mills and other factories polluted the air and water. Yet those who stayed too long at southern resorts met a very busy Grim Reaper—the mosquito. High temperatures and stagnant water created ideal breeding grounds from early spring to late fall.

Malaria is a parasite transmitted by *Anopheles* mosquitoes common across the United States. Breeding in stagnant fresh water, preferably in sunlight, the mosquitoes spread two strains of malarial parasites. *Plasmodium falciparum* frequently killed. *Plasmodium vivax*, a more common strain, rarely killed. Instead, sufferers endured weeks of chills, shivers, headaches, nausea, an enlarged spleen, and fever. These symptoms spiked every one to three days depending on the parasite's incubation cycle. The strain could lay dormant in the human liver for up to four years. Mosquitoes quickly spread malaria each year while those already infected could experience relapses. In mid-October 1877 Joseph Price, the owner of a Florida orange grove, described the pain of the auger and the thrill at the passing of the summer fever season: "I have felt new life and energy in me ever since 11 a.m. to day. In first place, yesterday being my twenty first chill day—a critical one for a convalescing 'chill man'—and I missing my chill, made me feel very joyful." Residents consumed quinine to ward off the effects of malaria. One visitor to Florida pined, "All through the country are springs of sulphur, magnesia, and iron. It is a pity there are not quinine springs in a country where chills and fever are so prevalent as in many portions of the south and west, and where, indeed, they must continue to prevail so long as people persist in living in natural swamps, or cultivating them artificially in the midst of their cities." Located among the piney woods and cypress swamps of the Florida Panhandle, the town of Perry regularly bore one of the highest infection rates in the South. Approximately 50 percent of the population suffered from malaria into the 1920s.[8]

Yellow Jack victims suffered more egregiously. *Aedes aegypti* mosquitoes carried the virus. The species breeds in stagnant fresh water collected in logs, cisterns, or other such locations. The mosquitoes primarily reside in the very Deep South. Unlike malarial victims, yellow fever survivors gained immunity and were not carriers. Instead, mosquitoes acted as the reservoir. Yellow fever outbreaks were not a yearly occurrence, especially when freezes or dry spells disrupted mosquito populations. The disease therefore reappeared sporadically, often when boats from the Caribbean or Latin America reintroduced yellow fever by transporting infected passengers or mosquitoes. Typically epidemics erupted in July, lasting until the first freeze in autumn. Those struck by the disease, if a mild strain, suffered flulike symptoms for a week. A more lethal strain brought chills, fever, and muscle pain. Soon, liver failure and jaundice occurred. Victims hemorrhaged from the gums, nose, and stomach. They vomited congealed blood. Roughly a week after the onset of the disease, renal failure occurred, marking the sufferer's last hours. Mortality rates stood between 10 and 60 percent. An outbreak of Yellow Jack in New Orleans in 1853, for instance, killed more than eight thousand victims—half of the city's mortalities that year.[9]

Diseases held a death grip on the tourism industry. Quarantines left communities isolated. Residents of Bay Saint Louis, for instance, petitioned the Mississippi State Board of Health in 1898 to slacken its quarantine policy in case of a yellow fever outbreak in New Orleans. Prosperity depended on maintaining unfettered access to the city. They argued, "The City of Bay St. Louis is practically immune, nearly every subject in the town having had yellow fever during the last summer." The petition then explained, "We are virtually a suburb of New Orleans dependent in summer upon those who resort to our shores. These people cannot risk being quarantined away from their business on the one hand or from their families on the other, and unless some reasonable intercourse can be secured those out of whom our poorer classes live will go elsewhere for health and recreation." Worse, negative publicity from the epidemics repelled investors. Varina Davis, widow of the former Confederate president, realized the literal cost of disease in 1905, when an outbreak ravaged Louisiana and Mississippi. Davis wrote of her desire to divest acreage from the family's coastal retreat: "I hoped to sell the Beauvoir land but yellow fever came and I could not do it without an immense sacrifice."[10]

During the nineteenth century, Americans blamed the miasma produced by sewage, decaying vegetation, and stagnant waters for deadly maladies. Southerners especially suspected marshes and swamps. Although hated by the largely pro-Confederate population of occupied New Orleans, Union general Benjamin Butler, afraid an epidemic might weaken his garrison, ordered frequent street cleaning. Flushing gutters and removing rubbish unwittingly diminished mosquito breeding grounds. Such cleanup campaigns became a standard weapon against Yellow Jack. After the 1878 yellow fever epidemic spread through the Mississippi River Valley, decimating the population of Memphis, southern communities refined their approach. They modernized sewerage systems, improved garbage disposal, and organized health boards to disperse the latest medical information to the public. Convinced that germs rather than mosquitoes spread yellow fever, southerners used quarantines, fumigation, pots of burning tar, and disinfectants for protection. As the yellow fever outbreak that killed Seymour worsened between New Orleans and Mobile, for example, news came of the death of thirteen-year-old Thomas Lovejoy in Beaumont, Texas. The regional press looked with suspicion on his family's business—they ran a boardinghouse. But more attention was given to the boy's job. A report announced, "The little fellow was a newsboy and among other newspapers he handled a New Orleans paper."[11]

Quarantines and evacuations proved the most successful means of controlling yellow fever, especially as medical experts recognized that the disease typically arrived via ships. Vessel quarantines were common, damaging the region's reputation for commerce. Cargos such as bananas rotted. Travelers and immigrants endured long waits in the summer heat while ships, persons, and baggage received treatment with lime, steam, or sulfurous gas. When the disease slipped past these stations, communities cut contact with infected areas, often turning back trains or wanderers at gunpoint. W. C. B. Sollee recalled the panic in Jacksonville when Yellow Jack appeared in 1888. Desperate evacuees crowded the railroad station and "when the trains pulled out they were jammed to the guards with refugees—packing the platforms, hanging on to the guard-rails and even clambering up on the tops of the cars." Sollee stayed behind, securing the homes of his friends: "I found food in vessels ready to cook, bureau drawers partially emptied and left wide open, and other evidence of a panic-stricken populace. Jacksonville was practically depopulated." Famed educator E. Warren Clark likewise observed the exodus of thirty thousand Floridians from across the state: "Every train on the Southern lines has a State inspector on board. Certificates are required, and mails and baggage are fumigated. Every suspected Floridian is watched, and his name and destination telegraphed to every station." Clark proposed using coastal camps as shelters for Floridians, declaring "that they have sea-side resorts available in their own State without taxing the hospitality, and endangering the health, of neighboring Southern States." Winter retreats for northerners could house southerners in fever season because "all the better class of people keep out of Florida during the Summer."[12]

Conducting research in Cuba, army medical officer Walter Reed revolutionized understandings of Yellow Jack when, through experiments undertaken in 1900–1901, he identified the mosquito as the disease vector. His evidence killed two pests with one figurative swat. Linking diseases such as malaria and yellow fever to the insect made control of the bloodsucker imperative. Across the South, communities moved against the mosquito—action that made the 1905 yellow fever outbreak in the New Orleans area the last to afflict the United States. Fear of Yellow Jack lost intensity as a result, but concern inspired the war on the mosquito well into the twentieth century. As late as 1967, Orin Evans of the Florida State Board of Health promoted mosquito eradication by linking the insect to potential yellow fever outbreaks. Even the language Evans used to describe the mosquito's presence suggested disease. Patrolling the state's mosquito control districts, Evans informed Bay County residents, "We begin working in the county with the heavier infection rate . . . and then work our way to the lighter infected areas."[13]

A crusade for mosquito eradication emerged in the decade after Reed's discovery. New Jersey, burdened by saltwater mosquitoes, pioneered research on mosquito control. California boosters closely followed. In the South the 1905 outbreak in New Orleans encouraged assaults on the mosquito menace. Systematic oiling of ponds and waterways as well as ditching of marshes to improve drainage occurred. The *Biloxi Daily Herald* in 1915 editorialized, "But the one greatest drawback to the South—the one greatest enemy—is the mosquito." Known to carry the "germs of malaria and yellow fever," the Mississippians speculated that mosquitoes carried other illnesses in its "poison." Only the obliteration of the insect would allow the South to reach its potential. For coastal communities, the struggle amounted to a "mosquito war."[14]

Mosquito control emerged as a major reason for incorporating beach outposts. The matter was so significant that when Virginia Beach incorporated in 1906, becoming the only incorporated town in Princess Anne County, newly elected mayor E. P. Holland made his "first communication to the first council of the town" about mosquito eradication. He called for filling in or pumping salt water into nearby Lake Holly, a breeding ground for the malarial mosquito. He also advocated a cleanup campaign to remove debris such as bottles as well as measures to ensure oiling of stagnant waters and the screening of cisterns. The mosquito was the "most pressing matter" confronted by the town. Nearly fifty years later, Holland's letter to the council still served as a rallying cry. Reflecting on why Surfside Beach, south of Myrtle Beach, incorporated in 1964, longtime councilman Archie Benton identified mosquitoes as the chief catalyst. He recalled, "I think they incorporated to get the services. We were down here in what's known as the 'Low Country.' The mosquitoes are bad unless you do something about controlling them and you know, all the sanitation, picking up your trash and all this."[15]

Boosters well understood the connection between mosquito control and tourism. Eliminating the threat of malaria and yellow fever opened the door to extending the tourism season year-round. Certainly travelers worried. A Boston family driving to Florida in June 1924 noted that they had passed through "much country which might harbor malaria and we added quinine pills to our diet, intending to make it a Sunday habit."[16] Assorted county and state programs and departments worked to alleviate such concerns.

Some southerners pursued a natural solution to the mosquito menace. Officials in Brewster, Florida, where infection rates for malaria ranged between 40 and 80 percent annually, pioneered the use of minnows to consume mosquito larvae in 1920. Other southern communities followed suit. C. I. Simpson of Biloxi proposed "stocking the waters with mosquito destroying minnows" within a twenty-mile radius of the city. An official for the Gulf and Ship Island Railroad traveled to San Antonio in 1922 to observe how bats had "suppressed" that city's mosquito population. Laws in Texas set high fines for killing a bat, since each of the flying mammals could devour more than three thousand mosquitoes each night. Convinced, railroad executives based in Gulfport bought a roost capable of holding sixty-five thousand bats, "a number sufficient to rid the coast of mosquitoes." Lifelong residents such as Archibald Boggs noted how the antimosquito efforts had reduced the annual summer infestation to "intervals varying from one to four years." But Louisiana's attempts to suppress mosquito populations through marsh fires backfired. Without marsh grass as shelter, the winds carried the pests to Mississippi. Gulfport's mayor proposed that Louisiana and federal officials use poison gas instead of fire. The situation dismayed Gulfport resident John Lang: "The marsh mosquito carries no disease but is simply a pest and nuisance and may be sent to remind us that this is not quite paradise."[17]

Biloxi emerged as a center for mosquito eradication in the 1920s. Galvanized by an outbreak of dengue fever in 1922 and subsequent years of heavy mosquito populations, boosters along the Gulf Coast looked to coordinate their efforts. New Orleans mayor Martin Behrman, who led the city through the 1905 yellow fever outbreak, organized an October 1925 summit of Gulf Coast mayors along with state and federal officials. The officials raised funds for mosquito surveys and programs for suppressing the bloodsuckers. Southerners found a champion in Mississippian Byron "Pat" Harrison, who had moved to the coast after gaining his law degree. After three terms in the U.S. House of Representatives, Harrison won election to the U.S. Senate in 1918. Acutely aware of the mosquito problem, he gained $25,000 in federal funding for the two-year Salt Marsh Mosquito Survey of the South Atlantic and Gulf States. The U.S. Public Health Service hired Dr. Thomas Griffitts to conduct a comprehensive study of mosquito breeding grounds from Virginia to Texas. Headquartered in Biloxi, Griffitts benefited from Harrison's continued support. The senator arranged for an additional $10,000 in 1927 and $15,000 in 1928. Armed with Griffitts's initial reports, southern states with budding coastal resorts now urged the federal government to facilitate mosquito eradication districts.[18]

The Depression brought New Deal largess to the antimosquito crusade. Directors of the Civilian Conservation Corps, Civil Works Administration, Tennessee Valley Authority, and other agencies undertook mosquito control projects. The mosquito control program established in Virginia Beach during the mid-1920s expanded. Under President Roosevelt, for instance, Virginia Beach and neighboring areas spent more than $250,000 on mosquito control—$180,000 coming from federal sources. Relief workers dug five hundred thousand feet of ditching to drain lowlands and cleared underbrush that sheltered mosquitoes. Oil spraying occurred regularly. The local newspaper in December 1939 warned, "Without an ever-vigilant system of control, the community must have recourse to smudge pot, mosquito netting, repellants and other means of protection, and, of course, a corresponding decrease in the patronage of visitors." To safeguard the future, the state legislature authorized a mosquito control district in the Virginia Beach area in 1940 largely paid for by a special county tax.[19]

For the Florida Panhandle, only the stable fly, also known as the dog fly, rivaled the mosquito. Though present in many parts of the United States, the insect thrived along coastal New Jersey and in Lakes Michigan and Superior, some lakes in the Tennessee River Valley, and northwestern Florida. Similar in appearance to the housefly, the dog fly's skin-penetrating proboscis made the pest a severe threat to tourism. The insect prefers feeding on livestock or other animals. But development near the beach not only displaced farms but also positioned more and more people as ready meals. The stable flies congregated behind coastal dunes during northerly winds. When not breeding in soggy hay or cut grass, they laid eggs on beached seaweed. The *Panama City News Herald* in March 1939 warned, "Annually, the health and wealth of the entire coastal region of Northwest Florida from Pensacola to Apalachicola is menaced by the presence of . . . the dog-fly." Bites were "vicious to the human." The damage to milk and beef production paled in comparison to the impact on tourism. Present throughout the year, the fly population peaks between August and December. "The span of the summer season in this immediate vicinity is reduced perceptibly because of the dog-fly and visitation at our beaches is immediately curtailed with the coming of the pest," complained the newspaper. The losses inflicted on Panhandle tourism represented an incalculable yet no doubt "staggering sum." Beach communities needed to take the bite out of nature.[20]

With programs targeting particular carriers of yellow fever and malaria, support for the eradication of all mosquitoes faded by the interwar period. Sportsmen, bird lovers, and naturalists starting in the 1930s decried the impact of mosquito eradication on the food chain. Taxpayers more eagerly supported efforts against a deadly threat than a mere buzzing aggravator. Virginia Beach boosters in 1934 complained, "Since malaria was stamped out here country people have regarded the mosquito more as an annoyance than as a major pest. The elimination of the insect, as an annoyance, was considered too costly." Funding for eradication proposals waned, though control programs continued.[21]

The Second World War marked a turning point in the fight against insects. The influx of soldiers made mosquitoes a threat to morale and to manpower. "The mosquitos and sand flies here have a larger army than the Russians and Germans put together," growled Anthony Costantini in a June 1942 letter home from his post in Palm Beach, Florida. He continued, "I didn't have any room on my body for them to grab another bite. Sleep was and still is out of the question." An Oregon native stationed in coastal Alabama wrote, "Speaking of itching, our barracks is alive with mosquitos."[22] Communities as well as state and federal agencies rallied against the bloodsuckers.

The solution came in 1939 via an insecticide produced by the Geigy Chemical Company of New York. Working with a chemical first synthesized in 1874, a scientist in Geigy's Switzerland office discovered the deadly effect of DDT on potato beetles. By late 1942 scientists at the Orlando laboratories of the U.S. Department of Agriculture learned how to reproduce the mixture cheaply. The same lab developed the repellant DEET in 1954. Although Paris green, introduced in 1921, had marked the emergence of chemical warfare against mosquitoes, DDT demonstrated incredible potency. The Tennessee Valley Authority, in June 1943, tested aerial application of DDT. A single treatment killed mosquitoes for several months. For military personnel confronting tropical diseases, DDT became a vital weapon. *Time* cheered the insecticide in 1944: "It promises to wipe out the mosquito and malaria, to liquidate the household fly, cockroach and bedbug, to control some of the most damaging insects that prey on the world's crops." A wall treated with DDT killed flies three months later. Clothes dusted with DDT resisted lice even after eight washings. A bed sprayed with DDT killed bedbugs for more than three hundred days. The chemical showed little effect on humans. Yet fish and other wildlife suffered declining populations. The environmental impact worsened as mosquito control districts across the United States placed DDT in their arsenal.[23]

The desire to suppress pests was calculated against the cost of damaging insects vital to the lush tropical plants tourists expected. Galveston businessmen in 1946 expressed serious reservations about having DDT sprayed over the entire island via a duster for $5,000. The flyer "attempting to sell the proposition had been in islands of the Pacific where it had been used effectively." But some chamber members doubted the wisdom of a blanket application that would kill all bugs "including bees and other pollinating insects." Furthermore, mosquitoes would "only be eliminated until a wind blows in from the mainland swamps." The chamber preferred "house to house control and store to store control of garbage cans and garbage disposals" and a limited, though more expensive, program in the range of $15,000 to $20,000. By 1949 the chamber's Public Health Committee convinced city commissioners to spray DDT in alleys and streets. A subsequent meeting announced that mosquitoes were "eliminated in the city." However, chamber members eyed a broader mosquito control program reaching into the mainland because "unless they are eliminated for a radius of 35 miles they could not be permanently controlled in the city."[24]

While thousands of planes and trucks dispersed pesticides, residents increased efforts to protect themselves from insects. The *Panama City News-Herald* in March 1958 warned, "Unless we in Bay County launch our own private war on mosquitoes . . . it may require an arsenal of spray apparatus to control the dreaded pests later." Empty flower vases, ignored watering cans, old tires, stray tin cans, and other refuse needed patrolling lest the pest hatch "to perpetuate misery, inflame tempers and completely disarrange dispositions that can result in nightmares of proportions which would put most science-fiction movies to shame." The emergence after the Second World War of mass air-conditioning offered further protection from mosquitoes. Insulating and sealing homes for air-conditioning purposes reduced exposure to the pests.[25]

Environmentalists during the 1960s successfully rolled back usage of DDT. The miracle pesticide met its most eloquent critic in Rachel Carson. Publishing *Silent Spring* in 1962, Carson traced the impact of insecticides on the environment and on humans. DDT, which severely reduced wildlife populations, received special attention. In the mid-1960s Americans used more than 350,000 tons of pesticide annually. Carson's death from cancer two years later brought homage and dismay from coastal communities. Her best-selling 1951 book *The Sea Around Us*, an ode to the ocean, drew tourists to the shore. But her criticism of pesticides threatened to undo the efforts of beach communities to tame nature. Like DDT, Carson's writings were a double-edged sword. Yet even advocates of mosquito control lost interest in the insecticide. As early as the 1940s, some insects showed resistance. Selective use of other chemicals and means of suppressing mosquitoes slowly replaced DDT. By 1972 the United States banned the pesticide.[26]

The rise of environmentalism raised questions about pesticides, but mosquito control remained a staple of resort life. Control of the mosquito removed the seasonal shadow of death from southern beach resorts. Coastal boosters dreamed of year-round crowds, real-estate booms, and palatial hotels at shorelines no longer plagued by epidemics. Yet an equally deadly and far more powerful danger lurked offshore.

Nature's Eye

John Blagden's letter home to Duluth, Minnesota, brought relief to friends and family. He had been in Galveston for two weeks when, on 8 September 1900, the barometric pressure plummeted. Soon, sustained winds of at least 120 mph whipped through the streets. A fifteen-foot wall of water slammed ashore, inundating the city that stood just 8.7 feet above sea level at its highest point. Yet Blagden survived: "Very probably you little expect to get a letter from me from here, but here I am alive and without a scratch. That is what few can say in this storm swept city." The building in which he took refuge barely withstood the hurricane as it had "rocked frightfully in some of the blasts." The next morning Blagden saw a ravaged city. Corpses lay scattered in the wreckage: "I could not help seeing many bodies though I was not desirous of seeing them." Many survivors bore bruises and cuts. Those who had fled collapsing buildings were battered "from falling & drifting timber" that had also served as life preservers. Most now slept outdoors since few structures remained standing. As the wagons gathered the dead, the number of fatalities rose to more than six thousand. Some estimates placed the death toll at more than 8,000 of Galveston's roughly 37,700 residents. Including deaths on the mainland, the hurricane claimed between ten and twelve thousand lives. Property damage in Galveston alone amounted to $30 million, including the destruction of 3,600 residences.[27]

Hurricanes were a part of life along the southern coast. F. A. Woolfley of New Orleans described an August 1860 storm: "We had quite a blow here on the 11th & 12th and was as heavy and done as much damage as the blow in Augt 1856 did." Crops and lives were devastated, mainly in the buffering agricultural lands between the city and the Gulf. Woolfley noted how the northeasterly wind caused water downriver from the city to "come all over the place destroying the entire Sugar Rice & Orange Crops besides washing Cattle off the Bank in to the River—a great many lives were lost—some having taken refuge in trees were killed by thier [sic] falling and some when the storm commenced attempted to cross the river for safety were drowned." Natives gained protection by avoiding coastal areas.[28]

Holding back the sea became vital for safety and development. Communities invested in coastal armor, replacing the natural shoreline with seawalls, riprap, groins, bulkheads, and replenished beaches. By the end of the twentieth century, an estimated 50 percent of the U.S. shoreline was armored. Boosters and real-estate entrepreneurs dismissed the opinions of those such as Alma Simmang Simpson, who, after a 1915 hurricane washed away the beach in front of the recently finished Galveston seawall, remarked, "After all, we are on only a sandbar; wasn't ever intended that people should live here . . . and sooner or later we will be in the Gulf of Mexico." Woolfley, however, would have appreciated such efforts. By the time he died in the late nineteenth century, he owned a "Cottage" in Bay Saint Louis complete with accommodation for seven (plus three servants) as well as finery to host dinner parties of up to a dozen guests. Such an investment needed protection.[29]

Galveston did not succumb to the seemingly mortal blow of 1900. Instead, residents launched engineering and political marvels that rippled across the nation. A new style of municipal government was created—popularly known as the Galveston Plan—that discarded councilmen and their political wards. The plan centralized municipal authority under a small number of commissioners elected through at-large contests. Each commissioner administered a municipal department, such as waterworks and sewerage, finance and revenue, or police and fire services. Hundreds of American municipalities experimented with the new arrangement during the Progressive Era. Furthermore, the city issued $1.5 million in bonds to build a three-mile-long seawall standing some seventeen feet above mean sea level. A massive grade-raising project lifted Galveston by some five to twenty feet. With surviving structures placed on jacks, engineers pumped sand beneath the foundations. The magazine *Confederate Veteran* in 1903 equated the effort to the "wonderful recuperative powers and energy displayed" by southern cities immediately after the Civil War. Galvestonians embodied the "self-reliant" nature of the "Southern people"—role models for an audacious New South. The seawall and sand-pumping, completed in 1904, cost $3.5 million, half of which was provided by local sources. Over the next two decades, Congress funded seawall extensions to protect area military installations.[30]

A 1915 hurricane proved the seawall's value. Louise Bache reported how some Galvestonians retreated to the recently built Rosenberg Library, designed as an emergency shelter. Alma Simmang Simpson had just returned from the Panama-Pacific International Exposition in San Francisco, an event that heralded that city's recovery from the 1906 earthquake. What Simpson now witnessed heralded the wisdom of Galvestonians. She wrote, "The streets were a raging ocean, it looked as if the whole island were a Gulf." Several houses slid off their foundations. Roofing slates cluttered the streets. Sand washed out from beneath pavement. The storm surge smashed buildings opposite the seawall—"for miles the wreckage was piled neatly, timber upon timber, like a shelf." Telegraph lines were down. Railroad tracks were washed out. With bridges damaged, boats connected Galveston to the mainland. But few died and most buildings survived. Simpson boasted how the "seawall is intact; it is this seawall that saved the city; this broke the force of the water." "As much of town as I've seen is a wreck," wrote nurse Nellie Watson after riding out the storm. She added, "The sea-wall saved the city from utter destruction."[31]

The lessons of Galveston's 1915 hurricane—only slightly less intense than the 1900 storm—resonated along the southern coast. A weak hurricane had already tracked up the Atlantic coast of Florida. The Florida Panhandle absorbed a moderate storm in early September, but later that month a powerful hurricane with sustained winds of 145 mph moved through the Gulf toward New Orleans and the Mississippi shore. In addition to battering homes and businesses, several New Orleans landmarks took damage, including the Saint Louis Cathedral and, irreparably, the Saint Louis Hotel. The devastation was worse in Mississippi.[32]

Within a week of this 1915 hurricane's landfall, a mass meeting mulled "plans for making Biloxi seaworthy." Hundreds of Harrison County citizens gathered at the courthouse in Gulfport. Of all the damage, nothing grated more than the condition of the beach boulevard linking Biloxi and Gulfport. Boats had washed ashore. Some homes were off their foundations; others lay strewn across the sand. A "well-known citizen" stressed that the "principal asset of Biloxi is its beach front." The security of the beach boulevard was essential as American car ownership skyrocketed and as vacationers sought beachfront access. He concluded, "We must either progress or confess our weakness before the world." The call to action galvanized residents.[33]

Ranking third in assessed wealth among Mississippi counties, Harrison County residents refused to lose status, especially as the vulnerability to storms sent property values plummeting. A minimal wall could provide protection without hindering access or views of the beach. The short wall sheltering nearby Bay Saint Louis became a model. Judge George Dodds reasoned, "No granite wall is needed . . . and neither is a wall like that in front of Galveston necessary. A wall, built on a less imposing scale will protect the beach, our property and the property of the coast traction company." A consensus emerged. The *Biloxi Daily Herald* boasted that locals had met "for a common purpose—that of adopting ways and means of providing funds with which to build a thoroughly modern north and south highway through the county, to build a boulevard of approved standardization between Pass Christian and Biloxi, and to let the coast section of the county create itself into [a] separate district and issue bonds for the erection of a sea wall such as would give the beach front protection from gulf disturbances for all time in the future." Believing in the promises of prosperity offered by a seawall, Harrison County voters supported a new highway sheathed in coastal armor.[34]

Progressive Era faith in science and engineering—combined with the proven success of the Galveston seawall—convinced coastal southerners, beginning with New Orleanians and their Mississippi neighbors, to invest in concrete fortifications. Harrison County appointed the Seawall Commission in 1916 to protect beachfront homes. By 1928 a twenty-six-mile seawall armored part of the Mississippi shore. New Orleans too moved to fortify its lakefront, vulnerable to Gulf surges, from future storms.[35]

Events along the Mississippi coast demonstrate how beachfront communities thrived from the security—real and imagined—provided by coastal armor. Construction of the seawall, designed as waterfront stairs, began in 1925. Funding came from a gasoline tax, passing a portion of costs onto vacationers driving the coastal boulevard, part of the Old Spanish Trail. Traffic counts into the late 1960s regularly placed the coastal road as the busiest anywhere in Mississippi.[36] Some Floridians complained of this exploitation of motorists along a highway key to their own tourism industry. A concerned citizen, exaggerating the length of the seawall, contacted Robert "Bert" Dosh, the prominent editor of the Ocala newspaper: "They built a seawall along the coast from the Alabama to the Louisiana line—it is three counties wide—and along a part of it built a boulevard. AND THEY ARE NICKING MOTORISTS FOR FOUR CENTS A GALLON TO PAY FOR IT, not only the highway but the seawall." The Mississippians' actions clearly shook Floridians uncomfortable with the competition and the exploitation of drivers "on the greatest highway in the nation."[37] Mississippians were siphoning travelers' money to promote their own tourism industry. The Biloxi press praised the coastal fortification: "We urged its value as an advertisement, as a unifier, builder and binder of communities; as employment of labor, as a contributor to trade, as a bestirrer [sic] of life here; as a protector of highways, of putting up a front to disaster, as a beautifier which would attract the attention of the country." With Bay Saint Louis and Galveston as examples, the Harrison County seawall inspired nearby Ocean Springs and Pascagoula to invest in coastal armor. New houses of "American and Spanish design" crowded lots while businesses worth millions, like the aptly named Edgewater Gulf Hotel, vied for beach frontage. Truck farms, schools, libraries, hospitals, and churches all facilitated the economic growth born of security from future storm surges.[38]

Like the Galveston seawall, the Harrison County seawall was an engineering marvel. Mark Woods, president of the firm contracted to build the wall, hired a New Orleans advertising company to document the construction. Woods ensured the film was viewed by "all the engineering societies in the country and before the meeting of railroads boards in various places over the country." For boosters eager to sell coastal property, moving images of cranes, concrete mixers, and pile drivers were not as exhilarating as a "moonlight scene on the Gulf adjacent to the wall showing the silvery sheen over the rippling water when the moon is shining brightly and a gentle breeze is blowing."[39] Such romantic imagery promoted the seawall as a conqueror of nature. Potential property owners rested easy that the Gulf had been tranquilized. Recognizing the economic boon of the $3.4 million project, the mayors of Biloxi, Gulfport, Pass Christian, and Long Beach declared Seawall Dedication Day on 10 May 1928, a formal holiday celebrated with bands and a seventeen-gun salute from coast guard vessels. A pair of Soviet travelers surveying the United States during the Depression expressed awe upon encountering Mississippi's coastal boulevard and seawall: "It is hard to astonish people after they had seen Ford's plant, Boulder Dam, the San Francisco bridges, and the New Orleans bridge. But in America everything proved possible." With their automobile seemly converted into a "motorboat," the Russians exclaimed, "What effort, what money were needed to build it all!" The seawall was a stunning success.[40]

Yet ownership of the beach remained a question wherever seawalls appeared. In 1927 Hortense Davis of Pass Christian organized support for zoning laws restricting construction between the coast highway and the seawall in Harrison County. Property owners along the shore claimed ownership of land to the waterline, though easements had carved the road and seawall across their lots. "In regard to the Mississippi Coast, if we consider that the seawall is built at the expense of the public, not of the property owners and that it was designed, not for the protection of private property, but for the protection of the road, I do not see how any property owner can feel he has a moral right (though he may have a legal right) to construct a building for profit on the beach side of the front road, or sell his property to another for such a purpose," reasoned Davis. She argued that the "rights and privileges of the general public, the taxpayers and the property owners who either for esthetic reasons or for protections of their property values" opposed beachside construction, trumped the "rights of a few individuals" who restricted physical and visual access to the beach. Similar debates emerged wherever coastal armor funded by tax dollars appeared. In the Jim Crow South, the argument served as a harbinger of civil rights protesters' claims to colorblind access to the sea.[41]

Resort towns along the southern shore worked vigorously, though often frustratingly, to maintain open vistas of the beach. Seawalls created a firm border between sea and land, though entrepreneurs often breached these barriers to gain space nearest bathers. The promise of high tax returns or hefty leases could compromise municipalities burdened by costly beach maintenance and infrastructure needs. Beautiful views attracted tourists. But more tourists meant more strain on the sewerage pipes, garbage crews, police forces, and other public services and systems.

The shore was prime real estate for private and government exploitation. Virginia Beach officials invested in a concrete boardwalk and seawall during the interwar period. Soon questions of profiting from vacationers strolling the boardwalk arose. "One of the assets of Virginia Beach has been the declared policy to keep its waterfront free from commercialism," explained that city's newspaper in 1939. Shops were barred from the boardwalk. Litigation in the 1930s had granted Virginia Beach a "vested right in what is known as Ocean Avenue and no constructions of any sort could be erected on that strip of land." As a result, "summer houses and what-nots" were forcibly removed. The aim was to "see the waterfront kept free from the Atlantic City type boardwalk" crowded with glitzy—and tacky—beer gardens and other amusements. But commercialization was not entirely banned. Within weeks, city officials granted permission to two entrepreneurs who lined the boardwalk with "addresserphones." The system "periodically" broadcasted stock reports and police notices from 8 a.m. until 8 p.m. It was also "used for advertising purposes."[42]

Businessmen such as those in Galveston recognized the dilemma of public beaches. Under the legal principle called public trust doctrine, individuals and businesses claimed a proprietary interest to tidal lands, shorelines, and navigable waters, but the state's interest remained paramount. The Texas legislature in 1949 pioneered bills that declared beaches public property. The Galveston Chamber of Commerce hotly debated the costs and benefits of maintaining public beaches. John McCray believed beaches should be private. He decried "a Saturday and Sunday on the beach—people camping anywhere they please, no roadways, no policing, no cleaning up of the beach." McCray continued, "People should be encouraged to come to Galveston to spend their money, and a majority of the people who come to the beach bring their boxes filled with food, beer, ice and do not spend a penny in Galveston." Some beaches were leased and maintained by the county. The city, for instance, cleaned and policed Stewart Beach Park, though the crowds, as McCoy noted, overwhelmed police and cleanup crews. On the other hand, privately held beaches not only drove away some tourists but also soiled the reputation of the city, chiefly when property owners failed to tidy their shoreline: "Galveston is criticized every year for not keeping its beaches clean. The city and county do not have the revenue to maintain the property." Worse, ensuring public access to the beach threatened future prosperity. Some businessmen reasoned, "By being able to fence off the beaches, it would speed development of the western end of the island where many new summer homes are being erected. If the beaches are declared public, it would certainly stop this development."[43] Most businessmen waffled lest they drive away either vacationers or real-estate investors. James Bradner finally forged a consensus. He contended "that since the people who use the beaches are not people from Galveston but from over the State, that the State should take the leadership to see that the beaches are properly policed, maintained, etc."[44] Texas declined such an expensive responsibility. But by 1966 the state attorney general vigorously defended public access to the Gulf, forcing Galveston to "remove protective fences which have the approval of the county" as well as ordering the removal of "some beach houses."[45]

As development raised property values, placed more Americans and structures in harm's way, and decreased public access to the beach, the federal government became more involved in armoring the coastal environment. The agency most responsible for shoreline defenses has long been the U.S. Army Corps of Engineers. Created in 1802, the corps initially trained engineers and prepared fortifications. The role expanded in 1824 when the U.S. Supreme Court ruled, in *Gibbons v. Ogden*, that the commerce clause of the Constitution granted federal oversight of interstate trade, including transportation routes. Congress soon passed the General Survey Act of 1824 empowering the corps to clear interstate waterways as well as facilitate road and canal construction. Faced with severe coastal erosion in his state, U.S. senator Walter Edge of New Jersey pushed for expanding the role of the corps during the 1920s. The Rivers and Harbors Act of 1930 established the corps' Beach Erosion Board. The board advised states on techniques to combat erosion. With state budgets slashed during the Depression, Congress passed the Flood Control Act of 1936. The act granted the federal government power to protect public and private property from inundation. The Act for Improvement and Protection of Beaches Along the Shores of the United States, also passed in 1936, authorized construction of erosion control projects by federal agencies. After the Second World War, the corps increasingly devoted resources to fight coastal erosion. Covering up to 33 percent of costs in 1946, Congress agreed to bear 50 percent of costs after the Ash Wednesday storm of March 1962, a destructive northeaster that ravaged the coastline from North Carolina to Maine for three days. Congress covered 70 percent of costs for protecting public lands. A dramatic change in corps policy had occurred. Until 1956, the corps had refused to assist with beach replenishment projects, seeing such efforts as maintenance rather than construction. Beach maintenance added significantly to the burden undertaken by the corps. In 1963 the Coastal Engineering Research Center replaced the Beach Erosion Board. The center, eventually located at the corps' Waterway Experiment Station in Vicksburg, Mississippi, facilitated dialogue between experts within the corps and private engineers.[46]

A series of laws in 1972 further expanded the role of the corps. Under the Clean Water Act, the corps was authorized to issue permits for dredging and filling efforts. The Marine Protection Research and Sanctuaries Act empowered the corps to grant permits for offshore dumping. Congress also passed the Coastal Zone Management Act to curtail escalating expenditures on coastal armor. Congress allayed states' reluctance to surrender authority over their shoreline by creating a voluntary program seeded with federal grants targeting coastal management. The standards restricted pollution, oil drilling, and other activities jeopardizing coastal ecosystems. By 1985 twenty-eight of the thirty-five coastal states and territories participated. Environmental groups ardently supported the legislation. When the act faced renewal in the mid-1980s, Shirley Taylor of the Sierra Club of Florida urged support: "Overdevelopment pressures are the most severe on the coast where everybody wants to locate. Controls are badly needed!"[47] Furthermore, Congress passed the Coastal Barrier Resource Act in 1982. The legislation designated 188 undeveloped islands and mainland beaches on the Atlantic Ocean and Gulf of Mexico as part of a coastal barrier system. The act prohibited federal subsidies for highways or bridges as well as eliminated new federal flood insurance along six hundred miles of beachfront.[48]

Such legislation reacted to the massive post–Second World War construction boom and the growing popularity of costly sand replenishment projects wherever development occurred. As in 1900 and 1915, the 1947 hurricane season galvanized coastal southerners. A storm with sustained winds of 155 mph slammed into Fort Lauderdale in September. The hurricane was the worst to hit southern Florida since 1928. That hurricane, immortalized in Zora Neale Hurston's *Their Eyes Were Watching God*, killed more than 2,500 people as 140 mph winds sent Lake Okeechobee over the dikes. The lessons of 1928 had been learned, however. Stauncher building codes and the stronger Herbert Hoover Dike surrounding Lake Okeechobee minimized damage. Improved transportation systems sped evacuations. As a result, only seventeen Floridians perished. Citrus groves suffered the most costly damage.[49]

Upon entering the Gulf of Mexico, the hurricane tracked straight for New Orleans while whipping coastal Mississippi and Alabama with winds and waves. Though weakened to 100 mph winds, the storm pushed a tidal surge of at least fifteen feet into the Mississippi coast. Angela Moynan thought the water was a "good 35 feet high on the beach." The next day she bought a camera. She joked, "There wasn't anything else you could do unless you possessed a derick [sic], incinerator or a hurse [sic]." Fellow resident Marila Green described her experience in a letter to her mother in Illinois: "I myself was really scared mostly because I've never been thru any floods, cyclones or any thing like that. I kept saying what a wonderful city Chicago is."[50] Thomas Davis Berry mourned, "Many homes were totally destroyed. Many homes were injured. Many homes lost thousands of dollars in value and had no insurance to cover their loss." Counting himself among the uninsured, Berry sold part of his beachfront land to raise money to replace the roof and water-damaged plaster.[51] Twelve died in Louisiana, and twenty-two perished in Mississippi. Tourists were "barred from gulf coast resort areas" as officials in Mississippi and Alabama issued "shoot to kill" orders to National Guard and army troops patrolling against looters.[52]

As property owners restored homes and businesses, Mississippi politicians increased the effectiveness of the seawall. Petitioning for federal assistance, Harrison County officials in 1949 planned to lay three hundred feet of refurbished sand beach in front of the now twenty-eight-mile concrete barrier to weaken future storm surges while also bolstering tourism. One of the earliest such beach replenishment projects occurred at Coney Island. Between 1921 and 1923, New York officials spent $4 million to construct a three-mile-long beach consisting of 1.5 million cubic yards of pumped sand. Mississippians had something similar in mind. The federal government paid half of the nearly $4 million cost while Harrison County covered the rest via a gasoline tax. In 1951 hydraulic pumps finished spraying more than 1.4 million cubic yards of sand onto the shore.[53] Boosters proclaimed the beach "The World's Longest Welcome Mat." The gentle slope supposedly eliminated undertows, and bathers could wade out some 1,500 feet before losing footing. "So safe no lifeguards are required and so long it will never be overcrowded," assured local historian Ray Thompson in 1956. Other resort communities used the beach as a model. Places such as Virginia Beach envied how Mississippi had not only seemingly "whipped a serious erosion problem" but gained national publicity as well.[54]

Virginians had good reason for watching their counterparts in Mississippi. In September 1950, Virginia Beach councilmen Robert Simpson and W. W. McClanan Jr. pleaded with the governor for emergency aid after "disastrous tides and winds pounded and tore at the boardwalk with such force . . . that sheet piling on the face of the wall was torn away for a distance of three blocks and the sea washed under to erode dirt fill . . . leaving gaping holes." The corps proposed jetties and beach replenishment at a cost well over $1 million. Charles Gardner and other hoteliers feared inaction. He observed thousands of vacationers "compelled to laze on the lawns and even on the hard boardwalk" because so little beach remained.[55] Finding the money to repair the damage became the topic of "all conversations among Virginia Beach people." All agreed that a town of slightly more than five thousand residents could not bear the expense on top of an "already heavy tax burden" necessary for sustaining the resort's infrastructure. Instead, city leaders hatched a plan by which "10 or 12 representative men outside of Princess Anne County" would urge the Virginia General Assembly for the money; if they refused, the same men would propose legislation allowing for local option of alcohol sales to raise the revenue. If assembly members refused either choice, Virginia Beach leaders threatened to act independently. The unnamed proponent of the plan believed it the "duty of our county and town governments to protect the life and property of its citizens by openly licensing such operations as now are illegal in order to pay the bill." The proposal expressed "open defiance of law and order" because "people have the right to help themselves."[56]

Others balked at such outlawry, fearing the negative publicity. Instead, the Beach Erosion Company, a private organization of local property owners, received permission from the corps to sink two ships and a barge in hopes of trapping sand and breaking the waves. A bulldozer stretched the remnants of the beach.[57] Sidney Kellam, head of Virginia's Conservation and Development Commission, agreed that the city should not "single-handedly" fend off the Atlantic since the resort "brought many thousands of tourists into the Old Dominion."[58] By February 1952 the governor appointed the Virginia Beach Erosion Commission to oversee an initial $350,000 outlay. The five members of the commission over the next decade typically included hotel operators, restaurateurs, bankers, and other businesspeople "directly affected by the tourist business." The city inaugurated an annual Sand Festival Day in August 1952 to celebrate the $1 million replenishment program and to remind travelers that beaches—widened with 1.4 million cubic yards of sand—again awaited them. Revelers enjoyed "The World's Largest Wiener Roast," a yacht parade, live music by Jimmy Dorsey's orchestra, a bathing beauty contest that subsequently became the Miss Virginia Beach pageant, and a "mock football game between two teams of girls." National print and television news media covered the event. The Virginia Beach Erosion Commission subsequently purchased a hydraulic line dredge named "City of Virginia Beach." The machine drew a hundred thousand cubic yards of sand annually from nearby lagoons and creeks to preserve the beach.[59]

The restored beach, seawall, and boardwalk equated to money in the bank. When Hurricane Barbara swept past with 80 mph winds in August 1953 with little damage, locals boasted of the city's "quick return on its million dollar plus beach restoration investment, a whopping dividend that can hardly be measured in dollars and cents." Just as Mississippi's Harrison County and sites in Florida served as an example to Virginia Beach boosters, Virginia Beach inspired Wilmington, North Carolina, and other nearby Atlantic communities eager to "halt the eating away" of their shorelines.[60] The piping system that carried sand from Owl's Creek and Rudee Inlet to pumping stations along the beach became the envy of Ocean City, New Jersey; Miami Beach, Florida; Santa Barbara, California; and other cities with dire erosion problems. Representatives from these communities flocked to Virginia Beach during the 1950s and 1960s to observe the replenishment process. Even the Ash Wednesday storm of 1962 failed to shake confidence. Gales of 30 mph and waves cresting eight feet above normal ripped away forty feet of seawall. Ruby Phillips reported, "Homes in the $100,000 price range were undermined by the battering surf to the point of breaking in half and many residents stood helplessly by and watched their home crumble and their furniture float off down the street." The cost for repairs in Virginia Beach alone ran in the tens of millions. Yet, with procedures in place, agencies quickly repaired the beach for the summer tourist season. The federal government's Office of Emergency Planning covered most of the costs for restoring 220,000 cubic yards of beach. Beginning in June, a truckload of sand drawn from nearby Seashore State Park was dumped onto the shore every six minutes for ninety days.[61]

Fighting the sea proved increasingly expensive. Sand replenishment cost more than $3.5 million in the first fifteen years of the Virginia Beach Erosion Commission; $2.4 million of that figure came from city coffers. Expenses for maintaining the Harrison County, Mississippi, beach completed in 1951 stood at $253,897 in 1955, $326,897 in 1956, and $432,784 in 1957. By the end of the decade, seawall and beach maintenance costs surpassed $750,000 annually. Tom Cook reported, "There appears to be a growing fear that the spacious sand beach stretching along the county's coastline, designed in 1949 to provide protection from tropical storms and erosion as well as to attract myriads of tourists, may some day become a burdensome millstone around the necks of taxpayers." Though a special two-cent gasoline tax hit the "pocket books of tourists and residents alike," the cost of the beach outpaced tax revenue.[62] More than seventy workers cared for the beach while an additional crew of seven engineers and one bookkeeper supervised. Salaries, dredging, and miscellaneous costs such as repair equipment, parts, and gasoline exhausted the budget. Erosion was constant. After Hurricane Camille, the width of the beach shrank to fifty feet in some spots, requiring a $2 million replenishment effort undertaken by the county and federal governments. Dredges gathered two million cubic yards of sand, restoring the beach to a width of 265 feet. The effort also removed a grounded barge, splintered pier pilings, and other storm damage. The 130 storm drain conduits that opened into the Gulf were also fixed. Engineers optimistically gave the restored beach a thirty-year lifespan.[63]

The lessons learned by Virginia Beach and Harrison County were repeated all along the southern shore. Development led to expensive seawalls or sand replenishment projects to protect increasingly valuable beachfront property. In 1970 Harmon Shields, Florida's director of marine resources, replenished sand for worried Bay County officials because beaches near Panama City were "eroding at an enormous rate." After Hurricane Eloise ripped across the Florida Panhandle in 1975, the federal government sponsored a beach renourishment program costing more than $1 million. Yet the 232,000 cubic yards of sand sprayed ashore offered meager protection. Alton Colvin, representing the corps, warned officials that this restoration project only offered protection from a so-called "five year storm" bearing waves six feet above mean sea level.[64]

Dredging sand to nourish beaches provided protection from future storms but could also harm tourism and the beauty of the shoreline. Whereas early dredging easily found deposits of white sand similar to beach sand, repeated dredging and erosion lowered the supply. Offshore dredging frequently raised sand mixed with shells and clay. The dredging project at Panama City after Hurricane Eloise stirred loud protests. Jake Roudenbush, who owned two beachfront motels in Panama City in July 1976, condemned the renourishment program: "We have black beaches now, instead of white ones." The dredges muddied the water and raised poor-quality sand. The dirty sludge pumped onto the beach, argued Roudenbush, sent tourists fleeing to less worn resorts in Fort Walton Beach and Destin. Luckily for Panama City, promises that the sand would whiten from weeks of exposure to sunshine and the elements proved true. Yet these were not the same sugary-white strands as before Eloise. Seashells were abundant on the new beach. Over time, shells act as natural cement, hardening the beach. Commenting on changes to South Carolina's Grand Strand, Eatofel Arehart criticized "all the renourishing we're doing to the beaches. . . . The beach looks nothing like it looked." Arehart particularly missed the large dunes enjoyed as a child. Dunes around Myrtle Beach during the interwar period seemed to "have reached to the sky." Interviewed in 1993, Arehart lamented, "Well there's no sand dune there now."[65]

Since the Galveston hurricane, destruction created opportunity. More formidable structures replaced older buildings and roads damaged by storms. After a powerful 1926 hurricane deflated Florida's real-estate bubble, a Fort Lauderdale banker dismissed the death and devastation. He boasted, "This storm has done a very important job for us." By ending the land craze, the storm allowed locals to retrench. The banker explained, "We needed normalizing. This storm did that job. It is painful and certainly a most undesirable way to do things, but it happened and we might as well admit that good will come from it." The *Christian Science Monitor*, in the aptly titled report "Florida Finds Way Clear for Better Growth" from September 1926, declared such views common among coastal businessmen.[66]

Moreover, hurricanes created publicity. Some businessmen even tried to use the hurricanes to their advantage. After a 1949 hurricane hit Galveston, a chamber member rushed a plan to his colleagues. He lamented that boosters had "passed up a good publicity stunt the day after the hurricane in that we didn't take pictures of bathing girls on the beach . . . to show that we are not bothered by a hurricane and to indicate what beautiful weather we have following such a storm." Hurricane Hazel washed ashore near Myrtle Beach in 1954, severely damaging the tourism infrastructure. Asked what remained standing along the beach, Lynnie Gore announced, "Nothing hardly at all." Mark Garner likewise witnessed the storm and its impact. He was hired six years earlier to manage the chamber of commerce. He subsequently started the *Myrtle Beach Sun* newspaper. Recalling Hurricane Hazel in a 1992 interview, Garner declared, "By that unfortunate natural disaster, Myrtle Beach gained tremendous amount of fame." He continued, "I recall my wife and I were in New Hampshire and stopped into a motel and were checking in, and the lady who checked us in said, 'Well I don't [know] anything about South Carolina, but I know that the hurricane hit Myrtle Beach." Raised awareness ironically bolstered rebuilding efforts as "stronger and better . . . 2 and 3 and 4 story motels" replaced smaller oceanfront cottages.[67]

The aftermath of Hurricane Camille in 1969 revealed how a storm could encourage more, rather than less, development. The recently authorized federal flood insurance program for home and business owners had not come into effect by the time of Camille. Yet regulations for federal emergency response aid were adjusted to erase biases against rural areas. Money for the National Weather Service was increased so the agency could better track storms.[68]

Locally, residents, particularly whites, along the Mississippi coast witnessed rapid rebuilding. Though federal officials in the U.S. Office of Education, Office for Civil Rights, and the Department of Health, Education, and Welfare used recovery funding to spur desegregation in Harrison County, most recovery funding favored white businesses and residents. "The particular configuration and structuring of state, federal, and municipal authority in the aftermath of the hurricane did much to further marginalize the poorest members of southern Mississippi and checked their recovery rate relative to that of the middle class," explains historian Mark Smith. President Richard Nixon directed the bulk of the recovery money—$100 million of federal aid—through Mississippi governor John Bell Williams's Emergency Council, the agency responsible for planning the Gulf Coast's long-term economic recovery. Ten of the twelve members were wealthy white realtors, bankers, lawyers, and corporative executives. Funding for shopping centers, golf courses, marinas, and hotels sparked a quick recovery for the tourism industry, though, as Mark Smith argues, the jobs were "likely nowhere near enough to absorb jobs lost or postponed in manufacturing and agriculture." The poor suffered high unemployment, lost possessions, and destroyed homes with relief aid disproportionately directed to whites instead of blacks. Gerald Blessey, a Biloxi native and mayor during the 1980s, likened hurricanes to the urban renewal projects under President Lyndon Johnson's Great Society. Blessey remarked, "Downtown had a lot of people living there, then, so downtown itself was a neighborhood, until Hurricane Camille and urban renewal wiped it out. I'm not sure which one was worse." Fellow Biloxian Charles Breath agreed. After the hurricane, real-estate speculators "really got rich" by buying battered properties. "Lots that before the hurricane would sell for $5,000, now would go for ten, twelve, and fifteen thousand dollars," explained Breath ten years after Camille. Investors with portfolios filled with beachfront lots campaigned for a full recovery. Devastation brought better zoning and building codes as municipal governments, businessmen, and homeowners braced for the next storm. In 1980 longtime white resident Henry Fortner observed the probusiness changes wrought by Camille: "I think the Coast as a whole is probably in better condition now than it would have been. . . . You can't make a person tear down his place of business because it's old and ugly and ramshackled. But the hurricane tore it down for us."[69]

Beachfront motel and hotel owners along with homeowners vigorously resisted intensifying efforts to distance structures from the surf. Sandra Vann, operator of the Treasure Island Motel in Panama City Beach, explained in April 1986, "We love the beaches and agree the natural beauty was not preserved and properly planned for 30, 40, 50 years ago when roads were built and property divided." She continued, "No one foresaw the erosion due to time, storms and unnatural causes." Wave action had damaged four rooms of her establishment, and under new state setback requirements, she feared a demolition order for part of the motel. Buying the property in 1978, Vann had felt safe behind the private, thirteen-year-old seawall and the "over 100 feet of beach" in front of her business. Built "over 35 years ago," the motel had witnessed the slow encroachment of the Gulf. But preventing the defense of private property seemed outrageous. Referring to a recent storm, Vann sneered, "We also wonder if the people of Tallahassee are still without power and telephone service since the same 'God' that Governor Graham said is telling us not to be here also was telling the citizens there that the lines should be removed."[70]

Preserving vegetation vital to a beach's health proved equally daunting. In 1939 Mary Leigh repeatedly witnessed vacationers ripping "stately sea oats" from Virginia's dunes. Despite the importance of the sea oats in trapping sand and state laws protecting the plants since 1926, tourists and even some natives plucked oats for decoration or souvenirs. Leigh noted that the vegetation was "ruthlessly pulled, to be placed in some cottage or home, there to stay a few short months, or even gathered for commercial purposes from others' property." William Gatewood faced a similar problem after he repaired dunes near his cottage after the 1962 northeaster. He sowed wild oats and lined the tops of dunes with fencing to catch airborne crystals. The highly effective fences gathered more than sand, however. Gatewood explained that "groups, small and large alike, descend upon these fragile fences and break them up for fire wood in order to enjoy a beach beer party." Worse, his dunes were decorated with a "quantity of beer cans, liquor bottles, and trash which will fill a twenty gallon trash container at the end of one night's gathering."[71]

The investment in beaches required clearing the sand for bill-paying tourists. In 1939 Virginia Beach officials banned dogs from the beach. Myrtle Beach police patrolled against "Jitter Bug Bums" and vagrants. By 1965 the city council, like that of many coastal communities, prohibited sleeping on the beach at night. Automobiles were also banned from beaches by the mid-twentieth century. Galveston businessmen in 1964 found that of "all the cities with beaches the Chamber of Commerce has contacted, not a single one allows automobiles on the beach except Galveston." Horses too came under fire. In March 1968 a "battle tinted with shades of the Old West" erupted in Panama City. Mike Darley described how moteliers "who also hold title to most of the silvery sands" decried the locals who "almost daily" rode horseback along the beach. After their child stepped in the "hoss droppings," the parents stormed into the motel lobby threatening to cancel their two-week stay "and never come back."[72] The Bay County Motel and Restaurant Association mobilized. No county or municipal ordinances banned horses from the beach. However, the association did not seek such a law. Officially referring to the droppings as "horse stuff" lest publicity draw attention to the fouling, the association asked state health officers to intervene. They thereby circumvented local officials sensitive to the political muscle of wealthy horse riders. Association president Barney Gray explained, "The beach is no place for both horse and humans, and since we depend on the people for a living they come first." Outmaneuvered, representatives of the horse riders promised to "stay away from the beaches proper."[73]

Yet few things damaged tourism profits more than, in the words of a Virginia Beach resident, "that old bugaboo—hurricane notices." Locals feared the angst stirred by hurricanes. Coastal resorts handled news of storms with great care. The display of storm flags by the U.S. Weather Bureau to warn bathers of rough surf garnered heated reactions. For instance, some residents of Myrtle Beach in the early 1950s—even in January when few vacationers came to the Grand Strand—condemned the system. Congress had created the bureau in 1870 to oversee, initially, weather stations along the Great Lakes and Atlantic coast. First operated by the Army Signal Corps, Congress transferred authority to the Department of Agriculture in 1890 and then, in 1940, to the Department of Commerce. The bureau used readings to issue advisories and make forecasts vital to commercial interests. Coastal development during the twentieth century made predicting storms even more vital for safeguarding lives. In 1967 the agency was renamed the National Weather Service.[74]

In Myrtle Beach, Waldo Jones initiated the flag system in the late 1940s after an unexpected spring gale threatened the local Ferris wheel. Jones and his associates climbed the amusement ride in the dark to secure it with ropes. Despite opposition, Jones defended the storm warning flags. Representatives of civic organizations as well as city officials feared the negative impression conveyed by the flags: "Many visitors do not know the meaning of the flag and the color of red develops a 'fear phycosis' [sic] causing alarm. Since Myrtle Beach is a resort catering to visitors and tourist [sic] the flag creates 'great economic loss.'" The flags were more appropriate for a "seaport town" rather than a beach resort. The protesters pleaded to local Weather Bureau meteorologist John Cummings that "modern means of communication" such as telephones and radio made the flags obsolete. Cummings explained that flags had operated along parts of the coast for twenty-five years and, although principally for maritime use, such systems saved "hundreds of lives during hurricanes" as well as other storms by "warning people to take proper precaution." Cummings refused the request to remove the flag in the interest of public safety.[75]

Hurricane tracking was a newborn science in the mid-twentieth century. In the 1930s Captain W. L. Farnsworth of the Galveston Commercial Association gained Weather Bureau support for a federal storm patrol bill. The legislation, passed by Congress in June 1936, authorized military aircraft to follow hurricanes at sea. Miami emerged as a particularly important base as military planes scouted meteorological disturbances in the Caribbean, Gulf, and Atlantic during the 1940s. The United States adopted increasingly sophisticated techniques during the 1950s. Hurricanes now received female names to facilitate research and tracking. In 1954 Hurricane Hazel ravaged Myrtle Beach while Hurricane Carol swamped North Carolina's Outer Banks before slamming into New England. The storms left more than $700 million in damage. The next season Hurricanes Connie, Diane, and Ione tore into the Outer Banks before drenching the mid-Atlantic states. Responding to the rash of hurricanes, the federal government improved tracking know-how. The State Department in 1955 negotiated for a network of twenty-eight weather stations scattered across Caribbean islands. The air force utilized three specially equipped hurricane observation planes. The navy maintained camera-equipped rockets to fire into the storms.[76]

No matter the physical or psychological costs, hurricanes strengthened the bonds within and between coastal communities. "Sectionalism, business and group rivalries, political beliefs, the wet and dry issue, religious differences and a plethora of other matters often sharply divide West Florida and West Floridians, but in times of general emergency and stress there is no cleavage," declared the *Panama City News-Herald* after the 1947 hurricane ravaged the Gulf South. Rather than take advantage of a resort's devastation, coastal residents united to lend aid "for humanity and the public welfare." When Hurricane Camille smashed into the Mississippi coast in 1969, Myrtle Beach residents adopted crippled Gulfport "because it is similar to Myrtle Beach in size and geography." The South Carolinians donated nearly $8,000 to aid Gulfport's rebuilding effort.[77]

Despite attempts to tame hurricanes, memories of past devastation lingered. As resorts rebuilt on a bigger scale after a storm, residents often recalled less fortunate places. In Louisiana an 1856 hurricane swept clear a large hotel and settlement consisting of more than a hundred cottages along with several hundred residents on Last Island, a popular Gulf resort for New Orleanians. For Texans the disappearance of Indianola, a city of five thousand residents washed away in an 1886 hurricane, haunted coastal boosters as much as the Galveston storm. Floridians recalled the fate of Saint Joseph, once the largest city in the state, before it vanished under a tidal surge in 1843. Clarence Gay asked in 1958: "Has the tragedy of the 1840's hopelessly haunted the future of this historic piece of Florida ground, or have some venturesome souls . . . Realtors, maybe! . . . set forth to down the ghosts of St. Joseph." As Hurricanes Hugo (1989), Andrew (1992), and Katrina and Rita (2005) made clear, no concrete walls, restored beaches, or whitewashed reporting could successfully contain nature. To live on the coast meant risking life and fortune.[78]

Litterbugs

Resorts with small permanent populations needed to satisfy tourists' expectations while also supplying municipal services capable of accommodating vacationers in peak tourist seasons. Tourists paid much of the cost of such services as well as maintenance of seawalls and beach replenishment. Government expenditure of millions on refurbished beaches brought positive publicity but also concerns over the trash left by sunbathers. Beach communities, as in Virginia Beach, condemned the litterbug—"the most nefarious, malicious and difficult-to-eradicate insects known to man"—but avoided strict laws or harassment of visitors lest they go elsewhere. Conquering the worst of human nature and satisfying tourists' expectations proved as daunting as killing mosquitoes and repelling hurricanes.[79]

What nature provided, tourism boosters embellished. Clarke and Marjorie Wilson of Biloxi urged hotels and motels to landscape. They argued, "The visitor in a hurry often gets his main impression of the area from the motel. He expects to see the South, the deep South, with flowers the year 'round and a touch of the tropics." In order to "give the tourist what he is looking for," businesses were encouraged to plant palms, magnolias, banana plants, hibiscus, azaleas, and "Confederate jasmine." Clumps of bamboo enticed as "something most tourists have never seen." Citrus trees, offering satsumas, lemons, grapefruit, and kumquats, as well as guava, pear, and peach trees suggested warmth and natural bounty. Municipalities regularly invested in tropical foliage. The Myrtle Beach City Council in 1961, for example, purchased seventy-five palmetto trees for highway beautification. Improving "part of nature" made for "good business." Larry Boulier worried, "The Palmettos planted along beer-can highways between our sister-cities have added an attraction for many and yet if these trees were small enough, we would find some of them pulled up and carried away."[80]

Beach communities drew on the best talent to craft a vacationer's paradise. John Harris, a Galveston businessman, was so impressed by Desmond Muirhead's book *Palms* (1961) that he paid all travel expenses and fees for the landscape architect to visit the Texas city. Another businessman covered food and lodging. Muirhead's visit in May 1967 provided a seven-point blueprint for a more tourism-oriented Galveston as the profitability of the docks waned. First, Muirhead supported establishment of experimental botanical gardens overseen by Texas A&M University. The gardens would identify plants suited to Galveston while encouraging citizens to "grow acclimated plants." Muirhead reasoned, "In addition to providing a useful service for experimentation purposes, the gardens are a magnificent tourist attraction." He also urged the removal of utility poles by burying unsightly wires. Muirhead recommended replacing "ratty and derelict" Washingtonia palms with Canary Island date palms. Muirhead also "strongly encouraged the extensive planting of oleanders and the creation of an Oleander Festival to publicize the native plants." Most importantly, he advocated beautifying the "beachfront with any plant that will make a showing," banning beachfront billboards, and planting hedges along roads leading into Galveston. Furthermore, he called for "one new golf course for every 20,000 inhabitants." To boost tourism, Muirhead highly favored a 3 percent hotel tax with which to "hire a public relations, not advertising firm, to 'beat the drum of Galveston.'" The chamber appreciated his desire to put "the city on the map with a favorable impression to potential visitors rather than being known because of Hurricane Carla," which had hit in 1961. Although not all the recommendations were followed, chamber members leaned heavily on Muirhead's expertise over the next decade.[81]

Maintaining a manicured resort required fighting an endless war on litter. Rooted in the Progressive Era's City Beautiful movement, beach towns regularly organized cleanup campaigns. To maintain the renourished beach in Harrison County, Mississippi, officials in 1951 bought a beach sanitizer in addition to bulldozers. The sanitizer combed the sands with steel teeth to a depth of eleven inches, scooping bottles and other trash at a rate of more than two thousand square yards per hour. Rings, sunglasses, wristwatches, and other valuables lost by sunbathers were separated and kept at the county maintenance headquarters for tourists to retrieve.[82]

Similar efforts appeared elsewhere during the 1950s as tourism burgeoned. The Council of Garden Clubs of Princess Anne County and Virginia Beach lamented the beer cans, bottles, paper, and other trash "continually thrown" onto the streets and the renourished beach. Protecting the beach from erosion and trash became the number one issue in the municipal campaign of 1954. Luxury taxes gathered mainly on cigarettes and motel rooms brought $180,000 annually for erosion control, advertising, and refuse collection. The new city council intensified efforts to safeguard the cleanliness of the restored beachfront by considering extra police for "Sunday patrol of the waterfront" as well as publication of handbills publicizing ordinances "against taking beer cans and soft drink bottles on the beach." Within months, pressure mounted on the board of supervisors of Princess Anne County to pass ordinances that prohibited "garbage, bottles, trash and litter on the beaches or water" as well as tighter regulations of dumping grounds and "automobile graveyards" marring drivers' impression of the area. J. Malcolm Firth in 1967 complained to Virginia Beach officials that greater services were needed for tourists. He proposed adding "drinking fountains, and shower accommodations on the beach proper (Clearwater, Fla. has both of these as well as most other resorts.)" Firth also urged removal of litter: "In the spring and fall, the beach should be cleaned every day if one is to anticipate outsiders, such as Canadians, to make it attractive for them. A machine to do this work is used in other seaside resorts."[83]

Despite calls to clean beaches and laws against littering, resorts acted with caution. The Galveston Chamber of Commerce declined to sponsor a spring cleanup campaign in 1946. City officials lacked the equipment "to do the job." The businessmen concluded that such a campaign if not handled "satisfactorily—would amount to 'bad publicity' just when season is about to open." In 1951, meeting at Fort Morgan State Park on the Alabama coast for their tenth annual convention, the National Association of State Park Directors debated the best means for conveying rules to visitors. A. H. Nall, representing Mississippi, declared, "We could save much money, if we could make the people put their garbage in the garbage can. However, those are small things and we do not worry too much about them." For Mississippi, free access to parks and lax rule enforcement made for happy locals and tourists. C. West Jacocks, director of state parks for South Carolina, concurred. Fewer rules made for "keeping them [visitors] happy and making them want to come back again to the parks." Presenting vacationers with too many orders stirred their ire. Jacocks explained, "You can make a lot of people angry in your park as soon as they get there, if they are faced with a number of signs. . . . The first few things that hit the park user are 'Not Allowed' 'Not Allowed' 'Not Allowed'. Before he even gets into our park, he is already mad." Jacocks had changed the tone of signs in state parks to a "positive approach rather than a negative one" by emphasizing what was allowed instead of what was prohibited. The state park directors reflected a sentiment common within tourism-oriented enterprises. For example, the Virginia Beach press commented, "It is quite natural for the vacationer to become a bit careless away from home and drop trash and paper along our streets and on the beach." A community dependent on happy tourists needed to pick up after their guests rather than simply "look to the city government to take care of all our problems." Richard Webbon, a city official, agreed. Dismissing calls for strict enforcement of litter laws in 1967, he explained, "Many of the offenders are tourists and we certainly don't want to drive people away. Enforcement of the law should be a last resort."[84]

The soft approach to litter law enforcement stirred anger. In 1958 a Myrtle Beach resident observed a family in a parked car near the beach. Suddenly the father opened the car door and "dropped an amount of napkins, chicken bones, Jello and potato salad on the ground." The angry resident confronted the litterbugs: "Now we residents have garbage cans which you are welcome to use and if you do not pick up every drop of that garbage I shall swear out a warrant for your arrest." Others criticized municipal leaders. Mrs. W. Peyton May of Virginia Beach rebuked politicians and businessmen in 1967: "Afraid of injuring the feelings of a littering tourist? So—who wants tourists who throw around beer cans and whiskey bottles? (not to mention soft drink ones as well)." May concluded, "That type of tourist is probably more trouble than profit to businesses and authorities." Ann Clark of Chapel Hill, North Carolina, saw Grand Strand beaches in summer 1971 strewn with "trash of all description." Most discouraging, she "actually saw a child's sand castle decorated with at least a dozen beer cans." Clark complained to the press and to the mayor of Myrtle Beach.[85]

As population and crowds grew, beach resorts confronted the consequences of dumping raw sewage into the sea. As early as the 1920s, tourists complained of the shortage of toilets. In January 1926 William Golloway of North Canton, Ohio, enjoyed a vacation with some friends on Daytona Beach's shores, though the resort was crowded "like a beehive." The popularity of their outhouse proved particularly vexing. One friend sought "to keep people out of our toilet but I think we will have to put up with it." The strain on sewage systems led to careless handling of human waste. Florida governor Millard Caldwell, in a December 1945 speech, rebuked complacency as an "enemy more insidious and dangerous than the combined Germans and Japanese." Demobilization of the federal government required the mobilization of more state and local resources. He not only called for additional mosquito control to "make our cities and towns and the country more comfortable for our homefolks and visitors and, at the same time, win the battle against disease," but also action to halt the conversion of lakes, bays, and streams into "cesspools" that served as "hourly repositories of raw sewage."[86]

The Galveston Chamber of Commerce typified the growing angst about human waste dumped in surrounding waters. An official in March 1946 noted "two schools of thought on this." One view held that salt water killed germs, and the other argued that the tide "flushed" the channel twice daily. But increasing tourist numbers and expanding permanent populations made conditions difficult to ignore. Members believed that "Galveston was definitely at fault and couldn't very well ask neighboring communities to stop practice until new system put into effect here." Tourism lay at the center of their concerns. The chamber leadership recorded, "It was pointed out that some doctors were advising parents to not allow their children to play on the beach due to polluted water which was certainly very bad publicity in view of advertising beach." Luckily, surveys by the U.S. Health Department promised to be "free of charge and without publicity." Harry Black, who headed the chamber's Anti-Pollution Committee during the late 1940s, recommended a low-key approach. In May 1947 he reported that "due to the summer season being on, the best thing would be to stay in the background, and in the meantime try to get Houston to go ahead and call the regional meeting, rather than have Galveston take the lead in calling the meeting as originally proposed." Galveston businessmen were content to prod from the rear. They did, however, believe in maintaining an active role in any joint effort of nearby communities "regardless of any unfavorable publicity which may result from any meetings." The matter was severe, especially as tourists feared the pollution as a cause of polio. In June 1948 businesses "not alone in the downtown mercantile area, but on the beach front" suffered a 25 percent decline in receipts from the previous year due to "unfavorable publicity regarding pollution of Gulf waters." Business leaders eager to quell the resulting "polio scare" consulted with three Houston newspapers to repair Galveston's damaged tourism industry.[87]

Waste management grew in importance. Biloxi by 1957 faced a health crisis. Harrison County health officer Dr. A. N. Morphy noted how rapid urbanization produced dangers: "In three-fourths of the area of the city the people have to rely on septic tanks, cesspools, or pit privies, and in the majority of this area these have ceased to function properly, and are allowing raw sewage to run out on the surface of the ground and into the ditches and storm sewers." The soil was "so saturated that there are no absorptive powers remaining." Leakage threatened swimming and oystering in the Back Bay as well as the Gulf. Although Virginia Beach built a sewage disposal plant in 1938 and enlarged the facility in 1951, the state water control board reprimanded the city for water pollution resulting from improper sewage disposal in August 1961.[88] Rapid development overwhelmed municipal systems, forcing costly expansions and tighter regulations.

Disposal of rubbish also became problematic. In November 1945, for instance, the Galveston Chamber of Commerce convinced Houston mayor Otis Massey to reject a plan to dump garbage thirty miles offshore. David Damon of Panama City lambasted the burning of trash at the city dump in 1967: "Until recently, the prime offender has been our manufacturing industry creating an offense to the nose, damage to property and devolving land. Now the general public had added an offense of its own." Tourism formed "our multimillion dollar industry," yet the lack of a cleaner rubbish disposal system created a "public nuisance sufficient to discourage, if not kill, this particular goose that lays golden eggs." Damon concluded, "Imagine the reaction of a family fleeing the heat and odors of the city for the fresh air and sunshine of the Gulf Coast only to find the air heavy with the stench of a burning dump."[89]

The changing nature of trash, which included more packaged grocery and fast-food items, worsened conditions. The development in the early twentieth century of the automobile, chemical, and electronic industries as well as a more consumer-oriented economy, meant more packaging, synthetics, and toxic products. Per capita disposal of all waste—including agricultural, industrial, mining, and consumer—rose from 2.75 pounds per day in 1920 to 5 pounds per day in 1970. The dramatic increase in discards, especially as the "throwaway" culture emerged after the Second World War, severely strained means of disposal. Environmentally conscious Americans no longer tolerated the traditional means of dumping waste along the waterfront as fill, common from colonial times through the nineteenth century. Plastics and other synthetics used for everything from utensils to coolers washed ashore.[90]

Nuclear waste posed a more serious threat. A firestorm of protest erupted after the National Academy of Sciences in 1959 identified several sites in the Atlantic and Gulf for dumping radioactive materials. Congressman Thomas Downing, speaking for Virginia Beach, condemned the recommendation of a location only twenty-five miles off the resort city. Business organizations such as the Galveston Chamber of Commerce likewise denounced the federal plan to license the disposal of radioactive materials offshore.[91]

Tourism challenged competing industries that damaged the environment. Panama City's paper mill exemplified the tension between manufacturing and tourism. Local resident Robert Keeler asked in 1968 why the mill continued to spew "forth tons of obnoxious filth" damaging to people, property, and "our beaches and waters." Florida governor Reubin Askew, speaking at a Keep Florida Beautiful luncheon in 1971, declared, "In short, Florida—nature's Florida—is better than any artificial 'upper or downer' for helping what ails you. And it is our job, my friends, to see that neither can, bottle, plastic wrapper, billboard, nor pulpwood chain saw transforms what we have to offer into little more than a 'bad trip.'"[92]

Oil exploration was particularly controversial. The discovery of oil at Spindletop near Beaumont, Texas—barely twenty miles inland—in 1901 revolutionized the oil industry. Before 1901, Standard Oil controlled the industry by controlling the Pennsylvania fields. The costs of shipment by rail hindered competitors. Pipeline construction at the time cost an expensive $5,000 to $6,000 per mile. Close proximity to the Gulf made pipelines more cost effective since vessels could cheaply carry the crude to global markets. Rival companies, marking the corporate integration of the oil industry, flocked southward to construct drilling rigs, pipelines, refineries, and shipping facilities. Prospectors quickly realized that the Gulf contained resource-rich sea bottoms vital to energy-hungry Americans. Historian Tyler Priest labels the Gulf of Mexico the "most explored, drilled, and developed offshore petroleum province in the world." As Americans crowded into automobiles, the value and demand for oil increased. Companies tapped oil reservoirs beneath Louisiana wetlands by the 1920s. In the 1930s prospectors tested the offshore shallows of Texas, Louisiana, and Mississippi. In a 1938 clash of competing economic interests, oilmen who courted the Mississippi legislature for offshore drilling rights faced "spirited" opposition from hotel operators, fishermen, and their allies. Protesters asserted that more than 80 percent of businesses along the coast opposed the legislature's plan to lease nearly five hundred thousand acres in Mississippi Sound to oil exploration companies in return for an eighth royalty interest on any oil produced. Oil exploration went forward but under close scrutiny. Similar concerns struck the Galveston Chamber of Commerce during the 1930s as the oil industry drilled deep into Texas soil and politics. Tourism-dependent businessmen such as Harry Levy "stressed the need of curbing the oil pollution on the beach and in navigable waters."[93]

After the Second World War, oil exploration stretched to Alabama and Florida waters as well as farther offshore as new technologies facilitated drilling at greater depths. The unsightly derricks required closely monitored camouflage. In the 1970s drilling off Galveston only occurred during the "off season" between October and May. Rigs were removed by May 1st, when wells were capped and "painted to blend with the background." The chamber of commerce reported, "At one mile, it would be hardly noticeable from the beach."[94]

Practices on commercial and military vessels further fouled the waters. H. M. Abbot of Massachusetts expressed ambivalence on visiting the beaches around Miami in January 1955: "Too cold for us but beach was lovely except for oil in sand from tankers." Galveston and Virginia Beach particularly suffered from traffic to and from the crowded ports at Houston and Newport News, respectively. U.S. naval ships regularly ignored federal regulations during the 1950s by dumping oily bilgewater offshore as vessels headed to base. Commercial vessels also "badly abused" the laws. As a result, clouded surf, oil slicks, and tar balls soiled the beaches. The problem forced the Virginia Beach mayor and other city officials to meet with the "top brass" of the Fifth Naval District in July 1957. As the "largest single operator" in Hampton Roads Harbor, the U.S. Navy was the biggest headache for the tourism industry. Private and foreign shipping firms were also contacted. Politicians and businessmen from Virginia Beach maintained a "constant alert" to safeguard their expensive investment in beaches.[95]

The oil crises of the 1970s raised awareness of American wastefulness. As Americans conserved oil, they accepted simpler pleasures offered by nearby nature. They also viewed the crises, which demonstrated American dependence on foreign nations, as a challenge to family life and leisure. Fears of an oil rush in the Gulf of Mexico galvanized environmentalists eager to prevent spills or seepage damaging to coastal ecosystems. Under pressure, President Jimmy Carter declared 1980 the Year of the Coast. Environmentalists over the next decade organized an annual Coastweek, held in October. The celebration, endorsed by numerous governors and Congress as well as groups such as the Coast Alliance, Sierra Club, and League of Women Voters, raised awareness about the consequences of development and pollution. Beach parties, nature walks, canoe trips, workshops, photography contests, and a media blitz educated Americans about the nation's shorelines.[96]

Pollution during the 1960s and 1970s caused beach communities to reconsider their creed of exploitation. Historian Arnold Toynbee famously suggested that monotheism lay at the heart of the pollution problem, since polytheistic faiths typically linked gods to particular animals, landmarks, or weather phenomena, thus inspiring respect as well as worship. Lynn White, a medieval historian, went further when *Science* published his influential "The Historical Roots of Our Ecological Crisis" in 1966. White blamed Christianity by teaching that humans possessed mastery over the world. The argument gave William Hutter, a Biloxi resident "steeped in Christian traditions," pause. The polluted waterways, littered roadsides, endangered animal populations, and clouded skies required "more serious dialogue" about environmental damage.[97]

Elemental Forces

By the end of the twentieth century, engineers, builders, and boosters had crowded the shores with businesses, homes, and coastal armor. Writing in 1973, Mark Hodges of Myrtle Beach questioned boosters' long-held view that the "bigger a thing is the better it becomes." He feared the consequences of the expanding tourism industry: "Condominiums are sprouting almost as fast as the plants they replace, motels are going up in a matter of weeks, and untouched seashores are quickly fading from the scene." Traffic and pollution threatened the coast. Hodges asked, "Are we prepared to turn the Strand into a composite Coney Island South–Miami Beach North and doom Conway streets to be an eastern version of the Los Angeles Freeway?" In 1989 Joyce Watters, a college student in Panama City, remarked: "Today the traveler doesn't stop here to get away from it all; he stops to get to it all."[98]

Whether suppressing mosquitoes, holding back the seas, or attempting to preserve nature to exploit it, boosters came to realize that the ecosystem challenges the illusion of human-built security. Like the Galveston storm of 1900, Hurricane Katrina ravaged the Gulf Coast in 2005. The storm surge punctured New Orleans's levees and topped the Harrison County seawall. A year after the hurricane, Gulfport native and poet Natasha Trethewey interviewed a woman struggling to reestablish normalcy. She mused, "It was like a bomb had went off. And now everywhere is slabs, just slabs." More than 230 coastal Mississippians had died in the storm. Some eighty miles away, journalist Chris Rose likewise pondered the consequences of the levee breaches that left most of the Crescent City an aquatic Pompeii, killing more than 1,500 New Orleanians and making Katrina the deadliest hurricane to hit the United States since the 1928 Okeechobee storm. Referring to the thousands of rank refrigerators dumped onto curbs as residents rebuilt, Rose pondered:

> In Refrigerator Land, the levees all are made of sand
> And there's no gas, no food, no water, and no sewage.
> But in Refrigerator Land, we will make our final stand
> Because anything beats rush hour in Baton Rouge.

Like victims of past natural disasters, Rose determined to build stronger coastal defenses so that residents and tourists could still get to it all.[99]

The tourism industry provided African Americans escape from the cotton fields but also forced them to adopt a servile manner expected by white travelers. Here, waiters stand prepared in the dining room of the St. James Hotel, in Jacksonville, Florida, c. 1885. State Archives of Florida, Florida Memory.

Tourism was a New South industry. Here, c. 1905, the electric power station for the Great Southern Hotel in Biloxi ensures travelers access to the latest technology. Note the Mediterranean architecture of the tower. Detroit Publishing Company Photograph Collection, Library of Congress Prints and Photographs Division.

Malaria and yellow fever plagued the American South into the early twentieth century. This illustration by Matt Morgan, published in *Frank Leslie's Weekly* in 1873, shows yellow fever as a monster strangling Florida as Columbia, the female personification of America, calls for aid. Cabinet of American Illustration, Library of Congress Prints and Photographs Division.

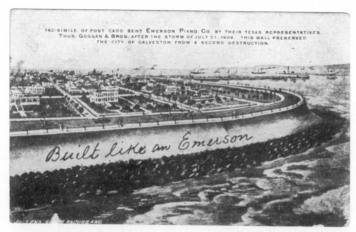

FAC-SIMILE OF POST CARD SENT EMERSON PIANO CO. BY THEIR TEXAS REPRESENTATIVES. THOS. GOGGAN & BROS. AFTER THE STORM OF JULY 21, 1909. THIS WALL PRESERVED THE CITY OF GALVESTON FROM A SECOND DESTRUCTION.

Built like an Emerson

When the 1900 hurricane killed thousands in Galveston, survivors launched a massive rebuilding effort. The Galveston seawall became an engineering marvel that inspired coastal armoring projects across the United States. When a salesman likened the Emerson Piano Company's products to the sturdy seawall on a popular postcard in 1909, the company replicated the postcard. Author's collection.

The seafood industry along the Gulf Coast attracted a wide range of European immigrants, such as these working at the Biloxi shrimp processing plant operated by the Dunbar, Lopez, and Dukate Company in February 1911. National Child Labor Committee Collection, Library of Congress.

The opportunities afforded by the tourism industry attracted a diverse population. Stopping in Myrtle Beach on their way to Florida in 1946, a Greek family decided to remain in the flourishing resort. Their Kozy Korner restaurant became a downtown fixture during the mid-twentieth century. Author's collection.

The construction of U.S. military installations across the South fostered a year-round economy in beach resorts and undermined Jim Crow. Installations often dotted the shore to protect from invasion and to exploit the open water for safe pilot or artillery training. This parade of amphibious craft in Panama City in 1943 also demonstrates the importance of the military as an attraction. State Archives of Florida, Florida Memory.

NO, THIS ISN'T ME! BUT I'M SO TANNED THERE ISN'T MUCH DIFFERENCE! (HOPE YOU'LL KNOW ME WHEN I GET HOME)

White Americans linked tanning with racial inversion. A tan served as a kind of "brownface" in which white tourists could indulge in leisure and sexuality in ways often associated with people of color. This postcard from the 1940s suggests that a tan equated to blackness. Author's collection.

African Americans used wade-ins to challenge segregated beaches. The increased expenditure of federal funds on beach erosion projects after the Second World War brought federal protection of blacks' access to the shore. Here, the wade-in at Saint Augustine's beach in 1964 turns violent. State Archives of Florida, Florida Memory.

Beauty pageants emerged in the 1920s as a means of marketing sexuality within a framework that provided a veneer of moral order. These bathing beauties gathered in May 1926 to participate in the First International Pageant of Pulchritude hosted by Galveston. Panoramic Photographs Collection, Library of Congress.

Women in swimwear became a staple means of advertising beach tourism. This promotional photograph for the Florida Department of Commerce suggestively positions the inner tube to give a double meaning to the "Souvenir of Florida." State Archives of Florida, Florida Memory.

Beaches were sites charged with sexual energy. This promotional photograph taken in May 1950 for the Florida Department of Commerce emphasizes the romantic possibilities of a day along Panama City's shore. State Archives of Florida, Florida Memory.

GALVESTON ISLAND and FALSTAFF Brewing Corp. *Welcome You!*

WHILE IN GALVESTON,
TOUR THE SOUTHWEST'S NEWEST
AND MOST MODERN BREWERY

(left)
Alcohol was vital to the success of southern resort towns, which often flouted state prohibition laws to cater to tourists' desires. The Falstaff Brewery, operating in Galveston from 1956 until 1981, combined business with pleasure by promoting the facility as a tourist attraction in this brochure. Author's collection.

(below)
Despite the construction of seawalls and renourished beaches, southern beach resorts remain precariously exposed to nature. This photograph from April 2006 shows a ship washed ashore by Hurricane Camille in 1969 sitting on a Mississippi coast bulldozed by Hurricane Katrina in 2005. Carol M. Highsmith's America, Library of Congress, Prints and Photographs Division.

CHAPTER THREE

Black and Tan

Race, Tanning, and the Civil Rights Movement

Near Jefferson Davis's Beauvoir lay the Sea Shore Camp Ground of the Methodist Episcopal Church, a recreation center for white Methodists along the Gulf. Dedicated in 1872, the site had grown to a beach frontage of 1,400 feet and stretched two miles inland by the time Minnie Walter Myers visited in the mid-1890s. In her *Romance and Realism of the Southern Gulf Coast* (1898), Myers mused, "This camp ground proves that the good old customs are not all obsolete, and who knows but that these soul-stirring Methodist hymns, as they are carried far out over the gulf in wave after wave of sound, are not caught beneath the water and given back to us in that strange, mysterious music of the sea?" Religious devotion complemented natural wonder. For American tourists steeped in the romanticism of the nineteenth century, earthly marvels, whether at Niagara Falls, Mammoth Cave, or Myers's Gulf Coast, manifested the divine blessings enjoyed by the United States.

African Americans offered Myers a less tranquil tale. The emergence of vacation retreats for whites meant an increasingly restricted beachfront. "Some of the old negroes tell that in that long ago when their sea-shore revivals were held, many of their members 'came through' with religious ecstacy [*sic*], and rushing into the sea believed it to be the river Jordan washing away their sins," recounted Myers. Like the God of the Old Testament, the waters also brought retribution. Myers continued, "They say that the sea imprisoned these wild shouts and singing, and that the storms free these sounds and they come back to us in strange, fitful notes." The waves swept away troubles, but thunderous storms returned with punishing waves and wind. Myers unwittingly captured a metaphor for segregation and civil rights protests along southern beaches.[1]

Though blacks managed to purchase shorefront and enjoy the surf before the First World War, the development of coastal resorts for white tourists meant increased scrutiny of African Americans within these municipalities from the 1920s through 1960s. Increasingly, black enclaves came under assault by white developers through liens for unpaid taxes, zoning laws, and other legal means or through outright fraud and deception. Other black property owners became isolated from waterfront areas as white developers circumvented black communities, denying access to municipal services and improved beachfront. Not surprisingly, some African Americans came to understand hurricanes as divine punishment for whites' hubris—retribution for denying blacks communion with the sea. Lee Owens, a black Biloxian, recalled the beach replenishment program of the 1940s: "But when they put that beach there, those white folks went stone crazy. 'That's our beach. This ain't no nigger beach.'" He snapped back: "'No, it's God's beach.' I said, 'God going to move his hand after a while.' And God moved his hand, Brother John. He swept that beach off twice." The 1947 hurricane and Hurricane Camille in 1969 demonstrated divine disgust with Jim Crow.[2]

By the mid-twentieth century, white boosters and municipal leaders confronted erosion, both to segregation and to beaches. Resort communities increasingly depended on federal largesse to bolster the tourism infrastructure and the Army Corps of Engineers to buttress coastal armor. Yet federal aid meant federal scrutiny and increased exposure to the threat of federal lawsuits over segregationist practices. The strengthening of segregation along the beachfront between the 1920s and 1950s ultimately led to the demise of the color line during the 1960s. The denial of equal public access to restored beaches for everyone became untenable as civil rights activists increasingly challenged Jim Crow practices after the Second World War, often with the aim of disrupting local tourism industries while also targeting the renourished beaches funded with federal dollars. The result was, according to historian Nathan D. B. Connolly, "a widening whiteness and the requisite hardening of the boundaries of blackness." In other words, the diversity of vacationers, both domestic and foreign, encouraged acceptance of those with darker skin. Simultaneously, white urban boosters in the 1960s and 1970s, though speaking in support of a new colorblind society, created greater spatial distance between black neighborhoods and white tourists by cunning use of eminent domain, zoning, and other methods as part of slum clearance campaigns.[3]

Beach towns formed the Achilles' heel of Jim Crow. In a tourism industry that celebrated bronzed bodies, white skin lost the cultural currency that reinforced labor and class divisions in the agricultural economy—though racism certainly persisted. By the mid-twentieth century, state budgets heavily depended on tourism for tax revenue. When racial violence made international headlines, state legislators not only heard protests from coastal businessmen but also witnessed a sharp drop in sales taxes as vacationers avoided the turmoil. Segregation rested on a foundation of sand.

Sands of Babel

Vietnamese refugees crowded into fishing villages from Texas to Florida during the 1970s and 1980s. They aimed to rebuild their lives by plying traditional trades in new waters. Lien Thi Beale's father came to Mississippi to work a shrimp boat. She explained that "the first concept that everybody gets about Mississippi is the shacks and all that that you read in the history books" about racial violence. But the towns of Gulfport and Biloxi were a pleasant surprise when she arrived in 1983: "I didn't realize that the Coast was so different from the rest of Mississippi."[4]

The coast was the South's melting pot, a contrast to the cotton South rooted in sharecropping, debt peonage, and sharp racial distinctions. Geographers have recently defined a new cultural region, labeled the "Creole Coast," sharing "economic and social systems" within the thin ribbon of coastal lands stretching from Chesapeake Bay to the Texas Coastal Bend. Here, architectural styles, foodways, and vernacular speech reflect a considerable Caribbean influence dating to colonial times. Jim Crow had difficulty deciphering the ethnically diverse, racially complex, tourist-filled, and—in older port towns—partially unionized workforces. Places such as Galveston, Biloxi, Jacksonville, Norfolk, and points in between claimed either groups of color with ties to the French and Spanish colonial period or maritime populations that mixed a surprising range of peoples largely overlooked by historians of the region. From Texas to Florida, many older resort towns claimed both. Tourism reinforced such diversity.[5]

Trade bound seaside towns along the Gulf from Galveston to Pensacola and on the Atlantic from Saint Augustine to Charleston since the eighteenth century. Less rigid racial regimes on the Gulf, settled initially by the Spanish and French, produced populations that included significant numbers of free people of color. Even the English settlement of Charleston, established in 1670, claimed a sizeable free colored population. Cotton and slavery strengthened the shared economic interest during antebellum times as these settlements fell under the American flag. Concerns over disease and storms further linked coastal communities.

Creoles of color, often claiming French and Spanish ancestry, maintained a proud culture that resisted a black-white dichotomy. Historian Virginia Gould, in her study of antebellum New Orleans, Mobile, and Pensacola, writes, "Black, white, and racially-mixed Creoles recognized that they shared a unique culture that had evolved over generations of mutual experience. They realized that their identities were knit together by kinship, common interest, and culture." Such bonds, though strained by America's white supremacist culture, lingered after the Civil War. Few were as famous as Creole of color Homer Plessy of New Orleans, whose challenge of segregation failed when the U.S. Supreme Court established the legal principle of "separate but equal" in 1896. Lorita Nelson Jones, born in Biloxi in 1909, boasted of her Creole-of-color roots in a 1999 interview. When her parents left New Orleans for the Mississippi Coast after the Civil War, the French language still claimed their tongues: "They didn't speak no kind of English; all Creole. They speak that French."[6] The WPA's guide to Texas likewise noted that Galveston contained "Negroes—some of them, from Louisiana and West Indian islands speaking French patois." Whether due to a sense of cultural obligation or to prosperity from the seafood and tourism industries, those of African descent maintained a strong sense of their rights. A Biloxi native born in 1937, whose family fortune rested on decades of shrimping and hotel work, elaborated, "Daddy always subscribed to *The Chicago Defender, The Pittsburgh Courier, The Louisiana Weekly, The Times Picayune,* and *The Daily Herald. The Daily Herald,* we read that every day, and the others we read on Saturday."[7]

Conflicting definitions of Creoles muddied the racial waters. White New Orleanians, whitewashing their racial heritage and denying their African-blooded cousins, identified Creoles as an aristocratic people descended from white French or Spanish ancestors. Yet the Alabama supreme court defined "Creoles" as colored. Mississippians understood the term—spelled either *Creole* or *Kreole*—to mean "a person of mixed race in which both Negro and Indian blood may be present." The Mississippi Coast Motel Association endorsed the definition. In sharp contrast to white Louisianans' vigilant defense of Creole whiteness, Mississippians tied the term to poverty and miscegenation. A federal researcher visited the poor whites living in Kreole, the "dingy village dominated" by the Southern Paper Company, in the late 1930s. Although the name of the town came from a "variety of coffee-colored paper" made at the plant, the term cast racial suspicions on the poor white mill hands.[8]

In former Spanish outposts, such as Galveston, Pensacola, and Saint Augustine, African and Spanish descendants formed ties. Spanish colonial policy had encouraged slave runaways to seek refuge in Spanish settlements. The tactic undermined nearby English plantations while bolstering the population of Spanish colonies, making them more defensible. Takeover by the United States repressed these ties. But even as segregation and racism encouraged those of Spanish heritage to claim white purity, the economics of racism could have the opposite effect. Though racial suspicions hindered intermixing, poverty and violence often exposed the cultural fluidity of race. New Orleans native Sidney Bechet, a Creole of color who gained worldwide fame as a jazz clarinetist, visited his brother in Galveston around 1910. There he befriended a Mexican guitarist. One night, white policemen harried the two musicians, severely beating the Mexican before arresting both men. Bechet continued, "And it was while I was in jail there that I played the first blues I ever played with a lot of guys singing and no other instruments, just the singing. And, oh my God, what singing that was!"[9]

Along the Gulf Coast, especially in isolated enclaves, bloodlines entangled. Sherwood Anderson traveled to a barrier island near New Orleans in March 1935. He wrote to Gertrude Stein and Alice Toklas, "The place to which I went is an island inhabited since before the Revolution—French, Spanish, Indians, and Negroes, all gradually intermarried. They fish. There is no agriculture." But tourism too anchored the refuge. He explained that a "city man owned land on the island and built a ramshackle hotel, putting his mistress in charge." Anderson reveled in the surf, seafood, and unusual residents. Discerning lineages became difficult as storms demolished records and markers, such as headstones, and as some inhabitants passed as white.[10]

Whereas most coastal whites boasted of their Confederate heritage, blacks cherished a group of former slaves—Union veterans. Many African Americans abandoned plantation districts for nearby towns and cities after the Civil War. Urban centers, often containing federal army posts, provided more social and economic freedom as well as greater safety from violence. The region's largest cities sat along the coast. One African American, remembering his childhood in early twentieth-century Biloxi, noted the black veterans' presence at festivals such as Mardi Gras: "We had some Civil War Veterans, black. We'd be downtown watching the parade, and they'd sic us on the white boys, 'Get them.'"[11]

Like Creoles, other residents with a non-Anglo colonial heritage honored their ancestry. A tourist in Saint Augustine in the late nineteenth century declared the residents "entirely different from the rest of the mixture forming the United States." She continued, "They, too, are a compound, but of other ingredients, consisting of Spaniards and Minorcans, a few original English settlers, and but a small proportion of Americans. They speak a sort of Spanish patois; intermarry among themselves; and live as much apart from the surrounding population as though Saint Augustine were an island."[12] Like the French Creoles of the Gulf Coast, the culture and bloodlines of these Saint Augustine inhabitants faded by the twentieth century. But across Florida descendants of Spaniards shaped the politics of old colonial outposts blossoming into twentieth-century resort cities. Saint Elmo Acosta, the Jacksonville Park Commissioner in the late 1930s, boasted: "I am a direct descendant of Pedro Menendez, the early Spanish governor, and my relationship comes down through the Alvarez family." His great-grandfather, Antonio Alvarez, had served as mayor of Saint Augustine. The commissioner showed particular pride in his family's donation of the bells to the cathedral in Saint Augustine. A WPA interviewer noted Alvarez's "olive skin" and "small piercing brown eyes."[13] When WPA interviewer Barbara Darsey ventured to the hamlet of Venus, Florida, in 1938, she found middle-aged Maria Gonzales. Her married name, Morgan, created confusion over her racial lineage. The sunrays that darkened her already brown skin intensified the bewilderment. Gonzales remarked, "Sometimes people ask me if I am Spanish because I am so dark of skin an [sic] have such big dark eyes."[14]

Places with colonial French and Spanish roots possessed prominent Catholic populations reinforced in ports such as Galveston, New Orleans, Mobile, and Pensacola by Irish and Italian immigrants, a sharp contrast from the heavily evangelical Protestant inland areas. The international reach, history, and principles of service central to Roman Catholicism challenged segregationist codes. Throughout much of the nineteenth century, Catholics of all colors worshipped in the same churches in contrast to the racially separate congregations common among Protestants. Bishops in the early twentieth century labored to institute segregation—a process historian James Bennett in his study of New Orleans called "Americanization"—via the creation of all-black parishes, though those parishes preserved class and Creole identities. Interracial worship declined as the white Catholic hierarchy marginalized people of color. Yet many African American laity resisted, attending through at least the 1940s the neighborhood "white" churches at which their ancestors had worshiped, though in segregated seating areas. Loyce Searight, born in central Alabama, came to Biloxi in 1947 while still a child. Although a Methodist, his exposure to Catholic schools revealed the possibility of greater interracial contact. Though far from color-blind, Our Mother of Sorrows, a Catholic school, "was integrated in that the faculty was all white nuns, and we had one African-American teacher. And the students were all black, and quite an experience, quite a transition from where I came from in Alabama because all the teachers there were black." Describing life along the Mississippi Coast, he noted how African Americans "used to call this God's country." The resurgence of the Ku Klux Klan in the decade after 1915, which espoused anti-Catholicism and anti-Semitism as well as racism against African Americans, alienated Catholic southerners. Many white Catholics, including priests and bishops, were certainly racists. But the colonial legacy of Catholicism, the Church's international reach, and its teachings tempered Americanization of the religion in regard to race.[15]

By the early twentieth century, a flourishing seafood industry emerged along the Gulf, born of the expanding railroad network, the new technology of refrigeration, and improved canning methods. Processing facilities employed cheap immigrant labor from eastern and southern Europe as well as desperate sharecroppers—black and white—suffering under the twin burdens of debt and boll weevils. Stefan Nesterowicz, touring Polish American communities in 1909, described how new arrivals landed in the oyster and shrimp canneries along the Gulf only to receive the "unheard of low pay doled out by the companies." Packing companies in Baltimore frequently shifted immigrant employees from Maryland facilities open during summer to operations in Mississippi during winter. In Biloxi these immigrants maintained a "little better life, thanks to the fact that there are Czechs and Frenchmen employed in the oyster industry, and these will not permit themselves to be so exploited." Nesterowicz identified more than four thousand Poles who participated in this migration. Yet a range of ethnic immigrants joined the Poles, including Dalmatian fisherman. Though most left the canneries by mid-February, a few remained. One Mississippian described how locals identified these motley ethnic groups as "Bohemian people." Travel writer Ernest Young explored the unique cultures along the Mississippi Sound in the late 1940s. He noted how shrimp and oyster fishermen in Biloxi belonged to "several small communities such as are common all along this section of the coast." These were insular settlements: "Each community tends to be almost exclusively of one nationality and tends to preserve its own customs, language and outlook on life." He encountered Slavs, Austrians, Czechs, French, and "some negroes." On the outskirts of Biloxi, Young found "descendants of Swiss and German colonists who are engaged in lumbering" while "others of French descent, speaking a French patois," raised poultry and cultivated orchards.[16]

Commercial fishing likewise drew assorted ethnic groups to the Gulf Coast. Nathan Alfonso's Sicilian father immigrated to Louisiana in 1898 to work the sugar cane fields. He freelanced as a fisherman, selling his catch at the French Market in New Orleans. In time, he moved to Mississippi. He used his savings to build fishing boats, hiring fellow Italians as crewmen. Glennan Anderson, a longtime Biloxi resident, noted the diversity of the coast's population in a 1979 interview: "You have your Austrians, you have your Yugoslavs, you have some Spanish, you have some French, and you have quite a few Italians. So you really have a cross section. And you have some Mexican. Now you've got Vietnamese." The range of peoples left Anderson tongue-tied. She joked, "In fact, there's some I still can't pronounce their names, I just abbreviate them."[17]

The docks birthed powerful longshoremen's unions, some boasting integrated membership dating to the late nineteenth century. Ernest Young was amazed by the strength of organized labor on Mississippi's coast: "At Gulfport the longshoremen comprise a small number of Greeks, a larger body of thrifty, progressive, hard-working Italians, and many negroes. The negroes are so advanced, politically, that they are organized in a powerful trade union and work under contract at standard wages." Young exclaimed, "This, in the south, is a miraculous achievement." Wilson Evans II of Gulfport, an African American, worked the docks as a longshoreman after the Second World War and was elected president of his union in 1950. Labor activism and voting rights went hand in hand. Evans explained, "And at that time we was voting very strong, and I had voted continuously since 1946." Evans noted that "one of the conditions of membership at that time was that you had to be a registered voter in Harrison County." The predominantly black International Longshoremen's Association, which Wilson headed until 1989, bolstered civil rights activism in the area.[18]

The South's strict racial code strained to discern multishaded natives, tourists, and immigrant workers. The Brinker family of Pennsylvania traveled to Florida in December 1940. In Saint Augustine they visited the Fountain of Youth. They recorded, "Greeted by girls dressed in Spanish costume." A few days later they watched Greek sponge divers in Tarpon Springs. Near Tampa, they stopped at "Japenese [sic] Gardens, a bit of Japan" complete with a "Japenese [sic] family living there." Florida contained a hodgepodge of ethnic and racial groups drawn together by history, by the sea, and by the tourism industry. As historian Chanelle Rose argues, the push to increase tourist traffic from Cuba and Latin America after the Second World War further muddled racial lines. The ability to speak Spanish or French often allowed travelers, despite possible African ancestry, to enjoy whites-only beaches, among other facilities.[19]

The so-called Conches exemplified the racial confusion. Natives of the Bahamas, the Conches—nicknamed for the shellfish that formed a staple of their diet—arrived in southern Florida in the early twentieth century. Employees of the Federal Writers' Project encountered several hundred Conches living in Riviera, a "bare fishing village" consisting of scattered "stores, open-faced souvenir stands, tourist camps, jook joints, filling stations, and a post office" along the highway approaching West Palm Beach. The Conches evidenced the more liberal racial society that evolved in the Bahamas after slavery. The researchers recorded, "Although the majority are Anglo-Saxon in appearance, with fair hair and blue eyes, some of them give evidence of Negroid characteristics. Occasionally in a single family one child will appear Anglo-Saxon, another Negro." Officials struggled to place the Conches in the South's racial caste system: "Listed as white people in the records of the Palm Beach County Board of Social Welfare, immigrant records list those with Negroid features as Africans, while citizenship applications classify them as West Indians. All of the children attend white schools." More befuddling, many Conches retained British citizenship. Local whites tried to accomplish by custom what the law could not. Though they "live among white Americans in Riviera," commented the WPA workers, "the adult Conches are almost completely segregated as far as social relations are concerned, due to the prejudice of their white neighbors." Some white Americans refused to allow their children to attend the local public school "where the Conches predominate." The racial animosity only heightened the confusion. Many Conches had come to deny miscegenation.[20]

The tourism industry, by its nature, engaged a diverse range of nationalities—both as employees and as customers. Interviewed in the late 1930s, hotelier Gertha Couric boasted of working in "some of the largest hotels in the South; Hotel Peabody in Memphis; the Tutwiler and the Thomas Jefferson in Birmingham; the Greystone in Montgomery, and others." These famed establishments shared an international clientele and, in some cases, affiliations with coastal resorts such as the Ocean Forest Hotel in Myrtle Beach. They also employed a diverse staff. Couric remarked, "A big hotel is like Port Said; a meeting place of the nations. In the kitchens alone, there may be Germans, French, Swedes, Italians, Greeks, and Americans." Such a "hodgepodge of humanity" speaking a "dozen different languages" complicated the divide between white and colored even though hotels typically reserved the most menial labor—from bellboys to waiters to dishwashers—for African Americans.[21]

In the early twentieth century, Greeks opened restaurants catering to the growing middle class in southern towns. They, along with Syrians, also started operating grocery and dry goods stores across the region. Immigrants found opportunity as tourists in their automobiles increased demand for eateries, overnight accommodation, filling stations, groceries, and other necessities. Gus Geraris opened his business in Elizabeth City, North Carolina, a town on U.S. Highway 17. He explained to a WPA interviewer why Greeks, many former sailors such as himself, settled across the South. Speaking little English upon arrival, Greeks took low-wage jobs such as dishwasher in a hotel or restaurant. Eventually they learned to cook, saving their money until finally having enough to open "a little restaurant." Dino Thompson's Greek parents left the shuttered Newport News shipyards for Florida in 1946. On the way, they stopped in Myrtle Beach. Seeing opportunity as well as a community of fellow Greeks and other immigrants, they purchased the Kozy Korner restaurant, a downtown fixture they would operate for decades.[22]

Like other immigrants, Greek newcomers, sensitive to their own marginal racial position, generally conformed to Jim Crow practices. After earning startup money as a steelworker in Pennsylvania, Peter Gournas moved in 1915 to Raleigh, North Carolina, to open his restaurant. Besides being a state capital, Raleigh rested on a major highway to Florida. The People's Cafe served blacks and whites through separate entrances. He employed three workers, all Greeks. A fervent Democrat, like most other Greek immigrants, Gournas adamantly opposed Greeks marrying anyone other than a fellow Greek or white American since marrying "anyone else is making his race even more foreign over here." Steve Loomis, another restaurateur in Raleigh, was more adamant. He sneered, "I hate Negroes, and I wish that the Government would give them a state by themselves and make them live in it." Loomis did not "cater to Negro trade." Yet ethnic arrivals such as Greeks and Syrians complicated the black-white dichotomy. Their support of Jim Crow reflected their racial ambiguity. As historian Sarah Gualtieri argues, groups such as Syrians and Italians were "not-quite-white" and thus subject to racism and violence, as when "white" Syrian grocer Nicholas Romey—often reported in the press under the Italianized misspelling "Romeo" or "Romero"—was lynched after a dispute with the police chief in Lake City, Florida, in 1929.[23]

A sampling of census records demonstrates the striking difference of coastal county populations from those of inland counties. According to the 1920 U.S.

Census, Florida's Bay County claimed five Frenchmen, twenty-four Germans, three Greeks, and one Pole, among others. Washington County, next to Bay County, contained three Germans, one Greek, one Pole, and no French residents. Mississippi's Harrison County contained 63 Frenchmen, 98 Germans, 22 Greeks, 58 Syrians, and 121 Poles, among others. While seemingly small numbers compared to the large enclaves of immigrants in cities such as Galveston, New Orleans, Jacksonville, and Norfolk, the figures are striking in comparison to neighboring inland counties. North of Harrison County, only one Frenchman, eleven Germans, ten Syrians, and one Pole lived in Pearl River, Stone, and George Counties combined. No Greeks lived there. According to 1940 U.S. Census figures, Horry County possessed seven Syrians, six Greeks, and one Lithuanian, among others. Of South Carolina's forty-six counties, thirty-two claimed fewer Syrians (sixteen had none), thirty-eight claimed fewer Greeks (eight had none), and twenty-eight had no Lithuanians. Though small in number, the diverse immigrant populations magnified the difference between coastal counties and more ethnically homogenous inland counties.[24]

Even the northern reaches of Gulf Coast counties marked another world of stricter racial codes. Reverend Harry Tartt, an African American born in Biloxi in 1908, warned, "There were times when it was not wise to stop at a filling station outside of the Gulf Coast, say, in the upper part of the county, of Harrison County." Doing so risked "bodily harm" for people of color. Such opinions were based on degrees of wrong. The coastal South sat in the shadow of the staunchly Jim Crow South. Earl Napoleon Moore, an African American born in Biloxi in 1914, remarked without irony: "Of course, we had it better than other sections of Mississippi. There was only one lynching here in Biloxi compared to other parts of Mississippi."[25]

Military installations and Cold War mobilization further diversified coastal communities. Foreigners receiving federal scholarships to study in the United States as part of Americanization programs frequently vacationed at the beach. Manuel Menendez, a Spaniard, married an air force nurse he met in Wiesbaden, Germany. By the early 1960s he moved with his wife to Tyndall Air Force Base in Panama City. Larry Hudson, a black man born in Biloxi in 1936, identified the tourism industry and the military presence as key to softening segregation along the Mississippi Coast. He declared, "Well, Biloxi has always been a tourist town. You know. And, with Keesler Field and the soldiers coming from various parts of the country, we didn't experience the harshness of segregation as the more northern portion . . . of, let's say, Mississippi."[26] A black barber in Biloxi since the 1960s fondly remembered that "here at Keesler they was sending in the guys from Africa and various foreign countries here to go to school. And I've dealt with all cultures of people." In the 1960s African American hotel worker Eleonora Hayes refused to surrender her bus seat to a white woman. The white passenger slapped Hayes and "and we went to war; World War III began." But this bus headed to Keesler, where Hayes planned to meet her husband. The military police and other riders testified for Hayes's defense. "I had half of Keesler with me," laughed Hayes.[27]

Military installations introduced local African Americans to peoples engaged in nationalist struggles worldwide. Lodie Marie Robinson-Cyrille, born in Biloxi in 1951, described her upbringing: "We had Africans in our household back in the '50s because there were African students being trained out at Keesler Air Force Base. So, in terms of cultural heritage, from as long as I can remember, seven, eight, I knew about Africa and our connection there because my aunt dated a lot of the people." Her perspective broadened: "That was one of the unusual things I think you wouldn't find in other places in Mississippi because it's on the Coast. So, you have a world perspective other than just the United States or regional, just Mississippi." Cold War programs that trained foreign military personnel from Africa, Latin America, or Asia at bases such as Keesler thus broadened the global perspective of the local black community by linking decolonization struggles with the persistence of the color line. Military service by African Americans likewise furthered this awareness. Indeed, officials in the federal government struggled with the contradiction of promoting democracy abroad in the face of Soviet propaganda advocating equality while much of the United States sustained white supremacy through laws, corruption, and violence.[28]

Military bases undermined segregation through the integration of the armed forces in 1948 and by raising wages. Lorita Nelson Jones, who had worked as a laundress at Keesler, recalled the shock of her first payday: "And when I got my first check, we couldn't believe it; we didn't know how to act. Forty dollars. We said, 'What this here?'" African Americans, denied access to whites-only stores and nightclubs, pursued their own consumers' republic. Tyrone Burton remembered his days as a barber in Biloxi, oftentimes trimming the hair of servicemen. Arriving in 1962, he proclaimed, "I was just like I was in New York. It was one of the greatest things could ever happen to me to see the growth and the way people were in this town, and business was booming." Biloxi native Vernon Jackson described how his uncle flourished by serving black military personnel: "You know, how he got his little clubs going, because he was working on Keesler, and all the soldiers, the black soldiers had to come down here on Main Street. They couldn't go—everything was segregated." Jackson's uncle seized the golden opportunity.[29]

The interior farmlands remained fields worked predominantly by African Americans and Anglo whites, even as growing coastal communities added ethnicities. After the Civil War, white planters pursued immigrants to replace freed slaves considered too unruly. Labor agents sought northern European immigrants, those considered most "white." Such efforts failed. European immigrants preferred northern, urban destinations, though some Italians took fieldwork in the South during the early twentieth century. Some plantation owners, most famously in Reconstruction-era Mississippi, hired thousands of Chinese thought more servile than former black bondsmen. Even as late as the 1920s, some landowners, such as Mrs. R. W. White near Camden, South Carolina, wanted to replace black fieldworkers with immigrants. With an eye on hiring Japanese immigrants already in California, she asked agricultural professor W. W. Long at Clemson College for advice: "Do you know of any good foreigners I could get." Horrified, Long forwarded the letter to U.S. Representative W. W. Smoak with added commentary: "No one would think of bringing Japs, Italians, Russians, and, in fact any of that crowd from the southern part of Europe and the Balkan States, but it would be a fine thing to get some Danes and people from northern Europe, along with a sprinkling of our western farmers."[30]

The sharecropping system, meant to tie tillers to the soil after emancipation, pushed laborers—black and white—from the fields by the late nineteenth century as debt levels rose. Even yeomen on the hardscrabble lands of the coastal plain looked for a better life beyond the cotton lands. African American farmer Andrew Stanley, born in 1902, remembered the community of black yeomen living in Horry County before developers arrived. Interviewed in 1993, he recalled the ill treatment received from whites during the Jim Crow era: "It was rough—they didn't want you around, they'd beat you, all of that you know, and feed ya out the door like a dog if you worked for 'em." Farm life barely improved by the 1960s, especially for black southerners. Ohioans driving through Georgia to the Sunshine State remarked, "Colored people hang clothes on fences bushes anything they can find. Plowing with old wood beam plows & mule." Affordable automobiles and the thrill of urban life encouraged flight from rural hardships during the twentieth century.[31]

Poor blacks particularly embraced the opportunities afforded by the South's tourism industry. Delmar Robinson, a Biloxi native, recalled his Louisiana-born grandfather taking a job with the Louisville and Nashville Railroad near the turn of the century. He combined his steady work on the railroad with his own entrepreneurship. With eight sons to aid him, Robinson's grandfather purchased freight wagons to deliver tourists' trunks from the train stations to the various hotels along the Mississippi coast. His drayage business also delivered three-hundred-pound blocks of ice to hotels. Others catered to the black laborers seeking jobs and the more liberal racial atmosphere of coastal towns. Clara Watson, also a Biloxi native, related, "But see, Biloxi, is sort of like the melting pot, you know, and you get people from everywhere. There were people who—I know there were people who came from the northern part of Mississippi who were really afraid." Watson's grandmother opened a rooming house since the hotels were "only for the rich that came down." Watson elaborated, "And they were people that were looking for work, and then I guess they were also looking for, you know, peace of mind, because there were so many blacks that were afraid of what whites would do."[32]

Black laborers expressed relief at finding work in the tourism industry. Tyrone Burton rejoiced after leaving rural Louisiana for a job in a New Orleans hotel in the 1950s: "And you can imagine operating a [*sic*] elevator, coming from the farm, plowing a mule and operating elevator, which was a toy. And I think I wrote just about everybody back in the country and say, 'Guess what! I got a job operating elevator.'" Burton's father bragged to neighbors: "You wouldn't believe my son is down there in New Orleans working at a job just pushing buttons. You imagine he leaving the farm just pushing buttons." In time Burton moved to Biloxi, where he thrived as a barber serving Air Force personnel who were required to "get haircuts all the time." Frank Bridges, born in Biloxi in 1923, recalled his days as a bellman at the White House Hotel, where he began after turning fifteen: "Sometimes you had good days, and sometimes you had bad days. You had a good day when they had conventions." He explained, "The average tip was about a dollar; and you had a good tip when you got four or five dollars. And if you got a party of several people, and sometimes they all would give you from one to five dollars. You would make from one to forty or fifty dollars sometimes on one party or in one day." Mark Garner, a former Myrtle Beach councilman and mayor during the 1950s and 1960s as well as the city's newspaper publisher, noted how the Grand Strand tourism industry was "now during the summer drawing workers, maids, and hotel personnel from Sumter. . . . We're getting from Williamsburg County, Florence, and Sumter and so forth. Pretty good distance for these people to come to work." For a hundred miles around Myrtle Beach, workers—many black—flocked to the jobs available along the Grand Strand.[33]

Tourists threatened the economic exploitation underpinning Jim Crow. In 1949 some Indiana tourists stopped in a Vicksburg, Mississippi, tearoom on their drive to Florida: "They used all colored girls dressed in Mammy Costumes. Lou tipped our waitress, she took it and gave it to the desk lady, she looked as if she would like to throw it in our faces for tipping the negro help they sure dont like we northern people." A traveler passing through Georgia and South Carolina in the 1960s likewise noted the economic role of tourism in reshaping race relations. He joked, "What's more I even gave a little colored girl a dime for an ice cream cone and didn't get lynched."[34]

Individuals unaccustomed to the mores of Jim Crow could easily misinterpret the subtle rules underpinning segregation. Surveying American resorts during the 1950s, Cleveland Amory recounted a popular tale about a white tourist in Palm Beach who greeted a black servant with "Hello, Uncle." A stunned bystander asked the African American whether the white woman was his niece. The servant responded, "No ma'am . . . when an old-time lady meets a colored man whose name she does not remember she calls him 'Uncle' as a term of respect." Though the term *Uncle* fit a tradition of ignoring blacks' names as a sign of their subservience, the practice made the most sense in close-knit southern communities where bloodlines were well known. Use of such terms at resorts spurred confusion and, ironically, acquired subversive meanings that blurred black and white.[35]

White southerners too misjudged the racially mixed global tourist market. Efforts to promote Jekyll Island in Georgia exposed the challenges confronted by segregationists. The island was developed as an exclusive winter reserve for the nation's elites, including the Vanderbilts, Morgans, and Rockefellers, in the 1880s. Their heirs lost interest, however, leading to the island's closure in 1941. In 1947 Georgia legislators purchased the twelve-mile-long island for a state park. By the 1950s a causeway connected the island to the mainland. Eager to draw attention to Jekyll Island's beaches while also giving Georgia a boost among Canadians, Governor Marvin Griffin in late 1952 offered survivors of a Nova Scotia mining disaster a free week at the resort. When the governor learned that miner Maurice Ruddick was black and that fellow white miners would not come without him, an embarrassed Griffin prepared a temporary colored section equipped with a trailer for the Ruddick family, a trailer for a cook and maid, and an additional trailer for a black family to keep the Ruddicks company. The state supplied light posts, septic tanks, beach chairs, and even sod. Although the Ruddick family was not allowed to interact with the white Canadian miners, the intrusion of blacks on whites-only Jekyll Island stirred celebration among African Americans in nearby Brunswick. They warmly greeted the miner who had shamed the state's Jim Crow practices. *Life* lampooned the governor for "an impulsive gesture that wryly backfired."[36]

Arthur Raper's sociological study of Thomasville, Georgia, in the 1930s exposed the impact of tourism on the South. Some thirty miles northeast of Tallahassee, the arrival of the railroad shortly after the Civil War brought thousands of northerners, birthing a winter resort. Large hotels sprouted. By the turn of the century, a "score or more rich families bought old plantations, which they used for general farming purposes, in a few instances, but usually for nothing more than hunting preserves." These absentee landlords sought "sunshine and rest" rather than crops. The town gained national recognition when President William McKinley visited.

Thomasville's tourism industry supported a prosperous black business district. During the Great Depression, the wealthy landlords buffered the economic hurricane. Three "rather prosperous Negro physicians, one very successful dentist, and a busy well-stocked drug store" cared for black clerks working at the "district headquarters for several Negro insurance companies." A number of "fairly prosperous restaurants, one being located in the proprietor's own two-story brick building," joined the "usual small businesses, such as shoe-shine parlors, barber shops, pressing clubs, and hat cleaning stands" filling the black section of Thomasville. This prosperity rested on the bedrock of wealthy northerners: "The bulk of the skilled and unskilled labor among Negroes depends upon the millionaire estates for employment and consequently a large percentage of them have year-round employment at a good price." Though peak employment occurred during the winter, hundreds of African Americans enjoyed "unusually auspicious conditions" year-round as they cared for the estates.

The eruption of racial violence revealed the complexity of tourism in the Jim Crow South. The community caught Raper's attention after a gruesome lynching in September 1930. Willie Kirkland, accused of assaulting a nine-year-old white girl, was shot about fifty times, dragged behind an automobile through Thomasville, and left lifeless on the courthouse lawn. The African American manager of the Guaranty Mutual Insurance Company blamed the "poor white" residents of the majority black county who possessed a "jealousy of the Negroes' apparent prosperity and care-free countenance." The same anger would lead poor white southerners from the hinterland into Biloxi and Saint Augustine for violent clashes with civil rights protesters in the 1960s. African Americans in Thomasville recognized their unique position—largely free from local white control yet dependent on the patronage of northern vacationers. In the aftermath of the lynching, local blacks' greatest fear was not racial violence per se but the consequences of racial violence. "The Negroes are very much afraid that the tourists will avoid Thomasville," wrote Raper. Under the circumstances, most blacks wanted "to let the lynching drop." They feared that the violence "will make northern people a little leery about coming to Thomasville and investing their money in plantations, and hunting lodges, and other Thomasville enterprises." White legislators and businessmen dependent on tourism taxes and revenues would face similar fears in the 1960s. The example of Thomasville highlighted the sensitivity of resort owners and employees to racial friction. It also demonstrated the tension between the wilting agricultural sector and the budding tourism economy.[37]

The tourism industry of the New South rested on fantasies of happily servile African Americans. Paul Green, a native of North Carolina, voiced a typical romantic imagining of race among white southerners. As a soldier stationed at a camp outside Charlotte in 1917, he and his comrades encountered a black farmer who "had been thro' the Civil War and knew how to sympathize with soldier boys." Green despaired, "When these old landmarks of an institution that is dead are gone, the South will have lost one of its quaintest attractions." Blacks' docility enhanced the tourist experience. A Massachusettsian returning from Florida via steamer in 1913 admired the staff who seemed unfazed by the rolling sea: "Couldn't help wondering how the negro waiters never seemed to be sick at all. They were usually smiling and happy. They would carry the biggest loads of dishes, without letting them fall." She then noted how those same waiters were forced to pay for broken dishes. An Illinois family visiting Saint Augustine, Florida, in 1931, "took a ride around town in horse & carriage driven by colored driver which is the common way for sight seeing." Another tourist to Saint Augustine in 1939 remarked, "The negro guide was awfully witty and had a ready answer for any query. He was better than any comedy."[38]

For white tourists, a trip to a southern resort during the Jim Crow era was a journey laden with expectations of black servility. J. E. Rawlings in December

1904 savored a gourmet meal and the service: "Finger bowls and napkins after each course, a darkie in a dress suit to jump at each call." Genevieve Pearce Moore, a primary school teacher from North Carolina, recorded daily entries during trips to West Palm Beach in 1941 and Myrtle Beach in 1943. One entry from her vacation to Florida merely recorded: "Col girl here to wash. Boy in yard." Regarding her weeklong holiday in Myrtle Beach, she penned, "Good breakfast abt 930 / Dinner 6 to 8 p / waiter looks as if drunk night before." For Moore, the service of African Americans was central to her beach vacations—one of the rare things worth recording besides her first ocean swim and a sunburn. A tourist from Los Angeles marveled at the Old South charm encountered along the Mississippi Coast. Visiting in 1950, she wrote, "All these homes are real colonial plantation homes. How truly lovely they are." She then penned, "Even motels along the way are colonial with pillars. Darling."[39] Advertising celebrated the region's racial caste system. The Hotel Dixie-Sherman boasted of being Panama City's "most modern" hotel. An ad depicted a smiling African American bellhop loaded with luggage. His greeting headlined the ad, "Yassuh Boss—we're glad to have you back!" In 1962 the Sea Horse Inn in Virginia Beach offered a "Plantation Buffet for those with a yearning for lavish foods of the by-gone era" while waitresses "in appropriate costume will complete the plantation motif." One of the "prides of Palm Beach," according to observer Cleveland Amory, was the "afromobile," a "combination of a two-seated chair in front and the business end of a Negro-pedaled bicycle behind." Similar rolling chairs powered by blacks were a staple of boardwalks in Virginia Beach and Atlantic City. Resorts into the 1960s regularly hosted shows featuring blackface performers.[40]

Despite the advantages over agricultural labor, the psychological and physical burden that tourism-related work placed on African Americans could be overwhelming. The hotelier Karl Abbott regularly traveled between his resorts in New England and Florida. Once, in the 1890s, he stopped at a restaurant in Savannah. An inebriated Georgia "cracker" sat nearby. When a roach raced across the drunkard's table, the Georgian asked the black waiter why "this restaurant is all cluttered up with cockroaches." The waiter, not seeing the insect, declared the restaurant was a "strictly first-class place" without a roach problem. The cracker set his pistol on the table. He then asked, "Nigger . . . what did you distinctly see run across this table?" The frightened waiter quickly concurred. Abbott recalled, "He was just one heartbeat from death." Ernie Pyle unexpectedly encountered a tearful "bellboy and jack-of-all-trades" at a Miami hotel in the 1930s. Pyle wrote, "Have you ever seen a grown-up man standing by himself crying? I can't describe just what it does to you." The future war correspondent was shocked; this was the same bellboy who "always smiled good morning." Asked to explain his sobs, the bellboy responded, "I'm just so lonesome." A native of northern Alabama, the twenty-one-year-old worked from 6 a.m. until midnight. He had spent the previous six years traveling around Florida from job to job. Pyle related, "He could never be anything but a dishwasher, bellhop, gas pumper. And in Florida, where labor was surplus, you didn't hold even those jobs very long." He was denied an education, regular employment, and time for friends and family. "We felt pretty useless," remarked Pyle.[41]

Federal welfare programs, particularly those launched under the Great Society, alleviated a degree of racial repression and economic exploitation even as federally funded slum clearance programs destroyed black communities across the region. The actions of black workers revealed the role racism and low wages had long played in controlling the tourism industry's workforce. Larry Boulier noted "some acute shortages of waitresses and cooks and other workers" in August 1966. Particularly troublesome were the employees who worked for a week, collected their paycheck, and quit without notification, applying for a job at another hotel or restaurant sometime later. Boulier, sharing the sentiment of other white employers, moaned, "Part of a national disease, a deterioration in personal responsibility with its biggest downward trend occurring after the election of 1964, manifested itself in a number of restaurant kitchens in this broad tourist area." But welfare programs did not equate to prosperity.[42]

Blacks working in coastal resorts were marginalized, often forced by segregation laws, racial customs, and low wages to live in shantytowns purposely excluded from the city limits so as to avoid the expense of providing municipal services. Harlem, an area of more than two square miles bordering Myrtle Beach, contained an all-black population of roughly six hundred residents in homes without municipal water or sewer systems. Garbage trucks ignored the area. Galvanized by the civil rights movement, Harlemites petitioned for annexation to Myrtle Beach in May 1968. City officials stonewalled behind legal technicalities requiring annexed areas to pay the cost of water system extensions. Frustrated, Harlemites presented the city council with an envelope containing $766 for the estimated $20,000 project. Although annexation would wait, the city agreed to finance the new water system in November 1968. Mayor Mark Garner, with the help of the biracial Community Relations Council, launched Operation Friendly Hand in March 1969 to improve race relations.

The program raised $50,000 to eliminate some open drainage ditches, often used as garbage dumps, in black neighborhoods.[43]

Yet life remained tough for Harlemites. University of South Carolina students Glenda Miller and Elizabeth Phillips ventured into the neighborhood in 1971. Here, Myrtle Beach was a "place to work, not relax." Adults toiled in motels, restaurants, laundries, and other businesses for less than minimum wage and under forty hours a week. The end of the tourist season worsened the poverty. Irving Campbell, at age five and only five blocks from the coast, had only recently seen the ocean. Miller and Phillips reported, "The Campbell children and many of their neighbors have never seen this other world of beautiful motels, hotels, restaurants, amusement parks, beaches and recreation areas. In fact, the Campbells have never seen a bathtub, a lavatory, a telephone, electric appliances and other modern conveniences which are normally taken for granted." Families huddled in the small two-bedroom wooden shanties common to Harlem. In winter they pulled planks off back walls to burn for heat. Severe rains flooded their dilapidated homes. In 1972 James Richardson, one of Harlem's white landlords, evicted his tenants in order to build a warehouse: "I've been giving the people there the lumber as I've been tearing the houses." A female resident with two children paid six dollars in rent from each week's twenty-eight-dollar unemployment check. When she got evicted, the cheapest housing she found was $125 a month.[44]

Conditions in black areas of other southern resort towns were equally squalid. When Gerald Blessey became mayor of Biloxi in the 1980s, he hired the city's first black police chief. He also, despite a "lot of opposition from some white leaders about spending that much money in the black neighborhood," undertook the revitalization of black areas "that, believe it or not, still had outhouses because they had no sewerage." In the Virginia Beach area, black neighborhoods such as Seatack and Burton Station likewise retained outhouses into the 1980s. Indoor plumbing was nonexistent into the 1990s.[45]

When white boosters first beckoned vacationers and real-estate buyers to the southern coast in the late nineteenth century, they crafted magnets of leisure for the haves and magnets of opportunity for the have-nots—all the while dispossessing the farmers, many of them black, who had staked their futures on the once-affordable lands. The Mediterranean architecture popularized by developers unwittingly offered more than an allusion to the warm, sunny climate along the southern shore. Actual Mediterranean peoples—Greeks, Italians, Syrians, French, Spaniards, and others, whether immigrants or by descent—claimed outposts in places such as Myrtle Beach, Panama City, Biloxi, and other waterfront towns. The celebration of the Mediterranean recalled a Roman empire capable of incorporating diverse peoples without surrendering much political and economic might, much like the white boosters along southern shores.

Bronzed Bodies

Born in Osaka, Japan, in 1887, Kosaku Sawada came to the United States in 1906. He spent four years in the newly developed rice fields between Galveston and Beaumont, Texas. He then moved to Grand Bay, Alabama. Taking his savings, he tapped the "orange tree boom" as developers, homeowners, and farmers along the Gulf capitalized on the association of citrus with tropical climes. The satsuma, a tree native to Japan, became popular at the turn of the century since it withstood freezes to 15° F. The area from southern Louisiana to the Florida Panhandle gained a reputation as the "Satsuma Belt." By 1923 Sawada opened Overlook Nursery on thirty acres. A deep freeze wiped out many of the satsuma groves across the Gulf South later that year. Sawada diversified, buying eighty more acres of "much better land" suited for shrubbery. All the while, the widower raised four children, sending one son to Auburn University, another to Spring Hill College, and two daughters to the upscale Crichton Academy in Mobile. By the time he died in 1968, Sawada, by importing varieties from Japan, had crafted hybrids of camellias, flowering cherries, and other plants that could better withstand the deep freezes and extreme heat of the Gulf South. His efforts earned him an honored place in gardening clubs across the region.[46]

WPA interviewer Ila Prine met Sawada in 1939. Prine noted, "More than three decades of outdoor work under the hot Southern sun have burned his skin from yellow to brown." The transformation caused by the strong solar rays of the Gulf Coast was not lost on Sawada. Describing a trip to Japan in the early 1920s, he expressed surprise that "people thought I was a Filipino." Sawada laughed, "One day, I was standing on a street corner scanning a newspaper. Some children passed by and said, 'Look at that Filipino reading a Japanese paper.'" In this case, sun exposure altered perceptions of race and ethnicity. Although black and white Alabamans, with limited exposure to any Asians, would likely have missed the subtly of skin colors in discerning Filipinos from Japanese or other peoples of the Pacific, Sawada's encounter with the Japanese children offers a telling account of racial confusion caused by tanning.[47]

A tan threatened to obscure the color line. Whites in Jim Crow America obsessed over racial passing under the one-drop-rule racial caste system. A white society that considered appreciation of jazz music or a taste for black-eyed peas a possible telltale of mixed bloodlines needed to allay concerns over tan skin. Whites, as the beach craze emerged during the interwar period, thus reaffirmed racial markers beyond skin tone, chiefly blonde hair, and rigidified segregationist practices along the shore.

The loss of white skin bore cultural burdens in the American South. In the early nineteenth century the term *rednecks* served as a means of differentiating Presbyterians—many of Scottish descent whose ancestors wore red scarves—from the growing middle-class culture based in towns. In the 1820s Anne Royall visited Fayetteville, North Carolina, where she encountered "*Red Necks*, a name bestowed upon the Presbyterians" who shunned the arts. Royall joked how Fayetteville contained "a theatre, just finished, (look out, Red Necks!)." The association of rednecks with cultural conservatism evolved to include poverty and violence after the Civil War as poor white fieldworkers competed with freed slaves on the labor market. In 1914 the *Crisis* explained the situation in textile industries across the region: "It is in the upcountry, however, where the mills are, that the 'red necks' or 'hill billies' have flocked to the towns. They are working for a wage. They hate the Negro for economic reasons." Southern politicians, like James Vardaman of Mississippi or "Pitchfork" Ben Tillman of South Carolina, stirred these whites' racial hatreds as well as criticism of their unabashed race-baiting. One author lampooned how "Col. Loud Eloquence" skillfully played upon the "passions and prejudices of the red-necks and the hill-billies" by encouraging them to "do what they believe to be right about the damned niggers, regardless of all the Yankees between Cape Cod and hell." The shame associated with the term *redneck* only faded as agriculture waned as the primary source of work across the region. After the 1960s white southerners, now largely urbanized and suburbanized, increasingly celebrated their redneck roots much as Italians and other descendants of European immigrants participated in the white ethnic revival born out of the civil rights movement.[48]

Until the interwar period, *tan* served as an implicitly racial term. Thérèse Yelverton, visiting from England, encountered white South Carolinians obsessed with racial definition during the tumultuous 1870s: "Two-thirds of the population of Charleston were said to be black, or 'black and tan,' for the shades and varieties are numerous." Tan as a recognition of color gradients within the black community evolved into a means of questioning whites' bloodlines.

Whereas "redneck" disparaged poor whites and their white supremacist extremism, "tan" criticized white advocates of racial egalitarianism. A Noah Webster dictionary from 1868 defined "tan" as: "To make brown; to imbrown by exposure to the rays of the sun." The phrase gained political heft as exposure to African Americans culturally blackened whites. Caroline Elizabeth Merrick, in her 1901 memoirs, recounted the well-worn image of corrupt Reconstruction governments. She lambasted how "the iniquities of carpet-bag governments and the diabolisms of 'black and tan' conventions for a long time kept respectable men out of politics. It was indeed too 'filthy a pool' to be entered." Reconstruction-era terms *black and tan* and *lilywhite* for the two groups vying for control of the Republican Party survived into the early twentieth century. The "Lilywhite Republicans," commented political scientist Albert Hart in 1910, sought to "build up their party by disclaiming any partnership with the Negro or special interest in his welfare." Even in Alabama, which hosted the powerful yet accommodationist Booker T. Washington, the opposition to the Lilywhites had all but collapsed. Hart observed, "In Alabama there are still 'black-and-tan Republicans'—that is, an organization of Negroes and Whites, and one of the most rabid Negro haters in the South is a dignitary in that organization." The once powerful party in southern politics had faded. Yet the former Confederates' derogatory label of Republicans as advocates of racial cooperation lingered. Whites who associated with blacks were "tan"—a backhanded means of questioning their racial purity without committing slander or libel. Even Lilywhite Republicans could not escape the burn.[49]

Tellingly, the term *black and tan* faded from popular use after the First World War, though it still appeared occasionally into the 1950s. The phrase even drifted northward. The Chicago Commission on Race Relations surveyed the city in the aftermath of the deadly 1919 race riot, sparked when colored swimmers in Lake Michigan drifted onto the white beach. The Commission particularly condemned "'Black and tan' resorts, which present a much-criticized association because of the vicious elements of whites and Negroes in contact there." By the 1920s, however, the rise of beach resorts and pageants celebrating white bathing beauties sapped "tan" of its usefulness. Southern politicians likely recognized the danger of suggesting miscegenation to a white electorate journeying in growing numbers to beach resorts where they acquired a bronze sheen. The rise of conservative southern Republicans such as Strom Thurmond in South Carolina also made the political party, once an anathema, palatable.[50]

White Americans were aware of the racial confusion possible through tanning. Historian Devon Hansen, in her study of sunbathing, noted how white women in the early twentieth century were particularly concerned that "their tan skin might lead them to be categorized with African Americans." William Hubbell, whose parents moved to the Mississippi Gulf Coast from New Orleans in 1909, when he was a young child, recalled the concern his mother displayed about skin tone. On the eve of the First World War, Hubbell's mother planned a trip to Philadelphia to visit relatives. Hubbell described a key part of the preparations: "My sister and I were on this beach in the summertime so much we were almost burned black. I remember well that my mother tried to keep us in the house. She said 'I want to bleach you out before we take you up to Philadelphia.'" Dark-skinned children riding with a white woman through backwoods southern hamlets could certainly raise eyebrows if not worse. Alma Simmang Simpson of Galveston observed female swimmers in 1915: "The girls looked as brown as Fiji Islanders, you hardly could tell as they walked whether they were men or women, they really looked tough from the outdoor life. I thought some of them might be Mexicans from their looks." Even in the late twentieth century, one southerner complimented her grandchildren's tans after beach vacations with the exclamation: "Just black!" Another southerner recalled an aunt affectionately known by her nickname "Mammy." As a teenager, the aunt had so enjoyed sunbathing that her relatives lampooned the change in skin tone.[51]

Tourists too recognized the racial implications of tanning. In the early twentieth century, tanning, according to historian Catherine Cocks, was racial play—"a kind of brownface, a playful experiment in becoming nonwhite that stemmed from, encouraged, and literally embodied a renovated relationship between civilization and nature." The tan was "transient, the underlying whiteness always liable to reappear," yet the darker tone submerged whiteness while it lasted. Charles Jackson of Maine wandered into New Iberia, Louisiana, after spending weeks hunting and fishing along the Gulf Coast around 1910. A small boy approached Jackson and asked if he was Cuban, an ethnically and racially ambiguous identity. The unshaven sportsman believed his worn appearance, which included "a Mexican hat and the sunburn, made up the part." A New Yorker vacationing with friends in Florida in 1953 recorded the irony of possessing a dark tan and riding in the white section of public transport: "We all have the start of a tan and so it shouldn't be too long until some of us move to the back of the bus." A postcard from the mid-twentieth century depicted a dark-skinned Sambo-esque character in a grass skirt on the beach. The overhead blurb announced, "NO, THIS ISN'T ME! BUT I'M SO TANNED THERE ISN'T MUCH DIFFERENCE! HOPE YOU'LL KNOW ME WHEN I GET HOME."[52]

As white Americans darkened their skin tone, blonde hair became a marker of racial whiteness and a definer of beauty within an American culture fixated with sun and sand. In the late nineteenth century, white women adopted blonde hair as a fashionable style. Those without natural blonde hair used chemicals to lighten their locks. Some of the earliest reports of "peroxides" or "forced blondes" appear in newspaper coverage of summer beach resorts during the 1890s. The *New York Herald* in 1894 noted that along "Long Island Sound bleached blondes were as plentiful as the women themselves." Blonde hairpieces grew popular, too. "The demand for blond hair far exceeds the supply now that so many false pieces are used in the fashionable coiffure," explained the *Baltimore American* in 1903. Beachfront recreation encouraged greater appreciation of blondes as lighter hair was celebrated as a fashionable contrast to darkened complexions, just as darker hair, according to one commentator, "makes a fair complexion seem far more beautiful than it is in reality." Blonde hair continued to increase in popularity as more Americans flocked to the shore.[53]

The celebration of blondes in beauty pageants and on film offered reassurances of white vitality. "Virginia is in the same latitude as North Africa and south of this line no blonds have ever been able to survive in full vigor," argued racial theorist Madison Grant in *The Passing of the Great Race* from 1916. He continued, "There rays beat heavily on the Nordic race and disturb their nervous system, wherever the white man ventures too far from the cold and foggy North." Yet the crowds flocking to the beaches, the urban growth of the emergent Sunbelt, and the rise of celebrities such as Mae West and Jean Harlow disproved such theories about blondes during the interwar years. By the 1960s the hair care firm Clairol even offered a product named Born Blonde. One ad campaign simply stated that "many women never make the most exciting discovery of all: they should have been born with blonde hair."[54]

Since the interwar period, a tan has served as a sign of well-being and a fashion accessory for white Americans. Those possessing a deep tan had escaped the office or assembly line to enjoy the outdoors. Research in the early twentieth century discovered that sunlight killed bacteria, quickened healing, increased resistance to disease, and invigorated tuberculosis patients. The discovery of vitamins during the 1910s and 1920s—and particularly the skin's ability to turn sunlight into vitamin D—encouraged tanning. By 1927 the Children's Bureau of the U.S. Department of Labor prepared a folder titled "Sunlight for Babies." The *Biloxi Herald* urged readers to request a copy since "mothers are fast learning of the advantages of sun bathing for their little ones." The growing interest in tans encouraged skin darkeners. Rejecting homemade concoctions, Americans turned to chemists and other professionals to improve tanning during the interwar years. The Delta Drug Company advertised its Gaby brand suntan lotion to Myrtle Beach vacationers in 1937: "GABY is not a grease or frying oil—it is scientific preparation that positively prevents sunburn and promotes tan." A tan also provided a souvenir of a health-rejuvenating holiday. According to Catherine Cocks, "a tan was strictly a seasonal accessory" that demonstrated the wealth to vacation. During the 1940s Meredith Drug Store in Virginia Beach hawked a "secret formula" capable of preventing sunburn or blisters while giving a "smooth and even tan." Tans served as beauty marks by the mid-twentieth century. Beauty expert Alicia Hart told readers in July 1960: "Choosing a suntan cream that's right for you is as personal a matter as choosing the correct lipstick shade." She informed readers in 1962: "It's true that one of the most flattering cosmetics a woman can wear is a healthy sun tan."[55]

Beach newspapers treated tanning with care given the racial implications. Newsprint—with black, white, and shades in between—forced publishers to adopt techniques that clearly conveyed race. Nowhere was this more apparent than in ads depicting women enjoying the sun. Such ads regularly used sketches rather than photographs. When a Virginia Beach store advertised its swimwear in 1958, readers saw three women with dark gray skin, suggesting the deep tan gained from the beaming sun depicted overhead. While one wore a wide-brimmed straw hat, the other two possessed what appeared to be blonde hair.[56] The *Myrtle Beach Sun-News* from 1972 similarly juxtaposed a tanned blonde and a white woman with dark hair in the "What's Going On" column.[57] The white hair color as depicted in newsprint provided a reassuring sign of the women's whiteness. An atlas issued by State Farm Insurance from the 1950s through the 1960s offered the strongest clue of blonde hair as a racial substitute for white skin on bronzed bodies. The cover presented in vivid color American landmarks and people. Situated amongst the South's cotton fields stood several African Americans. Their brown skin was identical in color to the female sunbather depicted in South Florida. Only her yellow hair marked her as white.[58]

Racial Riptide

Inspired by Harrison County, New Orleans boosters in the 1920s, under the authority of the levee board, started a seawall along Lake Pontchartrain shaped as stairs to accommodate water sports spectators, convert marsh into suburban neighborhoods, and offer tourists a shoreline drive. Despite their city being a major metropolitan area, New Orleans boosters mimicked shoreline drives and beaches popularized by coastal developers in Florida and Mississippi. White businessmen of the Association of Commerce retreated from their 1924 proposal to construct a five-mile-long island chain in Lake Pontchartrain that offered "acres of very valuable land, bathing beaches far in the lake, driveways, parks, resort hotel sites, and an extensive frontage for lakeside residences." The more modest plan to craft an armored lakefront, shoreline drive, and beach nevertheless provided the increasingly tourist-oriented city with a foothold in the coastal tourism market—though tourists never flocked to the city's shores as hoped. This all served, however, as a whites-only paradise. Concerns that black bathers depreciated real-estate values along the newly crafted shore fueled debate about racial accommodation. Completed by 1928, the seawall blocked blacks from accessing long-popular beachfronts used for picnics, family gatherings, or just a swim. Though racial restrictions also applied to municipal tennis courts, golf courses, and swimming pools, the exclusion from lakefront beaches stirred extraordinary anger.[59]

Individuals on both sides of the color line pressured white authorities. The Federation of Civic Leagues, an African American organization, urged the levee board to designate a permanent site for black bathers, preferably at a beach called Seabrook. At a levee board meeting in February 1929, several associations representing white property-holders condemned any accommodation for black bathers. Alexander Tureaud, spokesman for the federation, took exception when a protester claimed that blacks' "presence would give a bad impression to our visitors." He replied that "an out-of-town visitor would leave here with a feeling of horror" if confronted with the discrimination faced by black New Orleanians. Speaking for the levee board, Commissioner John Klorer declared that "some provision will have to be made for the negro population on the lake front since there are 100,000 in the city who pay a considerable amount of taxes." The levee board, following Klorer's lead, bucked white public opinion and unofficially designated Seabrook as New Orleans's black beach.[60]

The Seabrook controversy exemplified the activism sparked by white suppression of African Americans in coastal communities. African Americans and Creoles of color with a long history of civil rights activism remained vigilant. Rumors continuously surfaced that the levee board might designate another section of the lakefront as the city's black beach. Year after year the levee board delayed improvements.[61]

Black bathers forced the issue by flocking to Seabrook. "Seabrook is drawing the colored population of the city like the magnet draws the needle," declared the *Louisiana Weekly* in 1933. Along the seven-mile seawall, two beaches, one at Spanish Fort and another at Milneburg, bore signs designating areas for whites. Both possessed lampposts as well as lifeguards. Although a black entrepreneur opened a bathhouse at Seabrook called the Sea Side Inn, the city's unofficial black beach offered few perks or safety measures. The levee board strictly regulated the Sea Side Inn. Proprietor E. J. Lamothe, who personally hired four lifeguards, was limited to a structure designed to accommodate a bar, sandwich stand, and changing rooms. The levee board reserved the right to demolish at a moment's notice a large hall for parties and dances.[62]

By 1939 the levee board publicized a blueprint of a modernized, blacks-only beach facility on Lake Pontchartrain to be constructed by the WPA. The levee board selected a site on the outskirts of the city known as Little Woods, a place used by both races for bathing and picnicking. A large concrete bathhouse with locker rooms, showers, a restaurant, and a lobby formed the centerpiece of the proposal. Public telephones, a parking lot, and a playground were to be installed. Engineers planned to dredge sand for an improved beach measuring 1,000 feet long and 225 feet wide. A viaduct would allow pedestrians to walk under the railroad line separating the beach from the mainland. Two fences that extended into the water to prevent waves from eroding the beach heightened the sense of isolation. The *Louisiana Weekly* reported, "It had been rumored that these . . . were fences to keep the swimmers from going in front of privately-owned camps in the vicinity of the beach."[63]

Black civic organizations rallied protesters. Little Woods was seven miles from Seabrook and fourteen miles from downtown. What most angered black residents, however, was a letter from a "representative committee of colored people" released by the levee board expressing approval of the new location. Within days, the local NAACP and Interdenominational Ministerial Alliance disavowed any connection to the committee. Several of the twenty alleged committeemen declared their signatures forgeries. Others denied any knowledge of the document, much less having signed it. A petition signed by fifteen thousand black New Orleanians urged the development of the beach at Seabrook instead of Little Woods. The Negro Youth Congress organized its own petition drive, gathering more than five thousand signatures. However, when this petition reached Leon Tujaque, the president of the levee board, he declared, "But these have been sent too late." The board had made its decision. White officials named the new site Lincoln Beach.[64]

Wade-ins erupted at Seabrook in May 1941. When police chased off a group of a hundred blacks one Sunday afternoon, they vowed to return the following week. Black New Orleanians' anger over the levee board's denial of the Lincoln Beach concession to a black entrepreneur heightened the tension. White officials, according to a widespread though unsubstantiated rumor, had awarded the permit to a white man "who runs the biggest Negro gambling joint in town." Harold Lee of the Louisiana League informed local activists of the need "not to allow any arrest to be made until they decide to make a test case." However, rain coupled with police harassment defused further protests at Seabrook.[65] During the Second World War, the Army Air Corps established a base near the beach. City officials invoked military security to justify an ordinance banning swimmers from Seabrook. A frustrated Harold Lee commented to a friend in 1944: "You will remeber [sic] that trouble has arisen each year since 1938 concerning a place for the Negroes to swim at the lake front. Each year the League has finally gotten them the right to go in at Seabrook by threatening court action. As the decisions of the Supreme Court are clearly mandatory in a case of this kind, the opposition has always folded up at this point. We have never been able to identify the source of the opposition. Everyone claims he is not initiating it, but puts the blame on someone else." The ban on swimming at Seabrook left Lincoln Beach the only outlet for black recreation on Lake Pontchartrain.[66]

The Lincoln Beach controversy exemplified the importance of beach access for African Americans living along urban southern shores. An unprecedented outrage united blacks. "Negroes of New Orleans have been 'sold out' in certain instances but the resultant cry was not as long nor as loud as in this matter of bathing facilities on the lake front, for in few other instances have so many of us been affected," commented the Louisiana Weekly. Worse, Lincoln Beach improvements promised by the WPA failed to materialize. Single men and women, families, young and old, rich and poor all felt the sting of beach segregation. Poor blacks felt the sting of lacking basic luxuries, namely, the ability to rest and cool off, that equally poor whites readily claimed. Wealthier blacks felt the sting of not being able to vacation at places accessed by poorer whites whom they viewed as social and intellectual inferiors.[67]

The struggle for civil rights intensified as government resources concentrated on the tourism industry. African Americans along southern beaches understood their legal right to beaches when those strands were improved with tax dollars. They also understood the leverage granted by the publicity-sensitive tourism industry. Tourists sought fantasies of tranquil leisure, not hotbeds of racial conflict. Racial violence erupting across the southern interior—through which northern tourists passed—drained business and government coffers. African American protesters provided the surge to breach the bulwarks of Jim Crow society.

Before the Second World War, southern beach towns catered to a clientele who occasionally brought their black domestics. Sarah Evelyn Baylor recorded how upon a late-night arrival at Virginia Beach in June 1895 "everybody was asleep except the servants." In 1938 C. A. Donehoo of Gadsden, Alabama, contacted hotels on the Grand Strand about their availability. The Patricia Manor in Myrtle Beach responded with a colorful pamphlet that announced, "Hot-water heated and modern in every respect, Patricia Manor—operated on the American plan—affords delightful accommodations at very modest costs. Quarters, on the grounds, are maintained for your maids and chauffeurs." A family vacation meant keeping the luxury and status of black labor.[68]

Polite dismissals or stark signs policed the check-in desk against African Americans and Jews. The proprietors of Ocean Pines Motor Court in Myrtle Beach in 1940 boasted of Duncan Hines's approval and their facility's exclusiveness: "Ocean Pines Court is in a restricted residential section."[69] Most promotional literature was far less explicit. Signs risked offending guests' sensibilities, especially those with more liberal mindsets. Jewish traveler Leonard Lubman learned the hard way. Visiting Virginia Beach in June 1951, he and his family were told at one hotel that they would need "to write in" for a reservation. Insulted, Lubman asked whether the premises were restricted. The hotel manager confirmed his suspicions. Although he had "heard of such at the Beach many times," this was the Lubman family's first encounter with anti-Semitism. Lubman, a Second World War veteran, fumed: "I can't seem to recall that being called into the service was 'restricted.' Neither was death on the battlefield 'restricted.'" Though many of the offensive signs disappeared after the Second World War, custom, as Lubman discovered, remained strong. "In most states it is against the law to advertise resort hotels and restaurants as restricted, as people used to do," wrote cartoonist and veteran Bill Mauldin shortly after the war. Nevertheless, the "restricted sign is there in spirit if not in print."[70]

Tourism businesses accommodated segregation. Large hotels, such as the Edgewater Gulf Hotel near Biloxi, usually maintained a dormitory for their black employees, thereby exercising some control over their availability and behavior. Guests' employees could room as well. Smaller establishments could not afford such expense. In March 1939 two entrepreneurs in Virginia Beach planned a "deluxe service station and garage" for guests of beachfront hotels lacking adequate parking facilities. The two-story building contained a showroom and mechanic services and "31 rooms for chauffeurs" split into white and colored wings.[71]

The dependence on positive publicity, along with the confusion over policing race amongst strangers, meant that resort towns generally acted with moderation in accepting integration once the legal tide turned. Although Saint Augustine violently resisted integration with heavy costs to its tourism industry, Florida beach resorts tended to integrate peacefully, as Fort Lauderdale and Sarasota did in 1961. Historian Gary Mormino's observation of Florida carries weight in analyzing other beachfront communities in the South. Referring to the Saint Augustine standoff, Mormino writes, "The crisis symbolized the growing differences between the two Floridas—North Florida and South Florida—but also between rural and urban Florida, and between the beach and interior communities." Civility on civil rights safeguarded profits. Already thinking of themselves as part of a distinct locale separate from their respective states, officials in coastal resorts usually heralded their emerging urban centers as moderate havens that contrasted from the rural hinterland.[72]

Yet, across the coastal South, blacks until the mid-1960s enjoyed beaches at their peril and with a great deal of white hand-wringing. For example, the Galveston Chamber of Commerce in August 1937 "received numerous complaints concerning negroes bathing in the surf at various points along the beach, which was objectionable to visitors as well as local citizens." The members decided the "beach [should] be zoned and definite places be designated for both white and negro bathing." The businessmen consulted "with leading negro citizens to secure their cooperation in correcting the situation." By late October the mayor and city commission had offered their "full cooperation." The county commissioners, however, "refused due to the fact that they could not legally adopt laws or regulations segregating the races."[73] Denied legal solutions, the chamber parlayed with African American leaders. The consultations established areas between Tenth and Twelfth Streets and between the groins at Twenty-Seventh and Thirty-Seventh Streets as beaches for "negro bathing." The black population balked. A year later, as the chamber membership reflected on the tourist season in September 1938, they pondered the issue of segregation "on the Boulevard and beaches" as well as the possibility of developing West Beach as the designated colored-only bathing site. One member "pointed out that the situation had become acute and that something should be done before the next summer season." Yet the issue lingered. In September 1940 the businessmen again stressed that "some definite action would have to be taken" after hearing that "visitors had complained to them personally regarding the negro interference on the beaches over the Labor Day week-end."[74]

War preparations heightened concerns in Galveston. The arrival of approximately six hundred African American soldiers at the improvised Camp Wallace by October 1940 spurred efforts "to prevent the negros from monopolizing the beachfront." After Pearl Harbor, the installation quartered 1,600 black soldiers, and Galveston's businessmen sweated. One member explained that the "request to transfer these troops should be held in abeyance until Camp Wallace is definitely established." Chamber protests to federal officials occurred only after federal largesse was well rooted. Once the military installations were in place, the chamber strategized, "Southern congressmen should be requested to bring pressure on the War Department not to quarter negro soldiers in the South."[75] The chamber leadership worried over how the influx of black soldiers would strain the already meager beach access available to the city's "rather large negro population" at Twenty-Ninth Street and Seawall Boulevard. The specter of the Houston race riot of 1917 sent shivers through white Galvestonians "fearful of a possible recurrence." However, the secretary of war denied requests to divert black personnel, forcing city businessmen to contemplate the "proper handling of the negro troops on the beachfront during the summer months in as much as the facilities on the beachfront for the use of negroes were limited."[76]

The construction of the Pleasure Pier during the 1930s became a particular target for black Galvestonians and demonstrated how whites along the coast undermined campaigns for racial equality. Wise Adams, a black barber, and several associates peppered city politicians and businessmen with queries as to whether the facility would serve African Americans and, if not, whether they could proceed with a separate but equal pier at the colored beach resort at Twenty-Eighth Street. In September 1940 Adams explained that the "very limited" accommodations at Twenty-Eighth Street led to black vacationers "walking over one another on such days as June 19th, July 4th and Labor day; also on Sundays in summer time." The more than five thousand blacks who crammed the colored beach on peak days came "chiefly from nearby communities." Adams's plan marketed Galveston as a black resort, emphasizing how "we are only fifty miles away from the City of Houston, where the colored population is around 90,000, with no recreational features on Sundays." Adams had already cleared his project worth $300,000 with Morton Macartney at the Reconstruction Finance Corporation (RFC). The proposal called for a two-story concrete pier. The upper floor, with a capacity for five thousand people, contained an auditorium for conventions and special events. The lower floor possessed a dance hall, cafeteria, concession stands, and amusements for children. The pier would "prove a mecca and drawing card for colored persons all over the entire State."[77]

Adams and his partners understood the reluctance of municipal officials to construct a magnet for black tourists. They also recognized that the officials' use of a hefty RFC "loan for the white project" opened the door to New Deal financing for a black pier if the other site was not integrated. Adams goaded Mayor Brantly Harris, dismissing Harris's delay in improving black beach facilities until after the Pleasure Pier's construction by reminding "your honor that this will be after the municipal election and problematical."[78]

Both Galveston's white elite and federal officials quietly suffocated the proposal for a colored pier. A confidential memo to Harris revealed how bureaucracy, in service to the profit motive, crushed African American efforts at achieving equal accommodations: "The lowdown is this: While they do not say so in so many words of course, the RFC discourages such facilities for negroes because nine times out of ten they never do become self-liquidating." The memo outlined how the RFC rejected a similar project in Port Arthur, Texas, and liquidated the only other such project in Virginia by selling at "a big loss" to a black church congregation. The memo slipped into paternalism: "As Mr. Macartney explained it, and as we know, the southern negro expects to be looked after and seldom puts a thing of this nature over by himself." Macartney suggested that Galveston's white politicians submit a formal application in the knowledge that, after letting "it go through the regular channels," the RFC would "not in all likelihood approve the project."[79]

Adams and his fellow activists sensed the conspiracy. By May 1941 they turned up the pressure. Adams warned the mayor: "We are of the opinion that the legislative enactment has all the earmarks of unconstitutionality, we do not desire to jeopardize the possibility of anyone's recreational facilities, however we do feel that our own civil rights are about to be jeopardized." Legal action loomed. Harris fired off a letter to Bob Nesbitt, his liaison in Washington, D.C., declaring that Adams and his colleagues were "not representative of the true Southern negro, but are trying to stir up trouble." He seethed over Adams's attempt "to get me to say that the negroes will not be allowed on the recreation pier, with the idea of going to court and trying to stop it." Harris played for time, explaining to Adams that the decision to serve whites or both races depended on the eventual managers of the pier. But the politically astute mayor believed Adams's group might use the controversy against the national Democratic Party. He also feared the threatened lawsuit might reach the ears of the RFC, causing them "to get skittish" about the Pleasure Pier. Harris wanted Nesbitt to handle the "ticklish question" by seeing if Macartney favored a loan for a "small pier, probably just a fishing pier with a dance hall on it, something very, very modest" valued under $100,000. If the RFC refused, Harris stressed that he "would like to be lifted off the spot by a letter" from Macartney stating the RFC's position. The delaying tactics used by the RFC and Harris worked. Military occupation of the unfinished Pleasure Pier undermined Adams's efforts. In June 1942 the War Production Board banned construction of all amusement projects. The battle for racial equality on Galveston's shore would wait until well after the smoke cleared off the beaches of Normandy and Okinawa.[80]

As white officials replenished beach sands and developed coastal real estate for white tourists, African Americans witnessed tighter restrictions on beach access, as further evidenced by events along the Mississippi Coast. Lorita Nelson Jones fondly recalled family gatherings along the shore in the early twentieth century. Every Sunday French-speaking Creoles of color boarded trains in New Orleans for a day on the beach. They would "come and go to people's houses, and they'd sit down, and they'd have their dinner and stuff and talk French." These day-trippers also enjoyed the surf, though oftentimes whites would "run them." Wilson Evans II was born in the Black Belt of central Alabama in 1924. His parents moved to Gulfport in 1929. Evans remembered, "During that time I could go on the beach; you could go on the beach, yes, no problems with the beach when I was growing up. They used to have beach parties, fish fries." Evans recalled, "The problem developed with the beach was after they pumped the sand in." He continued, "There was no signs posted." Others also noted a change once beach replenishment occurred in the early

1950s. Earl Napoleon Moore, a Mississippian, remembered beachfront gatherings of African Americans during the interwar years: "Well, my mother went down on the beach. She tried to teach me to swim on the beach, which was in the daytime, but most of the Negroes went down there at night, because they had to work in the daytime, but at night you'd find plenty of them down there." Segregation tightened its hold on the shorefront when municipal officials and tourism boosters restored the beach. Jim Crow "became worse." Moore explained, "They didn't want them down there, laying in that *white* sand." Beach improvement heightened racial tensions and led whites to redouble their efforts to exclude blacks from the coast.[81]

As sharecropping and textile mills gave way to industrial farming and diversified urban economies, white southerners earned larger salaries and vacation time. Beach resorts tapped this market, hardening racial divisions in these communities. In September 1949 Galveston Chamber of Commerce members noted that newspapers had "received numerous letters cursing Galveston because of the great amount of space the negroes are taking up on the beaches." The businessmen recorded that "the white people are pretty bitter about it." Remembering that roughly "15 years ago the same problem arose," white civic leaders believed that the situation was "getting out of hand." A committee conferred with the African American community. The suggestion of distant West Beach as a colored-only strand was rejected. Clara Watson, an African American born in Biloxi in 1933, understood beach replenishment and increased segregation as synonymous with an influx of white southerners from interior counties. She identified the evolution of segregation along the Gulf Coast: "And then I guess I never realized that there was that much segregation on the beach until—what really happened in reality, the northern whites, meaning northern Mississippians, when they started coming down here, they felt that the black people were living too good. And they wanted to try and segregate it as much as they possibly could." These northern Mississippians came because "of the beaches," altering Biloxi's old claim as a "summer area for wealthy people to come during the wintertime."[82]

The cooling waters of the Gulf of Mexico or Atlantic Ocean nevertheless beckoned blacks as well. African Americans near the Atlantic coast trekked to American Beach, outside Jacksonville, and Atlantic Beach, near Myrtle Beach. In the Florida Panhandle, blacks enjoyed Johnson Beach on Perdido Key and Wingate Beach near Pensacola. Blacks from southern Mississippi oftentimes journeyed to New Orleans's Lincoln Beach. Wilson Evans II regularly took his family to Louisiana: "Primarily my kids went; we would go over there on the weekends or on special days and swim and do whatever we wanted." Blacks without the time or resources to reach New Orleans instead headed to Waveland. Others found refuge at Gulfside. All along the shore, African Americans carved places of leisure, though under the strain of Jim Crow.[83]

Beyond these enclaves, black beachgoers were largely left high and dry between the Second World War and the Korean War. Wartime mobilization and calls for patriotism undermined protests. Fears of Soviet conspiracies further hindered black activism. However, the U.S. Supreme Court's *Brown* decision in 1954, followed by the Emmett Till lynching in Mississippi and the successful Montgomery bus boycott in 1955, galvanized African American protests.

Biloxi and Saint Augustine were places limited by the conservative, rural mores of Mississippi and northern Florida, respectively. Their long history of tourism meant that these resorts also showed more sensitivity to the local convention circuit. For instance, when the Mississippi Press Association gathered for their eighty-third conference in June 1949, they journeyed to one of the state's few resorts: Biloxi. Here, association president James Arrington of Collins, a hamlet in central Mississippi, stressed white solidarity. He barked, "There is no place in Mississippi journalism for journalistic Judases nor quislings of the quill." The violence that erupted in these towns during the 1960s sent shockwaves through other southern resorts. Moderate segregationists soon realized that defense of Jim Crow threatened tourism. Furthermore, the prosperity of coastal resorts was wedded to the tranquility of the southern interior. White businessmen and politicians from coastal towns leaned on state legislators and governors to quell any violence.[84]

In 1959 African Americans in Biloxi launched Mississippi's first nonviolent protest of the civil rights movement. Dr. Gilbert Mason, who orchestrated the campaign, aimed "to gain equal access to God's Gulf Coast beaches for all of his children."[85] Born in Jackson, Mississippi, Mason spent time during the late 1940s in Chicago between semesters at Nashville's Tennessee State University. He then studied medicine at Howard University in Washington, D.C. After graduation, he learned that the only black doctor serving the Biloxi area's approximately ten thousand African Americans planned to move to Detroit. Mason bought the practice in 1955. He soon chafed under Mississippi's stifling segregation: "For a man who loved swimming and who had gloried in the free use of the parks in Chicago and Washington, D.C., the idea that a marvelous oak-lined public beach was forbidden territory was just too much to abide." Blacks venturing onto the twenty-six-mile beachfront of Harrison County faced harassment except for a "few dozen yards opposite the Veterans Administration Hospital in Gulfport or in a designated area called the Rice Fields opposite the Episcopal church in Pass Christian." Mason recalled, "However, if Negroes ventured onto the beach to enjoy it for themselves, they generally got cursed, harassed, spat upon, kicked, hit, or run off by white ruffians or property owners from across the highway." An "inconsistent policy" of segregation meant that blacks, even in seemingly designated spots, "never knew when or where they might encounter embarrassment, intimidation, or removal from the beach." On the afternoon of 14 May 1959, Mason and eight friends waded into the water near the old Biloxi cemetery. Run off by police, Mason rallied popular support as well as hired a white lawyer to document the use of public funds—local, state, and federal—to maintain the beach. With the local NAACP largely inactive and many local African Americans wary of drawing white anger over an invigorated NAACP, Mason spearheaded the new Harrison County Civic Action Committee along with a resurrected Biloxi Civic League.[86]

The protestors organized Operation Surf, a wade-in on Easter Sunday, 17 April 1960, at 1 p.m. When Mason arrived near the Biloxi lighthouse, he found himself alone. Mason stripped to his swimming trunks and marched into the Gulf. Soon a motorcycle cop arrested Mason for disturbing the peace and disorderly conduct. Although a small wade-in simultaneously occurred in Gulfport before police and Mayor R. B. Meadows personally asked the protesters to leave, only Mason was incarcerated. When Mason appeared at his trial the next day, black Biloxians packed the courtroom and called for another wade-in the following Sunday. Judge Schwan feared convicting Mason lest the doctor appeal the decision, causing higher courts to review the circumstances. Instead, Schwan took the case under advisement, meaning he never ruled. Such was standard practice for civil rights cases—a policy of delay. Schwan's move received the blessing of Governor Ross Barnett and the Mississippi Sovereignty Commission.[87]

Free on bail, Mason prepared for the next wade-in. About 125 protesters joined the doctor at his office on 24 April. Divided into three groups, they headed for the coast. Municipal, county, and state authorities, knowing about the wade-in, had spread the word amongst the "meanest and most virulently prejudiced and irresponsible elements in the white community." Biloxi police chief Herbert McDonnell arranged to have only a "skeleton crew" of officers on duty. Mason recalled, "By the time I got back to the lighthouse the shit had hit the fan. Hordes of snarling white folks poured onto the beach at the foot of Gill with bricks, baseball bats, pipes, sticks, and chains and attacked our unarmed black protesters. The law enforcement officers were just standing around." Throughout the week, white gangs along the coast sporadically stopped automobiles with black drivers and fired guns or tossed Molotov cocktails at black-owned homes and businesses. The nearly decapitated body of Bud Strong, a mentally challenged young black man, was dumped in front of Beauvoir. A black teenager was beaten to death while in police custody in Pascagoula.[88]

As Mason returned to court, this time charged with public fighting and obstructing traffic, radio stations and newspapers across the country carried the story of the wade-ins and rioting. The state legislature pushed through the "Mason Bill," which increased fines and prison sentences for those responsible for public disturbances, specifically referencing such actions on beaches. The black community responded by boycotting white businesses. African Americans flocked to the NAACP. The U.S. Justice Department in May 1960 filed suit against Harrison County and Biloxi for denying blacks access to the beach. Local blacks also launched successful voter registration drives. Though the city commission form of government with its mayor and at-large commissioners prevented blacks from gaining a post in the municipal government, the African American vote became a catalyst for moderate white candidates. Segregationists on the Mississippi coast folded under the pressure. In 1961 conciliatory Daniel Guice replaced the segregationist Laz Quave as mayor of Biloxi. Guice appointed blacks to municipal positions and hired the city's first black police officers. Billy Meadows, the mayor of Gulfport during the 1960s, worked closely with the integrated longshoremen's unions to end segregation quietly to salvage the tourism industry. For some local whites, Meadows's efforts earned him the sobriquet "the nigger mayor."[89]

White homeowners countersued, claiming the beach as an extension of their lots regardless of government funding for beach maintenance. In June 1963 seventy protesters, including three whites, joined Mason in another wade-in as Mayor Guice, two city commissioners, an extensive police presence, and even FBI agents stood guard. Homeowner Mrs. James Moore Parker ordered the protesters arrested. Much changed in the next few years as Mason and his associates fought Parker's trespassing charges. The Civil Rights Act of 1964 integrated public accommodations. In August 1964 public schools in Biloxi became the first to integrate in Mississippi. The Voting Rights Act of 1965 bolstered the black electorate. But the issue of beach ownership hindered the integration of the Mississippi shore. In August 1968 the Fifth Circuit Court of Appeals declared the beach public lands. In 1970 the federal courts overturned the trespassing convictions from the 1963 wade-in. Tyrone Burton, arriving shortly after Mason's wade-in campaign, chafed from the segregationist culture lingering at restaurants and other businesses in Harrison County. But he was in "hog heaven to . . . take the kids out on the beach."[90]

Racial conflict depressed sales tax revenues, a key source of local and state finance. Negative publicity caused by the rioting in Harrison County in 1963 increased with the lynching of three civil rights workers in Philadelphia, Mississippi, in June 1964. State sales tax revenue plummeted. Legislators raised the sales tax rate from 3 percent in 1963 to 3.5 percent in 1964 but still failed to offset the decline. Mississippi's legislature borrowed more than $8 million to cover budget gaps. Following the Philadelphia murders, tourism business along the coast dropped by 50 percent. A chamber of commerce member in December 1964 pointed to a shocking hotel occupancy rate of 8 percent that winter season. Although football teams playing in New Orleans's Sugar Bowl frequently spent December training in Biloxi, Syracuse University opted for Pensacola. A Biloxi spokesman explained, "They said they were afraid for the safety of their Negro players if they came to Mississippi." The official also reported receiving calls and letters from travel agents nationwide who asked, "Is it really safe to send out people to Mississippi?" Segregationists in the Mississippi state house and inland communities dragged their heels into the 1970s, but Jim Crow practices were becoming unaffordable given the growing dependence of local and state budgets on sales taxes linked to tourism. The Gulf Coast was a bellwether.[91]

Similarly, racial unrest in Saint Augustine made national headlines as the city planned for its four hundredth birthday celebration. Activists among the four thousand blacks in the town of fifteen thousand staged sit-ins in June 1963 after municipal leaders stalled discussions about integration. Ardent segregationists responded by attacking the homes of local NAACP leaders. Nightly gun battles erupted. Holstead Manucy, a friend of the sheriff who named him an honorary deputy, organized the gun-toting "Manucy's Raiders." "My boys are here to fight niggers," exclaimed Manucy. In July 1963 advisors to the U.S. Commission on Civil Rights branded Saint Augustine a "segregated super-bomb aimed at the heart of Florida's economy and political integrity."[92]

Cecil Musselwhite, an investigator for Governor C. Farris Bryant of Florida, echoed a common concern among boosters: "I know too that all the NAACP wants is to get one picture of a little negro down in the street with Police and white men standing over him in Florida." Such an image would give "Florida a bad name," diverting vacationers and conventioneers.[93] Since the early 1950s, for example, upscale Miami Beach hotels had been catering to large conventions with interracial memberships as owners attempted to fill rooms during the off-season. Florida officials therefore kept vigilant in order to curtail any racial violence. In October 1962 a Klan representative from Tallahassee bemoaned how Florida "had had more peace in the past 20 months then [sic] at any time in the past eight or more years" and blamed the "Governor's constant vigilance and aggressiveness in meeting racial problems."[94]

However, the situation in Saint Augustine escalated. The protests drew international attention as more civil rights activists arrived, including college students from as far away as Bates College in Maine and major figures such as Martin Luther King Jr. Efforts to integrate whites-only Anastasia Beach in June 1964 led to violent clashes. A Danish television cameraman was beaten. When a state trooper cracked a nightstick over a young segregationist's head as the youth attacked black swimmers, local law enforcement expressed outrage. Resisting the Civil Rights Act of 1964, James Brock, owner of the Monson Motor Lodge and president of the Florida Motel and Hotel Association, poured acid into the lodge's pool to flush out an integrated cadre of swimmers. Photographs of Brock committing the attack became iconic of the civil rights struggle. When Brock, initially a hero among segregationists, complied with the act in July 1964 by serving blacks in his restaurant, vigilantes tossed Molotov cocktails into the diner. Pressure from federal and state officials combined with the economic cost of the violence brought an uneasy calm by late summer 1964. Journalist Larry Goodwyn reported that "motel and restaurant owners who depend largely on the tourist trade and, hence, are considerably more flexible on racial matters" finally asserted themselves. One merchant explained, "It is fashionable to talk about peace now—we've taken a $7-million loss in the tourist trade, you know—but underneath there is this uneasiness you feel every time some nigger gets beaten up."[95]

Boosters in Myrtle Beach, led by Mark Garner and especially W. Horace Carter, likewise resisted Klan-inspired racial violence. Few places in the South were as tense as Horry County, which witnessed a significant Ku Klux Klan revival after the Second World War. The Klan thrived in the Jam, a "very isolated, rough community" some thirty miles from Myrtle Beach along the South Carolina border. Moonshining was the bedrock of the economy. Tabor City, North Carolina, became a Klan hub. One of their first targets was Charlie Fitzgerald, an African American who operated an interracial dance hall called Whispering Pines in Myrtle Beach. Fitzgerald paid the county sheriff to ignore whiskey sales and racial mixing. On 26 August 1950 the Klan paraded through Myrtle Beach in twenty-six cars. The rally ended at Whispering Pines where Klansmen fired hundreds of rounds into the crowded hall. They kidnapped Fitzgerald, whipped him, and cropped his ears. Others rushed fellow ghoul James Daniel Johnson to the hospital. He had been accidentally shot through the heart, the only casualty from the barrage. When doctors removed his robes, they discovered Johnson's police uniform. He was an officer in nearby Conway. The attack sparked a swift reaction. W. Horace Carter, publisher of the *Tabor City Tribune*, raged against the Klan, winning a 1953 Pulitzer Prize and the mayoralty of Tabor City. Carter's close friend Mark Garner, publisher of the Myrtle Beach newspaper and a regularly elected figure in the municipal government, also rebuked the Klan's wizards, dragons, and ghouls.[96]

Civic leaders struggled to ease into integration while holding protesters at bay. Gerald Friedberg and his wife, a white couple from Brooklyn, joined Reverend Isaiah DeQuincey Newman, executive secretary of the South Carolina NAACP, in attempting a wade-in at Myrtle Beach State Park in August 1960. State police and plainclothes officers from Myrtle Beach blocked entry to more than a dozen protesters. Officers followed the cars to hotels in Atlantic Beach. A journalist reported that most cars carried license plates from New York and New Jersey with "very few South Carolina automobiles." When a federal court order required integration of the state park system, South Carolina legislators closed the parks as of September 1963. In Myrtle Beach, Henrietta Abeles, who operated a rooming house, described the tense situation: "Here there is absolutely no move toward integration. I hate to think what will happen when the NAACP starts putting pressure. Horry County being what it is." Yet Abeles noted a distinction between Horry County's Klan-ridden hinterland and Myrtle Beach. Abeles explained, "The Federal government has built a school at the Base for colored and white children. It has also taken away the contract from Bennett & Hucks undertakers because they refused to care for colored soldiers." Faced with the closure of the state parks, the people of Myrtle Beach spoke with one voice. Abeles recorded, "We had a town meeting which I attended, and it was voted unanimously to reopen them integrated rather than keep them shut. However several other counties voted otherwise. Myrtle Beach has a good many northerners."[97]

African Americans demonstrated with reluctance in Myrtle Beach. When the Horry County School Board dragged its feet on integration plans in 1970, negotiators on the Black Committee headed by Reverend Rufus Daniels of Conway called for "economic sanctions and selective buying aimed at the Grand Strand." Demonstrations were planned for Horry County towns, but blacks in Myrtle Beach balked. Some feared violence while others, according to newspaper accounts, believed such actions "detrimental to the beach's tourism." The incident "widened the rift between coastal and inland Negroes."[98]

Virginia Beach surrendered quietly to integration. The *Virginia Beach Sun-News* in July 1963 praised the "peaceful approach" negotiated by civil rights activists and municipal leaders for integrating public accommodations.[99] Although Virginia Beach schools would not achieve full integration until 1969, the process was largely without incident. School superintendent E. E. Brickell boasted of the calm enjoyed by Virginia Beach during the 1960s: "There have been no incidents of any great significance, no riots, no demonstrations. People sat down across the table and worked things out."[100]

As in Virginia Beach and Myrtle Beach, economic interest trumped the desire for maintaining segregation in Galveston. The thought of negative publicity terrified Galveston business leaders. In March 1963 the race relations committee of the chamber of commerce noted the determination of the city's African American population: "The local Negros want total integration in the hotels, restaurants and theatres, and were very hostile at the first meeting; however, they were told that a gradual plan would be best with no publicity, and the hotels have agreed to integrate the hotels and dinning [*sic*] rooms for conventions only." The gradual plan meant that blacks would still "not be allowed to use the swimming pools or club facilities." These restrictions too crumbled. By 1967 civil rights activists complimented the Galveston Chamber of Commerce. Whereas some southern chambers still prohibited black membership, the Galveston chamber actively recruited black members.[101]

Panama City avoided conflict through negotiation with civil rights activists, under unusual circumstances. Sheriff M. J. "Doc" Daffin dominated Bay County, Florida. He won every election between 1952 and 1971, dying of a stroke while in office. Daffin rose to power when Bay County and Panama City were among a few southern communities to hire black policemen just after the Second World War, though these officers were restricted to black neighborhoods. Atlanta had done so in 1948. Charleston and Jacksonville followed in 1950. Daffin's main opponent in 1952 campaigned against hiring black deputies.

The new sheriff, however, used these positions as valuable patronage to gain black votes.[102]

But in 1961 Governor Farris Bryant removed Daffin on corruption charges. Edgar Jones, a black resident of Panama City, informed investigators that "most Negroes know that Sheriff Daffin was behind the protection of the moonshine and bolita operations" in the county. Bolita was a widely popular lottery-style game brought to Florida by Cubans. Through Roscoe Owens, "a big Negro at this time," Daffin allegedly maintained an extensive trade in illegal liquor and gambling. Bryant appointed Panama City commissioner Charles Abbott to clean up the county. The new sheriff discovered Daffin lurking in peculiar company. When police arrested Otis Lee for allegedly raping a white woman in June 1961, special investigator Elmer Emrich found Daffin publicly criticizing the charges and suggesting that the "confession was obtained through force." The preliminary hearing witnessed a courtroom "filled with negroes." The only white person in the audience was Daffin, who sat with his black former deputy, Joseph Lee, uncle of the defendant. The NAACP paid for the lawyer. When the white defense lawyer Mayo Johnston dropped the case—he informed Sheriff Abbott that he had initially "put his fee so high that he did not consider the NAACP would continue to retain him"—Daffin intervened. Attorney Leo Jones, the state legislator for Panama City, accepted the case. Jones owed Daffin. The former sheriff, according to Abbott, had "secured the Panama City negro vote" in the legislator's last election.[103]

Daffin manipulated the civil rights issue to rally his black power base before the next election in 1963. Blacks in Panama City in June 1961 planned to push integration of public buses. Abbott learned from Timothy Youngblood, the local leader of the NAACP, how "local money was being given to negro ministers in Panama City to finance the efforts to cause disturbance." Black informants revealed that Daffin "was contributing money and was behind these efforts on the part of the negroes." In July 1961 the Youth Council of Panama City, with aid from the NAACP, staged several sit-ins at the lunch counters of Walgreens, Christo's Variety Store, and Harlan's Drug Store. Pickets marched outside. African Americans were advised to boycott segregated stores. Civil disobedience, such as drinking from white water fountains or using white dressing rooms in stores, was also encouraged. Immediately, white businessmen and officials contacted Daffin, apparently cutting a deal to restore Daffin's badge in the next election. Emrich reported to the governor that the former sheriff, upon hearing accusations of "instigating several racial incidents" during July, visited a number of "his negro confidants" to tell them to quell the protests. Daffin and "his supporters in the negro quarters of Panama City" now worked to remove Youngblood, whom they were "unable to control." Black ministers in Panama City again received "considerable financial support" from Daffin to oppose the local NAACP leader.[104]

Tranquil race relations returned to Panama City. With prosecutors unable to convince witnesses to testify, Daffin exonerated himself at the ballot box. He received the most votes of his political career in 1963. The new sheriff rewarded his black supporters by supervising school integration. The restoration of peace revitalized tourism as well as Daffin's political future and his profitable moonshine and gambling empire.[105]

Sandblasted

High school senior June Foster was a proud New Orleanian in 1954. As winner of the Miss Lincoln Beach competition, she walked among prominent figures of African American culture. Her photograph graced the pages of *Jet* twice. The October issue showed her receiving a kiss from crooner Nat King Cole. The December photograph was a full-body shot of Foster in swimwear and heels. Images of Harlem's "Miss Sepia Cover Girl," Detroit's "Miss International Sepia," the Golden State's "Miss Bronze California," and Chicago's "Miss Bronze America" accompanied Foster's picture.[106]

The promotion of beauty and tanning hit home to African Americans with naturally dark skin. Terms such as *sepia* and *bronze* blurred distinctions between white and black when praising tans. Even Foster's victory is ironic given that the Supreme Court's *Brown v. Board of Education* decision that year overturned the principle of "separate but equal." The ensuing decade of civil rights protests, court rulings, and legislation revolutionized the world of Foster and her fellow bathing beauties.

After the Civil Rights Act of 1964, formerly colored-only resorts declined. Some former patrons deserted sites such as American Beach and Atlantic Beach for the better facilities now available. Others discovered owners, such as the black shareholders in Seaview Beach near Norfolk, selling off their lands in 1965. Elsewhere, white public officials abandoned maintenance of sites once devoted to people of color. Lincoln Beach, for instance, closed when the Lincoln Beach Corporation terminated its lease after the act went into effect. Proprietors of Pontchartrain Beach, an amusement area for whites opened during the interwar years, reacted by fencing the grounds, adding a gate fee, and charging for each ride. Yet whites increasingly abandoned Pontchartrain Beach as blacks flocked to the site. The decline in revenues led to the site's closure in September 1983, leaving all New Orleanians without a lakefront strand. Little wonder that the national black press's celebration of sunbathing during the 1960s and 1970s faded over the 1980s. Integration was a tide that waxed, then receded.[107]

CHAPTER FOUR

Beach Belles

Femininity, Religion, and the Sexual Revolution

James Gauker was a long way from home in 1944. An Indiana native and new-lywed, the young airman found himself in Myrtle Beach practicing bombing runs over the Atlantic Ocean. The weeklong exercises distracted from the oth-erwise monotonous routine of army life. Gauker wrote his wife about how his crew "buzzed the beach & just about scared the people to death out there." But flying low over bathers' heads was not the only thrill enjoyed. He also expressed amazement at how the town easily subverted gender conventions. The soldier described his first trip into Myrtle Beach: "Last night we went to town & its [*sic*] a very piss poor place to be called a town. Everything is for intertainment [*sic*]. I saw lots of almost naked girls which were hard to pass up." Gauker elab-orated, "They don't wear anything but bathing suits. . . . I haven't seen any-thing like that for a long time." Most of the women Gauker spotted were local girls "around 16 or 17" years old, and everywhere he and his friends went the "girls . . . whistled at us." Rather than feign revulsion, Gauker promised that Myrtle Beach provided an ideal location for a young couple to indulge their sexuality away from neighbors' eyes. Gauker fantasized, "Some day I hope to bring you to a vacation spot like this & all we will do is lay around love, swim & just have a hell of a good time by ourselves. I'm sure you would enjoy it even if you can't swim."[1]

Coastal resorts such as Myrtle Beach and Biloxi, where Gauker also trained, were (and remain) a contradiction. As developers marketed their coastal re-treats in the late nineteenth and early twentieth centuries and guarded against diseases and storms, they crafted places that balanced the local mores of the largely rural white South with the more cosmopolitan market of Yankee and foreign travelers. On one hand, these were gaudy tourist towns where vacation-ers escaped the fetters of cultural convention, particularly in regard to sexuality. On the other hand, such towns remained very southern places embedded in a conservative culture that set white women on pedestals and heralded feminine piety to justify Jim Crow. As Larry Boulier reported in 1958, for example, Myrtle Beach was surrounded "by a traditional south, it accepts many of its better customs such as knocking off work on Sundays, [and] showing good attendance at church." That said, the economic prominence of the beach exposed resort towns to the gale-force winds of cultural change blowing across the twentieth-century United States. Longtime Grand Strand resident Bertha Staley observed how "it takes awhile for real new styles to reach from California or New York to get down to South Carolina and especially Horry County." But arrive they did. Boulier noted that even many of the permanent residents were transplants with "an 'old home town' somewhere." J. Stewart Lomanitz, a transplant to Panama City, joked, "We came, we saw, we stayed." The arrivals diversified, even liberalized, southern culture. As promoters mimicked the beach culture born in Southern California and beckoned urban Yankees to the shore, beach resorts became oases from the more conservative southern hinterland.[2]

Heavenly Reminders

After the death of Booker T. Washington in 1915, Mary McLeod Bethune emerged as a leading spokesperson for blacks' higher education. Born in 1875, the South Carolinian attended Scotia Seminary in North Carolina and Moody Bible Institute in Chicago. She then settled into teaching African American children in Georgia and Florida. In 1904 news of black crews working for Henry Flagler's Florida East Coast Railroad reached Bethune. She investigated: "I found there dense ignorance and meager education facilities, racial prejudice of the most violent type—crime and violence." Venturing on to the "beautiful little village" of Daytona Beach, Bethune established a school for African American children; her first class in October 1904 held five girls and her own son. Parents paid fifty cents a week in tuition. Within two years, 250 pupils enrolled. Soon she bought "Hell's Hole," a local dumping ground. There she built the Daytona Normal and Industrial College with discounted, donated, and discarded materials from the contractors and entrepreneurs accruing fortunes from Florida real estate. Bethune chuckled, "I had learned already that one of my most important jobs was to be a good beggar!" In 1932 her facility was renamed Bethune-Cookman College after merging with a nearby training center for black schoolteachers. Even during the Great Depression, the college hosted more than four hundred students on a 32-acre campus with an additional 178 acres held as an investment—all valued at \$800,000 by 1937.[3]

The beach had been a godsend for Bethune. "I did my best missionary work among the prominent winter visitors to Florida," explained Bethune. "I would pick out names of 'newly arrived guests,' from the newspapers, and write letters asking whether I could call." She thus met benefactors such as millionaire James Gamble of Proctor and Gamble fame. Though frequently invited to speak at African American institutions nationwide, she reserved the winters for fund-raising. Bethune, for instance, initially refused an invitation to attend the Colored Activities Day at the Florida State Fair held near Jacksonville in March 1930. The short trip up the coast seemed inadvisable: "You know we have to work Florida vigorously during the tourist season in order to secure funds for the maintenance of our work." She relented, however, after the organizer clarified that prominent African American "educators and business men, from different sections of the Country," themselves vacationing in Florida and likely enjoying the amenities of the black-only American Beach, would be in attendance.[4]

Bethune's success reveals the fertility of coastal sands for the program of uplift—racial and religious. Walter Grover's recollections of Galveston at the dawn of the twentieth century ring true for many boosters along the southern coast: "It must not be inferred . . . that the citizens of Galveston devoted all their time to pleasure they did not; they were strictly business, and of a very religious nature." John Thomas Woodside, the developer who launched Myrtle Beach as a resort during the 1920s by buying more than sixty thousand acres along the coast, recalled telling fellow South Carolinians how "[he] was going to buy the property and all that [he] made out of it personally, [he] was going to give to the cause of Christian education."[5]

Attachment to a moralistic work ethic restrained hedonism among tourists through the early twentieth century. Devotion to work carried special resonance among white southerners who prided themselves on modernizing the regional economy damaged by civil war even while hallowing the plantation past. Vacations needed an element of edification or philanthropy to justify time away from the office. Furthermore, as timber executives, railroad tycoons, and real-estate promoters developed the southern coast, they enticed residents, workers, and vacationers who desired the trappings of civilization. Churches and schools granted respectability and an air of permanence to resort towns.

The building boom supplied ample excess that facilitated construction on the cheap, as Bethune and others discovered. Moreover, the influx of wealthy white vacationers bearing sentiments of paternalism and philanthropy common in the early twentieth century made financing, while not easy, certainly easier than in interior sections of the South less visited by potential white benefactors. As Bethune realized, even black workers tied to the tourism industry could afford tuition rates unmanageable for sharecroppers. The alchemy of drawing gold from sand caught attention.[6]

The Chautauqua movement popularized the rural retreat as more than a place for the infirmed. As editor of the *Sunday School Journal*, Methodist minister John Heyl Vincent advocated nondenominational outdoor summer schools during the 1870s to prevent children from backsliding between academic years. In 1874 he established a camp on Chautauqua Lake in New York. Families boarded at the site for the annual educational and recreational program. The concept quickly spread across the country. Dozens of Chautauqua camps, opened in rural settings often near lakes or springs, beckoned Americans eager for an enlightening vacation. In the South these facilities catered to the winter market. The proliferation of Chautauqua programs created a circuit, sharing musicians and lecturers. Educators, reformers, politicians, religious figures, and others addressed the latest issues.[7]

Located on a natural lake some thirty miles from the Gulf, DeFuniak Springs in Walton County, Florida, emerged as one of the most popular Chautauqua sites in the South. The Pensacola and Atlantic Railroad, a subsidiary of the Louisville and Nashville Railroad, established the town in 1884. To promote travel and settlement, the company simultaneously established a Chautauqua camp. Northerners were the target market. Visitors, as common for such programs, enjoyed a wide range of activities. The railroad, in a promotional brochure from 1915, hawked the "splendid lectures on literature, travel, economics, Biblical literature, art, elocution, story telling and their kindred subjects, while various forms of high class entertainment such as concerts, feats of magic, monologues, illustrated travelogues, motion pictures, scientific experiments, Shakespearean Plays and uplifting productions of all kinds render De Funiak Springs an ideal place for spending the winter months, free from the snow and cold, among the balmy breezes of the Southland." Attendees enjoyed the largest Chautauqua auditorium in Dixie. The building, steam heated and equipped with electric lights, seated four thousand spectators and boasted a stage large enough for a hundred performers. Nicknamed the "Adirondacks of Western

Florida" and "A Little Venice," DeFuniak Springs offered more than recreation and edification. The Chautauqua also supplied moral lessons. "The Biblical hour which, with the Sunday service, forms the great bulwark and strength of the Chautauqua movement, is duly emphasized," noted promoters.[8]

The Chautauqua camps of the late nineteenth and early twentieth century marked a transition between the elite spring and mountain resorts prominent during the antebellum period and the more hedonistic forays to the beach after the First World War. The legacy of the Chautauqua remained strong, if obscured, by the mid-twentieth century. For boosters, the combination of na-ture and recreation with family togetherness provided a marketing scheme that resonated with Americans. Southern beach communities retained a mor-alistic tone. Venues such as Pirateland Amusement Park near Myrtle Beach and Frontierland near Panama City couched entertainment in the rhetoric of education and family. As historian Susan Sessions Rugh notes, family vacations by twentieth-century Americans were often "pilgrimages" focused on a "grand narrative of national greatness" forged by visiting historic sites, recreations of the past, and natural wonders.[9]

The ample accommodation, transportation links, cultivated scenery, and entertainment facilities of coastal communities attracted religious-oriented encampments. Statewide or even regional religious gatherings formed key components of the early convention trade. Such meetings filled less busy parts of the calendar. In June 1908, and over the subsequent decade, Biloxi hosted the Seashore Divinity School. The ten-day program, besides capturing national press coverage, regularly attracted more than a hundred ministers from Missis-sippi, Louisiana, and Alabama to hear lectures on the Bible as well as politics. The Seashore Camp Meeting, begun in 1873 and still active under the name Seashore United Methodist Assembly, followed two weeks after the school in mid-July, drawing thousands of attendees from Louisiana to Georgia. The summer camp and conference grounds became, according to one local histo-rian writing in the 1950s, a "Mississippi Gulf Coast landmark" that served as "the annual Mecca for Methodists."[10]

Beaches shaped religious practices and rituals within southern coastal com-munities. Virginia Beach boasted of the numerous Sunday school programs hosted along the shore. The *Princess Anne Times* in 1915 proclaimed, "That Virginia Beach possesses all the advantages required to make it an ideal resort for Sunday School picnics is being evidenced every day by the arrival of one and some times two schools from the same town or city—Norfolk, Portsmouth and Berkley sending their schools to breathe the pure free air of the ocean." Baptists, Episcopalians, Methodists, Presbyterians, and others flocked to the Virginia coast. Such Sunday schools remained a staple of the town's life. Born in 1927, Jean Bruce of Norfolk recalled parents taking their children to the beach every Sunday after church during the summers. For churchgoers, a Sunday at the beach provided time for reflecting on God's creation, enjoying the surf, and sharing time with friends and family well into the night, when small fires lit the shoreline. Galveston, Panama City, Myrtle Beach, and other coastal resorts likewise drew pious southerners to their shores.[11]

Bob Jones stood among the more prominent religious figures to see the southern coast as an ideal spot for his purposes. A native of Mobile, Jones understood the attraction of the Gulf, eventually acquiring acreage near Panama City for a self-named college devoted to fundamentalism. Alabama governor Bibb Graves delivered the keynote address at the groundbreaking in 1926. When the doors opened in fall 1927, eighty-eight students from seven states enrolled. The campus consisted of five buildings of Spanish design. Besides studying, students cultivated the surrounding twenty acres for produce, milked twelve dairy cows, and worked an on-campus canning factory. Even in the depth of the Depression, some two hundred students attended. The focus on Christian instruction and the location of the college on a bay earned students the nickname "swamp angels" from locals. However, in 1933 Bob Jones relocated the college to draw a broader student body, not to mention resurrect the institution's faltering finances. Jones moved the college to Cleveland, Tennessee, and then, in 1947, to Greenville, South Carolina, where the university remains today. To honor Jones and to recall the community's religious heritage, Mayor Montel Johnson of Lynn Haven and Mayor M. B. Miller of Panama City in 1976 welcomed Jones's widow, sons, and alumni to the unveiling of a historic marker at the site of the first college in Bay County. The Jones family and other guests visited the beach after services.[12]

A devout Christian, Edgar Cayce settled in Virginia Beach to explore psychosomatic healing in 1925. The native Kentuckian regularly placed himself into a hypnotic trance from which he diagnosed human ills, predicted events, and recalled past lives. Virginia Beach residents embraced Cayce. He organized the Association of National Investigation in 1927 to engage in psychic research and to devise practical applications for its esoteric studies. Financier Morton Blumenthal of New York, who used Cayce's readings to judge the stock market, funded the establishment of a hospital based on the psychic's teachings in

1928. Blumenthal also underwrote the establishment of Atlantic University to popularize Cayce's work. Dr. William Mosley Brown left Washington and Lee University to head the institution. Although the university opened in 1930, the Depression, which erased much of Blumenthal's fortune, led to its closure by early 1931. Later in the year, Cayce, his wife, and his secretary were arrested for fortune telling while visiting New York City. Undaunted, supporters from Norfolk and Virginia Beach encouraged Cayce to incorporate the nonprofit Association of Research and Enlightenment to promote his psychic work and teachings on a permanent basis. More than five hundred members joined during the organization's first decade. The local press eulogized Cayce upon his death in 1945: "Arising each morning at dawn to watch the sun rise out of the ocean and to read his Bible by its light. A few visitors, always church on Sunday, in which he was intensely interested, an occasional visit to the movies, fishing, working in his garden or his shop, answering correspondence and giving his daily 'readings' filled his life." Another editorial began, "Edgar Cayce, Christian gentleman, is dead." Far from dismissing Cayce as an eccentric, Virginia Beach celebrated the psychic as a devout resident.[13]

African Americans also carved religious outposts along the coast. Robert Jones, the first black bishop in the Methodist Episcopal Church, established Gulfside Assembly in Waveland, Mississippi, in 1923. The site consisted of four hundred acres with a half mile of Gulf frontage. As a local historian commented, the site provided the "only place in America where Negro Methodists can gather in large groups on their own property to consider religion and its related problems." Jones managed to create an impressive facility. In addition to religious instruction, the site hosted the Gulfside Vocational School for African American boys as well as gatherings of Boy Scouts and 4-H clubs. Administrators rebuilt on a grander scale after the 1947 hurricane. In addition to a chapel, an assembly center, and a dining hall for five hundred diners, the site added the Gulfside Inn with a capacity for two hundred guests. By the 1970s the successes of the civil rights movement and devastation caused by Hurricane Camille eroded interest in a facility born of segregation.[14]

Observers noted the architectural prominence of religion within resort towns. In her study of Galveston, historian Elizabeth Hayes Turner details how churches transformed from small wooden buildings to imposing stone structures between 1870 and 1920. In an age of increased activism by women, churches became "more homelike and more comfortable for women and their families as they insisted upon edifices and programs complementary to their tastes, sensibilities, and needs." As if to remind hedonistic vacationers of God's watchful eye, Myrtle Beach residents constructed churches with towering steeples. In 2003 Will Murdock, a regular at the beach since the 1950s, described the skyline. Murdock recorded that "three sentinels stand over downtown Myrtle Beach, as they do in thousands of small Southern towns—the spires of the First Baptist, First Methodist and First Presbyterian churches." Murdock well understood their purpose, explaining how "the churches keep watch over the traditions and morals of a town that many feel has already lost its way." Not surprisingly, the large number of devoted Christians and political conservatives who called Myrtle Beach home maintained a firm grasp on activities despite the area's reputation for carnality—so much so that some observers have nicknamed the town "Mayberry-at-the-Beach." As historian Harvey Jackson III has argued about the Gulf Coast, the "very culture that gave rise to the Redneck Riviera was also a culture full of churchgoers who wanted to visit the beach for the family activities it offered." Some large churches in cities such as Atlanta and Birmingham had purchased older motels along the Florida Panhandle by the 1980s, converting them into youth retreats.[15]

Few grasped the relationship between architecture and morality better than the University of South Carolina medical students who opened the short-lived Deliverance House in Myrtle Beach during the early 1970s. Determined to address then-taboo subjects such as venereal disease and birth control, the students received funding to convert an old beach house into a health clinic. The city of roughly 12,000 boomed to more than 250,000 during the summer, representing a "massive concentration of youth." Rollin Reeder, a manager at Deliverance House, stressed the importance of appearance: "The intent was not to turn this place into a reminder of the 'establishment.' In fact, very few visible repairs were made. The old house possessed a comforting attraction that may have been defeated with too much 'paint.'"[16]

Boosters pointed to church structures as vital to turning tourists into permanent residents. "What draws the visitor and new resident?" asked the *Virginia Beach Sun-News* in 1952. The "fine sand beach" topped the list, followed by the "matchless weather." But of things man-made, churches crowned local glory. The editors celebrated the variety and growth of religious faith symbolized by places of worship: "There are our fine churches . . . the new Jewish synagogue, the fine Catholic church, even now planning expansion, the new Baptist house of worship, the rapidly expanding Methodist building program, the excellent facilities existing for the adherents of the Presbyterian, the Episcopal and other faiths." Schools, golf courses, country clubs, civic organizations, and progressive municipal leaders completed the list. For many Americans, according to a Panama City journalist, the "appearance of a church is a sign of progress" and a "symbol of civilization."[17]

Campaigns to promote church attendance often equated religion with nature. The awe inspired by the outdoors equaled the faithful reflection fostered inside houses of worship. One ad depicted a pond surrounded by woods: "You'll find quiet in woods like these, but not a silence. The wind whispers through the trees. Birds murmur softly. Insects squeak tunelessly. The soft lap-lap of water against the shore is like distant drum-beats. There is infinite peace, but never silence." The advertisement added, "Much closer to you is another haven of peace—your church. Here too you will find quiet, but no dead, spiritless silence." When a Presbyterian minister in Venice, Florida, opened a drive-in church in the 1950s, he discovered that the sermons carried extra meaning given the location. As *Life* reported, the congregants enjoyed an "extra spiritual dimension, brought on by the sun, the pines and the birds."[18]

Given the difficulty of sustaining churches in towns with transient populations, resorts emphasized interdenominational religion. In Galveston, as Elizabeth Hayes Turner argues, the "insecurities caused by tropical storms and tropical diseases" taught church-related charity workers the "value of responding swiftly and effectively in groups to the existing crises." During the 1920s, after the Methodists constructed the first church at Myrtle Beach, visitors "of all denominations," according to local historian Blanche Floyd, attended the services until their own houses of worship pierced the skyline. The effort to bring God to the beach encouraged both interfaith cooperation as well as a "close community spirit." The wisdom of investing resources in the construction of multiple large churches to accommodate the summer influx of vacationers seemed foolish given the small permanent population. In 1938 the editors of the Myrtle Beach newspaper philosophized, "We can see no reason why there should not be built a great big church and everybody on the beach go to that church."[19]

Such unity represented a growing movement that stretched beyond the nation's coast. A liberal spirit of religious unity blossomed in the late nineteenth century, exemplified by the World's Parliament of Religions at the 1893 Columbian Exposition in Chicago. Interdenominational cooperation in Virginia, for example, dated to the 1875 formation of the Sunday School Convention in Richmond. Over time, "Protestant forces of Virginia have been learning to trust each other and to work together," remarked one observer. The Virginia Council of Churches, founded in 1944, represented fourteen Protestant denominations united to promote Christian devotion. Committees on inter-racial cooperation, ministry to migrants, evangelism, and leadership develop-ment eased adjustment to the modern world by strengthening a shared faith in God. Programs such as the annual "Cooperative Christianity Sunday" spread the word among Virginians. The interdenominational cooperation attracted prominent religious leaders. Evangelist Billy Graham, for instance, premiered his second film in Myrtle Beach in August 1953. A 1977 guidebook to the Grand Strand reminded vacationers of their religious obligations: "Even though you may be here on vacation, Sunday is still a day of worship and relaxation on The Grand Strand. So we have provided you with a list of churches in the area. There is probably one of your denomination nearby, but all local churches wel-come visitors." Given fears of atheistic communism during the Cold War, inter-denominational efforts reinforced the moral strength of American democracy and capitalism.[20]

Businesses and churches encouraged church attendance to bolster moral standards and patriotism. Resort towns regularly beckoned vacationers and residents to "GO TO CHURCH," as one newspaper headline proclaimed with the subtitle "to the Church of your choice." Hotels and restaurants figured prominently as sponsors of such advertisements. One typical headline—above a listing of several dozen business sponsors—stated, "Ministers of all faiths and the community-minded firms below persuade you to read this Spiritual Values page and make it a part of your life. . . . It is your heritage."[21] Business-men within the tourism industry pushed church attendance to demonstrate that they had the "Best Interests of The Community at Heart" and to temper guests' behavior. Floridians in the Panhandle proclaimed in 1939: "For his own benefit, every one of us should participate in the spiritual life of Panama City, a phase of community activity from which everyone benefits and which every-one can enjoy." Carl Compton, in a 1951 sermon given at a Baptist church and subsequently published by the local press, asked vacationers, "Have you aban-doned all efforts to serve Christ in the summer at Myrtle Beach?"[22] Another ad, titled "Attend the Church of Your Choice," urged young men to take their sweethearts to Sabbath services. "There's not a girl in the world who wouldn't deeply appreciate and treasure the respect such an invitation implies." An ad in the *Galveston Daily News* in 1970 asked, "Some say you find God just as well in a garden, in the woods, or on a golf course as in a church—that God is everywhere. But be honest about it. Are you not more apt to think of weeds, or mosquitoes, or a poor shot than you are of God? And after all, you have made this outing to seek pleasure."[23]

Shirkers could not escape the deeply religious culture. The dependence on vacationers and rapid expansion of resort communities encouraged openness to the various faiths espoused by tourists and transplants. In Virginia Beach, pastors of Protestant churches regularly joined forces to canvas residents. Armed with survey cards, congregants, as happened in 1933 and 1939, fanned out to "cover the entire Town." The census workers encouraged new residents (and backsliders) unaffiliated with a local church to join, especially since many retained ties to churches in their former communities or primary residence. The size of the undertaking encouraged unity among the denominations. Furthermore, the joint effort opened doors to census takers seeking to record details of family size and religious belief. Rather than being annoying proselytizers, the surveyors appeared as neighbors welcoming newcomers into the Virginia Beach family. Since 47 percent of children in Princess Anne County on the eve of the Second World War did not attend Sunday School, educators maintained, through donated funds, the Non-Sectarian Religious Program. Started in 1937, the lessons taught during the school day by consecrated instructors emphasized a general Christian morality stripped of denominational theologies. During the 1950s the Panama Transit Company of Panama City offered free bus rides on Sunday if they informed the driver that they were either heading to or from church. In 1965 communities along the Grand Strand embraced a national campaign by the fraternal Elks Association to ring all church bells at 11 a.m. on the Sunday of July Fourth weekend. Mayor W. E. Cameron of Myrtle Beach proclaimed Independence Day as Bell Ringer Day, "a patriotically and spiritually inspired day of rededication to our Flag and the great American heritage of freedom."[24]

Beach communities delicately balanced religious values with the sexuality unleashed by beach vacations. Downtown sites captured the odd blend of religiosity and sexuality. The Pavilion, a public dance hall and arcade, served as Myrtle Beach's tourist hub. Dances hosted at the Pavilion were regulated affairs. From the 1930s through the 1950s, teenagers and young adults wore formal outfits onto the dance floor, and parents closely supervised the activities. For the religious, the Pavilion was the gathering place for sunrise services each Easter. Yet the Pavilion regularly hosted wrestling tournaments during the 1950s as well. None were more popular than matches between women, who would "forget their feminine beauty and physical trimness, much admired by male spectators, and will go to the mat to win, each for herself."[25] Capacity crowds packed the facility to witness the "thrills and chills during their hour of hair pulling, head banging and leg twisting." A similar blending of faith and hedonism occurred at other beachfront facilities, whether the publicly owned Pleasure Pier in Galveston or the privately owned Miracle Strip Amusement Park in Panama City. Organizers declared the "largest Christian event ever to hit these parts" when Jesus Celebration '82 attracted more than six thousand people to Panama City over Labor Day in 1982. "The park is open for Christian-oriented entertainment as opposed to the other days," remarked a local pastor.[26]

Ads commonly blended the profane with religious imagery. In July 1941 Virginia Electric and Power Company ran a large ad headlined by a suggestive pun: "Absence makes the meat grow TENDER." Below, a smiling housewife wore a bathing suit and large sun hat modeled as a halo. Life was literally a beach vacation for wives with electric appliances. Such equipment freed women from the hard work of the patriarchal household. The ad explained, "While she's browning in the sun . . . her dinner roast is browning in the oven." Dargan's Grill of Myrtle Beach, which boasted of selling the "coldest beer in town," welcomed visitors to the Sun Fun Festival and Miss Universe Pageant with a large newspaper ad in June 1958. The central image likewise depicted a young woman in a bathing suit, the sun carefully positioned to form a halo effect.[27]

Southern beach communities adapted to modern ways to draw young vacationers. Ruth Millet of Tennessee noted the stark difference in dating habits from her youth and those she witnessed in the 1950s. In the early twentieth century, girls "went in heavily for the helpless, 'aren't you wonderful' routine." Those of the Cold War era tried "her best to out-water-ski, outputt, outbowl any boy she can. And if she wins, she doesn't worry for a minute that she might have damaged his masculine ego." Many fretted over juvenile delinquency and a decline in morality. Millet, however, thought the new courting customs "easier, more relaxed and more fun." For beach promoters, preserving outdated views of gender roles threatened local pocketbooks.[28]

The women's liberation movement in the 1960s caused many southerners to voice muted support for greater freedoms regarding sexuality. The sexual revolution challenged notions of propriety. Swimwear grew skimpier. Films, magazines, and theater performances displayed nudity, included profanity, and offered a more frank discussion of sexual matters. Dale Sims, a student at Gulf Coast Community College in Panama City, embraced the openness. Rather than ban explicit films or publications such as *Playboy*, Americans needed to encourage free expression and individualism. Writing in 1966, Sims dismissed "laws regulating sex—not as an endorsement of either premarital or extramarital sex—but in the firm belief that such personal conduct should be left to the private determination of the individual and is not rightly the business of government in our democracy." When Frances Moore interviewed fourteen women in Myrtle Beach about "Women's Liberation," all voiced support for equal pay for equal work and an equal opportunity for employment. "What they're not in favor of is being quoted, by name, in the newspaper," added Moore.[29]

The delicate balance between marketing sexuality and repressing sexuality proved difficult. Stephanie Pace, a Myrtle Beach high school student during the early 1970s, satirized efforts to suppress open discussion of sexuality. Pace, through her newspaper column, protested the decision to expel two high school seniors who, rather than engage in premarital sex, decided to marry. Pace decried the hypocrisy of officials who classed the young couple with "troubleshooting pinkos who go around yelling about civil rights, heretics who cause trouble, people screaming about dignity." Festivals meant to celebrate young women easily declined into crude displays of sexuality. At the Grand Strand's Miss Waves Pageant of 1970, "a group of rowdies had gathered rocks and beer cans with the announced intention of pelting the pageant group if Miss Tennessee was not chosen." Contestants from other states "complained of having to listen to indecent remarks by the crowd." One bathing beauty raged, "I felt like we were cattle on an auction block."[30]

Activists struggled to overcome conservative attitudes toward southern womanhood. Joan Senyk chafed in the resort and retirement community of Fort Walton Beach, Florida. Writing to the state chapter of the National Organization of Women (NOW) in January 1974, Senyk, who had a teenage daughter, asked for information about public or private high schools "available for liberated persons, or just women." She grew so frustrated that she volunteered to establish a local chapter of NOW. Florida director Karen Coolman warned Senyk of the difficulty in breaching religiously and politically conservative communities of the South: "Sometimes organizing can be an up-hill effort, especially in the Fla. Panhandle (I'm telling you!!!)." Senyk understood the wisdom of not pressing too hard against local mores. She informed her superiors, "With the very conservative attitude here we feel we have a lot of education to do before 'making enemies.'" Expanding beyond Fort Walton Beach into the surrounding county was nearly impossible.[31]

The struggles of the Fort Walton Beach NOW chapter exemplify the slow pace of change in perceptions of women across Dixie. By August 1974, when Senyk left for a job at Auburn University, the chapter claimed only twenty-nine paying members and a mailing list of barely a hundred. Once Robin Rothrock of Fort Walton Beach assumed leadership, the NOW members surveyed attitudes toward rape among Okaloosa County prosecutors, hospital officials, and policemen. They not only raised awareness of the issue but also convinced the Fort Walton Beach Police Department to hire its first female officer to facilitate rape investigations.[32] The NOW members of Fort Walton Beach countered the impression that "NOW makes all women look bad because militant libbers are unladylike and rude." In the patriarchal South, the NOW members also had to overcome the shame felt by some husbands who faced ridicule for being "henpecked or emasculated" if wives—65 percent of NOW members were married—joined. Equally important for a NOW chapter in the South, the Fort Walton Beach members stressed that they did not need to "agree with every nationally accepted position." Rather, the chapter labored to inspire southern women. "We have been raised, more or less, to be passive and dependent," complained the members.[33]

The Panama City NOW chapter further revealed the role of tourist resorts in drawing out-of-towners, including retirees and college students, thereby providing a space—however scant—for liberal causes. Melissa Miller, a college student in Panama City, convened the city's first NOW gatherings in November 1973. Distracted by her studies, Miller passed responsibility to Pam McCormack. In October 1974 McCormack described how the chapter languished as collegians "went away for the summer and nothing happened." Fewer than the ten members needed to start an official chapter attended. McCormack informed the state headquarters of their quandary: "We have discovered that we are all from out of the state and are a bit stumped as to how we can broach the apathy of the local residents." To attract a larger base, McCormack proposed expanding the "chapter's reach and be known as the 'Bay County Chapter', since Panama City proper is not that large." In January 1975 the Panama City–Bay County chapter, claiming only six dues-paying members, went inactive. McCormack concluded, "Apathy is rampant in this particular part of Florida." Southern conservatism prevailed.[34]

Suitable Bodies

Looking back on the state's long history of summer tourism, a Virginia Beach journalist in June 1939 reminded readers of the once-ample clothing donned by bathers. Between the American Revolution and the Civil War, Virginia tourism centered on the thermal and mineral springs of the cooler, mountainous counties where the "fashion and wealth of the Tidewater during summer months" went on display. Antebellum grandeur faded as more Americans accrued the wealth and time for leisure. A revolution in fashion resulted. Quoting a period guidebook, the newsman described how swimwear at the springs typically consisted of "a large cotton gown of a cashmere shawl pattern lined with crimson, a fancy Greek cap, Turkish slippers, and a pair of loose pantaloons—a garb that consumed little time in donning or doffing." As middle-class Americans flocked to the beachfront in the twentieth century, the trappings of refinement and propriety shed from bathing gear for both sexes. Each thread lost exposed more skin, launching fresh debates over morality and the purpose of a vacation.[35]

Christian values held that women be faithful stewards to their children, husbands, and community. In April 1928 Mrs. Alonzo Richardson of Georgia, director of the General Federation of Woman's Clubs, spoke to the Mississippi chapters at their convention in Biloxi. She emphasized, "That every effort of woman was for the perfecting of the American home." Rapid changes in technology and culture were no excuse for distraction. Richardson "declared that there is nothing the matter with the American home, that we are living in an age of Sports, Speed and Splendor, moving minds, motor wheels and high gear. But the wise woman takes time to adjust herself to this high tension and her first need was time for prayer." Tourism boosters along southern beaches bore the task of easing the contradiction between sexual indulgence and sexual piety. To accomplish this, local leaders accentuated the religiosity of their communities and women bathers. A veneer of divinity disguised a multitude of sins.[36]

At the dawn of the twentieth century, women, at least those not among the elite, frequently sewed their own swimwear. The mother of adolescent Sarah Blackford bought cloth—grey with white dots—to sew her daughter's bathing outfit while on vacation at Virginia Beach in June 1895. One observer of American culture in 1908 joked, "The paucity of material in a bathing suit is the stock theme of the newspaper humourist, and the paragraphs that have been written on the young woman who goes to a shop and asks for a 'sample' and triumphantly exhibits it to her husband as the material out of which she is going to make her bathing suit are endless." Alma Simmang Simpson of Galveston found her husband quite taken by the bathers in "risque looking" swimwear encountered on a trip to California in 1915: "The bathing suits here caught Jack's fancy immediately; they looked about the size of a postage stamp."[37]

Beachfront attire exposed bodies. The warmer climate of the Deep South led many to don looser and thinner clothes whether at the beach or not. Raised in a more conservative upstate community, Glennan Anderson expressed shock when she moved to the Mississippi coast just after the Second World War: "I thought the people were the worst-dressed people I had ever seen. I wasn't used to a resort town. We didn't wear sun-back dresses, and we didn't wear shorts and go around half naked." That underwear companies such as BVD entered the burgeoning swimwear trade during the interwar period reinforced the perceived impropriety of beach dress on town streets. Placing Olympic swimmers and Hollywood stars in ad campaigns eased some anxiety about respectability, but the association with bedtime wear raised eyebrows for Americans shocked by the rapid exposure of bodies after the First World War.[38]

Beaches, by encouraging bathing and thus degrees of nudity, naturally emerged as sexualized spaces. David Carr, a black man who worked near Myrtle Beach for much of the twentieth century, remarked on the way women's attitudes changed over the decades. Carr laughed that "women dressed then [in the early twentieth century] with long knee pants and then when they'd see us coming, they'd pull that down. Now [in the late twentieth century] it's up here and they'd see us coming and pull it up." Beach communities required vigilance in policing moral codes and changing attitudes toward sexuality.[39]

Beauty contests provided a framework for displaying female bodies without discarding morality. The first coastal resort to host a beauty pageant was Rehoboth Beach, Delaware, in 1880. The gimmick, meant to draw tourists, respected the mores of the era by not requiring women in the "Miss United States" competition to don swimwear, despite the bulky designs. Australian professional swimmer Annette Kellerman ushered in a new age of lighter swimwear in 1907 when she was arrested at Revere Beach outside Boston for wearing a form-fitting, one-piece suit without a skirt. She later pushed boundaries as the first woman to appear nude in a movie, *Daughter of the Gods* (1916). By the interwar period, bathing beauty contests and one-piece suits featuring bare arms and legs were commonplace. Pageants grew in popularity nationwide. Across the South, bathing beauty competitions emerged from farm demonstration agents' work promoting healthy living and modern clothing styles. Town boosters used pageants to draw business and add glamour to events such as tobacco auctions. Tobacco queens, maids of cotton, and a slew of other title winners honoring agricultural products from peanuts to strawberries soon populated the countryside. In her study of the phenomenon, Kathleen Blain Roberts shows that the "dangers inherent in showcasing woman-as-commodity were tempered by showcasing woman-as-commodity crop." Beach communities, lacking such ploys, exercised greater caution. Municipal leaders in Saint Petersburg, Florida, hired John Lodwick in 1918, the first press agent in the world employed by a city. He quickly publicized plans for a beauty contest. To oversee the Festival of States, inaugurated in 1921, Lodwick organized the Purity League and personally measured the women's bathing suits. His efforts publicized the skimpy swimwear while suggesting moral standards of dress.[40]

The 1920s marked the golden age of bathing beauty competitions, gimmicks meant to market sex and draw tourists. Galveston challenged Atlantic City, which founded the Miss America Pageant in 1921, with its own parade of swimwear-clad women aged sixteen to twenty-five years old. From a one-day, local affair launched in 1920 to coincide with the opening of the tourist season on so-called Splash Day, the pageant evolved into the three-day International Pageant of Pulchritude in 1926. The event included a Miss United States competition followed by an international contest. Organizers offered the highest prizes of any beauty contest in the country—the 1927 grand prizewinner received $2,000 in gold along with the title "Miss Queen of the Universe." Women from around the world, including winners from Austria and Brazil, competed in swimwear, sportswear, and evening gowns. For five years Galveston captured international headlines and profited from the 250,000 spectators. The Great Depression ended the affair in 1931.[41]

Although promoters in Belgium adopted the international event before folding in 1935, the concept of a Miss United States to rival Miss America remained alive but homeless. Virginia Beach businessmen contacted Bob Thompson, president of the floundering Miss United States Beauty Pageant and owner of a film travelogue company, to bring the competition to their shores. In 1939 the resort hosted its first national beauty contest with participants donning pajamas, sport clothes, bathing suits, and evening gowns. Winners received a screen test with MGM Studios in Hollywood. The onset of the Second World War ended the pageant. On a much smaller scale, in 1952 the town launched the Miss Virginia Beach competition, part of the annual Sand Festival celebrating the town's replenished beaches.[42]

The Miss Universe Pageant reemerged in its current manifestation after a controversy involving Miss America sponsor Catalina, a California-based swimwear firm. Yolande Betbeze, a Mobile, Alabama, native and winner of Miss America 1951, refused to pose in the company's scanty bathing suits. Catalina responded by withdrawing sponsorship of Miss America. The firm launched the Miss USA Pageant in Long Beach, California, in 1952 along with a revitalized Miss Universe competition. Miss USA continued in Long Beach until moving to Miami Beach during the 1960s. Since 1972 the pageant has moved for two- to three-year stints in different American cities, including Biloxi from 1979 until 1982, Mobile in 1989, and South Padre Island from 1994 until 1996. Miss Universe, since 1972, has moved to a different international city each year.[43]

Bathing beauties captured publicity for resorts and the warm climate. Pictures of "hot" women caught the public's eye. Florida boosters in January 1936 circulated a photograph of a beachgoer clad in newspaper. The *Panama City News Herald* boasted, "The cold blizzardy North is 'hot news' in Florida and this bathing beauty thought up a novel way of using newspapers, emblazoned with storm headlines, for her suit to spread the tidings." Competitions celebrated places, climate, and friendliness. Pageants rallied locals and energized tourism promotion campaigns. In 1949 boosters in Biloxi consulted state officials, chiefly the Mississippi Agricultural and Industrial Board, about creating and hosting the "Miss Hospitality" competition—a contest that culminated in a statewide "Hospitality Month" meant to raise Mississippians' awareness of tourism's value. The emphasis on beauty and charm highlighted traits important to attracting travelers, a point that made the contest popular into the twenty-first century. When Governor Fielding Wright crowned the first winner, he declared, "As Mississippi's queen of hospitality you will officially represent to the nation and to the World the traditional courtesy, charm and hospitality which are a Mississippi heritage." Twenty-year-old blond Katherine Wright of Pascagoula gladly accepted her duties by "representing the state in travel shows and other activities" while endeavoring "to show the true Mississippi hospitality." Other contests, such as the Miss Northwest Florida competition launched by Fort Walton Beach promoters in 1950, aimed at regional markets. The 1954 title, for instance, went to the seventeen-year-old, blue-eyed blond Adalyn Bush of Camilla, Georgia—some forty miles north of the Florida line.[44]

When not displaying bathing beauties at competitions and festivals, businesses hired swimwear-clad women for advertising stunts and stage performances. Cultural critic Charles Merz noted the emergence of swimsuited vixens in advertising during the Jazz Age: "What we have here is emphasis upon youth, beauty, and the one-piece bathing suit, adapted to the needs of industry and commerce." In 1925 Gulfport hosted the Mississippi Gulf Coast Beauty Pageant parade with floats and contestants "presented by the various business concerns of the city." The procession discharged its "freight of pretty girls" at a downtown theater where the "bathing revue" was judged. Far from a summer festival, the pageant occurred in December and aimed to draw Christmas shoppers to Gulfport stores. The Beach Theatre and Nite Club of Panama City enticed customers with beauty queens from Florida, Georgia, Alabama, and Tennessee over the July Fourth holiday in 1947. An advertisement showed photographs of six young women in swimwear but also listed the nearly fifty towns represented, stoking regional pride. Such a combination boded well for profits, so much so that the club filmed the contestants for replays.[45]

Photographs of swimwear-clad women enjoying the sand became commonplace after the First World War. These often mimicked provocative shots of film stars. Men very rarely appeared. Photographs and sketches celebrated thin white women, typically teenagers or those in their early twenties. Local newspapers combed area beaches. Caroline Long of Columbus, Georgia, unwittingly became a promoter while vacationing in Panama City during the summer of 1961. The town newspaper carried her photograph on the front page, explaining that the Georgian, "although a tourist herself, no doubt served as a very effective tourist attraction as she poses prettily. . . . The 17-year-old lass looks capable of attracting most any tourist." All coastal newspapers contained such photographs.[46]

Hollywood increasingly defined fashion—and propriety—despite efforts to censor sexually suggestive scenes or revealing clothes. The Crown Theatre in Biloxi enticed ticket buyers in April 1920 by featuring Mack Sennett's collection of Hollywood starlets known as Sennett's Bathing Beauties. Sennett, founder of Keystone Studios—famous for its Keystone Kops films, among other silent-era classics—frequently featured the women in comedic short films. When not on camera, the starlets raised the profile (and profits) of the studio by barnstorming. The Crown Theatre advertised in bold print: "THE FIRST BATHING GIRLS OF THE SEASON—ONLY, 'WE WON'T GO NEAR THE WATER.'" This was not just an attraction for men. Women could see the most fashionable swimwear worn by Hollywood actresses. "COME AND SEE THE LATEST, PRETTY, PACIFIC COAST BEACH COSTUMES," proclaimed the promoters. If that was not enough, the Crown Theatre informed Biloxians of the wild success of the show in Louisiana, where 38,000 "broke all attendance records in New Orleans" during the eleven-day run. The press regularly carried photographs of actresses in new, revealing designs. For instance, the *Virginia Beach News* in June 1935 showed "motion picture star" Maxine Reiner giving readers an "eyeful" by modeling a rubber bathing suit ideal "for Beach Wear."[47]

The parading of bathing beauties came naturally to boosters who thought of their beach communities as feminine. Beautiful scenery was likened to female attractiveness. Leisure was likewise feminized, contrasting with the hardworking male breadwinner. Journalist William Rivers reported on the impressive development of Saint Petersburg, Florida, during the first half of the twentieth century: "St. Pete is as frankly publicity conscious as a model trying to break into the movies." Even businesses with little association to bathing or the beach utilized images of bathing beauties. McCall's Café of Panama City boasted of its downtown location, twenty-four-hour service, and diverse menu. Advertising in the *Panama City News Herald* in October 1935, the restaurant owners included a small sketch showing tuxedoed men at tables with women in evening gowns. Such supposedly haute cuisine was juxtaposed with a sign depicting a female figure in mid-dive. "EAT AT THE SIGN OF THE BATHING GIRL," beckoned the ad. Smiths' Inc., also in Panama City, boasted of being the king of used cars during the 1950s. To capture eyes, the car dealer ran ads of a woman in a two-piece bent in a diving position. "A sight for shore eyes," cracked the caption.[48]

Promotion of bathing beauties was not merely exploitation of female sexuality. Surveys suggested that images of swimsuit-clad women spoke to a major segment of the tourism market—single working women with the wealth to vacation and mimic beauty queens or film starlets. Paul Ross reported on evidence gained from travel agents in the late 1930s. Wealthy women generally traveled in pairs, preferring long ocean cruises. Ross explained that women of the "clerk-stenographer class travel alone in search of husbands, prefer short cruises or motor trips, spend 2–3 weeks vacationing," and frequently spent all their savings. Most strikingly, more than 60 percent of all travelers were women. One travel agent declared, "Women travel to show off, to 'put on the dog.'" In contrast, wealthy men preferred isolated rural camps in the woods or boating trips in secluded locations while men of the "clerk-stenographer class" either went on "motor trips to the seashore or boating." Unlike women, men rarely spent all their savings while vacationing.[49]

The marketing of exotic dancing during the interwar and postwar periods reinforces the view that beauty pageants were aimed as much at women as at men. The Gayety Burlesk Theatre in Myrtle Beach encouraged patrons to "Bring the Ladies." Two shows nightly offered audiences of men and women comedy acts in addition to performances by dancers such as the "Blonde Bomb Shell Grace Reed." Sometimes such venues even targeted families. The Buccaneer Lounge on the Mississippi coast enticed customers with a changing array of acts during the 1950s. Madalyn King, a former Miss Omaha and Miss America contestant, tap-danced. Eleanor Lee sang while Charles and Rita Jenkins provided comedy and dance. This was wholesome entertainment. However, Cegon, the "Oil Bath Girl," supplied "Something New in the Exotic Art." And Kalantan—"Exotic Afro-Cuban Bombshell" with a "Heavenly Body"—tantalized with her scantily clad frame during three late-night dance performances. The audience enjoyed full-course dinners every night, including Sundays, and could purchase a child's plate for their youngsters, although the stage and restaurant formed separate venues. Playland Park siphoned patrons by hiring Mitsi Ray, promising that the "supple and agile darling of the French Music Halls with her exhibition of muscular control and manipulations of the body will thrill and amaze every one." Far from a seedy, male-oriented venue, Playland Park maintained twelve amusement rides and featured amateur hillbilly music competitions in its Moulin Rouge theater. An ad even showed a child enjoying an ice-cream cone.[50]

As swimwear shrank, beach towns plunged into a debate about proper dress. This debate raised two interlinked questions: (1) how little should bathers don? and (2) how far beyond the beach was swimming attire appropriate? Such issues increasingly arose after the First World War as scantier outfits promoted by fashion designers, Hollywood, and other cultural merchants—such as California or Florida boosters—challenged American attitudes toward propriety as outdoor recreation at municipal pools and beaches grew popular.[51]

Events along the Mississippi Sound exemplified the tensions over propriety. Born in New Orleans, John J. Kennedy moved to the Mississippi coast in 1897 to make his fortune as a restaurant and hotel entrepreneur. He therefore understood the concerns over swimwear when, in 1919, he became Biloxi's first mayor under the new commission system of government. Kennedy and the commissioners in April 1920 enforced a municipal ordinance restricting bathing suits. One resident complained, "The Beach is made for bathing parties . . . so lets [sic] have these suits worn along the shores and not into the photograph galleries and business houses as well as to be paraded down Howard avenue for show." Yet defining respectability was no easy task. City officials reassured locals that "costumes will be required to come within a re-spectable calling of the law and it is proposed to enforce the ordinance during the summer at which time Biloxi will be filled with bathers from all parts of the south." The language reflected the ambiguity of defining proper cuts of swimwear, the hesitancy to enforce an ordinance that might anger tourists, and the need to safeguard southern sensibilities. Outraged, a New Orleans man who frequented the Mississippi coast condemned the ban on one-piece swimsuits in a letter to Kennedy. The form-fitting outfit facilitated swimming and proved safer since the extra cloth of older suits so weighed down bathers that wearers could drown. He elaborated, "It is an old and mistaken idea that clothing fosters either modesty or morality." The mayor responded with legal gymnastics, stating that the one-piece suit was not banned while in the "wa-ters of the Mississippi sound" but restricted when in "full view of pedestrians" along the beachfront boulevard and neighborhood streets. Beachgoers needed to cover up onshore. Kennedy hoped the municipal ordinance made bathers "both comfortable and moral." Police chief George Bills soon after arrested Fred Randall and Leo Bickman. Each was fined five dollars for walking along the beachfront boulevard in a one-piece bathing suit. The Biloxi newspaper praised the arrests, though noted that Biloxi's actions had "caused comment from all parts of the country."[52]

Other communities concocted different means of sheltering eyes. A Virginia Beach ordinance during the interwar years required pedestrians to cover the upper portion of their bodies west of Atlantic Avenue, which ran parallel to the shore. "The present day abbreviated bathing is bad enough without having to see the scanty put on," complained one Virginian. Hotels, motels, cottages, and rooming houses posted the law, which carried a minimum two-dollar fine. Furthermore, the municipal government licensed bathhouses where beachgo-ers could change for a small fee. Yet bathers proved reluctant to pay. Instead, they parked in seemingly secluded residential neighborhoods before swapping their street clothes for swimwear. "They attempt by the use of towels, some wearing apparel or other non-transparent material to screen the car windows but this is not always done with the utmost of success," lamented the *Virginia Beach News* in July 1939. The newspaper condemned the "repulsive and ob-noxious" practice that hindered "those attempting to enjoy the pleasures of their front porch." However, the fear of bad publicity and the possible loss of business led "the police department to be subservient to the pleasures of the visitors of the Beach."[53]

Beaches kindled sexual flames. A cartoon from the *Panama City News Herald* in 1939 showed three women on a beach fixing their makeup. One declared, "This is the third straight winter I've come to Florida to land a husband." The beach was for romance and pregnant with sexual energy. Claude Dunnagan encouraged men "having trouble with your gal-friend, or if your marriage needs a morale booster" to venture for a nighttime drive along the Grand Strand. The moonlit ocean—and the privacy supplied by the automobile—provided "a sure remedy for a lagging romance." In 1953 a Florida lifeguard joked with a female New Yorker about her sunburn. A friend recorded, "After all according to him, Alice does not have leoprosy [*sic*] (her dusty, peeling arms), but rather summer syp——s." British commentator Alistair Cooke likewise observed, "For to most Americans Florida is not a state but a state of mind, not a place to live at all but a place to work off a year's inhibitions in a few determined weeks of pleasure." His remarks held true for many a beach resort. Military personnel, especially, celebrated the sexual implications of the beach. Exercises off the Carolinas regularly received the code name "Exotic Dancer." The mobilization of 50,000 troops, 550 aircraft, and 35 ships for the training maneuvers labeled "Exotic Dancer V" in 1972 flooded coastal recreation areas with men eager for a good time before and after the combat simulations.[54]

The Second World War dramatically altered American attitudes toward sexuality and courting, causing swimwear to shrink even further. Men such as Gauker found themselves stationed at coastal training bases where women's clothing was more spartan than in interior towns. Those shipped to the Pacific or Europe encountered a range of beaches and women with darker skin or less rigid attitudes toward sexuality. Pinups further popularized scanty swimwear. American women felt added pressure to capture men's eyes. The U.S. Census in 1942 warned southern women that they already outnumbered men by a slim margin. In the South 99.6 men existed for each 100 women. Migration to northern and western factories depleted the male cohort. Figures were better in the North, where 100.4 men courted each 100 women, and in the West, where 105.7 men sought the attention of each 100 women. Stricter immigration laws during the 1920s caused a sharp decline of foreign bachelors. The Second World War widened the imbalance between sexes. Bullets, shrapnel, and disease killed just over 405,000 men and left hundreds of thousands more physically or mentally scarred. Some ninety thousand servicemen had married foreign brides by 1946. Journalist Edmond Lebreton remarked that the "poor girl was up against hard lines, matrimonially speaking, even before she kissed the boys goodbye and saw them off to war." Southern belles, at least, found relief in the "mighty big share of the Army camps" established across the region. Yet the shortage of men encouraged sexual openness. One commentator described the numerous "unmarried women tourists" in the late 1940s as "frustrated stenographers who have read too many love story magazines" and, upon seeing veterans serving as guides or lifeguards, "get pitter-patter ideas in their hearts and often write long, passionate letters." Though advice manuals on courtship stressed female submissiveness, women felt pressure to compete for mates by revealing more of themselves to men's eyes.[55]

For resorts that long sought to separate beachwear from proper downtown dress, the improvisations made by fashion commentators created a conundrum. Renowned beauty columnist Alicia Hart, popular from the 1930s through the 1950s, celebrated beachwear: "There's no better place to have summer fun than the beach. And no nicer way to show it than in the sun clothes one wears on the sands." She urged vacationers to make their own accessories rather than go without. Hart advocated making a "dry-off dress" by attaching snaps to two beach towels so they could hang from the shoulders. A straw or canvas belt could be wrapped around the waist. For those wanting a poncho, Hart recommended taking a "big beach sheet" and cutting a hole in the center for the head. Beach bags made from two terry facecloths could also transform into sun hats.[56]

Myrtle Beach's Sun Fun Festival demonstrated a unique approach to the postwar embrace of swimwear, reversing long-held concerns about beachwear invading the streets. In June 1952 municipal leaders called on all residents and tourists to don swimwear from 6 a.m. until noon on the first day of the celebration or face either a fine or brief imprisonment in a temporary stockade. Three businessmen acted as judges while thirty-two local women served as attire inspectors. Those arrested were forced to don convict suits. The mayor and city council conducted business in swimwear, as did bankers and other townsfolk. Policemen patrolled the streets in bathing suits outfitted with holsters. *Life* magazine reported that those arrested included "a group who appeared in old-fashioned bathing suits (too modest), a man who appeared wearing only an out-size diaper (too immodest), and three Air Force officers who had picked that day to inspect Myrtle Beach as a possible leave town for trainees."[57]

Even scandalous swimwear lost some punch as Americans adapted to the international beach culture arising during the Cold War. Introduced in France in 1946, the bikini slowly gained acceptance. By 1960 bikinis accounted for 5 percent of American swimwear sales. But the style was also adapted to sleeping wear, accounting for 30 percent of bikini sales. Films and songs, such as Brian Hyland's hit "Itsy Bitsy Teenie Weenie Yellow Polka Dot Bikini" (1960), soon inspired more women to test the style. Anticipating that new designs "will probably be plentiful on U.S. beaches" in 1961, *Life* magazine noted how French designers offered daywear variations on the bikini. The magazine mused, "Fashions, like missiles, often need a trial run before they are ready for a bigtime launching."[58]

Soon bikinis were plentiful on American shores. Advertisers at home and abroad popularized the style. The French Government Tourist Office exposed the importance of swimwear in the global tourist industry when, in 1961, they ran an ad in *Harper's Magazine* asking, "What do French beaches have that American beaches don't have?" The ad answered, "In France, a beach is more than a beach. It's a chic resort or a primitive fishing village or a swanky movie colony or an off-beat artists' hangout. Want glamour? At Deauville, Cannes, Nice, or Biarritz you can ogle the world's teeniest bikinis." The popularity of French fashion and the desire to ogle or display bodies proved a potent combination among Americans. One woman commented in May 1965: "Last week half the racks were choked with bikinis, and the rest dripped enough black mesh, veiling and fishnet to make me think a school of tattered mermaids had just moulted there." Myrtle Garrick, owner of Myrt's Sportswear in Panama City, remarked in 1970, "There still are designers who create 'demure' suits that are for the feminine and modest women but the bikini is very popular and has been during the last few years." Many residents near beaches as well as tourists now wore swimwear all day as they accessorized with belts, hats, and sundresses. Garrick observed, "Some people on the beach don a swimsuit as soon as they get up in the morning. Practically their entire wardrobe is swimwear."[59]

Younger Americans, even in the South, defended a greater acceptance of sexuality during the 1960s. With films such as *Gidget* (1959), *Where the Boys Are* (1960), *How to Stuff a Wild Bikini* (1965), and *The Girls on the Beach* (1965) celebrating the sexualization of slender young women on American strands, locals faced the troubling task of keeping their houses in traditional order.[60] Women who pushed the limits of propriety risked disapproving looks, jokes, catcalls, and other harassment. A representative debate about dress occurred at Panama City's Gulf Coast Community College. A student remarked on the few young coeds who wore a "short mini-dress" on the first day of classes in 1967: "Perhaps she felt daring and sophisticated that morning, but it is doubtful if she felt that way later on in the day." Catherine Nix, dean of women, met with freshmen on two occasions to explain that the "extreme form of dress is forbidden." Several students ignored the warning. As one student observed, coeds still appeared in "dresses, skirts, and jumpers which, while perhaps fashionable in Paris, London, or Southern California, are absolutely out of place here at Gulf Coast." But such angst quickly evaporated, especially in a community where residents exposed their bodies on area beaches and dressed for relief from the stifling heat. By 1969 Ellen Caldwell noted the widespread popularity of miniskirts on campus. Caldwell chuckled, "The main problem concerning mini-skirts, it seems, is the fact that mini-skirts are comfortable. And anyone knows that when one is comfortable one forgets very important teachings, such as, how to bend down to reach an item, or how to sit properly in a chair, or how to slide into a car." Under pressure to modernize outdated clothing standards, the college administrators issued a five-point dress code for students in fall 1969. Besides prohibiting bare feet and unkempt hair or beards, officials issued rules that reflected the power of the beach to define everyday dress. "Swimming trunks or short shorts" were banned. "Any item of clothing in the category of beach wear" also faced sanction. Finally, administrators prohibited nudity in public places.[61]

Officials responsible for promoting tourism adapted to the international market. Mississippi's Miss Hospitality attended travel shows "gowned in traditional ante-bellum hoopskirt attire of the Old South" well into the 1970s. Yet most states made alterations. South Carolina officials, for example, constructed eight welcome centers, with the first to open in Myrtle Beach, by 1970. Putting a "lid on hoop skirts and ante-bellum hemlines," state administrators worked with Uniroyal to design new outfits for the hostesses behind the welcome desks and other important fairs and conventions attended around the world. The young women donned a "blue-and-white skimmer dress with sleeveless bodice and action pleats flaring to an above-the-knee hemline." For the winter, a "flaming red coat" was supplied. White boots and white, broad-brimmed hats completed the look. New York designer John Weitz, commissioned for the project, declared that "they may be modern, but they're still charming young Southern ladies."[62]

Most troubling for beach resorts, nude bathing offered escape from a world increasingly dominated by consumerism—ironic given the importance of barely clad bodies as a marketing ploy. American nudism emerged in the early 1930s, drawing inspiration from a German nudist movement birthed at the turn of the century. Originally participants argued for the healthfulness of nudism. For some bathers the naked body possessing an even tan demonstrated worldly sophistication liberated from American prudishness. Paul O'Neil, writing for *Life* in October 1967, observed, "It is possible to theorize that nakedness, as a social phenomenon, has sprung from all sorts of sources: unrest in the young, the epidemic feel of anarchy being reflected by the black rebellion and by resistance to Vietnam, disillusionment with the Puritan ethic, the 'freedom' theoretically being induced by the birth control pill, and the insistence by hippies that pleasure rather than toil is the true end of man." An emergent gay rights movement expressed through the arts and fashion also impacted attitudes toward the body. O'Neil remarked, "Nakedness (on the part of our fellow citizens, that is, rather than those of cynical Paree or the benighted Amazon) seems suddenly to have achieved acceptability in the U.S." This was far less so in the South. Nevertheless, nudists' efforts after the Second World War to free themselves from censorship, such as postal bans of nudist publications, led campaigners to challenge laws and practices that only permitted nude images of Africans and other people of color to be sent through the mail via magazines such as *National Geographic*. They likewise argued their right to bathe nude at beaches. Whereas nudists during the Depression sought to obscure the separation between nature and civilization, nudists by the 1960s symbolized political, social, and environmental protest.[63]

Clashes over nude bathing erupted sporadically along the coast. Few, except those in South Florida, dared breach this level of propriety. Doug Smith of Riviera Beach, Florida, condemned police raids on Air Force Beach in 1975. The secluded strand had grown popular for a small number of nude sunbathers. Rarely more than thirty congregated on the privately owned beach. When the *Palm Beach Post* carried a story about the beach, "huge mobs began to congregate, some to nude sunbathe, some to gawk." "Eventually the gawkers left because it wasn't the fantasy they expected (orgies)," wrote Smith to the Florida branch of the American Civil Liberties Union (ACLU). John MacArthur, the millionaire who owned the beach, had tolerated the small gatherings but now allowed the North Palm Beach police to arrest the nudists for public indecency. News that several national magazines planned to feature Air Force Beach gave MacArthur pause. The larger crowds and the risk of a lawsuit should someone become injured on his property worried MacArthur.[64] Far from riffraff, however, the nudists represented "professional people" and "several couples" who trekked from Miami and Fort Lauderdale. Retired schoolteacher Benjamin Sweeting was among them. Sweeting decried the attack on the nudists and for the intimidation of upstanding citizens who "cannot afford to be arrested and have their name in the paper" on charges of indecent exposure, thereby risking their careers. Sweeting hoped that the ACLU might intervene, as it had successfully done only months before in Dade County by arranging that arrests of nudists violated the First Amendment by infringing upon the freedoms of speech and association.[65]

But liberating the beaches for nudity carried costs. Florida nudist Jim Wiles complained, "The police are there only sporadically; the perverts are *always* there." Wiles described visiting a "virtually deserted beach" near Coconut Grove with his girlfriend in 1976. The nudists soon realized that they were not alone. A "paunchy, totally bald man" sat within nearby dunes. With one hand he held the *Miami Herald*; with the other hand he masturbated. Wiles commented, "Sick, confused, or sane, the man is using her as a sexual object—nothing more. She's not a person, she's merely something to beat off to, like a Playboy centerfold. If she has the right to take her clothes off, then he must be allowed to masturbate over her? And perhaps drool? Touch her? Rape her?" Constitutional rights to nude bathing crumbled under the pressure of voyeurism.[66]

Beach towns and state governments had little stomach for carving clothing-optional zones into state parks or municipal beaches. Even attempts to define proper beach attire remained difficult. Carole Agate, editorializing in the *Los Angeles Times* in 1981, decried discriminatory practices against women on the beach: "Laws requiring only women to keep their chests covered at public beaches stubbornly remain on the books, even though other laws that distinguish between men and women—limitations on women's work hours, rules that set different ages at which boys and girls may marry, provisions for alimony for wives but not husbands—are being declared unconstitutional at a rapid clip." Agate pointed to Clark Gable's bare-chested appearance in the movie *It Happened One Night* (1934) as the liberating moment when men could bare their breasts. Though arrests of topless men continued into the late 1930s, general disregard of the law led communities to rescind their ordinances. Agate reasoned, "When the sight of topless women of all sizes and shapes becomes commonplace, the concept of women's breasts as sex objects will go the way of their legs as sex objects."[67]

State officials nationwide labored to negotiate the rights claims of nudists with the fierce public reaction stirred by any change to clothing requirements. When nudists in the 1990s ventured to Ship Island—roughly twelve miles off the Mississippi coast—many residents condemned the activity. Sue Grace of Ocean Springs defended, "In my opinion, lumping nudists and adult sex shops together is a demonstration of pure ignorance." Yet her fellow Mississippians decried so much skin exposure as pornographic. Revisions of clothing standards presented a legal quagmire and courted a potential public backlash. When Florida officials revised clothing standards within state parks in 1990, for instance, resident John Wirth expressed outrage at the continued resistance to granting space for nudity. His letter to Governor Bob Martinez raised issues of decency that had plagued tourism boosters throughout the twentieth century. Wirth complained, "The pubic area is to be covered you say, where on a person does the pubic area start and stop? Does the hair designate the area? If this is so, would a person who shaves their pubic hair be arrested for having a small suit that covers only their genitals?" He continued, "This law also states that a female must not expose her breast from the top of the nipple to the bottom of the breast. Why is the skin on the top of the breast okay but as soon as it gets to the bottom it turns illegal? If it is the nipple that is the problem and every thing points to that, why can a male be topfree and a female must cover up?" Southern tourism boosters eager to attract the most vacationers preferred to look askance no matter how titillating the view.[68]

Given the association of beach vacations with sexuality, resorts continuously battled venereal disease. The onset of the Second World War sent officials scrambling to ease the minds of military leaders worried about losing troops to infection. One soldier recalled the health lectures common throughout the military. He described "a talk by the Chaplain in which he surprisingly didn't dwell on morals but stressed the use of prophylactics." Not everyone in uniform heeded the instructions. Galveston, as a major port and tourist resort, suffered shockingly high outbreaks of sexually transmitted diseases. Municipal leaders condemned federal proposals to convert the Pleasure Pier into a venereal disease clinic. Mayor Henry Flagg believed that "venereal infections carries [sic] with it the thought of filth" and that "you had just as well get a long piece of crape [sic] and string it from one end of the Galveston beachfront to the other if you convert the pier." Within two years of demobilization, Galveston, no longer under the stern eye of military commanders, witnessed a 50 percent increase in venereal disease rates. City leaders still waffled on opening treatment centers or clamping down on prostitution. One businessman in June 1948 noted how a "few women in clubs and bars had been picked up, but before one can be picked up it must be first determined whether or not she is a prostitute or somebody's wife." In a city crammed with tourists, inaction against unescorted women in taverns and other venues seemed wise as well as profitable. But this did little to quell the venereal disease problem. The American Social Hygiene Association in 1948 reported that, in proportion to population, Galveston had the highest infection rate for syphilis of any seaport in the United States. Again, in a 1970 study, Galveston reported the highest incidence of syphilis of any major American city with 200 cases per 100,000 population. Rates were highest among the poorest residents. Helen Smith further reported, "Gonorrhea, the other of the two most prevalent venereal diseases is so out-of-hand the health officials don't even have good estimates on it." Texas state health department official Bob Norton considered Galveston a "resevoir [sic] of infection" that spread venereal diseases across the state via tourists. He planned two free clinics to reduce the infection rate.[69]

Smaller resorts were not immune from infection. South Carolina after the Second World War regularly ranked in the top three states for venereal disease. Horry County claimed the highest infection rate in the state. One doctor reasoned, "But standards were always more relaxed, because people are coming here for vacations. They're away from home where their normal community standards operate; they're not under supervision of any sort, really. They're less inhibited and a little more likely to involve themselves in situations where they might contract one of the venereal diseases." Another physician remarked, "When you have this many people all together . . . you've got a pyramid situation; it's like a chain letter—buy one, sell two. It spreads quickly." The arrival of the birth control pill and the subsequent sexual revolution heightened risk as high school and college students along with adult vacationers increasingly trekked to the beach.[70]

Family Space

In a region where service jobs carried racial meanings and where Yankees were viewed as haughty money-grubbers, the tourist season grated against southerners' sense of community. Locals regularly expressed disgust with the antics of vacationers. Marie Gilbert recalled an adventurous couple who had an intimate rendezvous beneath her family's raised beach house—until chased away by her father. Longtime resident Mark Garner commented on the end of the tourist season: "As you say, you could closeup [sic] then, but that was the time then in the off season months that the community came together." The arrival of tourists fixated on their own pleasures even disrupted home life, especially since family-run rooming houses and motels predominated into the 1970s. Sigmund Abeles recalled growing up in his mother's rooming house in Myrtle Beach after the Second World War. He wrote, "The rest of my family used their living rooms only for their visitors, but in our case, since our home was public, we often would be interrupted by paying guests walking through and past our visiting families in dripping bathing suits, a beer in hand and Mom having to be gracious to all."[71] In 1976 the *Charlotte Observer* reported a more bitter opinion shared by Grand Strand residents: "Most permanent residents have moments when they feel like one working woman who said: 'by mid-May I want to spit on every golfer I see and pray for rain.'"[72]

Beach resorts therefore emphasized amenities that catered to families. Although men served as realtors and buyers, family grounded marketing efforts since the interwar period. W. W. Smoak, a real-estate agent in Myrtle Beach during the 1920s, received a reprimand for treating potential investors from Walterboro, South Carolina, but failing to sell. Remarking that four men escaped commitments to buy by saying they needed to consult their wives, Smoak's boss spat, "*In the future please qualify your prospects and take the wives or partners along so they can close at the beach.*" Developers of a nearby real-estate project named Arcady boasted that, unlike other resorts, the interests of women and children were not considered "secondary." Promoters trumpeted that they would "do as much for them as for the men." A brochure outlined the extensive facilities: "There will be golf courses for men and women, as well as special golf courses for the mothers and the children, salt and fresh water swimming pools for the young or timid, ball fields, archery butts, and indoor play-rooms for the children." The baby boom after the Second World War reinforced the strategy. James Elliott, reporting on affairs in Virginia Beach in 1951, declared, "Stretching in a leisurely way along the coastline for a distance of five miles, this is decidedly a resort for both medium and high income vacationers. What's more, the facilities are definitely keyed to satisfy the whole family." Hoteliers and even club owners offered playgrounds, some supervised by registered nurses. Children could also play games or ride ponies while parents spent the "whole day" fishing, swimming, or touring local sites. The babysitting was free. Businesses regularly harped on their religious devotion and family-friendly approach. The Kirklands of Panama City opened the Sombrero restaurant in the late 1950s. Customers into the 1980s were enticed by the resort's oldest Mexican eatery and appreciated its "friendly Christian atmosphere."[73]

However, urban-dwelling vacationers comfortable with franker discussions and depictions of sexuality pressured local businesses to spice up resorts. The newspapers of beach towns exposed how local values were challenged by the sexual mores of vacationing strangers, especially those from northern cities. Virgil "Red" Newton, managing editor of the *Tampa Tribune* from 1943 until 1964, noted the tensions between small-town and big-city expectations regarding coverage of sexual topics. Newton described the "difference of opinion between the big-city editors, who were interested in street and news-stand sales, and the smaller-city editors, who were interested in home delivered circulation." The different markets reflected different interests, one aimed to catch the eyes of passersby and the other to appeal to families. He elaborated how "big-city editors want less restraint in the handling of sex stories and more flamboyancy and flashiness in the Page 1 art; whereas, the smaller-city editors prefer the restraint in sex and the moderate tone of the family life covers, be they clichés or not." Newspapers in southern resorts, eager to placate resident subscribers, thus reinforced a conservative culture regarding gender roles and sex through an emphasis on the traditional family containing a male breadwinner, a doting housewife, and fun-loving children. Editors resisted the most extreme excesses trumpeted by northern press syndicates based in major urban centers such as New York City.[74]

Newspapers in beach towns shielded themselves with the rhetoric of family values even while offering risqué articles and ample images of scantily clad female sunbathers. To appeal to tourists without raising the ire of locals, businesses frequently supported tourist-oriented magazines or annual guides during the summer season. Myrtle Beach provides a prime example. Charles Joyner and William Darby began publishing the short-lived *Sun-Fun Magazine* during the mid-1950s to coincide with the similarly named festival in Myrtle Beach. The publication clearly targeted visitors. Consequently, the publication included advertising more suggestive of sexual encounters than those in the local newspaper. The Seacoast Telephone Company, for example, ran an ad about the superior long-distance service and rates available. An illustration depicted a woman in a bathing suit resting on a lounge chair on the beach. She was attended by three fully clothed men, one in a suit. One figure served her a beverage; another apparently offered a cigarette. The third man held the telephone while the woman spoke into the receiver: "I'm having a GRAND vacation!" The ad reversed gender roles, with men catering to the whims of a woman, but also carried a not-so-implicit hint of sexual freedom away from the prying eyes of home a long-distance call away. The *Grand Strand Tourist Guide* for 1974 contained a list of twenty-seven area churches as well as an ad for Pirateland and the Komo Mai Motel, which proclaimed itself a "Great Family Motel!" The back pages of the guide, however, advertised the Myrtle Beach Health Salon. The business offered "Swedish Massage—All Girl Staff." The supposedly professionally trained masseuses promised to massage away tensions between 10 a.m. and 3 a.m. This was the place, according to the ad, "Where Keyed-up Executives Unwind." In conservative Myrtle Beach, such promotions in the daily newspapers threatened a whirlwind of outrage—not to mention possible canceled ads and subscriptions. But irregular, tourist-oriented publications provided a firewall against damnation.[75]

Beach resorts confronted the uncertain waters stirred by communist threats from abroad and social upheaval from within by focusing on family life. Protests for civil rights by African Americans, women, and other groups combined with new laws and court rulings broadening Americans' rights created a conservative backlash. Many Americans in the 1960s feared the more frank discussions (and depictions) of sex in books, films, television shows, and plays. One commentator moaned, "We are drowning our youngsters in violence, cynicism, and sadism piped into the living room and even the nursery. Every Saturday evening in the Gunsmoke program, Miss Kitty presides over her combination saloon and dance hall. Even the five-year-olds are beginning to wonder what's going on upstairs." Milledge Leach of Panama City spoke for many when she offered a solution to the urban rioting, greater sexual frankness, and racial tension of the mid-1960s: "The thing that will stop this is more Christianity." By the 1970s Americans confronted defeat in Vietnam, crippling oil shortages, loss of manufacturing jobs, post-Watergate anxiety over the political system, and concern over a rising culture of narcissism. All of these, as historian Natasha Zaretsky has demonstrated, were interpreted as evidence of a faltering American family life. Zaretsky explains that the "family assumed the status of a victim, the primary locus of the nation's confusion and suffering" even while policymakers blamed those families for "producing young men unwilling to fight wars, workers unable to produce competitive goods, women no longer willing to mother, and consumers incapable of exercising appropriate restraint."[76]

Beach towns exploited their small-town religious roots, emphasizing the family in the process. When North Carolina newspapers in 1957 ran stories that Myrtle Beach profited by offering tourists "a little sin in addition to sun and sand," the Myrtle Beach press responded by stressing that "our churches are now bulging at the seams with visitors and that one of these churches is now having two morning services on Sunday." Yet locals needed to practice vigilance to keep the impression of the Grand Strand as a "family-type vacation spot." Kenneth Haynes, an African American reverend, noted the transition in Biloxi. When he first visited in the early 1960s, Haynes found a "family-oriented city" and "a Christ-conscious community." By the 1990s he saw a populace "more concerned about their economy than they are Christianity." Yet economics depended on fostering a religious aura. The political galvanization of evangelicals, a significant portion of the southern population who have vocally opposed abortion, gay rights, and feminism since the 1970s, has meant that the rhetoric of "family values" has allowed boosters to substitute the ambiguous phrase for direct religious references to Christianity, echoing earlier nondenominational rhetoric vital to bolstering tourist numbers. Indeed, evangelicals themselves adopted "family values" as a rallying cry to bridge theological differences with other religious groups, most importantly Catholics, so as to strengthen their political efforts.[77]

To protect their community's wholesome reputation, boosters organized unique national contests. When Virginia Beach launched the annual Sand Festival in 1952, the chamber of commerce invited Miss Virginia June Beach of New Jersey to serve as the first "Miss Virginia Beach." The young woman not only embodied, in female form, sexual energy but also supplied a constant and wholesome reminder of the resort. She became a walking and talking advertisement, as did similarly named women across the nation. Virginia Beach then attended Mary Washington College in Fredericksburg where, as a sophomore in 1954, she hosted a Thursday radio program called "The Chatterbox." Each time she interviewed guests, her name gave the resort free publicity on the airwaves. Her mother informed boosters several years later, "You might also be interested to know that New York City is still talking about the unusual circumstances which led up to Virginia being invited as guest of the Chamber and State and how the Sand Festival got started." Other beach towns copied the tactic. Myrtle Beach promoters in 1957 launched a national search for women named "Myrtle Beach." Contestants registered for an all-expenses-paid family vacation to the Grand Strand. The winner, Myrtle Beach of Fort Madison, Iowa, was selected because her family provided a "representative American family and the resort Myrtle beach [sic] prides itself on being a family beach." Beach's "blue eyes," twenty-two-year marriage, three children (named Sandy,

Marshy, and Rocky), and "active" role in her Methodist church and the PTA met the contest organizers' expectations.[78]

Other communities added their own wrinkle to contests designed to garner family-friendly publicity. To celebrate the fiftieth anniversary of Gulfport's incorporation in 1948, city officials and businessmen invited two couples—the Cubbages of Garland, Wyoming, and the Hairs of Williston, South Carolina—to celebrate their own golden jubilee. The highlight of the celebration was their vow renewal. The guests were showered with flowers, banquets, tours, and other prizes. Much was also made of their attendance at Sunday church services, one couple to the First Baptist Church and the other to the First Presbyterian Church, escorted by two members of the Gulfport Business and Professional Women's Club.[79]

The emphasis on family remained a staple of booster rhetoric. Archie Benton, a councilman in Surfside Beach who served for more than twenty years after being elected in 1972, noted how small municipalities attempted to control beach behavior. Benton boasted of how "mayors and the council people" successfully maintained Surfside Beach as a "family beach." The concern with supervising youth culture rested at the core of small towns' efforts. Benton commented, "Well we want the people that got young children and teenage children to come here and be comfortable, stay for a week, and not have to worry about some of the things that you see at a lot of beaches. That's where the family image comes in I think." Although not explicit in identifying the so-called things that made a beach antifamily, the emphasis on controlling "teenage children" suggests both a concern with regulating sexuality and a hesitancy to address the sexuality unleashed by the beach—as if the sheer mention of sex or alcohol would taint the town. Not surprisingly, communities along the Grand Strand celebrated native Vanna White when she gained fame during the 1980s for her role on the game show *Wheel of Fortune*. One guidebook from 1987 explained that "it's no small wonder that Vanna—who seems to embody perfectly the popular show's glamorous-wholesome dichotomy—has turned into a very hot property."[80]

Infectious Vacations

By the end of the twentieth century, sex had entered the mainstream of American society. Economist Ezra Mishan announced in *Harper's Magazine* in 1972: "Like other forms of pollution, sex pollution has become so ubiquitous that we hardly think to express our annoyance any longer." One college student in the Florida Panhandle remarked in 1990: "Our society seems to be fast becoming one in which public nudity is accepted. Contests to show more than just legs or tans are becoming a reality today not just in New York, Las Vegas and San Francisco—but yes, on the Redneck Riviera." The comment referred to the "truly obscene . . . beach club competitions" in which bars along the coast enticed customers not only with cheap shots and beer but also "wet t-shirt contests, creative banana eating contests and other better-left-unmentioned contests." Contestants off the street found themselves competing with professional strippers for cash prizes, raising the "sleazy" factor by encouraging contestants to strip or offer some other "gesture to win over the crowd."[81]

Beach resorts evidenced the changing sexual mores of Americans. Even while promoting religious virtues, promoters exploited the human body to draw tourists and increase business. The romantic setting of the beach could turn staid revivalists into adventurers. When "prominent young society girl" Lida Riley of Montgomery, Alabama, eloped to Biloxi with businessman Edward Hare of Troy, Alabama, in 1904, her parents were dumbfounded. They had all ventured to the Seashore Camp Grounds for the annual revival on the Mississippi Gulf Coast. Lida Riley was said to be an "enthusiastic Methodist . . . actively engaged in revival services" while her groom had traveled to Biloxi "ostensibly on a visit in connection with his religious obligations." But love and the adventure to the shore shunted convention. The *Atlanta Constitution* carried the story with the headline, "Desert Revival for Altar?" For subsequent beach visitors over the twentieth century, however, sex out of wedlock proved more enticing, though boosters tried to preserve a veneer of respectability. In 1974 a prominent Myrtle Beach prostitute elaborated on the development of the local sex industry: "The golfing season is the busiest . . . but this is getting to be an all-year-round town. Call girls come in from out of state—they follow the seasons, stay in hotels and go to a man's room, or he comes to hers." The easy cash tempted locals to skim some profits for themselves. Girls as young as sixteen hawked their services: "These girls probably have jobs on the side—they do it summer and winter here. There's very little of that given-away stuff, but they sell for so little it aggravates me. If they're going to sell, sell big."[82]

Richard Cole's 2002 novel *Redneck Riviera*, set along the Grand Strand, captured how the influx of tourists and chain hotels weakened the ability of locals to control the reputation of their community. Risqué bars and gaudy shops increasingly elbowed into the background the religious imagery of

Myrtle Beach. Cole's novel presents a modern Horatio Alger tale that celebrates the virgin-whore dichotomy of beach women. The book starts with Dolly Devereaux, a thirty-six-year-old reformed exotic dancer, proudly receiving a promotion to manager of the Fantasia Lingerie Store #23 in Myrtle Beach, leading her to dream of life beyond the trailer park and to ponder if *"it's even time to move up from Budweiser to Heineken's."* But the plot thickens as Dolly must redeem her daughter who became enchanted with the easy money earned by selling her body to tourists. The story of faith in bikinis is retold with a twenty-first-century twist.[83]

CHAPTER FIVE

Wet Lands

Moonshine, Gambling, and the Slow Death of Prohibition

In the late 1950s Thomas Allison, a "revenuer" at the Treasury Department's Anniston, Alabama, field office, traveled to the Florida Panhandle with his father-in-law to play golf. Returning home, they stopped at a "small beer joint" on the Florida side of the state line; many Alabama counties were dry. A woman sat in a rocking chair on the front porch. With the main entrance locked, she led her customers to the back door. Allison and his father-in-law bellied up to the bar; the woman opened two bottles of beer. She went pale when Allison opened his wallet. It was Sunday. The sight of Allison's badge frightened the bar owner, who violated the county's blue law banning alcohol sales on the Sabbath. She quickly blurted: "It's against the law to sell beer on Sunday in this county. It's not against the law though to give beer away." Allison insisted on paying. He explained, "Some of the locals had evidently given her some free advice about how not to get caught. After I showed her the badge and told her that I enforced the moonshine liquor laws only, she reluctantly took the money."[1]

Allison's account exposes the profitable, though complex, trade in alcohol—and oftentimes other vices such as gambling and prostitution—that satisfied the desires of travelers and locals alike. Giving lip service to the law on alcohol and gambling placated the more conservative, religious southern population just as beauty pageants allowed for the marketing of female sexuality within limits. Yet the persistent breach of prohibitions on alcohol and gambling satisfied the desires of travelers, including the same conservative southerners who indulged themselves while away from the prying eyes of home. As the tourism industry grew in importance to local and state economies over the twentieth century, the violation of state laws on alcohol and gambling became more open and sensational.

Entrepreneurs within the black market navigated laws that closed businesses on Sunday, restricted alcohol sales, banned gambling, and curtailed prostitution. Although resort boosters depicted their communities as moral bastions, an underground trade in vice thrived. The automobile made access to reclusive spots, transportation of contraband, and contact with consumers easier. In 1931, with some exaggeration, writer Georges Duhamel commented, "The automobile is a lever that increases all our vices, and that does not exalt our virtues." Towns from Galveston to Virginia Beach struggled with negative depictions of corruption. The political imbalance of southern legislatures favored rural—and thus more religiously conservative—counties over more liberal urban and resort areas. Ignoring state laws on vice thus represented local democracy and economic sense. The 1960s, however, brought greater federal oversight of local affairs, campaigns to ensure growing urban and suburban communities equitable representation within state legislatures, and the rise of the civil rights movement. Consequently, the illegal traffic in booze and gambling, long protected by politicians, police, and businessmen, largely ended and a modern era of increased legalization arose.[2]

Seashore Shine

Florida prohibitionists blanketed their state with tales of doom in the early twentieth century. "With the bar-room element so thoroughly interested in politics it is indeed high time for the real manhood of the State to assert itself," declared the State Temperance League in 1904. Prohibitionists saw a union of liquor dealers and bar owners corrupting state politics and eroding public morality. Some proponents stoked racial fears of drunken African Americans while a resurgent evangelical movement decried the lost ways of inebriated souls. Further galvanized by the First World War, many Americans considered prohibition a worthy measure to increase industrial efficiency and conserve grains for foodstuff. Though more and more states had instituted a ban on alcohol, a push for federal action gained momentum. In 1919 reformers cheered ratification of the Eighteenth Amendment, ordering a national ban on alcohol production and sales except for medicinal or industrial use.[3]

Moonshine claimed a long history in the United States. Backcountry settlers in the colonial era regularly converted their corn crops into whiskey. Liquor was less vulnerable to spoilage and easier to transport to market over poor roads. Settlers also found community through drinking. Through the early nineteenth century, annual per capita consumption of distilled spirits exceeded five gallons. Pioneers along the western frontier continued to distill their crops given the poor condition of internal improvements. After 1830 consumption declined to under two gallons of spirits annually, a level that has generally remained constant through the twentieth century. Distillers have harbored a strong suspicion of government ever since a federal tax sparked the Whiskey Rebellion in 1794, though Jeffersonian politicians rescinded taxes on liquor within a decade. During the Civil War, however, Congress again taxed liquor to reduce the national debt and sustain pension payments to veterans. The levy infuriated southerners, particularly—and ironically—in Unionist areas of the former Confederacy. These pockets tended to be in the most rugged parts of the South least suitable to plantation agriculture and with the most difficulty transporting crops to market. Meanwhile, temperance advocates gained traction in the late nineteenth century. State prohibition campaigns during the Progressive Era, culminating in the ill-fated Eighteenth Amendment, galvanized the black market for moonshine. Prohibition gave respectability to illegal distillers as many Americans spurned the national ban. Bootleggers, who often contributed financially to temperance advocates, enjoyed a lucrative market. Traffickers likewise paid kickbacks to politicians and law enforcement to ignore their activities.[4]

The southern coast was a major entry point for alcohol during national Prohibition. Ports such as New Orleans and Galveston experienced heavy liquor traffic. Smugglers also operated widely along shores, delivering contraband from the Caribbean, Bahamas, and Bermuda. Rumrunners found estuaries ideal for avoiding federal patrols and sand convenient for hiding deliveries. In April 1920 a small boat from the Bahamas ferried several cases of Canadian Club whiskey ashore at Gulfport, burying the contraband in the beach. Coastal resorts absorbed liquor like a sponge. In Mississippi federal agents launched a major offensive against smugglers and moonshiners over a weekend in late August 1927, destroying twenty-one "brewing plants" in Jackson, Hancock, and Harrison Counties. The raids netted 25,000 bottles of beer, 1,500 gallons of wine, 84 quarts of "genuine imported whiskey," 1,200 quarts of moonshine "colored, flavored and labelled [sic] as foreign stock," 100 quarts of "synthetic gin," and 63 gallons of pure moonshine. Such bootlegging and smuggling cast long shadows. E. J. Cain operated a shrimp boat along Bayou la Batre, Alabama, in the late 1930s. When approached by a WPA interviewer, Cain eyed him with suspicion. Though his boat no longer smuggled liquor from Cuba to Mobile, "revenue men" still kept track of the vessel.[5]

Liquor lubricated beach vacations. The *Princess Anne Times* decried the "frantic and nefarious prohibitive activities" raging across the country during the 1910s. Corrupt county politicians resisted, sheltering producers and sellers. New York governor Al Smith, immediately after his defeat in the presidential election of 1928, headed to the Edgewater Gulf Hotel for a week of relaxation— aided by highballs. Armand Fountain noted that life in Biloxi during the interwar years was lean. But he profited from producing beer and scuppernong wine, storing the jugs under the baseboards of his house: "I made my own home brew—enough to float this house with." In 1932 U.S. representative Tom Yon, a Democrat from the Florida Panhandle, voiced his constituents' "widespread dissatisfaction with prohibition."[6]

The suppression of bars stripped resorts of lively entertainment and places for social gathering. Many men had frequented saloons for their camaraderie. Many women, who had rarely entered saloons before Prohibition, increasingly chafed at the ban. Worse, restrictions on wine and liquor damaged the restaurant business, especially in historic towns such as Galveston, New Orleans, Mobile, and Charleston, where cherished recipes included these ingredients.[7]

By the time of Prohibition's repeal via the Twenty-First Amendment in 1933, American perceptions and practices of drinking had changed. Prohibition made the consumption of alcohol a political statement supporting individualism and liberty. Booze emerged as a fashionable beverage, a symbol of cosmopolitanism, linked to posh speakeasies and jazz clubs. Young women increasingly joined men in such places as they rebelled against dying Victorian moral standards that placed women on pedestals and restricted them to the domestic sphere. Furthermore, the continued enjoyment of liquor reflected a changing America in which automobiles shrank distances and made policing morals more difficult. One Floridian remarked in 1929 that the "bulk of small filling stations in Florida are bootleg joints with gasoline as a stall."[8] Some housewives, long championed as the greatest benefactor of prohibitionists since husbands could no longer spend wages on drink, made home brew to bolster domestic finances. With the Twenty-First Amendment, the battle against Prohibition fell back to the states. The wets had won the struggle to repeal national Prohibition, but the fight to rescind prohibition laws at the state and county levels had just begun. These became intense political debates about personal liberty and the tourism economy. As a result, attacks on state and local prohibition laws merged with attacks on laws restricting amusements on Sundays.[9]

Moonshine maintained a strong hold on the American South. Some championed the independence of home production. Charley Ryland enjoyed a secluded life along the rivers of Alabama. Asked in 1938 if he brewed his own whiskey, Ryland declared, "Hit's th' only way I'd drink it." Others likened moonshine to a cultural staple. In 1954 William Lundy shot a buck while hunting on Eglin Air Force Base. He boasted, "Boy, it felt good. Just like I had taken a good swig of homemade 'skeeter juice." Lundy was no ordinary deer hunter. At 106 years old, he was one of three living Confederate veterans. Moonshine was a cherished southern tradition.[10]

In conjunction with temperance laws, Progressive Era legislatures passed new blue laws while reformers urged stricter enforcement of those already on the books. For example, rural Mississippians, like many Americans, disapproved of modern encroachments such as movie showings and professional baseball games on the Sabbath, a day traditionally devoted to church-related gatherings and socials. Law enforcement officials in resort towns along with sympathetic judges frequently leveled meager fines against offenders, thus paying lip service to blue laws through a legal ritual that upheld the letter of the law while mocking its spirit.[11] Opinions in Mississippi demonstrated a common resistance to blue laws from resorts. In 1921 C. Von Tinglestadt of Biloxi sneered, "Now, in all fairness, do any of those who started this blue law enforcement for one moment imagine that tourists will come to this coast?" Others emphasized the hypocrisy of blue laws. A self-described conscientious citizen from Biloxi complained, "Yes these blue people can ride around up and down the beach on Sunday afternoon. There is plenty of gasoline stations open to supply them with gas and besides the chauffeurs don't mind working on Sunday. No [sic] if these chauffeurs would ask for their Sunday off these blue law leaders would want to kill him." Sporadic enforcement of the blue law against movie theaters ended in 1929 when a jury refused to convict operators of the Strand Theatre in Gulfport. Reporting on Mississippi's three coastal counties, George Coad of the *New York Times* observed, "Little by little they have ignored the blue laws and bit by bit they have amended other laws to give the State a more nearly reasonable attitude toward capital." The Mississippi legislature repealed the antebellum blue law banning all Sunday business in the late 1950s.[12]

The blue law debate marked a shift in American working culture, as more and more laborers enjoyed higher wages, shorter work weeks, and paid vacations. Sunday, a Christian day of rest, became a battleground over leisure time. New technologies such as the automobile and airplane required a service sector of hotels, restaurants, gas stations, and other businesses. The emergence of the two-day weekend and paid vacation made arguments for preventing labor on Sunday impractical. By the Second World War, support for blue laws ebbed, though many states retained watered-down blue laws into the late twentieth century.[13]

Blue laws threatened prosperity. As legal scholar Peter Wallenstein shows, the Virginia legislature's decision in 1932 to sanction gasoline sales on Sundays recognized the importance of tourism. Wallenstein argues, "tourism, by its nature, invalidated any assumption of an immutable sum of sales. If Sunday sales from customers in transit add a bonus to local sales . . . then Sunday sales did not simply spread a fixed sum of sales across an additional day." In other words, blue laws reduced business profits and tax revenues given the shifting demographics and economy of the South. In 1962, for instance, the Greater Myrtle Beach Chamber of Commerce supported changes to the state blue laws. The revision attempted to "prevent inroads into the commercialization of Sunday, and, at the same time, to permit the sale of articles and services that have become generally accepted as being reasonably essential to health, comfort, and our present-day way of life." The modernized blue laws would ensure "no curtailment of Sunday recreation and business activities . . . accepted as reasonably essential in the Myrtle Beach Grand Strand area and other resorts of South Carolina." The reform reflected the growth of tourism, cities, and powerful retail chains.[14]

As with blue laws, the struggle against prohibition took decades, typically fought one county at a time. After ratification of the Twenty-First Amendment, state legislatures quickly authorized the return of beer and wine to barrooms, restaurants, and stores, though under licenses granted by state and local Alcohol Beverage Control Boards (ABC), as the agencies were often called.[15] Liquor proved far more controversial. Virginia, Alabama, and North Carolina opted for the dispensary scheme for hard alcohol. The system involved the state ABC acting as retailer of spirits in communities desiring a store. The state thereby regulated access to hard alcohol as well as set prices. Sales by the drink were banned. Virginia established its state dispensary system in May 1934. Stores operated in Richmond, Norfolk, Virginia Beach, and other metropolitan areas. The authorized sale of booze coincided with a vigorous federal crackdown on moonshiners. Protecting legal liquor safeguarded tax revenues for cash-strapped municipal, state, and federal governments during the Depression. However, as some Virginians complained by 1940, the high taxes on alcohol hindered tourism and made it "profitable for the bootlegger to operate in competition." Fear of state crackdowns encouraged the collusion of county and municipal officials with illegal distillers.[16]

Other legislators, as in Texas, Louisiana, South Carolina, and Florida, authorized a state ABC then passed the legalization issue for beer, wine, and liquor to the counties via local option legislation. Unlike Louisiana, Texas and South Carolina resisted by-drink sales of liquor into the 1960s. Mississippi opted for a different course. The Magnolia State legalized beer in 1934 but otherwise maintained prohibition into the 1960s.

The tourism industry made alcohol a boon. For example, the ABC store in Virginia Beach witnessed a tenfold increase in sales during the summer. In November 1934 the store's two employees processed approximately $300 in sales each Saturday. Such was common for "small town establishments." That contrasted with the $3,000 worth of liquor typically sold every Saturday during the summer when six employees catered to customers.[17]

Even after legalization, conservative southerners prevented sellers of intoxicating beverages from blatantly hawking their wares. The Virginia ABC quieted wholesalers and retailers in 1938 by banning the words "beer" and "wine" from signs. Signs advertising liquor were also prohibited. Instead, stores could only announce that they carried an ABC license in letters not exceeding five inches in height, "making it rather difficult for the nearsighted to learn whether he can or cannot buy a glass of beer," joked one Virginian. The order altered the streetscape of Virginia Beach. The local newspaper reported, "Many small Neon beer and wine signs in Virginia Beach must go, together with a good number of small highway signs located along the roads leading to the Beach." A similar tightening of the law occurred in South Carolina. The South Carolina ABC stipulated in July 1939 that merchants could carry no advertising on their buildings "but the name of the dealer, the number of his license, and the words, 'wholesale liquor dealer', or 'retail liquor dealer.'" Proprietors also needed to operate on a cash basis. The *Myrtle Beach News* reported, "Illegal signs were therefore being painted out; necessitating new coats for the entire buildings." Under Mississippi's local option law enacted in the mid-1960s, liquor stores were required to mask the interior. The measure, like those in South Carolina and Virginia, was short-lived. A string of robberies convinced the legislature to permit storeowners to uncover windows in 1968.[18]

Dry advocates saved their most vitriolic attacks for by-drink legalization. In 1946 Chauncey Leake seethed over the "abominable taverns and drinking places" in Galveston. He expounded, "No systematic attempt is made by our merchants or citizens to make Galveston a clean, neat and pleasant place for visitors to come. On the contrary we develop all sorts of rackets to irritate and fleece them." As late as the 1960s, prohibitionists, such as Baptist preacher Joe Tuten of Biloxi, raged against legalization proponents: "Murder is one of the first of crimes and I think we might as well legalize murder as something like this." Through the 1960s, prohibitionists in local-option states campaigned for new referendums to reverse the wet tide in counties with alcohol sales. Prohibitionists emphasized the role of alcohol in worsening crime rates, increasing alcoholism, and decreasing highway safety. They seized on a two-year study published in the *Journal of Criminal Law, Criminology, and Police Science* shortly after the Second World War. The analysis showed that 72.7 percent of persons arrested had been drinking. They also cited a 1962 study by Rutgers University that the "34 states with liquor by-the-drink have 50% more alcoholics per capita than do the 12 states with bottle sales only." Prohibitionists attacked the cost of regulating by-drink sales and dismissed claims that liquor boosted tourism. The example of Gatlinburg, Tennessee, loomed large by attracting more than three million tourists annually without authorizing any liquor licenses.[19]

State restrictions preserved scattered, highly localized black markets for illegal hooch, breeding political corruption. Cooper Darby, who headed Mississippi Gulf Coast Community College during the 1930s before becoming chancery clerk in Harrison County, noted that residents of coastal Mississippi "never have really believed in enforcing" prohibition. "Everybody knew that there were places where you could get whiskey everywhere," explained Darby. Elected officials therefore reflected the will of local voters and ignored state prohibition laws. Wilson Evans recalled how his mother operated a bustling bar, complete with slot machines, for fellow African Americans in De Lisle, Mississippi, after the Second World War: "It was part of Harrison County, and my mother had connections with the sheriff. You know, you just didn't run a nightclub back in those days." Payoffs to law enforcement became standard practice for proprietors of liquor and gambling joints. When conventioneers or tourists came to the coast, they flocked to illegal bars. Even state legislators could not resist the temptation. Biloxi businessman William Hubbell recalled one particular gathering of state legislators at the coast: "These same legislators that were so dry, that had been on record for voting against legalized liquor for so long, believe it or not, they were going around that hotel not with one highball but one in each hand!" When the Virginia Beach police department bought five new patrol cars and a Cadillac for police chief Reeves Johnson in 1950, rumors swirled about hefty kickbacks from local bars and gaming halls. "That the police are parties to a pay-off from the interests which control gambling and the bootleg sale of whiskey by the drink in the so-called 'clubs' is a widely accepted concept," declared the *Virginia Beach News*.[20]

Resorts closed ranks when threatened by investigators. When a grand jury in 1950 indicted twenty-three individuals in Virginia Beach for gambling while ABC officers raided illegal bars, residents who aided the investigations were shunned. A country club denied privileges to a member who had testified. A business owner who revealed information to the grand jury lost contracts and had his delivery truck driver threatened. The Virginia Beach chapter of the American Legion denied use of its meetinghouse to an organization with a member subpoenaed by the grand jury—a person who proved too outspoken for local tastes.[21]

During the 1960s Bay County sheriff M. J. "Doc" Daffin faced allegations that he protected an extensive network of moonshine and bolita operations. State investigators gathered evidence suggesting the complicity of Panama City police chief Ira Ross. Roscoe Owens, whom an informant described as a "big Negro at this time," allegedly handled the cash pickups for the sheriff. Investigators thought I. M. Kickliter served as the white boss of the bootleggers while Sollie Culverhouse, a white woman, managed bolita operations. Edgar Jones, another informant, had once been close to the sheriff and maintained ties to the moonshine trade. In one incident Daffin arrested Jones and James Hooten for the burglary of a Jitney Jungle store, from which they stole sacks of sugar to sell to moonshiners. Daffin interrogated them, eager to learn of any upstart bootleggers. Jones further "accused the Sheriff of getting it [sugar] from the jail supply" to furnish stills under Daffin's protection.[22]

To safeguard their interests, Daffin, Ross, and Panama City chief of detectives Doc Barron leaned on Jones to incriminate John Henry Stanley, a Panama City policeman who offered state investigators testimony that, Barron explained to Jones, "was very bad and would hurt Ross." Hooten recalled how "Officer Stanley had been 'knocking off' some of the men selling whiskey for Doc Daffin and they wanted Stanley put out of the way." Barron urged Jones to implicate Stanley in the Jitney Jungle burglary. An hour after Barron left Jones's cell, Ross arrived to urge the prisoner to testify that Stanley had told Jones locations where the police were staked out in return for a cut of the loot. Another half hour passed before the sheriff had Jones brought to his office. Daffin denied Jones, facing a fifteen-year sentence for the burglary, an attorney and refused to allow Jones's uncle to post bond. When Jones and Hooten refused to accuse Stanley, Daffin, according to Jones, "went to pieces." He ordered a deputy to "put them on cold steel," removing the mattresses from their cells and refusing them any visitors. Jones and Hooten still resisted. Despite such reports, state investigators in July 1961 admitted encountering "purely rumor and suppositions" that nevertheless "established the extensive unmolested nature" of gambling and moonshine operations in Bay County. Investigators, a few months later, had gathered enough evidence for the governor to remove Daffin from office, only to see him win the next election.[23]

Even state intervention in county affairs met resistance. A sting operation at the Town Pump and Boulevard Room near Pensacola, Florida, in 1961, led to the arrest of Betty Mendoza and Rita Johns. When the Beverage Department agents went before Justice of the Peace Walter Lagergren, they met a "tirade" about entrapment and the policing of morality. Lagergren asked agent R. H. Comfort to define "lasciviousness or lewdness." Comfort replied, "When I told him that I had been fondled publicly by the girl and that she in turn had placed my hand upon her female sexual organs publicly, he then stated 'Well, isn't that what men go in there for?'" The judge lambasted the "do-gooders in the Legislature." Adult activity such as boozing and prostitution was acceptable. Lagergren encouraged a "European viewpoint on morals" in which women were either chaste or "a prostitute and classed as such." He disdained a new state law prohibiting b-drinking, in which hired women hustled men to buy overpriced beverages. "It's the prerogative of the girl to ask the man to buy her a drink if they previously had established a friendly relationship," explained the judge as he dismissed the charges.[24]

Stills dotted the landscape and smuggling rings thrived. Born in 1904, Andrew Stanley of Horry County recalled liquor distilled from cornmeal and molasses. John Taylor, a fisherman and packinghouse worker who lived in a shack on the Pascagoula River in Mississippi regularly purchased illegal whiskey called "stoop-down." Jim Kelly, recalling life along the Mississippi coast in a 1979 interview, asserted that the area long claimed a "terrific amount of moonshiners."[25]

Most of the moonshine trade was concentrated in the South. Federal statistics on stills destroyed by agents in 1955 identified the extent of bootlegging: North Carolina (2,673 stills), Georgia (1,865 stills), Alabama (1,703 stills), South Carolina (1,421 stills), Tennessee (1,345 stills), Virginia (707 stills), Mississippi

(663 stills), Kentucky (633 stills), Florida (424 stills), Texas (65 stills), and Louisiana (9 stills). In comparison, Michigan only had 107 stills raided. A report from May 1960 identified sixty-one stills destroyed in Horry County over the previous year. In 1961 Florida agents in the Panhandle destroyed dozens of stills. The officers busted thirty-four operations in Calhoun County, sixteen in Holmes County, fifteen in Washington County, thirteen each in Jackson and Okaloosa Counties, ten each in Bay and Walton Counties, two in Gulf County, and one each in Franklin and Liberty Counties. These represented 17 percent of the 671 stills discovered across the state that year.[26]

Stills particularly flourished near state and county borders. The ability to cross jurisdictions allowed producers to avoid crackdowns by entangling law enforcement in procedural red tape often involving municipal, county, state, and federal officials. In 1956, for example, Mississippi governor James Coleman instructed the highway patrol to rigorously enforce prohibition: "Enforce all the laws and that means the liquor laws. Don't let me hear tell of some bootlegger running over you or buying you." But he also noted that state troopers had no right to interfere with interstate transit, subject to federal law. Coleman clarified, "When you catch him and are convinced he is not in interstate shipment, break it, (the liquor), where you find it." The governor quickly added, "And remember, you're on patrol to chase violators of the law . . . not skirts." During the early 1960s bootlegger Jurow Gibson of Panama City received five five-gallon jugs each weekend from a still operator in neighboring Washington County. Gibson's liquor thereby crossed two counties and involved a municipality. Catherine Lewis of Horry County recalled the dangers of traversing the Jam, an area near the border with North Carolina. One snooping revenuer was burned in his car. "And law officers were careful when they went into a place like that," Lewis noted.[27]

Other operations stretched farther afield. The Gulf Coast from the 1960s through the 1980s harbored a criminal syndicate known as the Dixie Mafia, which trafficked in illegal liquor, gambling, and other criminal ventures ranging from dogfighting to contract killing. Dixie Mafia operations stretched across the South, though Biloxi served as headquarters. Mike Gillich, a Biloxian of Croatian ancestry who operated a bingo hall and nightclubs that doubled as strip joints and gambling dens, claimed leadership. The Dixie Mafia maintained ties with a similar criminal network known as the State Line Mob on the Mississippi-Tennessee border. The Mob was partly populated by criminals who had fled a 1950s crackdown in Phenix City, Alabama. City officials there, backed by local mobsters, catered to soldiers at nearby Fort Benning, Georgia, by providing illegal gambling, liquor sales, prostitution, and drugs. Reformers were literally beaten on the streets. In June 1954 Albert Patterson, a Phenix City resident, gained the Democratic nomination for state attorney general on a law-and-order platform. Patterson was gunned down days after the primary. The governor placed Phenix City under martial law. National Guardsmen patrolled the streets and supervised local elections. A grand jury subsequently issued 569 indictments. The brazen criminal syndicate was broken, but some found new opportunities with the Mob. During the 1970s the State Line Mob, notorious for violence, gained national attention for an assassination attempt on McNairy County sheriff Buford Pusser of Tennessee, whose war on the Mob inspired the film *Walking Tall* (1973).[28]

Still operators thrived, even within town limits. In November 1939 Virginia Beach children discovered a small still along with five barrels of mash hidden just two hundred yards from the police chief's home. Large stills were also common. U.S. Treasury agents uncovered a distillery three miles west of Pass Christian, Mississippi, in March 1960. Oliver and Fred Scarborough faced charges of operating a thousand-gallon still. Agents also seized sixty 60-gallon drums and one 950-gallon vat used for fermentation. The officials destroyed 4,180 gallons of whiskey mash. In 1962 the Virginia Beach Water Department investigated a leak. Whereas the average family used at most ten thousand gallons in a two-month period, the residence of Ray Hutcheson registered ninety thousand gallons. A repairman discovered no leak but a strong smell of whiskey. Police found a garage fitted with twelve 275-gallon drums, a specially built chimney, and hoses fitted with pumps that drained into the swamp at the rear of the property. The still produced 324 gallons every four days. The court, however, dismissed all charges for lack of evidence.[29]

For some, the desire for a drink represented a personal right. A. H. Nall, director of Mississippi's state park system, commented on tourists who carried their own cultural expectations—and liquor. "The only real difficulty we have ever had to amount to anything has been involved with the drinking of alcoholic liquors in our parks," Nall informed fellow state park directors in 1951. He explained, "We found out that people from Louisiana are used to drinking beer and whiskey wherever they please. When they come to the parks in Mississippi, they think they should do it there." Pat Christy of Virginia Beach reasoned, "So if a cocktail is my pleasure, I certainly should be able to get it at Virginia Beach as I might in Washington, New York, or Miami." Clarke Mann, speaking for the Virginia Hotel Association in 1962, argued for "the right of the people to decide for themselves issues that by nature" rested at the local level. "That is in the finest Virginia tradition. It is the heart of States Rights," proclaimed Mann. The United States Brewers Association maintained a national campaign from the 1940s through the 1960s that equated beer with liberty. A spokesman described a 1910 photograph of beach bathers "smothered" in swimsuits more like "street-wear." The spokesman equated modern swimwear to the enjoyment of beer: "From where I sit, tolerance that lets us wear sensible, decent clothes—to give us sun and air and freedom—will keep that wholesome glass of beer a part of the American tradition." Another ad proclaimed, "Your familiar glass of beer is also a pleasurable reminder that we live in a land of personal freedom." The rhetoric of democracy and capitalism common during the Cold War eroded support for rigorous alcohol control laws.[30]

By the 1960s southern states considerably loosened restrictions as campaigns for by-drink sales on a local-option basis gained momentum. Larry Boulier of Myrtle Beach cited a national survey to show that South Carolina possessed the highest liquor prices in the nation. The legal stipulation that liquor be sold in stores and consumed in private proved counterproductive. His arguments echoed those heard wherever prohibition of spirits remained. Boulier questioned state regulations: "But in these efforts have we created a Frankenstein? When we make laws that draw illegal operators like flies, we open the door to other racketeering operations." He continued, "Before sun down, the bootlegger who delivers goods from the raw still has an advantage of price cutting. After sun down, he can match the bottled-in-bond price while the bootlegger handling the bottled-in-bond goods can get fabulous prices either by the bottle or the drink." Dawn-to-dusk stores, high-priced whiskey, and laws against spirits sold by the drink created a cocktail that inspired vice on par with "Chicago during the roaring twenties."[31]

Rather than boosting tax revenue, drawing tourists, and reducing crime, state statutes restricting liquor had the opposite effect. A 1960 editorial from South Carolina not only noted the "staggering" losses in tax revenue but also the cost of fighting bootleggers and corruption. From Virginia to Texas, proposals for by-drink sales appeared. In a poll of the Greater Myrtle Beach Chamber of Commerce in 1966, 90 percent supported extending hours during which liquor could be sold; 91 percent supported by-drink sales. In 1967 the Galveston Chamber of Commerce argued that long-standing laws banning by-drink sales were "impossible to enforce." Legalization "would provide a substantial source of income for the state." Freedom to purchase cocktails would also aid the tourism industry. "The economy of the state is hurt because of the present liquor laws which also negatively affect Galveston's economic gains in the tourist industry," argued city leaders.[32]

Proponents of liquor sales by drink snatched the banner of temperance during the 1960s. With tourism emerging as a billion-dollar industry in Virginia, advocates for by-drink sales, as in other southern states, stressed how "those visiting our state from other areas of the nation are genuinely disappointed when they do not find all the comforts of home offered them while visiting us."[33] The Virginia Hotel Association pointed to statistics from Oregon, Washington, and Idaho, all of which had legalized by-drink sales after the Second World War. Each witnessed a subsequent decline in alcohol consumption—by 10.5 percent in Oregon, 10 percent in Washington, and 37.3 percent in Idaho. In other words, those who purchased a bottle were less likely to consume only one or two glasses. The evidence undermined the view that alcohol by drink resulted in more drunken driving and crime. Statistics showed that Virginia ranked eleventh in per capita consumption of alcohol despite its by-bottle dispensary system. The argument convinced Henry Howell and Calvin Childress, both of whom served as Sunday school teachers as well as members of the Virginia House of Delegates representing Norfolk. They jointly authored a bill in 1960 to introduce a local-option, liquor-by-drink plan. Although the bill failed to leave committee, supporters formed the Virginia Local Option Reform Committee (VALOR) in 1961 to build momentum. The legislature sanctioned liquor by drink on a local-option basis in 1968. Virginia Beach residents supported legalization by a two-to-one vote.[34]

Arguments that bottle sales facilitated drunkenness far more than by-drink sales gained traction. In July 1967 the South Carolina legislature authorized the ABC to oversee a new brown-bagging law that allowed members of private nonprofit clubs to keep liquor in their lockers as well as permitted bartenders to pour drinks at public restaurants from a customer's bottle. The battle for by-drink sales in South Carolina lasted until February 1973, when the state legislature finally allowed such sales—but by bottle. Bartenders could only sell spirits via mini-bottle, thereby supposedly regulating the amount of alcohol in each cocktail. Rural county senators had struggled to delay passage of even this compromise measure. State senator John Martin of Fairfield mourned, "The people are going to realize that we have sold them down the river to get the tourist trade."[35] Even advocates were frustrated. Sue Collie, a lounge waitress in Myrtle Beach, commented, "I think it is the first step to liquor-by-the-drink but I still don't like it. It has cut down our tips because it's so expensive. It's a real hassle for blended drinks." Cocktails often required the sale of a mini-bottle even though only a portion was needed, thereby increasing waste. David Threlkel, a bar owner, complained that the Maryland tax on a case of mini-bottles was $4.50, whereas the South Carolina tax on a case amounted to $64.50. He elaborated, "The state is now having to hire extra people to keep owners from bootlegging and tax payers are paying for that too." Yet the mini-bottle law stayed on the books until 2005.[36]

Health concerns over moonshine facilitated the move toward liberalization of liquor laws. Brewers and distillers launched advertising campaigns that stressed the health benefits of alcohol as early as the 1930s. Targeting Mississippi, a beer ad for Schlitz hawked the beverage as a "health-giving predigested food." The company urged, "Order a case for your family." Though dubious, the health benefits of legal alcohol were better than illegal hooch. Moonshiners often welded stills with lead solder and used automobile radiators, likewise bound by lead solder, in stills. The lead leached during the distilling process. Worse, moonshiners occasionally gathered dirty jars from dumps, not cleaning them sufficiently before pouring their product. Blindness, convulsions, and paralysis could result. In 1961 at least eight persons died and thirty faced hospitalization from poisonous moonshine in the Winston-Salem, North Carolina, area alone.[37]

The rights crusade sweeping the United States during the 1960s challenged the last pockets of statewide prohibition—few places more so than Mississippi, where arguments over civil rights and state sovereignty brought scrutiny of state laws. Biloxi supervisor Dewey Lawrence decried the embarrassing failure of the ban: "Mississippi was the first state in the union to adopt a bone-dry law, and although it is a dry state, it is known to be the wettest state in the union, which is evidenced by the collection of black market tax."[38] The Mississippi legislature, without a plebiscite, in 1944 enacted a "tax levied on the sale of tangible personal property the sale of which is prohibited by law." More popularly known as the black market tax, the measure placed a levy on liquor and wine purchased by Mississippi dealers who imported the illegal beverages from states with legal sales. By the 1960s the state treasury reaped nearly $3 million annually from the tax. The *New York Times* described Mississippi as suffering from "legal schizophrenia." Illegal booze was big business in the Magnolia State. Estimates suggested liquor sales of approximately $35 million each year during the 1960s. Wholesale businesses in Louisiana, with some of the South's most liberal alcohol laws, lined the border. Attorney Clem Sehrt, representing the Louisiana Wine and Spirit Foundation, described the system in a 1960 interview: "A Mississippi liquor buyer coming to Louisiana first must have a federal tax stamp, then he presents himself to a Louisiana wholesaler. Then the Louisiana wholesaler has a list of these stamp holders, and so does the Mississippi collector who collects the Mississippi black market tax. Then Louisiana puts a 30-cent inspection stamp on each export case. The Mississippi truck driver then must depart on a specific route assigned to him." The black market tax amounted to $4.50 a gallon. "These buyers purchase 100 or 125 cases at a time," remarked Sehrt.[39] Even prohibition advocates noted that Mississippi had become "the laughing stock of the nation because of its double standard liquor laws." In Harrison County, Sheriff Curtis Dedeaux estimated that 40 percent of liquor along the coast escaped the black market tax as bar owners and retailers smuggled cases of spirits bought in New Orleans. Rankin County, in central Mississippi, claimed thirty retail liquor dealers and three wholesalers, according to federal liquor stamp records in 1960. These figures came from a county where nearly 75 percent of voters in a 1952 statewide referendum supported prohibition. The unofficial alliance of bootleggers and ministers undermined reform in the state.[40]

On 1 July 1966 Mississippi, the bastion of prohibition, became the last state to surrender to the wet tide. In the early 1960s local-option advocates launched a vigorous campaign. Wet legislators cleverly pushed for strict enforcement of prohibition. They supported a bill to send the National Guard to police the state's borders while making the possession, transportation, or sale of liquor a felony. Prohibitionists opposed the measure since a similar tactic had been employed in Oklahoma to dry up the state in preparation for a referendum that ended prohibition in 1959. The revolution in voting rights and the looming reapportionment of a legislature long dominated by rural counties tipped the scales in favor of wets. After fifty-eight years of statewide prohibition, forty-two of Mississippi's eighty-two counties voted to allow liquor stores and by-drink sales. The first legal shipment of whiskey into Mississippi arrived under police escort at the Broadwater Beach Hotel in Biloxi on 27 July 1966. The Mississippi ABC reported net earnings of almost $9.4 million on gross sales of $28.2 million in the first year. For a state struggling to offset negative publicity about racial violence and backwardness that hurt business investment and tourism, legalization filled state coffers with tax revenue as well as furthered the recovery of the tourism industry. The days of Prohibition were over.[41]

Skin Game

By his eighty-fourth birthday in 1958, John Herbert Peck had seen Florida transform into a tourist haven. Peck recalled how, in the late nineteenth century, the "Florida cracker . . . skinned alligators in the Summer and tourist [sic] in the Winter." Peck recognized the importance of cutting a profit from the tourist trade. And gambling provided one of the sharpest knives. Florida offered excellent opportunities for "'poets,' gamblers and thieves," chuckled Peck. Edgar Cole of Durham, North Carolina, agreed. Coming to Florida for work in 1909, Cole wrote his family about the "wickedest boys here I ever saw": "If I have had come down here twelve months sooner I would have been ruint [sic] for ever they curse drink and gamble all the time when not at work."[42]

Gambling claimed a long history in the American South. From colonial times through the antebellum era, betting on horse races and cockfights, among other sports and games, provided venues for planters to display wealth. The prestige of high-end betting, whether at illegal casinos or legal racetracks, remained through the twentieth century. For poorer southerners, wagering provided camaraderie, competitive play, and, according to historian Jackson Lears, "masculine self-testing, a highwire act without a net." As women increasingly gained employment after the mid-nineteenth century, they too took chances in lotteries, cards, horseracing, and other games, though a stigma against women gamblers persisted into the mid-twentieth century. Southern states slowly increased legalization of gambling—whether of casinos, lotteries, and horse or dog tracks—over the twentieth century. The region also continued to harbor more controversial gaming; Louisiana in August 2008 became the last state to ban cockfighting.[43]

Florida's treatment of gambling guided much of the legalization debate. Desperate for funds during the Depression, legislators authorized pari-mutuel betting on dog and horse racing in 1931. Jai alai fontons were legalized in 1935. A conservative Miami mother in 1939 despaired: "We don't drink, nor gamble on the horses nor dogs, which so many people do in a town like this." Yet legalized gambling proved a financial boon for highway construction, state universities, and other programs. By the 1960s Florida had approved harness, quarter horse, and summer horse and dog racing to take advantage of the rise in summer tourism. The sportswriter Jack Kofoed joked, "Though not so dependent as Nevada on professional chance taking, the state's financial britches would need patching if gaming were outlawed." By 1977 total state tax revenue from tracks and fontons amounted to more than $86 million annually. Only legalized slot machines, permitted briefly in the 1930s, fell to a repeal campaign for fear of enticing organized crime.[44]

The increased military presence in the South stimulated illegal gambling. The First World War spread interest in games of chance as soldiers visited casinos in Europe or gambled amongst themselves. Paul Green described the rampant gambling at his post in South Carolina in 1918: "The camp is happy tonight, and the dice are rattling in almost every tent down the line." Green prophesied that "it's easy for people to condone this gambling among soldiers, but mark my word, when the soldiers have become civilians again the old spirit will still be there." Cultural critic George Coad observed that many Gulf Coast politicians who condoned alcohol and gambling during the 1920s had been "in the army and all of them have had more contact with the world—or sin if you like—than their fathers had." The opening of more military bases during the 1930s and 1940s encouraged illegal gambling among bored soldiers with government pay. A soldier stationed in Florida in 1942 urged his friend to enlist: "You won't have a worry in the world. You will even learn to drink, shoot crap, and even how to pick up women. You can't miss." Hollis Alger, stationed in Mobile, Alabama, wrote home in 1943: "Today is pay-day. . . . There are several games going already, and one can pick from black-jack, poker, shooting dice, rummy and about any others."[45]

Law enforcement handled violators with velvet gloves. Floridians remained skeptical when Governor Fred Cone launched a statewide crackdown on illegal gambling in 1939. The *Tallahassee Democrat*, in an editorial carried across the state, mused, "Florida is more or less accustomed to March anti-gambling crusades on the lower east coast. At the end of the season on the gold coast, a drive against gambling establishments serves the purpose of showing the public that the officers are alert and determined to enforce the law." The newspaper added, "A drive in January or even in February would stop more gambling but would be regarded as somewhat rude by the operators, who are accustomed to being closed at a time when they are ready to close."[46] Raids by Virginia Beach police chief Dodson in 1939 led to guilty pleas from five proprietors of drug and confectionary stores, which had their pinball machines seized as gambling devices. Ironically, the court imposed a fine but returned the pinball machines on the grounds that the devices were not for gambling. Such generosity was common after raids. Despite the clear conflict of interest, the defense attorney representing the five operators also served as the municipal attorney.[47]

Local officials were deeply involved in the protection of the gaming market. Galveston endured a political controversy when, in 1939, Commissioner of Fire and Police George Gymer, with the unanimous support of the city's commission council, relieved Chief of Police Floyd Goodrich. Galvestonians understood that the accusations against Goodrich stemmed from his enforcement of the law rather than his lack of zeal. The *Galveston Daily News* summarized, "Gymer admitted under cross-examination by Owen D. Barker, attorney for Goodrich, that the chief had enforced the law, but he insisted that 'there are other things to take into consideration in running a police department.'" Gymer dodged rumors that police subsequently returned gambling equipment seized in Goodrich's raids. Gambling kingpins thanked Gymer by closing voluntarily until the publicity storm passed. They also feared that Goodrich might join state antigambling investigators championed by Governor W. Lee O'Daniel. A witness saw a truckload of roulette wheels and other gambling paraphernalia leaving downtown. The subsequent appointment of Chief of Police Dave Henry brought the obligatory raid to demonstrate lip service to laws against gambling. Policemen searched fifty local establishments. However, the sweep netted only five arrests at four locations where police seized gambling equipment, mainly slot machines, tip books, and policy tickets. Not surprisingly, expensive items, such as roulette or craps tables, were absent.[48]

The resiliency of illegal gambling depended on politicians, especially county sheriffs or municipal police chiefs, who spread the wealth. In 1963 a Bay County gambling ring protected by law enforcement made a minimum of twenty dollars per hour in each of four dens operating at various times out of trailers, motels, the American Legion Home in Panama City, or even outdoors. On an average fifteen-dollar pot, the house took two dollars. The ring collected $500 to $600 per week from each den. The profits split five ways: the gambling house owner, the owner's employees, the director of illegal gambling operations in the county, the liquor supplier, and law enforcement. Their astute use of illicit gains reaped electoral jackpots. Florida's Dixie County exemplified the political might of some sheriffs—and their political machines oiled by vice money—even when they no longer held office. State investigator William Jamison in 1963 found former sheriff L. E. Hatcher, who operated a Ford dealership, rewarding voters for their support behind a movie theater in the county seat of Cross City. Jamison reported, "He pays $5 per vote to most of the white voters and $2 per vote to other white voters and negroes." Hatcher, however, distributed buttons, not cash, lest he be incriminated in the vote-buying scheme. His former deputy sheriff, Lester Diggers, who owned a pool hall, handled the cash. The blue campaign button was worth five dollars, the white button two. Jamison noted that sitting sheriff Al Parker "pays off voters in a similar manner." Such was standard politics in many southern counties during the mid-twentieth century. Control of county offices meant control of an impressive underground economy linking liquor, gambling, and prostitution. Local elections were business decisions inseparable from a thriving black market.[49]

Illegal gambling entertained tourists. A visit to a gambling hall, fueled by alcohol, offered an exotic night out. A New York couple visiting Saint Augustine, Florida, in 1939 attended the "Kiwanis Club 'Night in Monte Carlo.'" They recorded their adventure in a travel diary: "Fred won $2.50 playing crap. I did the dancing. Met two very nice Spanish girls, Olga and Tina Cartyja. Both good dancers. After the Kiwanis, visited the Dutch Tavern and here had highballs, beer & more dancing. . . . Crawled home early in the morning." Bob Wilson, reporting for the *Richmond News Leader* in the late 1930s, declared, "Virginia Beach's average summer visitor pays his room rent in nickels, dimes and quarters put into the slots of gaming machines." Mississippi coast businessman William Hubbell noted how officials understood gambling to be essential to tourism: "The excuse they used was that this was a tourist center and the tourists wanted to gamble, so we had to have gambling to give them what they wanted." Florida agents investigating illegal gambling in Bay County during 1963 learned that "several Beach businessmen" met to voice support for gaming, legalized or not. A report identified H. Mack Lewis, president of the West Florida Gas Company, as allegedly informing area "businessmen that they needed to open the beaches to gambling if they were ever to attract tourists." The county sheriff sanctioned the meeting.[50]

The distinction between public and private gambling proved daunting. Panama City officials, as reported in the local press in January 1939, supported private games amongst friends, though ignored the difficulty of defining private gambling. Strict laws against gambling threatened personal freedom: "In fact we have nothing but contempt for the type of officer who raids negro dice games in the alleys or on the wharves, or who sneaks into a hotel or club room where a group of fellows are passing away the time with a little penny poker." When a Mississippi grand jury in 1959 called on law enforcement to "exert every effort to see that any and all gambling be abolished in Harrison County," illegal casino operators privatized. Proprietors issued membership cards to customers for a small fee. Though open to the public, these casinos were disguised as exclusive, private clubs with friendly games of chance. Harrison County sheriff Curtis Dedeaux opined, "I don't believe the law should break down the door of a private club where business or social people go who want to have a little game."[51]

Gambling represented a major untapped source of tax revenue. Moreover, legalization offered entertainment for tourists who might otherwise be fearful of entering an illegal operation. Prohibition had eased the stigma against gaming as some speakeasies doubled as casinos. The lessons of the Prohibition era loomed large. The *Virginia Beach News* argued for legalized gambling: "Not only will the game be fairer as to odds but straighter in operation and revenue producing to the State and the localities. It will largely destroy the illegal game as the abandonment of 'prohibition' destroyed 'bootlegging.'"[52] Whereas Florida and Nevada legalized gaming during the Depression, cities and towns in more conservative states fostered illicit gambling. Grenville Mellen, a New Orleanian who moved to the Mississippi coast in 1931, chuckled about the gambling in Harrison County: "It was like the scene that you used to see in the old motion pictures of the old western towns." The Northwestern Life Insurance Company surveyed gambling activity in the United States during the 1930s, revealing a major underground industry. Betting on horse races, legal and illegal, amounted to $2.2 billion. Gambling houses, bucket shops, and sports pools accounted for $800 million. Sweepstakes tickets drew $1.1 billion. Operators of lotteries, numbers games, and policy rackets pocketed $1.5 billion. Slot machines, pinball machines, and punch boards raked in $1 billion. Finally, Americans spent $500 million on bingo, raffles, and other such contests.[53]

A federal investigation of gambling activity near Keesler Air Force Base in 1951 revealed a common pattern for illegal activity. As with alcohol after Prohibition, the federal government ignored games of chance as long as federal gambling stamps were purchased. One observer remarked that "most of the stamps are purchased for the slot machines of country clubs and veterans' groups and fraternal orders whose memberships include those officials charged with protecting the county from the evils of wagering."[54] The implicit federal sanction undermined state bans, especially in counties chafing under the restriction. Congress had recently set an annual $150 tax on each slot machine. Biloxi mayor R. Hart Chinn therefore argued that the federal government "got the ball rolling on this whole thing." Military officials counted 1,257 slot machines, 72 blackjack games, 55 poker games, 31 dice tables, 11 race wires, and 10 roulette wheels operating across Harrison County. Estimates held that an eighth of the $4 million paid monthly to the thirty thousand personnel at Keesler went to local gambling dens. The president of the First Bank of Biloxi called gambling the town's biggest industry. Slot machine operators described how they paid monthly "fines" to Biloxi police chief Earl Wetzel while guaranteeing political campaign contributions to the sheriff and constables with countywide jurisdiction. Wetzel sent officers to collect $12.50 per machine each month. The payments were logged as "disorderly conduct fines" next to fictitious names that Wetzel himself admitted were "pulled out of thin air." Moreover, gubernatorial candidates, as one witness declared, regularly reassured coastal voters that the "Coast would be let alone as regards liquor and gambling." In November 1951 *Life* publicized the rampant illegal activity, complete with photographs. Criticizing the tranquil image of Biloxi crafted by the chamber of commerce, *Life* editors snarled, "They could have boasted the gambling joints, although illegal, offer a splendid opportunity for Biloxi's teen-age girls, who often work as change makers in them, and that they are well run because the guards and bouncers are off-duty policemen." Face-saving crackdowns on gambling and liquor occurred regularly, but both vices remained staples of the economy.[55]

Those businessmen reluctant to support illegal gaming could face considerable harassment. In 1949 Cyrus Scruggs, a motel owner in Duval County, Florida, received a visit from a deputy sheriff, justice of the peace, and representative of the local ABC. The three officials urged him to enter the gambling and prostitution racket under their protection. Scruggs refused. Officials, in turn, watched closely for liquor violations, arresting the owner forty-five times over the next thirteen years. The motelier informed a state investigator that he had suffered "constant harassment at a large expense . . . in court costs and lawyers['] fees." Eventually, he lost his liquor license for selling after hours. Scruggs admitted that he bent the law but that the intense scrutiny, including numerous police searches without warrants, made his business untenable. By 1962 Scruggs had taken his case to the Florida Supreme Court seeking to restore his liquor license so that he could sell his business and move to Virginia. The court upheld his request.[56]

Gambling nevertheless stirred greater unease than liquor. Whereas many resort inhabitants believed prohibition of spirits inhibited individual freedom and local democracy, illegal gambling increasingly seemed an invitation for racketeers and Mafiosi to corrupt community affairs. After all, prohibition benefited local producers and smugglers, whereas gambling, despite the protection afforded by county sheriffs backed by some business leaders, frequently involved national syndicates that coordinated sports betting, afforded headline entertainers, and supplied high-end gaming equipment such as roulette wheels or craps tables.

Investigative reports exacerbated fears among coastal residents of national crime networks operating in their community. The *Tampa Morning Tribune* in the late 1940s and early 1950s conducted several investigative series on "Tampa's blood-drenched underworld . . . ruled by a gambling syndicate of the dreaded Sicilian Mafia." The reporters described a $5 million lottery among other rackets in the Tampa area and claimed the mafia spent $100,000 on the 1947 municipal election, making the mafia the "No. 1 political power" in the city. A series covered fifteen unsolved murders linked to gambling over the previous twenty years. After exhausting coverage of Tampa, the newspaper sent reporters across Florida. An examination of federal slot machine license records found 627 license payments in Florida despite a state ban on the devices. Okaloosa County contained 115 of these slot machines. A reporter found the one-armed bandits "everywhere, in bus stations, in laundries, even next door to schools." Casinos also operated openly. Under pressure, the governor replaced Okaloosa County's sheriff and two constables. A subsequent survey of twenty counties uncovered "only two . . . in which the law enforcement officers were conscientiously on the job and in which there was no organized gambling." Indeed, the probe by the *Tampa Morning Tribune* attracted the attention of U.S. senator Estes Kefauver of Tennessee, who convened in Miami the first in a series of hearings by the U.S. Senate Special Committee to Investigate Organized Crime in Interstate Commerce.[57]

The Kefauver hearings of 1950–1951 raised public awareness of national syndicates of organized crime that facilitated illegal gambling. Kefauver, with an eye on the Democratic Party's nomination for president in 1952, ensured this through courtship of the press and, more importantly, the emergent television industry, which eagerly sought shots of crime bosses and tales of the underworld. Resort leaders launched dramatic raids both as an expression of outrage against alleged mafia strongmen and as a means of garnering positive publicity in the aftermath of the damaging testimony. Embarrassed by the Kefauver hearings, Florida governor Fuller Warren contacted the state's sixty-seven county sheriffs and nearly two hundred constables, giving them thirty days to close gambling establishments or risk suspension. Gambling opponents elsewhere looked upon Warren's action as a template for their states to follow given the reticence of locals to enforce the law.[58]

The federal hearings spotlighted activities that many tourists had not previously noticed as problematic. The president of the Society of American Foresters allayed members' concerns about their convention in Biloxi in 1951, shortly after hearings exposed the area's criminal underworld: "There is not much I can add except to say that I have attended at least a half dozen meetings in Biloxi in the last ten years and I was greatly surprised to read recently about the goings-on down there." Unless sought, "one does not know about it [vice] while there." He then reassured members that their gathering would be wet: "Of course it is well known that liquor can be bought illegally there as elsewhere in Mississippi." He added, "The good people of the State like to preserve the outward form in their social life, government, and religion."[59]

Even when successful, opponents of gambling claimed hollow victories. In Bay County tourism boosters pushed for the creation of a greyhound park. Twice, in 1951 and 1954, voters narrowly rejected the measure. Earl Gilbert, chairman of Bay County Sponsors of Progress with Morality, expressed jubilation: "Once again they have unmistakably indicated their determination to keep out the gambling and other sinister rackets and to maintain here a clean and wholesome moral atmosphere." Track opponents savored an empty victory. Neighbors in Washington County had earlier approved a track. Ebro Greyhound Park, on the southern edge of Washington County, opened in 1954, resting just fifteen miles from the coast and twenty-five miles northwest of Panama City. Nightly races, except on Sunday, occurred from early May through early September. Minors under eighteen were prohibited. However, until 1968 the track, conscious of the baby boom, supplied a nursery for vacationers' young children.[60]

Opponents of gambling clubs typically made little headway. Outraged citizens in Virginia Beach formed the League for Political Decency in March 1950. The league targeted incumbents in hopes of "eliminating the obnoxious and illegal gambling, 'nip joints,' and all assorted nefarious enterprises with their attendant racketeering and corruption." Locals in June reelected the incumbents by more than 60 percent of the vote. Within weeks Judge Floyd Kellam, head of the political machine in Princess Anne County and the person responsible for appointments to the county police force, called a grand jury to "investigate fully charges of gambling, illegal whiskey sales, nude entertainers, slot machines, and an alleged 'bag man', the collector from the gamblers." By the end of July, state and local police launched raids on thirteen Virginia Beach clubs known for illegal alcohol sales and gambling. But such action aimed more to quiet crusaders than to eliminate vice. Politicians, vice lords, and protection money formed a powerful bond.[61] Indeed, the defense attorney for some of those indicted by Judge Floyd Kellam's grand jury was his brother Richard Kellam. The fifteen sons of patriarch Abel Kellam, who had served as clerk of court for Princess Anne County, formed a network of political influence that stretched to Richmond and even Washington, D.C. Sidney Kellam, another brother, had managed the campaign of sitting governor John Battle while also serving as a "rising bigwig" under U.S. senator Harry Byrd. Harry Rumble testified to the grand jury: "To report matters in this county to any of the police officials is nil." He explained, "It is foolish for me to jeopardize my life, limb and property by going down and making a fool of myself when this court can't back you up."[62]

Few expressed surprise when juries acquitted all those accused of operating illegal gambling clubs in Virginia Beach. When political opponents again targeted the Kellam machine in Princess Anne County in 1951, they published ads condemning the "K-O-P-S—Kellam's Organization Party Stooges." Two years later a leader of the opposition movement, Clayton Davis, faced charges that he permitted whiskey in his restaurant. Confessing that 75 percent of customers wanted alcohol with their meals, Davis sighed, "I was a victim of pressure." Not that Davis had a clean slate. In the late 1940s a thief had robbed the slot machines in Davis's establishment.[63]

The example of Phenix City, Alabama, haunted boosters eager to promote gambling and drinking. In 1955 the Galveston Ministerial Association showed *The Phenix City Story* at a downtown movie theater with Hugh Bently of the Russell County Betterment Association providing a firsthand account. Bentley had launched a reform effort only to be "rewarded by persecution." The association claimed "high hopes" that the example of Phenix City would "stir the better people of our community to outright support of our efforts to make Galveston a place that thrives on the good, rather than advertising evil as a necessary part of our culture."[64] When Larry Boulier of Myrtle Beach ran for city council in the 1960s, he warned of the dangers involved in embracing illegal activity despite his own opposition to state restrictions on alcohol. Maintaining a "wide open city" that catered to the "accepted minor pleasures" sought by tourists required vigilance. Boulier noted how any "of our seasoned citizens will recall the deterioration of Phoenix [sic] City, Ala."[65]

In rare cases, however, officials publicly expressed support for gambling, drinking, and even prostitution. George Roy Clough, elected mayor of Galveston in 1955, made national headlines when he described the port as an "open city" but not a "wide open city." Clough had made his fortune in television and radio, so he understood the importance of publicity. Touting honest government, Clough also boasted that in Galveston a "man attending a convention can let down his hair and do some things he would not do in his own home town for fear his church pastor might see him." Clough even defended the city's unofficial red-light district: "We know what some of the girls that come to Galveston want there, so we put them in the right place for what they want to do." He reasoned, "If you were a farmer, you wouldn't raise chickens in the bedroom. You'd raise them in a chicken yard." When reporters for *Life* snapped shots of brothels and gaming in 1955, local toughs assaulted them.[66]

Clough briefly collapsed the wall of silence that protected vice. While in office, Clough accused Fire and Police Commissioner Walter Johnson, a staunch opponent, of regularly visiting "Margaret Lera's Ignacious House" and of being "paralyzed drunk with his chief of police in the Rod and Gun Club." Clough, at a meeting of Galveston businessmen, bluntly explained the standoff with Johnson as a battle over payoffs from vice. Clough had instructed madam "Dirty Neck" Jessie on how his administration dealt with brothels, barrooms, and gambling dens: "Well, I told her what I had told other people, I want you to move west to 25th Street. And you are going to have to be raided now and then; if you can pay Walter Johnson off, you can also pay the City some money." The rivalry between the mayor and the commissioner upset the black market. Clough's call for immediate raids clashed with the interests of Johnson. Clough complained, "But when I attempt to raid them and get a policeman to the house, the policeman is instructed to first inform these individuals where he is going so that when they get there, nobody happens to be there." Clough's issue hinged on the fact that he wanted raids to bring money to the city treasury; Johnson and his officers, in contrast, often pocketed the cash. After one night of raids, Clough celebrated the revenue gathered from fines: "I collected for the City of Galveston $700.15 in one hour and fifteen minutes doing the work that your chief of police is paid $604 a month to do and refuses to do it. Why? Because Mr. Johnson is a retainer for ladies in question and he is supposed to see that they have police protection." Clough believed raids were essential for creating positive publicity and revenue while regulating vice. Business leaders recognized that Galveston was not alone in handling vice in this way but, as one businessman complained, Clough needed to refrain from placing the city's corruption "in the limelight."[67]

Clough became an embarrassment. Many tourists considered Clough's open embrace of vice distasteful. I. H. Kempner spoke for many Galveston businessmen who saw the mayor as "not sound." The businessmen worked to "develop some way to keep him from parading the City of Galveston as a City of Vice." With Clough's compliance, Texas attorney general Will Wilson launched a crackdown on Galveston vice, padlocking gambling dens and brothels. In 1959 Galvestonians returned Herbie Cartwright, who had served for eight years before Clough defeated him, to the mayor's office. A report from *Time* in May 1959 described Galveston as a "wide-open sin city and the gaudy shame of Texas." "Prostitution flourishes in the houses of Post Office Street, one of the last unabashed red-light districts in the nation," continued the story. "After-hours gin mills and gambling joints thrive in defiance of Texas laws, under the tacit protection of kickback-hungry city officials." Efforts at reform sputtered. "From time to time, ambitious reformers have made feeble efforts to clean up Galveston, but the town has always quickly returned to its wicked ways, partly because the tourists like it that way—and also, apparently, because Galvestonians do, too," concluded *Time*. Rather than crush vice, Mayor-elect Herbert Cartwright and chamber representative David Nathan, at a meeting of businessmen, promised to "offset" and "override" the negative publicity.[68]

Federal oversight of county politics resulting from the civil rights movement curtailed black-market gaming. The more interventionist federal government emerged, for example, in its dealings with Clarence Earl Gideon, a drifter with a lengthy record of petty crime stretching from Texas to Missouri and, finally, to Florida. In the Sunshine State, Gideon worked as an electrician before slipping into gambling to make ends meet. Gideon was convicted in August 1961 for the burglary of the Bay Harbor Poolroom in Panama City, Florida. He was too poor to afford an attorney. County officials denied his requests for a public defender. A jury convicted Gideon, who received a five-year sentence in the state penitentiary. From behind bars, Gideon penciled a five-page petition to the U.S. Supreme Court. In the landmark *Gideon v. Wainwright* from 1963, the court ruled that poor and undereducated Americans needed a lawyer given the complexity of the legal system in the modern age. A fair trial required a right to a public defender. Gideon had won. In his retrial in 1964, Gideon's public attorney discredited the witnesses. The jury ruled not guilty.[69]

Gideon's saga marked a moment of transition for illegal gambling, law enforcement, and life in towns across America. The U.S. Supreme Court increasingly restrained the powers of law enforcement during the 1960s, thereby safeguarding the rights of the accused. Other cases, namely, *Baker v. Carr* (1962) and *Reynolds v. Sims* (1964), undermined the disproportionate power of rural counties by forcing legislatures to create equally populated representative districts, even within state senates. Federal oversight of county corruption and the professionalization of police departments further eroded the ability of county cliques to protect moonshining and gambling operations.[70]

Simultaneously, demographic changes and budget crises weakened opposition to legalized gambling. The focus initially rested on bingo. Though forms of the game dated to the nineteenth century, bingo in its modern manifestation appeared in Pennsylvania when a Catholic priest, desperate to raise money during the Great Depression, contacted entrepreneur Edwin Lowe in 1931. The game quickly spread to other dioceses and fraternal organizations such as veterans' groups. A mere 7 percent of Americans admitted playing bingo for money at the end of the Second World War. Yet five years later 22 percent of Americans admitted doing so. In the 1950s Americans spent $1 billion annually on bingo. Though illegal in the majority of states, this form of gambling thrived across the northern United States as few politicians or law enforcement officials risked confrontations with the Catholic Church or veterans' groups. Northern voters legalized bingo via state referendums by the late 1950s.[71]

The debate over the game drifted southward. The region's resorts stood on the frontlines as they pressed legislatures to appease vacationers, many from northern states. In 1967 the Florida legislature legalized, on a local-option basis, bingo "with certain restrictions designed to keep the game in the hands of homefolks, with the proceeds going to charitable purposes, and with 'jackpots' limited to modest size." Numerous Palm Beach County municipalities quickly legalized bingo "with an eye toward good relations with their senior citizens."[72]

The battle heated to a boil in the 1970s. Bingo presented the religiously conservative South, home to a large evangelical Protestant population with only small pockets of Catholics mostly located in cities and along the Gulf Coast, with a moral quandary. North Carolina, for example, allowed municipalities or counties as early as the 1940s to petition for exempting bingo from antigambling laws. As late as 1979, when the legislature legalized the game statewide, only a third of the counties had done so. Yankee retirees sought the game. Vacationing mothers of the baby boom generation, who had seen their children enter adulthood, now also possessed the time and resources to enjoy the camaraderie of bingo halls. A simple game of pure chance and low stakes, bingo was ideal for vacationers. For the mass of strangers visiting the beaches, the bingo hall supplied a shared experience of luck that erased differences of mental skill or financial standing. Bingo caller Archie McLellan from Myrtle Beach noted the value of the games at coastal resorts: "It's something a lot of older people do. Teen-agers have a lot of things to do, but the older people have nothing."[73]

States struggled to differentiate bingo from other forms of gambling. Senior citizens responded with outrage after a 1973 raid on the Golden Nugget Bingo Hall in Biloxi. "I think it is unfair to close the Golden Nugget and let other people such as our private clubs still play bingo," howled a self-described "Concerned Citizen." The Biloxian continued, "An awful lots [sic] of our senior citizens do not have a place to go anymore because they enjoyed playing bingo at the Golden Nugget. They don't care for bridge or canasta." When the hall reopened, the proprietor gave customers free bingo cards. Winners still received cash prizes while the hall reaped revenue from concession sales, though these ultimately failed to cover expenses. A public campaign pressured state and local officials to exempt bingo from antigambling laws. Odette Durocher of Biloxi spoke for local housewives who crowded the bingo halls along with senior citizens—the same demographic groups who had long been most vocal in their opposition to vices such as liquor and games of chance. Likening bingo to men's fishing trips, she explained that an evening at the bingo hall provided escape and excitement for women. When Myrtle Beach cracked down on bingo in 1976, officials faced outraged tourists. Dorinda Fisher, a forty-five-year-old grandmother from Huntersville, North Carolina, identified bingo as the only reason she came to Myrtle Beach: "You tell them it keeps grandmas off the streets." Jane Fagan of Asheville, North Carolina, concurred, "We are mad as fire." She added, "I am 41, and I've been playing bingo here since I was 15. . . . We just came to play bingo."[74]

South Carolina adopted a novel approach to legalizing bingo. Myrtle Beach officials warned private bingo operators in 1976 that their halls violated state law. In South Carolina bingo was only legal at county fairs when sponsored by a nonprofit organization. Representative Charles Hodges of Horry County exploited the loophole. In June 1977 legislators quietly sent a bill to Governor James Edwards that declared the Grand Strand a county fair between Memorial Day and Labor Day, thereby granting legality to bingo games in Horry County east of the Intracoastal Waterway during the tourist season. The governor refrained from signing the legislation, but the bill still became law. The Myrtle Beach municipal government quickly granted bingo licenses, ignoring the stipulation that nonprofit organizations sponsor the game. Ripley's Believe

It or Not on Ocean Boulevard claimed one of the first licenses. Jones Bingo Hall joined forces with the local Elks Lodge, sharing the profits under a safer legal umbrella. Elks spokesman A. B. Floyd boasted, "Bingo is essential to tourism in Myrtle Beach."[75]

The debate over legalized gambling intensified during the late twentieth century. Atlantic City's decision to legalize gambling during the stagflation of the 1970s received close attention. Moreover, several Native American tribes established bingo parlors on their reservations during the same decade, successfully holding off interference from state officials seeking to suppress the gambling. When the U.S. Supreme Court, in *California v. Band of Mission Indians* (1987), upheld the tribes' rights to offer gambling on their lands, a boom in casino construction erupted. Even rural southern towns such as Marksville, Louisiana, and Philadelphia, Mississippi, discovered full-fledged casinos on their outskirts as once-quiet Indian reservations joined the new gold rush.[76]

Fearful of losing revenue, southern legislatures loosened gambling restrictions. State-run lotteries and scratch cards appeared across most of the South by the 1990s. Mississippi turned to casinos. In 1990 Mississippi authorized casinos with the stipulation that gambling palaces rest on water. The first casino opened in Hancock County on the Gulf Coast in 1992. The recession of the early 1990s forced Mississippians to reassess their moral fortitude. State representative Charlie Capps from the Delta in 1998 cheered the state's twenty-nine casinos, located in only six of Mississippi's eighty-two counties. Capps pointed to the $235 million in taxes generated by legal gambling, with $153 million going into a general fund for statewide development and the rest to local governments hosting the casinos. "We've been able to do things with the money from gaming that we never would have dreamed of doing," defended Capps. "[Repeal of gaming laws] would be a huge loss to education, to human services, to mental-health programs." By 1998 Mississippi casinos collected $2 billion while creating thirty-two thousand jobs. The per capita income of Mississippians rose from $12,719 in 1990—the lowest in the United States—to $17,561 in 1996. Following closely on Mississippi's heels, Louisiana too opted for riverboat casinos with a land-based facility in New Orleans.[77]

Ironically, most beach resorts refrained from legal gaming, wary of duplicating Atlantic City where crime rates soared and development beyond the casinos never materialized. Even high-flying Galveston had been tamed by the 1970s. Paul Kleiber, a resident, considered the collapse of gambling a cause of the economic decay suffered by the Texas port. "Once Galveston did have the reputation and glamour of being a great tourist and fun city," wrote Kleiber. "It was primarily because of gambling etc., top entertainment (which gambling brought in and paid for) clean beaches, good weather, and some nice clubs, hotels and restaurants." Nevertheless, most communities, whether Galveston, Panama City, Myrtle Beach, or Virginia Beach, suppressed their gambling dens. These resorts turned away from that increasingly competitive gambling market and, instead, focused renewed energy on promoting their beaches—an attraction that Indian reservations, riverboat casinos, Las Vegas, and Atlantic City could not match.[78]

Rogue Waves

The arrival of vacationing students clashed with the promotion of morality along the seashore. Jesse Daniel Ames, widowed in 1914 after her enlisted husband died researching yellow fever in Latin America, maintained a busy life, advocating passage of the Nineteenth Amendment before campaigning against lynching during the interwar years. She sent daughter Lulu to Gulf Park College. On one hand, Lulu Ames encountered the Old South. She described how one classmate came from a "real old plantation with negroes . . . just like a story book." But Lulu also encountered a far more liberal South along the coast, at least with regard to carnality if not race. An April 1929 adventure to Bay Saint Louis exposed her to a "million house parties over there from New Orleans." University students, especially those in fraternities or sororities, savored the liberation afforded by beach houses. "They necked, and smoked and drank and went wild generally," recorded Lulu. "I was used to it more or less." Though the Great Depression dampened the exuberance of the Roaring Twenties, such battles over propriety returned as the baby boom generation came of age.[79]

The Second World War heightened concern over American youths. With many fathers joining the military—thousands never to return—and even mothers working shifts in war industries, commentators pondered the impact on children. Social critic Ruth Taylor argued in 1944, "Every act of juvenile delinquency convicts some adult of neglect or indifference amounting to criminal negligence." Vice conditions near military installations flourished. Many soldiers were teenagers or young adults away from home for the first time— and with regular paychecks, too. Soldiers, though honored, received criticism. As blackout restrictions eased along the Atlantic coast in late 1944, the electric company serving Virginia Beach refurbished oceanfront lamps with new bulbs and "expensive globes." Juvenile delinquents and "'visitors' in uniform" received blame when these globes lay shattered on the ground, victims of BB guns or brickbats. Youths also seemed more susceptible to the standards set by a rising consumer culture represented by Hollywood, radio, popular magazines, and comic books.[80]

Municipal ordinances regularly targeted teenagers who flocked to the beach without parental supervision. In Virginia Beach, "hell raising" beach parties with their "all night rowdyism" thrived just north of the city limits until state, county, and municipal officials coordinated regular patrols in June 1950. Youngsters often roamed the streets all night and occasionally pilfered or vandalized property. Most troubling, they often arrived without money. As elsewhere along southern shores, Virginia Beach, beginning in the 1950s, enforced an ordinance that banned sleeping in automobiles. Of twenty-nine teenagers arrested for the offense one weekend in June 1957, most came from out of town and carried less than a dollar. Fred Singleton, one of those arrested, asked, "Pray tell me, what harm can there be in sleeping in your own automobile at 5:00 a.m.? . . . Surely, one doesn't snore loud enough to disturb anyone." The decibels of the snore mattered less than its location. The Virginia Beach Hotel, Motel, and Cottage Association staunchly supported the ordinance. Targeting juvenile delinquency ensured that all tourists paid for a room.[81]

Alcohol vendors along the beach regularly served or employed minors. In 1952 Bay County sheriff Alva Thomas responded to underage drinking by heavily patrolling beachfront bars. Thomas warned, "Teen-agers from throughout the Southeast visit our beaches, and it is necessary that the beach areas be kept clean and decent and we intend to protect them." Yet beer dealers complained to ABC agents that the "short season forces them to take chances with beer sales to persons that appear to be of adult age." More troublesome were the minors who brought beer and whiskey from out of state, thereby circumventing local bans on underage purchases of alcohol. The Florida legislature clarified the legal limbo in the late 1950s by making alcohol possession for those under eighteen years old illegal. To draw customers, bar owners regularly hired underage girls. A Mississippi grand jury in 1956 revealed "several instances" of establishments in Harrison County employing teenagers as barmaids or waitresses. These bars also served minors alcohol. In the late 1960s, 70 percent of American adults drank alcohol—some 40 percent at least once a month. Among American high school students, 75 percent had consumed alcohol.[82]

Spring break worsened vice as young celebrants inundated beach towns. The annual rite dated to the interwar years, as high school and university enrollments grew. Ivy League students, particularly those on swim teams, honed their skills on Florida's Atlantic coast during their Christmas breaks. Word of the warm waters spread. Soon Fort Lauderdale, Florida, became a haven for students. In Mississippi fraternities and sororities maintained houses in Bay Saint Louis and Pass Christian. Newcomb College and Tulane University students from New Orleans regularly enjoyed the freedom and frivolity of the Mississippi shore. Even University of Arkansas students joined the "Easter house parties" as early as 1928. Some interwar spring breakers brought back potent mementos. Robert Walker, who worked in an Atlanta frat house during the 1930s, recalled students who returned from Miami with bottles of whiskey.[83]

As Americans entered their teenage years during the Cold War, they embraced the freedom of the beach. For young men a summer trip often provided, as described in a 1951 issue of *Life*, "a last big fling" before facing the draft and military service. Writing a decade later for the *Charlotte Observer*, Dwayne Walls described young North Carolinians' fixation with the dancing, sunbathing, and "all-night talking" enjoyed at the shore. "Most of all, there was a sense of freedom," wrote Walls. Those who escaped parental supervision gained the most freedom of all. Hotel operators complained that by 1962 Virginia Beach risked becoming little more than beer joints and honky-tonks catering to "rowdy youngsters." Spring break exacerbated unruly behavior. Stephanie Pace remarked on spring break in Myrtle Beach in 1972: "Families at Ocean Drive over the Easter weekend were about as commonplace as a cigarette machine in the recreation room at a Mormon church." Pace thought "campuses across the South must have been completely empty for all their students were down here."[84]

Panama City witnessed the most intense concerns over teenage havoc. The annual Alabama Education Association (AEA) holiday each April sent more than ten thousand high school students, mostly from Alabama's Jefferson and Montgomery Counties, flooding into Panama City during the 1950s. By 1958 students' misbehavior stirred the Jefferson County juvenile court to negotiate an extradition policy with the juvenile court in Panama City. Long Beach and other Panhandle resorts also complied with the request of officials in Birmingham, Alabama, to halt beer sales over the AEA holiday. Little changed, however. Student Warren Williams noted how AEA week in Panama City brought "increased sales of beer, wine, vodka, corn chips and suntan lotion" to "junior high school, high school, and college students" during the 1970s. As late as the 1980s, police handled students with velvet gloves rather than risk chasing away a profitable business; the AEA holiday now brought approximately thirty thousand to Panama City Beach alone. Bay County sheriff Lavelle Pitts commanded, "I've told the men not to arrest kids they catch with one or two joints if they can help it." Instead, the lawbreakers were warned to "hit the road."[85]

The influx of high school and college students during spring break spurred reformers' calls to regulate alcohol, gambling, and prostitution. Ministerial Association of Galveston representatives met with chamber of commerce directors on the eve of the 1956 spring break when a "number of school children will be coming to Galveston very shortly from various junior and senior high schools in Texas, Oklahoma and other neighboring states." The ministers identified twenty brothels operating in the city and eleven "so-called joints" where soliciting occurred. In previous years, numerous students had contracted sexually transmitted diseases while in Galveston. Others had gained entrance to gambling dens, where they played a variety of illegal games, including bingo. The religious leaders concluded with a threat. If the chamber did not "do something definite immediately" to eradicate these vices, the ministers promised "to write letters to school officials in the area of these vacationing children and inform them as to the condition here." The businessmen were wary of landing "in the middle of this unfavorable situation" by battling vice, yet damaging the tourism industry. The members reluctantly asked the police to increase patrols along the beachfront as approximately five thousand students flocked into the city. Robert Coleman concluded with a noncommittal stance typical of business leaders in coastal resorts: "If a resolution were adopted today it would not accomplish anything . . . but bad publicity for the city and we have had enough of that."[86]

Motel owners vigilantly policed teenagers and young adults. Before the expansion of motel chains in the 1960s, independent owners dominated the lodging industry. Yet all operators labored to belay public fears about immoral activities within the rooms. In 1964 a spokesman for the Quality Courts motel chain recognized the importance of dispelling public fears. Motels struggled in "the herculean task of living down the 'cabins of crime' label." The chain safeguarded its reputation just as independent owners did "by refusing service to those under the influence of alcohol, those objectionable in appearance, or of possible immoral intentions, or of questionable character." Motel owners supervised their guests with an eye on not only protecting their profits and property but also upholding their personal moral code. Gail Shackelford and her seventeen college girlfriends learned this lesson during their 1973 spring break in Myrtle Beach. Shackelford confessed, "The minute we pulled up at our motel trouble started." Shackelford complained, "The manager insinuated that some of the girls were of low moral standings. He did not have the right to judge us in this manner, evidently; he was judging us according to the way he suspects most teenage college girls to act." The manager "cursed" and "spied" on the vacationing students. Shackelford grumbled, "This man actually took account of where we went and when we came in for the next three nights. He forbid us to have any visitors during the day or night."[87]

The rise of spring break as an annual carnival for coming-of-age baby boomers exacerbated concerns over youth rebellion in the turbulent 1960s. When Hollywood turned Glendon Swarthout's novel *Where the Boys Are* (1958) into a film two years later, young Americans flocked to the beach for spring break. Swarthout, who taught English at Michigan State University, had spent two weeks with some of his honors students in Fort Lauderdale, the setting of the novel and film, as part of his research. In the early 1960s Fort Lauderdale witnessed an annual influx of fifty thousand students during the break. Nearby, more than a hundred thousand visited Daytona Beach, spending more than $5 million. By the 1980s Fort Lauderdale and Daytona Beach would each draw between 250,000 and 350,000 during the holiday.[88]

The impact of spring break carnality and rebellion rippled across the nation, affecting other holidays and events. In June 1961 the *Panama City News* noted how a "howling mob of young people spurred on by shouts of, 'This is better than Fort Lauderdale' battled police and smashed store windows" after a sports-car race in Elkhart Lake, Wisconsin. Around 200 rioters of the 1,500 young racing fans—some of whom had participated in a spring break riot in Fort Lauderdale that year—fought town police, vandalized downtown stores, threw beer cans and firecrackers, and slashed fire hoses meant to subdue the rioters. County and state police rushed to quell the violence. One officer noted, "They seemed to go for the uniform men." The rioters wore sweatshirts representing universities from across the country. Even patriotic occasions such as Independence Day could spark violence. Virginia Beach police fired fifty tear gas canisters and unleashed canine units on a mob of hundreds of young vacationers late on the Fourth of July in 1976. Police battled the brick- and debris-tossing mob for three hours.[89]

The Grand Strand witnessed some of the most egregious student riots during spring break. In 1967 half of the twenty-five thousand vacationers on Ocean

Drive, just north of Myrtle Beach, crowded into the streets on Saturday night of Easter weekend. Soon collegians, high school students, "some servicemen, and adults," most from North Carolina, joined in tossing rocks and bottles at police. Cries of "kill the cops" erupted. A man on a rooftop shouted, "Let's make this bigger than Lauderdale." Only the arrival of a large force of hel-meted police who unleashed fire hoses halted the rioters. A few officers toted automatic carbines. Officers commandeered a large seafood van to ferry the arrested to jail. In April 1970 Police Chief Merlin Bellamy of North Myrtle Beach faced down a "right good-sized crowd." For almost a half hour, a group of students shouted, "Kill the pigs, Kill the pigs" as they hurled rocks, bottles, and beer cans at policemen. During the 1974 spring break, reporter John Monk covered a "disturbance which reached near-riot proportions" as more than five thousand high school and college students crammed North Myrtle Beach in the wee hours of Sunday morning. The screaming celebrants blocked traffic. Some streaked; others rode naked on motorcycles; a few played games of nude basketball. Blake and Norma Whisnant, owners of the Stardust Motel, called the police but to no avail. Norma Whisnant described the revelers: "There were thousands of them—on top of guests' cars, on our building, on top of palm trees." When city, county, and state police arrived in force at 4 a.m., the crowd showered them with bottles and obscenities, then dispersed. Police Chief Bel-lamy declared, "We're the Ft. Lauderdale of South Carolina."[90]

Beach communities struggled to tame teenage behavior without applying too many restrictions. In 1963 officials in Virginia Beach converted the Alan B. Shepard Civic Center into a teen-friendly nightclub each Friday evening during the summer. The nightclub, restricted to those aged fourteen to eigh-teen, provided food service, nonalcoholic beverages, music, and dancing. Par-ents left their children in supervised care. The upscale decor further subdued the children. Supporters argued that "because of the nightclub motif with its candlelight and checkered tablecloths, the youngsters are automatically en-couraged, not by ruling but by own personal interest, to dress for the occasion and leave at home their usual somewhat sloppy resort attaire [sic]." The result emphasized "good manners and good grooming."[91]

Dance clubs for teenagers proliferated nationwide. Virginia Beach police-men Les Grover and Dave Wallace, drawing inspiration from a television re-port on a teen nightclub in Los Angeles as well as from the temporary Teen-age Cabaret in the Shepard Center the previous year, opened the Lampliter in May 1964. A board of directors consisted of students from Virginia Beach high schools. For a low membership fee, those aged thirteen to nineteen accessed the facility, open afternoons from Tuesday through Sunday. Doris Patrick, a mother, urged Virginia Beach teens to join the "plush night club." She stressed, "It is your Club—you can meet your friends, have a coke, shoot the breeze, listen to the juke box, or even do your homework!" In 1967 Ted Torok opened the Sandbox, a teen-friendly dance club in Virginia Beach supported by ministers and parents. Yet George Davis, speaking for the Virginia Beach Innkeepers Association, denounced the club as counter to the resort's family-friendly image. Attracting teenagers when they increasingly involved themselves with illegal drugs and protest movements, especially against the Vietnam War, seemed counterproductive given the focus on vacationing middle-class families.[92]

Other hangouts bore far more controversial names. In 1968 the Rotarian meeting hall in Kempersville, Virginia, for instance, not only served as a Pentecostal Holiness Church but also as the Purple Haze coffee house. The Purple Haze was founded by a "group of more-than-dedicated Virginia Beach teens who wanted 'a place to come and talk, discuss crucial things without being hooted down.'" Lonnie Cucinitti, a former student at Gulf Coast Community College, spent nine years in the U.S. Navy before working at a San Francisco coffee shop. After a few years, he rejoined his parents at Panama City, where he opened the Mushroom Factory, a Haight-Ashbury–style coffeehouse. In the mid-1970s controversy raged over the Slow Toke Saloon in Panama City. Allene Robbins spent nine years working at Emory University before buying the establishment and a motel. Her twenty-five-year-old son, Mike Robbins, explained that the name was a gimmick to attract customers, a tactic that worked. Business doubled, and the site became popular even during the winter. Other businesses disapproved of the marijuana reference and to the clientele. Motel owner Margret Colwell reported that "a boy and girl came out of the Slow Toke and got in the back of a van and took off their clothes. Then while some of the other patrons of the club stood around and applauded they performed a sexual act." Mike Robbins dismissed such charges as simple "jealousy" over the club's popularity. Under pressure, however, the name was changed to Slow Poke. Robbins sneered, "A place like The Hooker has topless dancers and they didn't have to change their name."[93]

The cultural upheaval of the 1960s replaced long-held concerns over alcohol and gambling with fears of drug use and rampant sex. Joseph Lowenthal interviewed a twenty-year-old college student from Virginia Beach who freely admitted to smoking marijuana: "I think it should be legal, with restrictions and control, like alcohol, those with hang-ups drink too." Given the drinking age of eighteen and that by-drink cocktails remained unavailable until January 1969 in Virginia Beach, teenagers frequently opted for more disguisable marijuana. One teenager explained why he smoked: "I enjoyed it more than drinking, which is a definite teenage factor in Virginia Beach." Whereas marijuana rarely appeared before the mid-1960s, younger Americans embraced the drug culture by 1968, raising concerns among police and parents who further publicized the trend. The police chief of Virginia Beach responded, "We've been putting pressure on the 'Hippie Movement' because past experience shows a large amount of the drugs have been connected with the 'Hippies.'" John Hogg of Virginia Beach observed of the younger generation: "As in Prohibition they consider themselves rebels in a righteous cause rather than criminals on the sly." By 1970 police encountered more frequent use of cocaine and heroin as well as more homegrown varieties of marijuana. A 1970 survey of the 2,100 students at Ball High School in Galveston found 26 percent had smoked marijuana, 13 percent had experimented with speed, 10 percent had tried LSD, 8 percent had gulped cough syrup, and 3 percent had used heroin.[94]

Students felt the scrutiny. A survey of students at Myrtle Beach High School in 1971 revealed a widespread belief that police unfairly targeted youths. Students also identified groups against which the Myrtle Beach Police Department discriminated. Of those surveyed, 18 percent believed out-of-towners received unfair treatment; 59 percent contended that law enforcement dealt unfairly with blacks; 72 percent believed police showed bias against "Long Hairs." The latter group represented a large portion of the rebellious young population. Cooper Terry, a twenty-four-year-old Vietnam vet from Danville, Virginia, certainly would have agreed with the survey. Terry had visited Myrtle Beach numerous times before his run-in with the law during the summer of 1971. Leaving a Myrtle Beach bar at 1 a.m., Terry was arrested for public drunkenness. Terry was released the next morning only after another policeman removed thirty dollars from his wallet to cover the fine. Terry remarked, "I was told I could appear in court on the 6th and appeal, but I was due back at my job in Danville prior to that time." Terry continued, "I know from other sources (a lot of people from Danville go to Myrtle Beach) that this sort of thing has been going on in Myrtle Beach lately." For Terry, his arrest was a "racket."[95]

Negative publicity about student drinking, spring break debauchery, drunk driving, and drug use inspired a crackdown. A conservative backlash during the 1970s and 1980s targeted teenagers and college-age adults even while encouraging efforts to legalize by-drink sales and gambling. Many states established eighteen or nineteen as the minimum drinking age after the Twenty-Sixth Amendment recognized the voting rights of eighteen-year-olds in 1971. Yet alcohol-related highway fatalities soon increased by more than 25 percent. By the 1980s the federal government threatened to withhold highway funding unless states raised their minimum drinking age to twenty-one. One by one, states submitted to the threat. Louisiana, in 1995, became the last state to raise its drinking age to twenty-one, closing a loophole that had allowed bars to pour freely to those over eighteen. States likewise toughened laws against drunk driving and adopted stricter enforcement measures. Vacationing students felt the tightening laws. David Fynn, a high school student from Atlanta, Georgia, took his holiday in the Florida Panhandle in 1987. He told a reporter, "I feel like I am under surveillance while I am on my Spring Break."[96]

A New Day

As civil rights activists pressed for equal voting rights, beach towns pursued their fair share of political power within their respective state legislatures. The *Biloxi Daily Herald* in March 1954 seethed, "Many states containing the largest cities in the nation are afflicted with the strange paralysis by which the small rural counties maintain a tight and stubborn grasp around the throats of the large urban counties." Equal representation by county in the Mississippi senate, as established by the 1890 constitution, meant that rural interests easily trumped urban interests—an imbalance made severe by the half century of migration off the land to the cities. Worse, state houses were rarely redistricted, further unbalancing representation between rural and urban areas. Virginia Beach leaders raised other issues, such as laws requiring two years of residency before new arrivals could vote. The *Virginia Beach Sun-News* lamented how "our election laws have not kept up with modern mobility." Coastal boosters further argued that political rights should reflect economic impact. Myrtle Beach reporters expressed dismay when telephone calls to Columbia to uncover tax revenue figures paid to the state government all "wound up in the same blind alley." With no answers after a week of questioning, the *Myrtle Beach Sun News* ran the headline: "How Much in Sales Taxes Does Myrtle Beach Supply? It's a Deep, Dark Secret."[97]

Reforms in the 1960s and 1970s reduced the incentives gained from illegal bootlegging and gambling. Federal oversight of local affairs and calls among locals to put police on a civil service system of employment reduced corruption. A Myrtle Beach newspaper declared in 1960, "Any salaried policeman should never have to depend upon an election to hold his job. Several members of the present County Police have attended FBI police schools as well as receiving training in fingerprinting work. In this modern age, it takes brains to be a good law enforcement officer who can and will work on details." Florida governor Reubin Askew concurred. Speaking at the 1971 gathering of the Florida Peace Officers Association, Askew noted that the "complexities of modern America and the pressures of urbanization" had revolutionized policing. Rather than merely handing out parking tickets or shooting it "out with a felon in some dark alley," the policeman of the 1970s also needed to "function somewhat as lawyer, psychologist, referee, marriage counselor, fireman, father, friend, coach, teacher, technician, tactician, obstetrician and statistician." The modern American police needed careful training to complement the badge.[98]

The black market for liquor and gambling collapsed. Police departments professionalized. The Voting Rights Act of 1965 and other civil rights legislation regulated local politics. U.S. Supreme Court rulings required reapportionment of state legislatures and safeguarded the rights of the accused. States weakened demand for moonshine by making liquor, particularly by-drink sales, more available. Even gambling became more acceptable as legislatures stretched loopholes for games such as bingo in South Carolina or casino gaming in Mississippi. Similarly to the post-1960s South Florida described by historian Nathan D. B. Connolly, boosters in burgeoning resorts along the southern shore sought "to assemble disjointed amoral and sometimes immoral cities into a moral metropolis, all while making as few public references to race as possible." White southerners of the Sunbelt South abandoned their hypocritical stance toward gambling and alcohol as they embraced the Sunbelt ethos of growth and free-market capitalism.[99]

Epilogue
Sunbelt Fetes

A new South is being born. The old South was ploughed under. But the ashes are still warm.
—Henry Miller, *The Air-Conditioned Nightmare* (1945)

Ed Kerr, writing for *Harper's Magazine* in 1958, called attention to a peculiar phenomenon occurring across the Gulf South states as timber companies and real-estate developers crowded once sparsely used lands. Although possessing a fourth of the nation's forest acreage, the South claimed more than 80 percent of the country's forest fires annually. In Florida, Mississippi, and Louisiana, arsonists caused 50 percent of these blazes. Yet the firebugs bore responsibility for 80 percent of the damage to timber stands since they specifically targeted these holdings. Kerr wrote, "In many communities, particularly near the Gulf Coast, this practice of 'burning the big man' has become more or less a pastime." Kerr noted the arsonists were most active in places where the "two forces" of industry and tourism squeezed small landholders by removing open range, restricting access to traditional hunting and fishing grounds, raising property tax rates, and turning hardscrabble farmers into employees. Scorching the woods hurt businessmen's pocketbooks and defiled a landscape to which tourists were drawn. For poor southerners such as Willie Kilcrease, a moonshiner and poacher in Florida's Okaloosa County, a well-timed forest fire ran off timber crews. John Shea of the U.S. Forest Service, who studied the problem of southern forest fires during the Depression, argued that the majority of attacks were "practically at the level of frustration" and that the pressure of development provided a "set-up, psychologically speaking, ready-made for numerous acts of aggression." While Hank Williams equated setting the woods on fire with a hot date in his 1952 hit song, the prevalence of southern arson revealed a region undergoing profound changes in the mid-twentieth century.[1]

The ashes of these conflagrations smoldered but did not halt coastal development. Real-estate and lumber interests launched an intensive publicity campaign against forest fires during the 1950s. Federal support led to more watchful efforts by the Forest Service. The profitability of neon-trimmed restaurants, well-stocked bars, tacky souvenir stands, and high-rise condos increased. By the 1980s the end of Jim Crow, the legalization of alcohol sales, the completion of most of the interstate network, and the deregulation of the airlines made the beaches of the American South more popular and accessible than ever. So popular were resorts that, by the late twentieth century, nostalgia for a past when southern coastal towns were what they had never been—quaint communities of friendly neighbors—arose. The design of a Seaside or Watercolor in Florida, developed during the 1980s and 1990s, respectively, recalled such an imagined southern past. Sanitized from the scene were broken roulette wheels, moonshine bottles, whites-only signs, DDT sprayers, and seawalls upon which most southern beach towns laid their foundation. It makes one wonder, as a Panhandle visitor did, what warm ashes rest beneath a resort when a sign reads "Rosemary Beach: A New Traditional Town on the Gulf. Established 1995."[2]

NOTES

Abbreviations

Archival Collections

ARC	Amistad Research Center, Tulane University
COHCH	Center for Oral History and Cultural Heritage, University of Southern Mississippi
GTHC	Galveston and Texas History Center, Rosenberg Library
GCCR	Galveston Chamber of Commerce Records, Galveston and Texas History Center, Rosenberg Library
HCOHP	Horry County Oral History Project, Waccamaw Room, Kimbel Library, Coastal Carolina University
LRC	Louisiana Research Collection, Special Collections, Howard-Tilton Memorial Library, Tulane University
SASC	Special and Area Studies Collections, Smathers Libraries, University of Florida
SCL	South Caroliniana Library, University of South Carolina
SHC	Southern Historical Collection, University of North Carolina at Chapel Hill
STDC	Stanonis Travel Diary Collection, Special Collections and Archives, J. Edgar and Louise S. Monroe Library, Loyola University New Orleans
THNOC	The Historic New Orleans Collection, Williams Research Center

Newspapers

BH	*Biloxi Herald*
BDH	*Biloxi Daily Herald*
GC	*Gull's Cry*
GDN	*Galveston Daily News*
LW	*Louisiana Weekly*
MBN	*Myrtle Beach News*
MBS	*Myrtle Beach Sun*
MBSN	*Myrtle Beach Sun-News*
MBSOBN	*Myrtle Beach Sun and Ocean Beach News*
PCDH	*Panama City Daily Herald*

PCH   *Panama City Herald*
PCNH   *Panama City News-Herald*
VBN   *Virginia Beach News*
VBS   *Virginia Beach Sun*
VBSN   *Virginia Beach Sun-News*

Introduction

1. Poe, *Tales*, 1.

2. James Edwards (10 December 1889), James Edwards Ledger, SASC. On depictions of southern swamps, see McIntyre, *Souvenirs of the Old South*, 68–95; Anthony Wilson, *Shadow and Shelter*, 3–103. On Progressive reform and the City Beautiful movement, see Melosi, *Sanitary City*, 103–204; William Wilson, *City Beautiful Movement*, 1–6, 281–306.

3. O'Rell and Allyn, *Jonathan and His Continent*, 295; J. E. Rawlings to Isabel Baker, (1 January 1905), Isabel Louise Ball Baker Papers, Virginia Historical Society; Rove, *Idea*, 33–43; Stanonis, *Creating the Big Easy*, 17–19.

4. J. E. Rawlings to Isabel Baker, (7 December 1904), Isabel Louise Ball Baker Papers, Virginia Historical Society; Muirhead, *Land of Contrasts*, 260–261; *WPA Guide to Florida*, 462. On urban amusements and travel in the late nineteenth and early twentieth centuries, see Cocks, *Doing the Town*, 9–40, 106–173; Peiss, *Cheap Amusements*, 11–55, 115–138; Costa, "Evolution of Retirement," 232–236; Harris, "Urban Tourism", 66–82; Short, "Confederate Veteran Pensions," 75–101.

5. S. M. Simister Diary-Scrapbook (10 October 1954), STDC; Knight, *Tropic of Hopes*, 65–80.

6. Beirne Brues, Diary of a Trip to Southernmost Florida (21 June 1924), STDC; Anna P. Kelly Diary (24 June 1927), STDC. On the erratic nature of racial customs and the impact on travel, see McMillen, *Dark Journey*, 10–14; Schweid, *Catfish and the Delta*, 13.

7. Leather Worker Union Diary (1902), STDC; Edith K. Miller Diary (1913), STDC.

8. Lassiter, "De Jure/De Facto Segregation," 28; Wolcott, *Race, Riots, and Roller Coasters*, 2–7.

9. Jeanelle Landstrom Family Diary (6–7 February 1931), STDC; Maude Lierch Diaries (30 October 1945; 7 November 1945), STDC; McIntyre, *Souvenirs of the Old South*, 101–131.

10. Pearl Noegel, Diary (1921), Noegel Family Collection, SASC; Our Trip to Florida Diary (4 July 1938), STDC; Hazel Timms Diary (10 May 1956), STDC; Rosemary Diaries (18 May 1951), STDC.

11. Kahrl, "Sunbelt by the Sea," 490–491; Kahrl, *The Land Was Ours*, 57. For recent work on African American beaches, see P. Nicole King, *Sombreros and Motorcycles*, 113–180; Phelts, *American Beach for African Americans*.

12. Cooper and Knotts, "Declining Dixie," 1083–1101. For recent research on southern tourism, see Karen Cox, *Destination Dixie*; Davis, *Race against Time*; Rushing, *Memphis*; Stanonis, *Creating the Big Easy*; Stanonis, *Dixie Emporium*; Starnes, *Creating the Land*; Starnes, *Southern Journeys*; Yuhl, *Golden Haze of Memory*.

13. Hoover and Ratchford, *Economic Resources*, 162–163; Woodward, *Origins of the New South*; Edward Ayers, *Promise of the New South*, 97.

14. Goldfield, "Searching for the Sunbelt," 3; Brownell, Introduction to *Searching for the Sunbelt*, 3; Shermer, *Sunbelt Capitalism*, 3–4. For discussions of the South as part of the Sunbelt, see Shulman, *Cotton Belt to Sunbelt*; Nickerson and Dochuk, *Sunbelt Rising*.

15. Stanonis, *Creating the Big Easy*, 22.

16. Kaufman and Pilkey, *Beaches Are Moving*, 24; Monmonier, *Coastlines*, 14–27, 58–67, 163–166.

17. Freidel, "Boosters, Intellectuals, and the American City," 115.

18. Connolly, "Colored, Caribbean, and Condemned," 33; Carl Abbott, *Boosters and Businessmen*, 109.

19. James Ingraham, "One Man's Work" (n.d., c. 1910), James Edmundson Ingraham Papers, SASC. Revels, *Sunshine Paradise*, 40–56; Richter, *Home on the Rails*, 65–84.

20. J. U. H. Barker, "The Camp Walton Country," *Gulf States Magazine* (August 1913), 4; "Big Total of $135,000,000 in South's New Hotels," *Atlanta Constitution* (8 February 1925).

21. McComb, *Galveston*, 338–345.

22. Leather Worker Union Diary (1902), STDC; "Wants Harbor on Gulf Coast," *Atlanta Constitution* (11 October 1904). For information on the Panama Canal and its political, diplomatic, and economic consequences, see McCullough, *Path between the Seas*; Maurer and Yu, "What T. R. Took," 686–721.

23. Ray Thompson, "The Father of Gulfport," *BDH* (7 March 1957).

24. Cooper Darby interviewed by Mike Garvey (13 May 1976), COHCH; "Influence of a Railroad on the Lumber Trade of Mississippi," *American Lumberman* (11 November 1905), 29; "Mississippi Should Make Gulfport the Outlet for Its Cotton Crop," *BDH* (7 September 1921); Ray Thompson, "Father of Gulfport"; Ray Thompson, "Gulfport's Most Famous Winter Guest," *BDH* (11 March 1957).

25. "Mrs. West, Widow of City Founder, Dies at Age 85," *PCNH* (27 August 1970); Loftin, "A Woman Liberated," 396–410.

26. Quote from "John H. Perry," *PCH* (30 September 1935). "W. C. Sherman, Bay Pioneer Dies," *PCH* (27 July 1967); "PCH Makes Bow," *PCH* (30 September 1935); Loftin, "A Woman Liberated," 406–408.

27. "Chapin Foundation Plays Vital Role," *MBSN* (8 November 1962); Mark Garner interviewed by Catherine Lewis and Randall Wells (20 November 1992), HCOHP. Ayers, *Promise of the New South*, 96–97. For the early history of Myrtle Beach, see Hourigan, "Welcome to South Carolina," 18–35; Stokes, *Myrtle Beach*, 10–17, 19–21.

28. Ruby Phillips, "90 Years Young," *VBSN* (3 May 1962); Sarah Blackford, diary (16 June 1895), Sarah Evelyn Baylor Blackford Diary, Virginia Historical Society. For background on Virginia Beach, see "B. P. Holland, 83, First Mayor of Virginia Beach, Presented Key to City at Special Council Session," *VBN* (10 November 1950); "Two Hotels, Few Cottages Was Virginia Beach 1889," *VBSN* (29 June 1961); Clark, *Spirit of the Times*, 93; Souther, "Twixt Ocean and Pines," 2–26.

29. "An Old Saying," *MBN* (5 March 1954); Harvey, *Urban Experience*, 83.

Chapter 1. Coastal Empires

1. J. Lewis Brown, "Why Men Migrate," *Outlook* (17 December 1924), 642. Historiography on the rise of the Sunbelt generally explores the demographic shift as a post-Depression trend with far less attention to the rise of regionalism and tourism during the interwar period. See, for instance, Schulman, *From Cotton Belt to Sunbelt*; Dochuk, *From Bible Belt to Sunbelt*. The term *Sunbelt* is laden with political meanings regarding the rise of the Republican Party and the emergence of military and retirement communities between California and Florida. Kevin Phillips is regarded as the person who coined the term in his 1969 study, *The Emerging Republican Majority*.

2. Brown, "Why Men Migrate," 643.

3. For examples of major works on the southern economy, all of which largely overlook tourism, see Ayers, *Promise of the New South*, 9–25, 96–131; Carlton and Coclanis, *The South, the Nation, and the World*, 9–11; Gaston, *The New South Creed*, 190–207; Wright, *Old South, New South*, 10–16.

4. "Time Arrives to Start Movement [of] Tourists South," *BDH* (9 October 1915); Pyle, *Ernie's America*, 289. For insight on the United States during the First World War, see Belasco, *Americans on the Road*, 24–30; Flink, *The Automobile Age*, 170–175; Kennedy, *Over Here*, 93–143.

5. Merz, *Great American Band Wagon*, 12. For information on car ownership, see Stanonis, *Creating the Big Easy*, 54; Flink, *The Automobile Age*, 189–193.

6. West, *Plainville, U.S.A.*, 211; Beirne Brues, Diary of a Trip to Southernmost Florida (14 June 1924; 20 June 1924), STDC; Jeanelle Landstrom Family Diary (10 February 1931), STDC; James Stevens interviewed by Catherine Lewis (25 September 1992), HCOHP; Ye Old Family Scrap Book (14 June 1949), STDC. For information on road conditions and construction, see Hugill, "Good Roads," 327–349; Lesseig, "'Out of the Mud,'" 50–72; Lichtenstein, "Good Roads," 85–110; Keith, *Country People in the New South*, 103–117; Preston, *Dirt Roads to Dixie*.

7. Edith K. Miller Diary (1913), STDC; Pindell, *Making Tracks*, 166.

8. "Transportation—Our Problem," *MBN* (30 July 1949); "Court Uphold MPSC on Restoring G&SIRR Trains," *BDH* (22 March 1954); Minutes of the Board of Directors of the Galveston Chamber of Commerce (9 November 1954), GCCR; "L&N Ordered to Continue Trains," *BDH* (24 April 1959); Ronnie J. Caire interviewed by R. Wayne Pyle (26 September 1979), COHCH.

9. "A Tourist Business Bottleneck," *MBSN* (27 August 1964); Hourigan, "Welcome to South Carolina," 44–51; G. J. Scott to Editor, *Life* (25 June 1951), 7; "Discuss East-West Roadway along Coast Area," *BDH* (25 June 1949). For information on the interstate system, see "Coastal Corridor Highway Pushed," *VBS* (22 October 1970); Flink, *The Automobile Age*, 175–176, 370–373; Tom Lewis, *Divided Highways*, 75–92.

10. Guy Middleton, "They Spread Sunshine with a Smile and Orange Juice," *PCNH* (21 April 1968); "S.C.'s First Welcome Center to Be Built at Little River," *MBSN* (19 January 1967).

11. Alperin, *History of the Gulf Intracoastal Waterway*, 4–5, 9–10, 16–17, 41–44; Noll and Tegeder, *Ditch of Dreams*, 45–99, 273–278; Stokes, *Myrtle Beach*, 36–38.

12. "Socastee Anchorage Basin under Construction," *MBN* (2 April 1936); Ann Diary (6 December 1946; 16 December 1946), STDC; Bissell, *How Many Miles to Galena?* 266; *Sunny Day Guide*, 2, SCL; Burman, *It's a Big Country*, 80–83.

13. "Atlantans to See Airport Opening at Myrtle Beach," *Atlanta Constitution* (14 August 1928); "Airline Service Opens May 14th," *MBN* (31 March 1950); "Civilian Aviation and Our Resort Area," *Myrtle Beach Daily News* (3 January 1956); "Gold in the Sky," *Myrtle Beach Daily News* (6 January 1956); "Airlines Bring $2 Million to Grand Strand Annually," *MBSN* (16 February 1967); Southern Airways ad, *PCH* (25 March 1958); "Just Reminiscing; Panama City, 1965," *PCNH* (30 July 1967); M. M. Frost to George Smathers (8 March 1957), Robert N. "Bert" Dosh Papers, SASC;. For information about air travel, see Catherine Barnes, *Journey from Jim Crow*, 137–142; Barry, *Femininity in Flight*, 13–16, 97–111; Bednarek, "City Planning and Municipal Airports," 349–375; Karsner, "Aviation and Airports," 406–436.

14. Sam Dawson, "Florida Economy Serves as U.S. Business Mark," *BDH* (26 March 1954); P. Ruffin to Mary McLeod-Bethune (26 February 1930), Mary McLeod-Bethune Papers, Amistad Research Center, Tulane University; Sal Romano to Editor, *VBSN* (10 September 1963); "'Sand in Your Shoes' Helped Burton to Decide to Change," *MBSN* (8 July 1965); James Gay, "Open Letter to People of Myrtle Beach," *MBN* (28 July 1950).

15. "$180,000,000," *PCH* (8 October 1935); "Asleep," *VBN* (10 March 1939).

16. Points, *America the Beautiful*, 46–47; "Southland Most Popular of Vacationlands in United States," *VBSN* (11 August 1960).

17. William Workman, "S.C. Tourist Trade Is Undeveloped," *MBS* (27 October 1950).

18. "Better Roads, Bridges Bring Visitors to State," *VBN* (3 July 1952); "Income from Tourists Is Fifth in S.C.," *MBS* (25 May 1951); "Virginia Enjoys Increasing Out-of-State Auto Travel," *VBSN* (6 August 1953); "To Sell Virginia to Virginians," *VBSN* (12 August 1954); Ray Thompson, "Tourists Spend with Us a Hundred Grand a Day," *BDH* (18 September 1956).

19. "Virginia Beach," *VBN* (16 June 1939); "Police Complete Town Census," *VBN* (5 January 1940); James Grotius, "Promoting Beach's Attractions Is Essence of Life for Laura," *VBSN* (6 April 1961); "Merger Carries by 5 to 1 Margin; All Areas Favor," *VBSN* (11 January 1962); "Virginia Beach Nation's 9th Largest in Area," *VBSN* (3 January 1963); Doris Padrick, "View of Virginia Beach," *VBSN* (29 August 1963); "Holiday Week-End Was Record Breaker," *VBS* (8 July 1965). For more perspective on the merger, see Carl Abbott, *New Urban America*, 203–211; Kahrl, "Sunbelt by the Sea," 493–495.

20. "Population Jumps 109% in Decade," *MBN* (10 August 1951); "The Next Ten Years," *MBN* (23 June 1950); "Myrtle Beach Developing in Eyes of Nation as Top Resort Mecca," *Myrtle Beach Daily News* (6 June 1956); Mary Miller, "Losing Base Compares to Myrtle Beach Disappearing," *MBSN* (27 January 1973); Henrietta Abeles to Sigmund and Gina Abeles (8 March 1960), Sigmund Abeles Papers, SCL.

21. Ray Thompson, "Tourists Spend with Us a Hundred Grand a Day," *BDH* (18 September 1956); "The Tourists Are Coming," *BDH* (23 April 1968); Billy Ray Quave, "Biloxi's Tourism Gets Early Start," *BDH* (3 June 1968).

22. "Paper Mill Biggest of Kind in World," *PCH* (21 February 1936); "Industrial Life of Panama City Expands," *PCH* (28 April 1936).

23. Jim Massey, "Panama City—New Records Ahead," *PCNH* (4 August 1947); Governor Reubin Askew, Governor's Conference on Tourism (20 October 1977), Reubin O'Donovan Askew Speeches, SASC.

24. "Four Upper Strand Municipalities Incorporate," *MBSN* (21 December 1967); "Strand Voters Call It North Myrtle Beach," *MBSN* (21 March 1968); Stokes, *Myrtle Beach*, 201.

25. "Panama City Beach Takes First Breath," *PCNH* (13 August 1970); "Merger at Beach Legal, Says Court," *PCNH* (30 March 1972).

26. Untitled Statement by Chamber of Commerce on Conditions in Galveston (n.d., c. 1955), Minutes of the Galveston Chamber of Commerce, GCCR; Stephanie Pace, "PACEing the Strand," *MBSN* (5 February 1972); "We Must Bury the Hatchet," *MBSN* (8 March 1962). For information on legislative apportionment, see Donald Bushman and William Stanley, "State Senate Reapportionment," 654–670; Douglas Smith, "Into the Political Thicket," 263–285.

27. Karl Abbott, *Open for the Season*, 43; "State Division," *PCH* (4 November 1935); Robert Sherrill, "Florida's Legislature: The Pork Chop State of Mind," *Harper's Magazine* (November 1965), 82–97; Connolly, "By Eminent Domain," 466–467. On the Pork Chop Gang, see Weitz, "Bourbon, Pork Chops, and Red Peppers," 3–10, 36–43, 225–233.

28. Stillman, "Florida," 90; "The Gulf Coast," *PCNH* (26 March 1982).

29. Bachelder, *Popular Resorts*, 299; Julius Lopez interviewed by Orley Caudill (2 August 1978), COHCH.

30. Holmes, *Six in a Ford*, 20–21; "Suddenly, Tourism Is Booming in South Florida," *PCNH* (4 March 1982); Kofoed, *The Florida Story*, 101; Tom Purdy to Susan Shughart (21 July 1969), Galveston Convention and Tourist Bureau, GCCR; "Extended Tourist Season," *PCH* (3 March 1958); Faris, *Seeing the Sunny South*, 88. For information on air-conditioning, see Cooper, *Air-Conditioning America*, 132–139, 142–176; Arsenault, "End of the Long Hot Summer," 597–628; Jeff Biddle, "Spread of Residential Air Conditioning," 402–423.

31. *The End of the Rainbow* (Valparaiso Realty Company, n.d., c. 1924), 13, SASC.

32. Merz, *The Great American Band Wagon*, 123, 125; Revels, *Sunshine Paradise*, 42–45; McDonough, "Selling Sarasota," 10–31.

33. "Mississippi Coast Super Chamber of Commerce," *BDH* (26 June 1922); "Mississippi Coast Week," *BDH* (30 November 1925).

34. "Biloxi Raises $25,000 Quota of $100,000," *BDH* (8 December 1925).

35. Ray Thompson, "The Famous Two Years $500,000 Was Spent Advertising the Coast," *BDH* (11 October 1957); Ray Thompson, "Tourist Excitement Thirty Years Ago," *BDH* (24 January 1958).

36. "Welcome Chicago!" *BDH* (16 October 1925); "How the Coast Looked to a Chicago Tribune Staff Man," *BDH* (26 November 1925).

37. "Advisory Board Witnesses Tourist Industry Growth," *BDH* (12 August 1973).

38. *Inlet Beach on the Gulf of Mexico*, 11; *The WPA Guide to Florida*, 494.

39. "Extended Tourist Season," *PCH* (3 March 1958); "Local Beaches Fast Becoming Mecca," *PCNH* (1 July 1962).

40. "Response to Ad Campaign to Up Budget," *Panama City News* (23 July 1954); "More Attractions Needed," *PCH* (13 March 1968); Michael Fiorelli, "City Could Do without Its 'Red Neck' Image," *GC* (17 March 1987). For a history of the so-called Redneck Riviera, see Harvey Jackson, "Rise and Decline of the Redneck Riviera," 8–30; "The Florida Room," 316–322; and *Rise and Decline of the Redneck Riviera.*

41. "Tourists Sight-See in Coastal Country," *MBN* (4 March 1937); "A Tourist Barometer," *MBN* (11 June 1954); "Easter Scenes around Myrtle Beach," *MBSN* (26 April 1973); "Churches on Strand Expect Huge Crowds," *MBSN* (1 April 1972); "State Shows 'Love' for Beach Area," *MBSN* (26 August 1972); "$42,000 Advertising Budget Adopted for City Program," *VBSN* (13 March 1958); "Dealing in Facts," *VBSN* (17 May 1956).

42. John Conder to All Salesmen (17 June 1926), William Wightman Smoak Papers, SCL; Myrtle Beach Sales Company to All Salesmen for Information (11 June 1926), William Wightman Smoak Papers, SCL; S. D. Cox interviewed by Catherine Lewis (6 November 1992), HCOHP; Meyer Eiseman Realtor ad, *BDH* (11 December 1925); Clifton-by-the-Sea ad, *GDN* (27 May 1927); Harry Fitzpatrick and Company ad, *BDH* (15 December 1925).

43. John Conder to Senior Salesmen (10 July 1926), William Wightman Smoak Papers, SCL; Sub-District Sales Manager to D. W. Gavin (1 July 1926), William Wightman Smoak Papers, SCL; John Conder to All Senior Salesmen (19 July 1926), William Wightman Smoak Papers, SCL.

44. *Arcady*, SCL; "The Beaches," *New Era* (July 1929), 9.

45. L. H. Simpson to W. W. Smoak (11 October 1926), William Wightman Smoak Papers, SCL; Haddock to Robert Dosh (9 June 1931), Robert N. "Bert" Dosh Papers, SASC; Mrs. Charles Stephens to Eleanor Roosevelt (18 December 1934), in Green, *Looking for the New Deal*, 92; Wright, *Old South, New South*, 226–227.

46. Olive Barrett Clower interviewed by R. Wayne Pyle (19 September 1979), COHCH.

47. J. W. McCann to W. W. Smoak (31 August 1926), William Wightman Smoak Papers, SCL; "Mississippi Coast Offers Unrivalled Advantages," *BDH* (26 June 1928).

48. "Chamber of Commerce for Virginia Beach Is Organized at Meeting," *VBN* (7 June 1935); "An Act," *MBN* (6 May 1937); "Myrtle Beach, the Place We Meet," *MBN* (9 June 1938).

49. "Faith in Myrtle Beach Property," *MBN* (7 May 1936); Edward Newton Reser to Claude Gordon (13 August 1931), Edward Newton Reser Letters, STDC.

50. Hardie and Ellis Realty Company, *BDH* (21 December 1925). On restrictive covenants and mortgage policy, see Freund, *Colored Property*, 45–139; Kenneth Jackson, *Crabgrass Frontier*, 190–218; Fox Gotham, "Urban Space," 616–633.

51. "Brilliancy Marks Opening of Edgewater Gulf Hotel," *BDH* (11 January 1927); Ray Thompson, "Chicago's Magnificent Contribution to the Coast," *BDH* (19 August 1957).

52. "Some Big Coast Events," *BDH* (13 January 1927); "Buena Vista an Institution," *BDH* (15 July 1927); "The War Moves Nearer," *VBN* (11 September 1942); "Myrtle Beach's Convention Headquarters," *MBN* (20 April 1951).

53. "Our Ocean Waterway," *VBN* (16 August 1940); Thomas Turner to Duncan Fletcher (22 September 1927), Thomas Yon Papers, SASC; "Opportunity," *GDN* (21 April 1940); "Library Is Favorite Spot for Vacationers," *MBSN* (4 July 1963); Catherine Heniford Lewis, *Horry County, South Carolina*, 155.

54. "Fort Massachusetts," *BDH* (16 April 1934).

55. "Building Dock at Ship Island," *BDH* (2 May 1934); Ship Island ad, *BDH* (11 May 1934); Ray Thompson, "Your Pleasure Is His Business," *BDH* (22 July 1957). On historic preservation movements, see Davis, *Race against Time*, 51–82; Stanonis, *Creating the Big Easy*, 141–169; Yuhl, *Golden Haze of Memory*, 21–52.

56. "Suggest Merger Shrimp Festival and Mardi Gras," *BDH* (19 June 1956).

57. "Carnival in Biloxi," *BDH* (1 March 1938); "Suggest Merger Shrimp Festival and Mardi Gras," *BDH* (19 June 1956); Jan Garrick, John McDermott interviewed by Tom Healy (8 September 1978), COHCH; "Beauvoir First Stop on Biloxi's Saturday," *BDH* (9 March 1954); "Beauvoir Offers a Glimpse into the Coast's History," *BDH* (12 August 1973); McComb, "Galveston as a Tourist City," 345; "Lotus Festival Next Big Event," *VBSN* (5 July 1956); "Sun-Fun Events Witnessed by Sixty Thousand People," *MBN* (11 June 1954); "Key to the City," *MBSOBN* (6 June 1956); "Sun Fun Days Strike Grand Strand Beaches," *MBSN* (5 June 1973).

58. "Definite Plans Made to Present 'Cavalcade of the Sea' on Beach during Summer by Local Society," *VBN* (4 March 1938); "Rebel Group Sets Campaign," *VBN* (3 April 1958); "'Confederacy' Well Received by Capacity Audience in Premiere Performance Here Tuesday Evening," *VBSN* (3 July 1958); "They Are Protecting Their Own Kind of Enterprise," *MBSN* (4 July 1968).

59. "Motorcycles Gathered at Ocean Drive," *MBN* (15 May 1953). For a more recent examination of the bike week festivities in Myrtle Beach and Atlantic Beach, see P. Nicole King, *Sombreros and Motorcycles*, 150–180.

60. "The New City Symbol," *VBS* (9 September 1965); "The New City Symbol," *VBS* (1 September 1966); "Tour Sign Goes Up," *VBS* (3 July 1968).

61. "Biloxi Scenes Will Be Taken," *BDH* (9 April 1920); "Myrtle Beach Movie Shown Here Tuesday," *MBS* (21 July 1950); "Playtown, U.S.A.," *VBSN* (21 May 1953); "New Film for City Approved," *VBSN* (16 July 1964).

62. "Training School for Waitresses to Open in Gulfport," *BDH* (6 May 1942); Minutes of the Board of Directors of the Galveston Chamber of Commerce (7 July 1950), GCCR; "Travel Conference to Stress Tourist Info, Hospitality," *VBSN* (2 June 1964); "Tourist Rental Laws Explained by Commission," *PCH* (6 March 1958).

63. "9 Conventions Scheduled to Meet in June," *VBN* (30 May 1935); "Ocean Forest Hotel Booked 42 Conventions for 1950," *MBN* (20 January 1950); Bama Byrd to Editor, *BDH* (5 May 1949); Ray Thompson, "Convention City," *BDH* (14 April 1956); Minutes of the Board of Directors of the Galveston Chamber of Commerce (14 October 1952), GCCR; Breakdown Spending—Conventioneers (22 August 1966), Galveston Convention and Tourist Bureau, GCCR.

64. "Mayor Dusch Gets Building Started Here," *VBSN* (11 July 1957); "Country's First Aluminum Dome Located Here," *VBSN* (12 July 1962).

65. "Ground Breaking Has Real Meaning," *VBSN* (11 July 1957); "Convention Center Exceeds Expectations First Year," *VBSN* (25 November 1958); "Council Quickly Gives Shepard Honors of City," *VBSN* (11 May 1961).

66. "Everybody Gets in the Act at Eight Flags Frontier," *BDH* (12 August 1973); "From the Pages of the Past," *PCH* (24 August 1967); "Val Valentine: Man of 1,000

Talents," *PCNH* (14 August 1970). On Disneyland and its impact, see Avila, *Popular Culture in the Age of White Flight*, 106–144; Kirse May, *Golden State, Golden Youth*, 27–66.

67. James Grotius, "Frontier City to Open in June Bringing a Taste of the Old West," *VBSN* (30 March 1961); "New Attractions Open This Year," *VBSN* (29 June 1961); "Anyone Want to 'Ride Shotgun' for This 5-Month Stagecoach Trip," *VBSN* (25 February 1964); "Stagecoach Due on Schedule Here July 4," *VBSN* (23 June 1964); Frances Moore, "Vacationing along Beach This Week," *MBSN* (9 July 1964). On the impact of Disney World, see Mormino, *Land of Sunshine*, 100–108; Richard Francaviglia, "Main Street U.S.A.," 141–156; David Johnson, "Disney World," 157–165.

68. "Crowd Estimated at 35,000 Visits Here for Fourth," *PCH* (6 July 1936); "100,000 Visitors Expected Here July 4th," *MBN* (1 July 1937); "Record Crowd Jams Myrtle Beach for Rainy Holiday," *MBS* (7 July 1950); "'Different Kind' of Fourth Crowd Is Area's Largest," *MBSN* (5 July 1962); "Estimated 75,000 People at Beach During Holiday," *MBN* (7 July 1950); "Record Crowd Observes Fourth Along Strand," *MBSN* (7 July 1966).

69. William Rivers, "Florida: The State with the Two-Way Stretch," *Harper's Magazine* (February 1955), 32; "The Public and Taxes," *VBN* (9 February 1951); "Town Revises Tax Laws," *VBN* (23 February 1951); "Tourists Can Lessen Tax Load—Kellam," *VBSN* (24 January 1963). For more on sales taxes and tourism, see Stanonis, *Creating the Big Easy*, 73–82.

70. Minutes of the Board of Directors of the Galveston Chamber of Commerce (10 January 1967), GCCR.

71. "Chamber Firm on Motel Tax Like Custer's Last Stand," *MBSN* (30 March 1969); "Horry Solons Beat Increase," *MBSN* (1 May 1969); "Measure Cites Tourism," *MBSN* (5 May 1975).

72. Mountains—Trip'O'Log Diary (1927), STDC; Beirne Brues, Diary of a Trip to Southernmost Florida (30 June 1924), STDC; "'No Trespassing' Sign Up on Nine State Arteries," *PCH* (24 October 1935); Joyce Pugh, "Tourist Boom Cuts Bay's Jobless Rate," *PCNH* (6 March 1982).

73. Janice Prendergast, "Combating Winter Doldrums," *GC* (14 October 1983); Daniel Day, "Upfront: Party Plans," *GC* (26 September 1985).

74. "Importance of Tourists for City Is Told," *PCNH* (8 July 1939); Governor C. Farris Bryant, Transcript of Ask the Governor (22 January 1962), C. Farris Bryant Papers, SASC; "New Film for City Approved," *VBSN* (16 July 1964).

75. Governor C. Farris Bryant, Transcript of Ask the Governor (15 January 1962), C. Farris Bryant Papers, SASC.

76. Governor C. Farris Bryant, Transcript of Ask the Governor (14 May 1962), C. Farris Bryant Papers, SASC.

77. "For More Winter Residents," *VBN* (14 December 1934); "'Winter' to Vanish in Old Dominion," *VBN* (3 July 1952); P. F. Murray to Editor, *VBSN* (17 September 1953); "Better Appearance," *MBSOBN* (4 January 1956).

78. Alden Horton to Editor, *VBS* (4 May 1967); "Shop Owners—Please Note," *VBSN* (6 October 1964).

79. Stephanie Pace, "PACEing the Strand," *MBSN* (2 September 1971).

80. "Pirates Seek Loose Culprit," *MBSN* (18 October 1962); "Culprit's Trial Slated Saturday," *MBSN* (8 November 1962); "Culprit Myth Exposed in City Hall Meeting," *MBSN* (15 November 1962); "An Editorial," *MBSN* (15 November 1962).

81. Stephanie Pace, "PACEing the Strand," *MBSN* (22 July 1971); Armstead, *"Lord Please Don't Take Me in August,"* 50–56, 93–94.

82. "Asleep," *VBN* (10 March 1939); "Let's Comb Beach," *MBN* (8 June 1951); Frances Moore, "Industry Is Needed, But Tourism Conflicts [*sic*]," *MBSN* (4 April 1971).

83. "George Veitt to Editor," *Princess Anne Times* (11 June 1915); "Fort Story," *VBSN* (1 July 1954); Mrs. Claire Grant Cook Scrapbook (12 July 1940), STDC.

84. Governor Millard Caldwell, Florida's Second Century (n.d., c. 1945), Millard Caldwell Papers, SASC; Mayor Brantly Harris to War Production Board (20 May 1942), Brantly Harris Papers, Rosenberg Library. On the impact of the Second World War on the South, see Chamberlain, *Victory at Home*, 15–39; Connolly, "By Eminent Domain," 176–184; Thomas, *Riveting and Rationing in Dixie*; Cobb, "World War II," 3–20; Pelt, "Wainwright Shipyard," 179–249, 370–375.

85. "Virginia Beach Has Assumed Atmosphere of Military Center," *VBN* (27 September 1940); "New City Filled with Military Posts," *VBSN* (3 January 1963).

86. "Biloxi Selected Site for Army Air Corps School," *BDH* (18 March 1941); "Great Project Secured," *BDH* (19 March 1941); "How Near 4 Millions [*sic*] to be Spent Here for Gunnery School Base," *PCNH* (30 April 1941); "Site for Tyndall Selected in 1940," *PCNH* (1 August 1947).

87. "Banner Season Expected as to the Result of Unusual Governmental Activities," *VBN* (30 May 1941); Dos Passos, *State of the Nation*, 94.

88. "Hotels Expect Good Business from Military in September," *VBN* (11 September 1942).

89. "Dimout Ordered," *BDH* (12 June 1943); "Lights On," *VBN* (5 November 1943); "Blackout Restrictions Rescinded by Gov.," *VBN* (18 May 1945).

90. "The War Moves Nearer," *VBN* (11 September 1942); "Army to Operate Warner Hotel for Civilian Personnel of Camp Pendleton," *VBN* (30 July 1943); "Beach Hotels Granted Right to Sell Rooms at Daily Rate," *VBN* (22 January 1943); "Rent Control Ruling Places Summer Home under the Ban," *VBN* (21 May 1943); "Army's Restricted Zone Covers Entire Beach Area," *VBN* (13 August 1943); Mormino, *Land of Sunshine*, 308–309; Revels, *Sunshine Paradise*, 87–93.

91. "New Vistas," *MBSOBN* (25 January 1956); "2,102 Dwelling Units Built in Gulfport in Nine Years," *BDH* (14 May 1949); "2,156 Dwelling Units Built in Biloxi since January '40," *BDH* (12 July 1949); "Local Chamber of Commerce Puts Beach in Eyes of World," *VBN* (7 December 1945).

92. "Fort Walton Beach Booming City," *PCNH* (20 August 1967); Don Hill, "Fort Story, Small by Comparison Has Big Impact on Virginia Beach's Economy," *VBSN* (24 January 1957).

93. "Dear Tourist," *BDH* (6 May 1954).

94. "Total of Keesler AFB Payroll Is Now over $5 Million Monthly," *BDH* (22 March 1960); "Finest Leaders Responsible for Security—White," *BDH* (15 May 1954); "Na-

tion's Armed Strength on Display as Services Mark Armed Forces Day," *VBSN* (13 May 1954).

95. "Air Show to Highlight Armed Forces Day at Eglin," *PCH and News* (18 May 1968); "Midshipmen Stage Assault Landing for Large Crowd," *VBSN* (25 June 1963); "Air Show Slated at Tyndall Today," *Panama City News* (25 June 1968); "Myrtle Beach Air Base Playing Big Role in 12th Sun Fun Festival," *MBSN* (6 June 1963).

96. "Soldier Reportedly Attacks Woman; New Manhunt Is Launched," *BDH* (10 April 1942); Paul Stults to Becky Stokes (21 July 1942), Paul M. Stults Papers, SASC-UF; Hunter Thompson, *Proud Highway*, 59; "Sun Spots," *MBSOBN* (4 December 1957).

97. "Explosion Is Felt throughout Beach," *VBSN* (17 April 1958); "New City Filled with Military Posts," *VBSN* (3 January 1963).

98. "Tyndall Jet Explodes in Midair," *Panama City News* (27 July 1954); "Air Force Investigates Crash at Myrtle Beach," *MBS* (20 August 1958); "Crash Is Described by Mrs. J. R. Martin," *MBSOBN* (20 August 1958).

99. "Beachcombers Hunt Drifting 'Mini-mines,'" *PCH* (17 July 1967); "Mini-Mines Blind Airman," *PCH* (18 July 1967).

100. Points, *America the Beautiful*, 2–3; "Travel Is Not a Luxury," *VBSN* (5 December 1963). For the best study of tourism, the travel gap, and Cold War foreign policy, see Endy, *Cold War Holidays*, 33–54, 182–202.

101. "Travel Curbs Could Upset Tourism Here," *MBSN* (11 January 1968); "U.S. Concerned by 'Tourist Gap,'" *PCH* (24 August 1967); "The Real Tourist Trap," *Life* (26 January 1968), 19; "Tourists Should Be Welcomed, not Tolerated," *Life* (2 August 1968), 30; "Tourism Funds Sought by City," *VBS* (11 February 1971).

102. "U.S. Concerned by 'Tourist Gap,'" *PCH* (24 August 1967); Governor Reubin Askew, Governor's Conference on Tourism (20 October 1977), Reubin O'Donovan Askew Speeches, SASC.

103. "Tourism Funds Sought by City," *VBS* (11 February 1971); Larry Boulier, "Crumbs from the Cracker Barrel," *MBSN* (13 March 1969); "Canadian Travel Show Visitors Get First Hand Tips," *VBSN* (1 September 1964); "Beach Takes Part in Canada," *VBS* (29 August 1968).

104. "Mrs. Julia Nelms Representing Beach at Canadian Event," *VBSN* (25 August 1960); "Summer Gone but not All Vacationers," *VBSN* (5 September 1963); "Officials Estimate 35,000 Canadians Visit Strand," *MBSN* (26 March 1970).

105. "Tourism Rise Is Predicted," *MBSOBN* (13 January 1961); *Leisureguide: The Grand Strand*, 11; "City Woos Canadians," *VBS* (6 April 1967).

106. Evelyn Moore, "Never Asked for a Raise," These Are Our Lives—WPA Interviews (n.d., c. 1938), Mississippi Department of Archives and History; Ford, *Where to Retire*, 7th ed., 7. On American attitudes to the weather and leisure in the twentieth century, see Meyer, *Americans and Their Weather*, 174–185.

107. Glennan Anderson interviewed by R. Wayne Pyle (29 September 1979), CO-HCH; "A Former Retreat for Summer Vacationers," *PCNH* (12 July 1976).

108. Ford, *Where to Retire*, 19th ed., 105. On how retirees affected southern communities, see Harvey Jackson, *Rise and Decline of the Redneck Riviera*, 109–110.

109. "About ODU," http://www.odu.edu/fusion/about/ (accessed 20 August 2012); "Gulf Park History," http://www.usm.edu/gulfcoast/about/gulf-park-history (accessed 20 August 2012); Ray Thompson, "Know Your Coast: Gulf Park College," *BDH* (26 May 1956); *Mississippi: The WPA Guide*, 296; "Bond Issue Aired," *GC* (4 September 1963); "Enrollment Statistics Reveal New Record," *GC* (17 October 1962); "Groundbreaking Plans Completed," *MBSN* (18 October 1962).

110. "Cows versus No Cows in Gulfport," *BDH* (13 April 1920); "Report Need for Stock Law," *BDH* (3 January 1927); "Constitution Prohibits Stock Law for Beach Front," *BDH* (2 April 1934).

111. "3 Killed, 18 Injured in Trailways Bus Accident," *BDH* (28 July 1954); "Adopt Motion to Fence Highway 49 in Beat No. 5," *BDH* (3 June 1957); J. Crawford King Jr., "Closing of the Southern Range," 53–70. Most studies of fencing laws focus on the rise of populism in the 1890s. See Hahn, *Roots of Southern Populism*, 56–65; Brown, "Free Men and Free Pigs," 117–137.

112. "Cows Win First Round on Fence Law," *PCNH* (12 April 1940); Ye Old Family Scrap Book (17 June 1949), STDC; Our First Trip to Florida Scrapbook (2 March 1954), STDC.

Chapter 2. Sand Storms

1. Muir, *Thousand-Mile Walk to the Gulf*, 2.

2. Ibid., 84.

3. Ibid., 29, 94.

4. Ibid., 133, 135–136, 141.

5. Grant, *Passing of the Great Race*, 38, 39, 76; Charles Alexander, "Prophet of American Racism," 73–90. On the limited immunity of African Americans to malaria, see Peter Wood, *Black Majority*, xviii, 88–89; Bell, *Mosquito Soldiers*, 12–13, 61–62, 81.

6. Robert De C. Ward, "Acclimatization of the White Race," 617. On the link between racial concerns and imperialism in the tropics, see Jacobson, *Barbarian Virtues*, 139–172; Love, *Race over Empire*, 23–25, 182–195, 199–200; Renda, *Taking Haiti*, 12–34.

7. "Guiteras Calls It Yellow Fever," *Atlanta Constitution* (10 September 1897); "Adopts Precautions," *Atlanta Constitution* (15 September 1897); "Biloxi Appeals for Help," *Atlanta Constitution* (19 September 1897). For perspective on the 1897 epidemic, see John Scott, "Yellow Fever," 119–128. On germ theory, see Warner, "Hunting the Yellow Fever Germ," 361–382.

8. Joseph Downing Price to Charles Simrall (18 October 1877), Charles Barrington Simrall Papers, SHC; Yelverton, *Teresina in America*, 160; Bell, *Mosquito Soldiers*, 10–11; Patterson, *Mosquito Crusades*, 109.

9. Bell, *Mosquito Soldiers*, 14–16; Humphreys, *Yellow Fever and the South*, 5–8.

10. "Coast Quarantine," *BH* (23 April 1898); Varina Davis to Emmie Durham (16 March 1906), Davis Family Papers, Archives and Manuscripts Division, THNOC.

11. "Touch of Fever Reaches Texas," *Atlanta Constitution* (23 September 1897); Bell, *Mosquito Soldiers*, 36–39; Humphreys, *Yellow Fever of the South*, 80, 86–87; Nelson, "Landscape of Disease," 535–567.

12. W. C. B. Sollee interviewed by Rose Shepherd (27 February 1936), Federal Writers' Project, SHC; E. Warren Clark, "Reminiscences of the Yellow Fever," *New York Evangelist* (27 September 1888); Humphreys, *Yellow Fever of the South*, 26–29, 83–89.

13. Doug Gilbert, "Panama City Battles Infectious Mosquitoes," *PCDH* (30 July 1967); Patterson, *Mosquito Crusades*, 8–9.

14. "The South's Worst Enemy," *BDH* (4 August 1915); "Mosquito War Cost $5712.51 Here in 1934," *VBN* (14 December 1934); "Residents of Surfside Beach 'Declare War' on Mosquitoes," *MBSOBN* (17 August 1960); Patterson, *Mosquito Crusades*, 23–26, 37–43, 48–52.

15. "Mosquito Control for Beach First Suggested by Mayor Holland," *VBN* (7 July 1950); Souther, "Twixt Ocean and Pines," 62–64; Archie Benton interviewed by Catherine Lewis (21 May 1993), HCOHP.

16. Beirne Brues, Diary of a Trip to Southernmost Florida (21 June 1924), STDC.

17. "Minnows and Mosquitos," C. I. Simpson to Editor, *BDH* (28 June 1928); Patterson, *Mosquito Crusades*, 110; "Bats to Be Used on the Mississippi Coast for Mosquito Eradication," *BDH* (20 June 1922); "Gulfport Believer in Mosquito Work," *BDH* (10 September 1921); "An Observation on Mosquitos," Archibald Boggs to Editor, *BDH* (14 September 1921); "Mosquitoes," John Lang to Editor, *BDH* (14 September 1921).

18. "Bill Authorizes Formation of Mosquito Control Areas," *BDH* (8 April 1928); Patterson, *Mosquito Crusades*, 116–119.

19. "Many Benefits Derived from Mosquito Control Activities," *VBN* (22 November 1939); "Mosquito Control Commission Cites Advantages of District," *VBN* (1 December 1939); "Mosquito Control Commission Now Functioning in District," *VBN* (5 July 1940); Patterson, *Mosquito Crusades*, 126–134.

20. "Let's Seek 'Real Relief,'" *PCNH* (17 March 1939); "Stable Fly (Dog Fly) Control," http://edis.ifas.ufl.edu/ig133 (accessed 27 July 2010).

21. "Mosquito: Farmers' Enemy," *VBN* (28 December 1934); Patterson, *Mosquito Crusades*, 136–138.

22. Anthony Costantini to Harry Engler (18 June 1942), Anthony Costantini Letter, STDC; Hollis Alger to Ellen Wright (2 June 1943), Hollis M. Alger Letters, STDC.

23. "Science: DDT," *Time* (12 June 1944); Patterson, *Mosquito Crusades*, 156–160, 210–214; McWilliams, *American Pests*, 189–193, 204–208.

24. Minutes of the Meeting of the Board of Directors of the Galveston Chamber of Commerce (10 May 1946), GCCR; Minutes of the Meeting of the Board of Directors of the Galveston Chamber of Commerce (17 March 1949), GCCR; Minutes of the Meeting of the Board of Directors of the Galveston Chamber of Commerce (20 May 1949), GCCR.

25. "Clean Up to Fight Mosquitoes," *PCNH* (29 March 1958); Cooper, *Air-Conditioning America*, 148–154.

26. "Rachel Carson," *VBSN* (21 April 1964); "Stop!" *VBSN* (5 May 1964); McWilliams, *American Pests*, 210–223; Patterson, *Mosquito Crusades*, 182, 210–211.

27. John D. Blagden to All at Home (10 September 1900), John D. Blagden Letter, GTHC; Greene and Kelly, *Through a Night of Horrors*, 3–5; McComb, *Galveston: A History*, 121–122; Elizabeth Hayes Turner, *Women, Culture and Community*, 29–36.

28. F. A. Woolfley to Martin Woolfley (15 August 1860), Dufour and Woolfley Families Papers, Archives and Manuscript Division, THNOC.

29. Alma Simmang Simpson to no name (27 August 1915), Alma Simmang Simpson Papers, GTHC; Inventory of Household Goods Contained in Cottage of F. A. Woolfley, at Bay Saint Louis, Mississippi, Dufour and Woolfley Families Papers, Archives and Manuscript Division, THNOC; Dean, *Against the Tide*, 58.

30. "Marvelous Showing from the City of Galveston, Texas," *Confederate Veteran* (October 1903), 471; Hardwick, *Mythic Galveston*, 113–188; Rice, *Progressive Cities*, xiii–xiv, 9–18.

31. Louise F. Bache Report (16 August 1915), GTHC-RL; Alma Simmang Simpson typed account (20 August 1915), Alma Simmang Simpson Papers, GTHC; Nellie Watson to Billy (21 August 1915), Nellie Watson Letter, GTHC.

32. Stanonis, *Creating the Big Easy*, 145.

33. "Mass Meeting of Citizens to Plan to Strengthen Biloxi," *BDH* (2 October 1915).

34. "Harrison County People Stirred by Storm Damage," *BDH* (5 October 1915).

35. Mary Ellen Alexander, *Rosalie and Radishes*, 119–120.

36. Ray Thompson, "Sea-Wall," *BDH* (31 May 1956); "Tally 27,230 Vehicles on Biloxi Beach," *BDH* (31 August 1968).

37. Haddock to Robert Dosh (n.d.), Robert N. "Bert" Dosh Papers, SASC.

38. "Building," *BDH* (5 November 1925).

39. "Making Film of Seawall," *BDH* (23 December 1925).

40. "Mayors Declare Holiday for Seawall Dedication," *BDH* (8 May 1928); "Program for Dedication of World's Longest Seawall," *BDH* (8 May 1928); Ilf and Petrov, *Little Golden America*, 358–359.

41. "Frank Discussion of the Harrison County Beach, *BDH* (16 September 1927).

42. "Preserve Our Waterfront," *VBN* (9 June 1939); "Novel Plan of Advertising to Be Given Trial on Walkway," *VBN* (16 June 1939).

43. Minutes of the Meeting of the Board of Directors of the Galveston Chamber of Commerce (16 June 1959), GCCR.

44. Minutes of the Board of Directors of the Galveston Chamber of Commerce (30 June 1959), GCCR; Dean, *Against the Tide*, 124–125.

45. Minutes of the Board of Directors of the Galveston Chamber of Commerce (12 April 1966), GCCR.

46. Pilkey and Dixon, The *Corps and the Shore*, 5–10.

47. Andrew Palmer, "Major Battle Looms Over National Coastal Protection Law" (November 1984), Sierra Club of Florida Chapter Records, SASC; Shirley Taylor, "The Florida Coast Needs . . . You!" (January 1985), Sierra Club of Florida Chapter Records, SASC; Pilkey and Dixon, The *Corps and the Shore*, 9–10.

48. Shirley Taylor, "Opportunity for Undeveloped Barrier Islands" (February 1985), Sierra Club of Florida Chapter Records, SASC; "A Chance to Expand Coastal Carrier System," *Barrier Islands Newsletter* (May 1985), Sierra Club of Florida Chapter Records, SASC.

49. "Worst Hurricane since '28 Lashes Florida East Coast," *PCNH* (17 September 1947); "Hurricane Warnings Flying from St. Marks to Pensacola as Storm Swings Northwest," *PCNH* (18 September 1947).

50. Angela Moynan to Susan Barkert (29 October 1947), Letter of Angela Moynan, THNOC; Mrs. W. C. Green Jr. to Mrs. Rose Lee (23 September 1947), 1947 Hurricane Scrapbook, Archives and Manuscripts Division, THNOC.

51. "Hurricane and Tax Appraisal," *BDH* (16 May 1949).

52. "Orleans Battles Floods, Mississippi Gulf Coast Is Reduced to Shambles," *PCNH* (21 September 1947).

53. "Two Long Beach Groups Urge Sand Beach Plan Start," *BDH* (14 May 1949); Ray Thompson, "Sea-Wall," *BDH* (31 May 1956); Dean, *Against the Tide*, 97–98.

54. Ray Thompson, "World's Longest Man-Made Beach," *BDH* (3 April 1956); "Erosion Solution?," *VBN* (8 June 1951).

55. "Town Makes Appeal to State for Funds to Combat Beach Erosion and to Repair Recent Damage," *VBN* (15 September 1950); Charles Gardner to Editor, *VBN* (1 December 1950).

56. "The Beach's Dilemma," *VBN* (29 September 1950).

57. "Councilman Simpson Asks That Town Managers [*sic*] Post Be Filled 'Immediately,'" *VBN* (4 May 1951).

58. "$80,000 Asked of State for Erosion Damage Repair Work on Local Beach," *VBN* (8 February 1952).

59. "Erosion Commission Is Named," *VBN* (29 February 1952); "The Sands That Come from the Sea," *VBSN* (11 December 1962); "'Sand Festival Day' to Celebrate Successful Erosion Control Here," *VBN* (14 August 1952); "Second Sand Festival Plans Underway," *VBN* (4 June 1953); "Permanent Maintenance of Sandy Beaches to Begin July 5," *VBSN* (5 July 1956).

60. "The Big Payoff," *VBN* (20 August 1953); "Many Areas Suffering from Loss of Shoreline," *VBSN* (2 May 1957).

61. "Ocean City Copies Beach Plan," *VBSN* (8 January 1970); Ruby Jean Phillips, "Storm Wreaks Havoc to Beachfront Here," *VBSN* (8 March 1962); "Sand by the Truckload," *VBSN* (21 June 1962).

62. "Battle with Sea to Last Forever," *VBSN* (24 November 1966); Tom Cook, "Study Shows Coast Beach Protection Expenditures Mounting," *BDH* (15 April 1959).

63. "Harrison Sand Beach Operation in April $44,612," *BDH* (21 May 1959); "Harrison County Beach Should Last for 30 Years," *BDH* (12 August 1973).

64. "Grand Lagoon Sand May Go to Beaches," *PCNH* (14 August 1970); Terry Witt, "Dredging Operations for Beach Renourishment Begin," *PCNH* (1 July 1976).

65. "Beach Dredging Hurts Business," *PCNH* (14 July 1976); Terry Witt, "Beach Sand Dredged from Gulf White after Bleaching," *PCNH* (18 July 1976); Eatofel Vereen Thompson Arehart interviewed by Catherine Lewis (16 April 1993), HCOHP. On dredging and sand quality, see Dean, *Against the Tide*, 111–116.

66. "Florida Finds Way Clear for Better Growth," *Christian Science Monitor* (27 September 1926).

67. Minutes of the Board of Directors of the Galveston Chamber of Commerce (7 October 1949), GCCR; Lynnie Edge Gore interviewed by Catherine Lewis (7 June 1985), HCOHP; Mark Garner interviewed by Catherine Lewis and Randall Wells (20 November 1992), HCOHP.

68. Zebrowski and Howard, *Category 5*, 233–234.

69. Interview of Gerald Blessey by Angela Sartin (2 January 2000), Community Bridges Oral History Project, COHCH. On federal efforts to link recovery funding to desegregation, see Mark Smith, *Camille, 1969*, 27–34, 49–53, quote from 53; Charles and Mary Breath interviewed by R. Wayne Pyle (16 August 1979), COHCH; Henry and Rita Fortner interviewed by R. Wayne Pyle (20 February 1980), COHCH.

70. "Motel Rebuilding," Sandra Vann to Editor, *PCNH* (2 April 1986).

71. "Readers Write," Mary Leigh to Editor, *VBN* (20 October 1939); "Letters to the Editor," William Gatewood to the Editor, *VBSN* (3 March 1964).

72. "Readers Write," E. F. Stone to Editor, *VBN* (12 May 1939); "Police Push Cleanup of 'Jitter Bug Bums,'" *MBN* (6 August 1949); "Sleeping on Beaches Is Prohibited at Myrtle," *MBSN* (15 April 1965); Minutes of the Board of Directors of the Galveston Chamber of Commerce (13 October 1964), GCCR; Mike Darley, "Hosses vs. Motels," *PCNH* (13 March 1968).

73. "Hosses-Beach Battle Tossed in State's Lap," *PCNH* (24 March 1968); Mike Darley, "Beaches Win Over Hosses," *PCNH* (31 March 1968).

74. "The Weather and Labor Day," *VBSN* (6 September 1956); Erik Craft, "Private Weather Organizations," 1063–1071; Joseph Hawes, "Signal Corps," 68–76; Wiser, "Weather, USDA, and the Farmer," 51–61.

75. "Letter to the Editor," Waldo Jones to Editor, *MBN* (24 March 1950); "Beach Voices Objection to Displaying of Storm Flags," *MBN* (30 January 1953); "Weatherman Says Flags Will Fly over Beach," *MBN* (6 February 1953).

76. "The Weather Bureau," *VBSN* (16 February 1956); Kenneth Gilmore, "Waiting for the Girls," *BDH* (5 July 1956).

77. "When Unity Counts," *PCNH* (25 September 1947); "Grand Strand Plans to Aid Gulfport Area," *MBSN* (24 August 1969); "Camille Fund Nears $8,000," *MBSN* (7 September 1969).

78. Clarence Gay, "Florida Today," *PCNH* (10 March 1958); Irene Ledesma, "Natural Disasters and Community Survival," 72–84.

79. "The Scourges of the City," *VBSN* (26 May 1966); McComb, *Galveston: A History*, 21–23.

80. Clarke and Marjorie Wilson, "Tourist Motels on Coast Have Special Responsibility," *BDH* (11 November 1957); Larry Boulier, "Sun Spots," *MBSN* (27 September 1961); Larry Boulier, "Larry Boulier in the Rough," *MBSN* (19 September 1963).

81. Minutes of the Meeting of the Board of the Directors of the Galveston Chamber of Commerce (9 May 1967), GCCR.

82. "Let's Comb Beach," *MBN* (8 June 1951); Ray Thompson, "Our Beach Sanitizer," *BDH* (23 July 1956). On the City Beautiful movement, see Peterson, "The City Beautiful Movement," 415–435; Szczygiel, "'City Beautiful' Revisited," 107–133.

83. "The Editor's Mail Box," Council of Garden Clubs of Princess Anne County and Virginia Beach to Editor, *VBN* (3 September 1953); "$1.329,563 Budget Is Proposed," *VBN* (6 May 1954); "Favor Ordinance," Charlotte Tilbrook to S. Paul Brown, *VBN* (2 September 1954); "Beautification Ideas," J. Malcolm Firth to the Editor, *VBSN* (25 May 1967).

84. Minutes of the Meeting of the Board of Directors of the Galveston Chamber of Commerce (15 March 1946), GCCR; Round Table Discussion IV: Park Rules and Regulations, Minutes of the Tenth Annual Meeting of the Association of Southeastern State Park Directors (6–9 November 1951), National Association of State Park Directors, Forest History Society; "Keeping City Clean Is Real Problem in Summer Season," *VBSN* (18 June 1964); "Beach Litter Laws: Enforce or Ignore?" *VBSN* (3 August 1967).

85. Larry Boulier, "Sun Spots," *MBSOBN* (17 June 1959); "Litter," Mrs. W. Peyton May to Editor, *VBSN* (17 August 1967); "Letters to the Editor," Ann Clark to Editor, *MBSN* (28 August 1971).

86. William O. Golloway Diaries (4 January 1926), STDC; Report to State by Governor Millard F. Caldwell (11 December 1945), SASC.

87. Minutes of the Meeting of the Board of Directors of the Galveston Chamber of Commerce (15 March 1946), GCCR; Minutes of the Meeting of the Board of Directors of the Galveston Chamber of Commerce (16 May 1947), GCCR; Minutes of the Board of Directors of the Galveston Chamber of Commerce (18 June 1948), GCCR.

88. "Points Out Need of Sewer System," Dr. A. N. Morphy to Editor, *BDH* (15 August 1957); "A Board Order That Puzzles City Officials," *VBSN* (24 August 1961).

89. Minutes of the Meeting of the Board of Directors of the Galveston Chamber of Commerce (16 November 1945), GCCR; "Rubbish Disposal Rapped," David Damon to Editor, *PCNH* (23 July 1967).

90. Tom Eleazer, "We'll Bury You . . . in Styrofoam!" *MBSN* (3 April 1973); Rathje and Murphy, *Rubbish: The Archeology of Garbage*, 30–37; Melosi, *Garbage in the Cities*, 190–194.

91. "Congressman Downing Protests Atomic Waste Disposal," *VBSN* (2 July 1959); Minutes of the Board of Directors of the Galveston Chamber of Commerce (11 August 1959), GCCR.

92. "Peeved about Pollution," Robert Keeler to Editor, *PCNH* (14 April 1968); Remarks of Governor Reubin Askew at Keep Florida Beautiful Luncheon (14 July 1971), Reubin O'Donovan Askew Speeches, SASC.

93. "Lease Opposed by Coast Group," *BDH* (26 January 1938); Minutes of the Meeting of the Board of Directors of the Galveston Chamber of Commerce (15 May 1936), GCCR. On the oil industry, see Arthur Johnson, "Early Texas Oil Industry," 516–528; Priest, "Extraction not Creation," 227–267.

94. Minutes of the Board of Directors of the Galveston Chamber of Commerce (8 June 1970), GCCR.

95. H. M. Abbot Diary-Scrapbook (13 January 1955), STDC; "Clean Beach Is an Economic Necessity," *VBSN* (27 June 1957); "War Declared on Oil on Our Beach," *VBSN* (25 July 1957).

96. Barbara Fegan, "Coastweek 85" (1985), Sierra Club of Florida Chapter Records, SASC; Zaretsky, *No Direction Home*, 77–88, 102.

97. "Cause of Pollution," William Hutter to Editor, *BDH* (26 July 1973).

98. Mark Hodges, "Unrestricted Tourism Dangers," *MBSN* (5 April 1973); Joyce Watters, "Beach Progress Noted," *GC* (3 October 1989).

99. Trethewey, *Beyond Katrina*, 17; Chris Rose, *1 Dead in Attic*, 106.

Chapter 3. Black and Tan

1. Myers, *Romance and Realism*, 105–106. The site remains in use as a religious retreat. See "Seashore United Methodist Assembly," http://www.seashoreassembly.org/about.html (accessed 1 July 2010).

2. Lee Owens Jr. interviewed by William Henderson (26 April 2000), Community Bridges Oral History Project, COHCH. For American spiritual views of nature, see Albanese, *Nature Religion in America*, 80–116, 153–198; Gatta, *Making Nature Sacred*, 71–100, 165–180, 195–198, 225–244; Sears, *Sacred Places*, 3–48. For general insight into segregation and leisure sites, see Mormino, *Land of Sunshine*, 97–98, 309–316; Phelts, *American Beach for African Americans*, 37–77, 119–125; Tuttle, *Race Riot*, 32–73; Weeks, *Gettysburg*, 92–98; Allnutt, "Negro Excursions," 73–104; Wolcott, "Recreation and Race," 63–90. For the most comprehensive analyses of leisure and Jim Crow, see Wiltse, *Contested Waters*; Kahrl, *The Land Was Ours*.

3. Connolly, "By Eminent Domain," 163.

4. Lien Thi Beale interviewed by Homer Hill (3 July 1995), COHCH.

5. Hardwick, *Mythic Galveston*, 150–151; Jordan-Bychkov, "The Creole Coast," 73–82.

6. Gould, "Defense of their Creole Culture," 27–42, quote from 36; Lorita Nelson Jones interviewed by Angela Sartin (7 November 1999), Community Bridges Oral History Project, COHCH. For more on Creole culture along the Gulf, see Dawdy, *Building the Devil's Empire*, 104–107, 130–137, 139–188; Jack Greene, *Pursuits of Happiness*, 124–169; Landers, *Black Society in Spanish Florida*, 229–254; Rebecca Scott, *Degrees of Freedom*, 61–93; Spears, *Race, Sex, and Social Order*, 155–220; Kein, *Creole*; Bragaw, "Loss of Identity," 414–418; Moreno, Hargis, and Coker, "Tom Moreno," 329–339.

7. *Texas: A Guide*, 267; Delmar Preston Robinson interviewed by Worth Long (26 August 1999), Community Bridges Oral History Project, COHCH.

8. "What Is a Creole?" *BDH* (18 June 1956); "A Paper Mill Don't Smell," These Are Our Lives, Works Progress Administration, Mississippi Interviews, 1939–1940, Mississippi Department of Archives and History. For insight into the debate over defining *Creole*, see Stanonis, *Creating the Big Easy*, 212–220.

9. Bechet, *Treat It Gentle*, 106, 108. On Spanish and Mexican relations to Anglo Americans, see Foley, *The White Scourge*, 40–63, 183–202; Carrigan and Webb, "Muerto por Unos Deconocidos," 35–60; Neil Foley, "Partly Colored or Other White," 123–144.

10. Anderson, *Letters of Sherwood Anderson*, 312; Yanner and Ybarrola, "He Didn't Have No Cross," 1–28.

11. Earl Napoleon Moore interviewed by Angela Sartin (9 November 1999), Community Bridges Oral History Project, COHCH. On freedmen's migration patterns, see Rabinowitz, *Race Relations in the Urban South*, 18–24; Ash, *When the Yankees Came*, 153–156; Fitzgerald, *Urban Emancipation*, 21–36.

12. Yelverton, *Teresina in America*, 143.

13. St. Elmo W. Acosta interviewed by Rose Shepherd (27 March 1939), Life Histories, Florida, Folder 998, Federal Writers Project, SHC.

14. Mrs. Texas Morgan interviewed by Barbara Berry Darsey (7 December 1938), Life Histories, Florida, Folder 108, Federal Writers Project, SHC.

15. Loyce Searight interviewed by William Henderson (20 October 1999), Community Bridges Oral History Project, COHCH; Bennett, *Religion and the Rise of Jim Crow*, 142–145, 210–213, 225–227; R. Bentley Anderson, *Black, White, and Catholic*, 7–25.

16. Nesterowicz, *Travel Notes*, 29, 32; William Hubbell interviewed by Bobo Morgan (24 November 1972), COHCH; Young, *North American Excursion*, 136. On the Gulf seafood industry, see Durrenberger, *It's All Politics*, 33–139; Nuwer, "Biloxi Fishermen," 325–352.

17. Nathan Alfonso interviewed by Michael Garvey (25 May 1976), COHCH; Glennan Alma Anderson interviewed by R. Wayne Pyle (29 September 1979), COHCH.

18. Young, *North American Excursion*, 187; Wilson Evans II interviewed by Orley Caudill (11 June 1981), COHCH; Donald Evans interviewed by William Henderson (26 October 1999), Community Bridges Oral History Project, COHCH. On waterfront unions, see Arnesen, *Waterfront Workers of New Orleans*, 119–203; Earl Lewis, *In Their Own Interests*, 15–17, 64; McComb, *Galveston: A History*, 111–114; Andrews, "Black Working-Class Political Activism," 627–668; Arnesen, "What's on the Black Worker's Mind," 5–18; Poliakoff, "Charleston's Longshoremen," 247–264.

19. Brinker Family Diary-Scrapbook (23 December 1940; 30 December 1940), STDC; Chanelle Rose, "Neither Southern nor Northern"; Connolly, "By Eminent Domain," 203–205.

20. Veronica Huss and Stetson Kennedy, "The Riviera Conches" (November 1938), Florida, Folder 120, Federal Writers Project, SHC. On the Conches, see Howard Johnson, "Bahamian Labor Migration," 84–103; Mohl, "Black Immigrants," 271–297.

21. Gertha Couric interviewed by Woodrow Hand (n.d.), Life Histories, Alabama, Folder 33, Federal Writers Project, SHC; Ocean Forest Hotel flier, John J. O'Leary to C. A. Donehoo (22 June 1938), C. A. Donehoo Papers, SCL.

22. Gus Constantin Geraris interviewed by W. O. Saunders (n.d.), Life Histories, North Carolina, Folder 1032, Federal Writers Project, SHC; Dino Thompson, *Greek Boy*, 1–2, 61.

23. Peter Gournas interviewed by Mary Hicks (n.d.), Life Histories, North Carolina, Folder 1033, Federal Writers Project, SHC; Steve Loomis interviewed by Mary Hicks (n.d.), Life Histories, North Carolina, Folder 1033, Federal Writers Project, SHC. On immigrants and the color line in the early twentieth century, see Ellis, "Greek Community in Atlanta," 400–408; Gualtieri, "Strange Fruit," 63–85; Jason Ward, "No Jap Crow," 75–104; Stathakis, "Almost White."

24. U.S. Census data taken from *The Great American History Machine*.

25. Rev. Harry Tartt interviewed by William Henderson (1 November 1999), Community Bridges Oral History Project, COHCH; Earl Napoleon Moore interviewed by Angela Sartin (9 November 1999), Community Bridges Oral History Project, COHCH. In 1900 two African American men, Henry Askew and Ed Russ, were lynched for the alleged rape of thirteen-year-old Christina Winterstein two miles from Biloxi. The sheriff arrested them and locked them inside a bathhouse. A mob seized the men and strung them up in a tree, then shot and burned the bodies. The *Atlanta Constitution*

stated that the "nauseating smell of burning flesh could be detected for miles around." "No One Recognized Members of Mob," *Atlanta Constitution* (11 June 1900). In 1908 a mob lynched Henry Leldy for the alleged rape of fifteen-year-old Eliza May Fauser. The lynching occurred a half mile outside Biloxi. "Negro Lynched by Biloxi Mob," *Atlanta Constitution* (11 November 1908).

26. Guy Middleton, "South Americans Enjoying Beaches," *PCNH* (20 August 1967); "Manuel's Quest for Meaningful Life Leads to White Sands of Gulf Coast," *PCNH* (1 July 1962); Larry Hudson interviewed by Worth Long (7 January 2000), Community Bridges Oral History Project, COHCH.

27. Tyrone Burton interviewed by Angela Sartin (20 September 1999), Community Bridges Oral History Project, COHCH; Eleonora Hayes interviewed by Angela Sartin (3 November 1999), Community Bridges Oral History Project, COHCH.

28. Lodie Marie Robinson-Cyrille interviewed by Worth Long (24 August 1999), Community Bridges Oral History Project, COHCH. For the rich literature on the United States, civil rights, and the Cold War, see Dudziak, *Cold War Civil Rights*; Borstelmann, *Cold War and the Color Line*; Horne, "Race from Power," 45–66.

29. Lorita Nelson Jones interviewed by Angela Sartin, Community Bridges Oral History Project, COHCH; Tyrone Burton interviewed by Angela Sartin (20 September 1999), Community Bridges Oral History Project, COHCH; Vernon Jackson interviewed by William Henderson (7 June 2000), Community Bridges Oral History Project, COHCH. On black businesses and community formation, see Ingham, "Building Businesses, Creating Communities," 639–665.

30. Mrs. R. W. White to W. W. Long (4 February 1925), William Wightman Smoak Papers, SCL; Mrs. R. W. White to W. W. Long (6 February 1925), William Wightman Smoak Papers, SCL. On efforts toward encouraging immigration, see Jung, *Coolies and Cane*, 73–106, 146–220; Bankston, "New People in the New South," 24–44; Pruett and Fair, "Promoting a New South," 19–41; Scarpaci, "Immigrants in the New South," 165–183.

31. Andrew Stanley interviewed by Randall Wells (3 October 1993), HCOHP; Part 1 of First Trip to Florida Diary (4 March 1961), STDC. On migration out of the South, see Gregory, *The Southern Diaspora*, 11–54; Grossman, *Land of Hope*, 98–160; Painter, *Exodusters*, 146–233. On the relationship between highway construction and farming communities, see Grantham, *Southern Progressivism*, 275–348; Keith, *Country People in the New South*, 103–117.

32. Delmar Preston Robinson interviewed by Worth Long (26 August 1999), Community Bridges Oral History Project, COHCH; Clara Griffin Watson interviewed by Angela Sartin (28 October 1999), Community Bridges Oral History Project, COHCH.

33. Tyrone Burton interviewed by Angela Sartin (20 September 1999), Community Bridges Oral History Project, COHCH; Frank Bridges interviewed by William Henderson (21 March 1999), Community Bridges Oral History Project, COHCH; Mark Garner interviewed by Catherine Lewis and Randall Wells (20 November 1992), HCOHP.

34. Spiral Memo Diary (25 July 1949), STDC; Richard Bissell, *How Many Miles to Galena?* 272.

35. Amory, *The Last Resorts*, 56; McMillen, *Dark Journey*, 10–14; Patricia Turner, *Ceramic Uncles and Celluloid Mammies*.

36. "Springhill Survivors on Segregated Spree," *Life* (8 December 1958), 49; Amory, *The Last Resorts*, 150–152.

37. "In Re: Lynching of Willie Kirkland at Thomasville, Georgia," Howard Washington Raper Papers, Series 3, Box 15, Folder 749, SHC.

38. Paul Eliot Green to Mary (12 August 1917), Paul Eliot Green Papers, SHC; Edith K. Miller Diary (1913), STDC; Jeanelle Landstrom Family Diary (12 March 1931), STDC; My Trip Diary (15 March 1939), STDC. On African Americans and the southern tourism industry, see Adams, *Wounds of Returning*, 54–107; Davis, *Race against Time*, 75–79; Stanonis, *Creating the Big Easy*, 220–232; Yuhl, *Golden Haze of Memory*, 127–156.

39. J. E. Rawlings to Isabel Baker (7 December 1904), Isabel Baker Papers, Virginia Historical Society; Genevieve Pearce Moore Diary, 27 March 1941 and 13 August 1943, SHC; My Trip Diary (22 February 1950), STDC. On the South and African Americans in the popular American imagination, see Karen Cox, *Dreaming of Dixie*; Kirby, *Media-Made Dixie*; McElya, *Clinging to Mammy*, 15–73.

40. Hotel Dixie-Sherman ad, *PCH* (28 April 1936); "'Old South' to Return with Special Party," *VBSN* (14 June 1962); Amory, *The Last Resorts*, 56; Kahrl, "Sunbelt by the Sea," 491; Simon, *Boardwalk of Dreams*, 19–44.

41. Karl Abbott, *Open for the Season*, 38; Pyle, *Home Country*, 328–329, 370.

42. Larry Boulier, "Help in Strand Restaurants Has Become Real Problem," *MBSN* (25 August 1966).

43. "Harlem Says It Wants In," *MBSN* (9 May 1968); "Harlem Gives All in Water Request," *MBSN* (8 August 1968); "Harlem Petition to Annex Fails," *MBSN* (7 November 1968); "'Friendly Hand' Given Impetus," *MBSN* (2 March 1969); Hourigan, "Welcome to South Carolina," 182–188.

44. Glenda Miller and Elizabeth Phillips, "Ghetto's Children Living in Shadows," *MBSN* (13 May 1971); "Tin Top Alley Blacks Moved," *MBSN* (1 January 1972).

45. Gerald Blessey interviewed by Angela Sartin (2 January 2000), Community Bridges Oral History Project, COHCH; Kahrl, "Sunbelt by the Sea," 496. For insight on the location of black neighborhoods, see Hourigan, "Welcome to South Carolina," 179–188; Rabinowitz, *Race Relations in the Urban South*, 97–124.

46. Kosaku Sawada interviewed by Ila Prine (20 January 1939), Life Histories, Alabama, Folder 66, Federal Writers Project, SHC; Camellia Society of Mobile Newsletter (November 2004), http://www.mobilecamellia.org/Newsletters/newsletter%20V1%20Issue%202o2.htm (accessed on 3 July 2010); Gainesville Camellia Society—Florida, http://www.afn.org/~camellia/camnames.html (accessed on 3 July 2010); Bill Ray, "Kosaku Sawada, American," American Camellia Yearbook (2007), http://www.camellias-acs.com/assets/Yearbook%202007%2005%20Kosaku%20Sawada,%20American.pdf (accessed on 3 July 2010); Ray Thompson, "What Happened to the Satsumas," *BDH* (14 February 1958); Rucker, "Satsumaland!" 60–77.

47. Kosaku Sawada interviewed by Ila Prine (20 January 1939), Life Histories, Alabama, Folder 66, Federal Writers Project, SHC.

48. Royall, *Mrs. Royall's Southern Tour*, 148, 151–152; "The Fortner Bill," *Crisis* (April 1914), 280; Billy Munday, *Black Shadow*, 49–50. On rednecks and the ethnic

revival, see Huber, "Short History of 'Redneck,'" 145–166; Jacobson, *Roots Too*, 177–205.

49. Yelverton, *Teresina in America*, 59; Webster, *Dictionary of the English Language*, 1009; Merrick, *Old Times in Dixie Land*, 105; Hart, *The Southern South*, 173–174.

50. Chicago Commission on Race Relations, *The Negro in Chicago*, 309.

51. Hansen, "Shades of Change," 42; William Hubbell interviewed by Bobo Morgan (24 November 1972), COHCH; Alma Simpson to unknown (27 August 1915), Alma Simmang Simpson Papers, GTHC; Julia Brock email to author (4 July 2010); Nicole King conversation with author (29 October 2011).

52. Cocks, *Tropical Whites*, 112; Charles Tenney Jackson, *Fountain of Youth*, 162; Rosemary Diaries (20 May 1953), STDC; "I'm So Tanned" (postcard, circa 1940s), STDC.

53. "At the Summer Resorts," *Chicago Daily Inter Ocean* (4 August 1895); "Peroxide Women Abroad," *New York Herald* (15 April 1894); "Is Blonde Haired Beauty Disappearing?" *Baltimore American* (15 November 1903); "Women Must Dye to Be in Style," *Boston Journal* (22 May 1904).

54. Grant, *Passing of the Great Race*, 84; "Veronica Lake's Hair," *Life* (24 November 1941), 59; Born Blonde ad, *Life* (23 June 1967), 33.

55. "Sunbathing for Infants Popular," *BDH* (20 August 1927); Delta Drug Company ad, *MBN* (1 July 1937); Meredith Drug Co. ad, *VBSN* (20 June 1941); Alicia Hart, "Choose Sun Lotion with Great Care," *BDH* (26 July 1960); Alicia Hart, "Beware of the Sun on a Hazy Day," *PCNH* (20 July 1962); Cocks, *Tropical Whites*, 114–122, quote from 122.

56. Rose Hall ad, *VBSN* (22 May 1958). For other examples, see Rowe & Long Music Company ad, *VBSN* (13 August 1964); Willner's ad, *VBS* (16 June 1966); Brumfield's ad, *BDH* (31 May 1954).

57. "What's Going On," *MBSN* (6 January 1972).

58. State Farm Road Atlas.

59. "5-Mile Chain of Islands to Protect, Develop, Beautify Lake Is Suggested," *Association of Commerce News Bulletin* (26 August 1924); "Give Us a Place on the Lake," *LW* (7 July 1928), 6; "The Lake and the Season," *LW* (14 July 1928), 6.

60. Minutes of the Regular Weekly Meeting of the Executive Committee (27 February 1929), Association of Commerce minutes, Louisiana and Special Collections, Earl K. Long Library, University of New Orleans; Resolution of the Federation of Civic Leagues, Alexander Tureaud Papers, ARC; Alexander Tureaud to Sepia Socialite (12 July 1939), Alexander P. Tureaud Papers, ARC.

61. "Parks and Beaches," *LW* (11 May 1929), 6; "No Place to Go," *LW* (26 June 1932), 6; "Bathing Beach Agitation," *LW* (29 October 1932), 8. For more detail on segregation on New Orleans's lakefront, see Kahrl, *The Land Was Ours*, 115–154.

62. "Go to Seabrook," *LW* (17 June 1933), 8; "Protect the Bathers at Seabrook," *LW* (16 June 1934), 8; "Protect Seabrook," *LW* (23 June 1934), 8; "Lake Bathers," *LW* (29 June 1935), 8.

63. "Work on Modern Negro Beach Well Underway," *LW* (27 May 1939), 1–2.

64. "Who Signed Beach Petition a Mystery," *LW* (15 July 1939), 1; "Deny Signing Beach Petition: Gets New Name—Lincoln Beach; 15,000 Sign Seabrook Petition," *LW* (29 July 1939), 1.

65. Clarence Laws to Mayor Robert Maestri (6 May 1941), Harold Newton Lee Papers, LRC; W. M. Duffourc to Clarence Laws (21 May 1941), Harold Newton Lee Papers, LRC; Harold Lee to Fontaine Martin (23 May 1941), Harold Newton Lee Papers, LRC; Harold Lee to Clarence Jackson (27 May 1941), Harold Newton Lee Papers, LRC.

66. Harold Lee to Base Commander (1 July 1942), Harold Newton Lee Papers, LRC; Harold Lee to Clarence Johnson (3 July 1942), Harold Newton Lee Papers, LRC; Colonel J. H. Houghton to Louisiana League for the Preservation of Constitutional Rights (30 August 1943), Harold Newton Lee Papers, LRC; Harold Lee to David Fichman (1 July 1944), Harold Newton Lee Papers, LRC.

67. "Things Which Concern Us," *LW* (5 August 1939), 8; "Who 'Represents' Us?" *LW* (15 July 1939), 8; "No Life Guards for Seabrook Bathers," *LW* (12 August 1939), 1.

68. Sarah Evelyn Baylor Blackford Diary (11 June 1895), Virginia Historical Society; Patricia Manor flier, Joe C. Ivey to C. A. Donehoo (22 June 1938), C. A. Donehoo Papers, SCL.

69. Ocean Pines Motor Court pamphlet (c. 1940), SCL.

70. Leonard Lubman to the Editor, *VBSN* (29 June 1951); Bill Mauldin, *Back Home*, 188–189.

71. "Posse Combs Area," *BDH* (7 April 1942); "Super-Service Garage-Hotel in Making at Virginia Beach," *VBSN* (31 March 1939).

72. Mormino, *Land of Sunshine*, 315.

73. Minutes of the Meeting of the Board of Directors of the Galveston Chamber of Commerce (6 August 1937), GCCR; Minutes of the Meeting of the Board of Directors of the Galveston Chamber of Commerce (22 October 1937), GCCR.

74. Minutes of the Meeting of the Board of Directors of the Galveston Chamber of Commerce (5 November 1937), GCCR; Minutes of the Meeting of the Board of Directors of the Galveston Chamber of Commerce (16 September 1938), GCCR; Minutes of the Meeting of the Board of Directors of the Galveston Chamber of Commerce (20 September 1940), GCCR.

75. Minutes of the Meeting of the Board of Directors of the Galveston Chamber of Commerce (18 October 1940), GCCR; Minutes of the Meeting of the Board of Directors of the Galveston Chamber of Commerce (21 February 1941), GCCR.

76. Minutes of the Meeting of the Board of Directors of the Galveston Chamber of Commerce (7 March 1941), GCCR; Minutes of the Meeting of the Board of Directors of the Galveston Chamber of Commerce (4 April 1941), GCCR. For background on the Houston race riot, see Haynes, *A Night for Violence*.

77. Wise Adams to Morton Macartney (30 September 1940), Brantly Harris Papers, GTHC.

78. Wise Adams to Mayor Brantly Harris (21 October 1940), Brantly Harris Papers, GTHC.

79. Confidential memo to Mayor Brantly Harris (n.d., c. October 1940), Brantly Harris Papers, GTHC.

80. Wise Adams to Mayor Brantly Harris (12 May 1941), Brantly Harris Papers, GTHC; Mayor Brantly Harris to Bob Nesbitt (21 May 1941), Brantly Harris Papers, GTHC.

81. Lorita Nelson Jones interviewed by Angela Sartin, Community Bridges Oral History Project, COHCH; Wilson Evans II interviewed by Dr. Orley B. Caudill (11 June 1981), COHCH; Earl Napoleon Moore interviewed by Angela Sartin, Community Bridges Oral History Project, COHCH. Emphasis in the original.

82. Minutes of the Meeting of the Board of Directors of the Galveston Chamber of Commerce (9 September 1949), GCCR; Clara Griffin Watson interviewed by Angela Sartin (28 October 1999), Community Bridges Oral History Project, COHCH. On the post-1945 economy of the American South, see Conkin, *Revolution Down on the Farm*, 97–122; Schulman, *From Cotton Belt to Sunbelt*, 174–205; Wright, *Old South, New South*, 239–274.

83. Wilson Evans II interviewed by Orley Caudill (11 June 1981), COHCH; Harvey Jackson, *Rise and Decline of the Redneck Riviera*, 66–67; Lodie Marie Robinson-Cyrille interviewed by Worth Long (24 August 1999), Community Bridges Oral History Project, COHCH; Rev. Harry Tartt interviewed by William Henderson (1 November 1999), Community Bridges Oral History Project, COHCH.

84. "Urges Mississippi Editors to Oppose 'Misled' Groups," *BDH* (10 June 1949).

85. Mason, *Beaches, Blood, and Ballots*, 1. For additional context of the controversy over beaches on the Mississippi Gulf Coast, see J. Michael Butler, "Mississippi State Sovereignty Commission," 107–148.

86. Mason, *Beaches, Blood, and Ballots*, 50–52, 56.

87. Ibid., 62, 66–67.

88. Ibid., 68, 72.

89. Ibid., 76, 84; Wilson Evans II interviewed by Orley Caudill (11 June 1981), COHCH.

90. Tyrone Burton interviewed by Angela Sartin (20 September 1999), Community Bridges Oral History Project, COHCH; "Trial of Beach Demonstrators Ends at Biloxi," *BDH* (28 June 1963); Mason, *Beaches, Blood, and Ballots*, 83–87, 115–123, 135–136, 139–140.

91. "Mississippi Hurt by Racial Strife," *New York Times* (20 December 1964).

92. Larry Goodwyn, "Anarchy in St. Augustine," *Harper's Magazine* (January 1965), 76, 77. For an overview of the civil rights movement in Saint Augustine, see Coburn, *Racial Change and Community Crisis*, 42–152.

93. Cecil Musslewhite to William Jamison (18 March 1962), J. Farris Bryant Papers, SASC.

94. National Klan Meet memo (14 October 1962), J. Farris Bryant Papers, SASC; Connolly, "By Eminent Domain," 268–271.

95. Larry Goodwyn, "Anarchy in St. Augustine," *Harper's Magazine* (January 1965), 75; Elmer Emrich to Governor Farris Bryant (6 March 1964), C. Farris Bryant Papers, SASC.

96. Catherine Lewis interviewed by Randall Wells (13 October 1993), HCOHP; Mark Garner interviewed by Catherine Lewis and Randall Wells (20 November 1992), HCOHP; Lee Braxton, "They Spoke Out for Decency," *Rotarian* (September 1953), 29; W. Horace Carter, *Virus of Fear*, 37–70; Hourigan, "Welcome to South Carolina," 71–73.

97. "Negroes' Bid to Enter Park Fails," *MBSOBN* (31 August 1960); Henrietta Abeles to Sigmund Abeles (September 1963), Sigmund Abeles Papers, SCL.

98. Thom Billington, "School Board Takes Firm Stand on Integration Plan," *MBSN* (22 February 1970); "Negroes Oppose Marching," *MBSN* (19 March 1970).

99. "Intergration [*sic*] Here Takes Quiet Air," *VBSN* (2 July 1963).

100. "Workshops Help Ease Local Desegregation," *VBS* (21 August 1969).

101. Minutes of the Meeting of the Board of Directors of the Galveston Chamber of Commerce (12 March 1963), GCCR; Minutes of the Meeting of the Board of Directors of the Galveston Chamber of Commerce (12 September 1967), GCCR; Minutes of the Meeting of the Board of Directors of the Galveston Chamber of Commerce (10 October 1967), GCCR.

102. "Progress in Racial Tolerance," *PCNH* (28 April 1952); "There Will Be No Colored Deputies When McCormick Is Sheriff," *PCNH* (4 May 1952).

103. Interview of Edgar W. (Jack) Jones (27 June 1961), C. Farris Bryant Papers, SASC; Elmer Emrich to William Jamison (12 July 1961), C. Farris Bryant Papers, SASC; Elmer Emrich to William Jamison (18 July 1961), C. Farris Bryant Papers, SASC.

104. Elmer Emrich to William Jamison (12 July 1961), C. Farris Bryant Papers, SASC; Youth Council flier (July 1961), C. Farris Bryant Papers, SASC; Elmer Emrich to William Jamison (6 August 1961), C. Farris Bryant, SASC.

105. Marlene Womack, "Out of the Past: Every Folk Knew the Sheriffs of Old," *PCNH* (27 August 2006).

106. "Kingly Kiss for a Queen," *Jet* (14 October 1954), 62; "Beauty Queens," *Jet* (23 December 1954), 10–11.

107. Hansen, "Shades of Change," 154–164; Kahrl, *The Land Was Ours*, 222–225.

Chapter 4. Beach Belles

1. James Gauker to Mommy [wife], 23 June 1944, James W. Gauker Papers, SCL; James Gauker to Mommy [wife], 22 June 1944, James W. Gauker Papers, SCL.

2. Larry Boulier, "Western Cities Are Different? . . . So Is Myrtle Beach," *MBSOBN* (1958 Program Report); Bertha Staley interviewed by Catherine Lewis, 21 August 1991, 25, HCOHP; J. Stewart Lomanitz to Editor, *PCNH* (13 September 1992). On the influence of California, see Kirse May, *Golden State, Golden Youth*, 13–26. On sexuality and race in the South, see Cahn, *Sexual Reckonings*, 13–15, 27–31; Gilmore, *Gender and Jim Crow*, 62–68, 86–87, 92–96; Ownby, *Subduing Satan*, 194–212; Stacy Braukman, "Nothing Else Matters but Sex," 553–556, 559–560.

3. Elmer Anderson Carter, "A Modern Matriach," *Christian Advocate* (4 February 1937), 79; Mary McLeod Bethune, "Faith That Moved a Dump Heap," *Who: The Magazine about People* (June 1941), 34.

4. Mary McLeod Bethune to G. W. Powell (24 January 1930), Mary McLeod Bethune Papers, ARC; G. W. Powell to Mary McLeod Bethune (27 January 1930), Mary McLeod Bethune Papers, ARC; G. W. Powell to Mary McLeod Bethune (7 February 1930), Mary McLeod Bethune Papers, ARC.

5. Walter E. Grover article (1938), GTHC; John Thomas Woodside autobiography, SHC.

6. Aron, *Working at Play*, 3–14; Adam, *Buying Respectability*, 153–180.

7. On the Chautauqua movement, see Aron, *Working at Play*, 111–126; Reiser, *The Chautauqua Movement*, 47–85, 139–150.

8. *Two Trains Daily via L&N* (pamphlet, c. 1915), SASC.

9. Aron, *Working at Play*, 124–126; Rugh, *Are We There Yet?* 41–67, quote from 42.

10. "Seashore Divinity School," *New York Observer and Chronicle* (3 August 1911); "Seashore Divinity School to Close Tonight with Address by Dr. Hoben," *BDH* (30 June 1915); "Sunday Big Day at Campground," *BDH* (23 July 1921); Ray Thompson, "Know Your Coast: Seashore Methodist Assembly," *BDH* (28 May 1956).

11. "Many Sunday Schools," *Princess Anne Times* (18 June 1915); "Vacation Bible School Held at Oceana," *VBN* (29 June 1945); Jean Miller Bruce interview (n.d.), James River Elementary School Oral History Project, Virginia Historical Society.

12. Larry L. King, "Bob Jones University: The Buckle on the Bible Belt," *Harper's Magazine* (June 1966), 54–55; "Bob Jones College Marker Unveiling Set," *PCNH* (3 July 1976); Ludelle Brannon, "Marker Unveiled at Site of First College in Bay," *PCNH* (4 July 1976); Deena McMurtry, "A Christian College That Cared," *GC* (9 December 1983).

13. "'Psychic' Lecturer and Wife Arrested," *New York Times* (9 November 1931); "Cayce, Psychic Diagnostician, Dies in Home at Virginia Beach," *VBN* (5 January 1945); "Edgar Cayce," *VBN* (5 January 1945).

14. Ray Thompson, "Know Your Coast: Waveland's Gulfside Assembly," *BDH* (15 March 1957); Kahrl, *The Land Was Ours*, 52–85, 241–248.

15. Elizabeth Hayes Turner, *Women, Culture and Community*, 42; Murdock, *Banana Republic*, 22; Harvey Jackson, "Florida Room," 23.

16. Reeder, *Project Myrtle*, 16.

17. "The Deep Channel," *VBSN* (2 October 1952); "You Are Invited to Attend the Church of Your Choice," *PCNH* (21 March 1952). On the history and meanings of church architecture, see Kieckhefer, *Theology in Stone*, 135–166, 195–228; Ryan Smith, *Gothic Arches, Latin Crosses*, 83–117.

18. "You Are Invited to Attend the Church of Your Choice," *PCNH* (17 July 1954); "Drive-In Church," *Life* (18 April 1955), 177.

19. Elizabeth Hayes Turner, *Women, Culture and Community*, 103; Floyd, *History*, 5; "Churches," *MBN* (27 October 1938).

20. "'Cooperative Christianity Sunday' Will Be Observed in State on 15th," *VBSN* (12 November 1953); "'Oil Town' Billy Graham's Second Film Opens Tonight," *MBN and Coastal Carolinian* (21 August 1953); *Leisureguide: The Grand Strand*, 7, SCL. On interdenominationalism, see Marty, *Modern American Religion*, 1:17–31, 3:277–330; Settje, *Faith and War*, 23–60.

21. "Ministers of All Faiths," *BDH* (26 March 1960).

22. "GO TO CHURCH," *VBN* (5 April 1940); "Go to Church Your Church Easter," *PCNH* (8 April 1939); "Attend the Church of Your Choice Sunday," *MBN and Coastal Carolinian* (22 June 1951).

23. "Attend the Church of Your Choice Sunday," *MBN* (7 December 1951); "Have a Problem? God Has the Answer," *GDN* (6 June 1970).

24. "Church Census Begins Sunday," *VBN* (10 November 1939); Rev. Reginald Eastman to Editor, *VBN* (8 March 1940); "Religious Education," *VBN* (9 August 1940); "Going to . . . Church Sunday," *PCNH* (4 May 1952); "Church Bells to Ring Sunday," *MBSN* (1 July 1965).

25. "Girls Feature Wrestling Card Saturday Night," *MBN and Coastal Carolinian* (9 March 1951); Eugenia Cutts, Belle Hood, and Harriette Stogner interviewed by Catherine Harris (8 April 1994), 14, HCOHP; Marie Gilbert, *Myrtle Beach Back When*, 25.

26. "Girl Wrestlers Thrill Spectators Saturday's Card," *MBN and Coastal Carolinian* (16 March 1951); "'Jesus Celebration '82' Set for Labor Day at Beach," *PCNH* (4 September 1982).

27. "Absence Makes the Meat Grow Tender," *VBN* (25 July 1941); Dargan's Grill ad, *MBSOBN* (4 June 1958). For other examples of the halo effect, see Austin's ad, *BDH* (26 March 1956).

28. Ruth Millet, "Modern Fair Sex Kicks over the Old-Fashioned Pedestal," *BDH* (15 September 1958). On changing dating customs, see Bailey, *Front Porch to Back Seat*, 13–76; Dorr, "Perils of the Back Seat," 27–47.

29. Dale Sims, "'Playboy' Philosophy Benefits Individual," *GC* (21 September 1966); Frances Moore, "'Other Sex' Lacks Sex to Get Top Jobs, Pay," *MBSN* (16 April 1970).

30. Stephanie Pace, "PACEing the Strand," *MBSN* (16 March 1972); "Miss Waves Pageant Won by Tennessee's Entrant," *MBSN* (18 June 1970); Watson and Martin, "Miss America Pageant," 106, 110–112, 121–122; Latham, "Packaging Woman," 150.

31. Joan Senyk to Karen Coolman (6 January 1974), Florida National Organization of Women Records, SASC; Joan Senyk to Karen Coolman (n.d.), Florida National Organization of Women Records, SASC; Joan Senyk to Karen Coolman (8 May 1974), Florida National Organization of Women Records, SASC.

32. Robin Rothrock to Karen Coolman (6 August 1974), Florida National Organization of Women Records, SASC.

33. "Satisfaction: Newsletter of the Fort Walton Beach Chapter of the National Organization for Women" (May 1974), Florida National Organization of Women Records, SASC.

34. Pam McCormack to Karen Coolman (9 October 1974), Florida National Organization of Women Records, SASC; Pamela McCormack to Margaret Barovich (10 January 1975), Florida National Organization of Women Records, SASC.

35. "Modern Bath Suits but in Days of Yore," *VBN* (16 June 1939).

36. "Declares First Need of Wise Woman Is Time for Prayer," *BDH* (19 April 1928).

37. Sarah Evelyn Baylor Blackford Diary (20 June 1895), Virginia Historical Society; Low, *America at Home*, 181; Alma Simmang Simpson to no name (27 August 1915), Alma Simmang Simpson Papers, GTHC.

38. Glennan Alma Anderson interviewed by R. Wayne Pyle (29 September 1979), COHCH; Cunningham, "From Underwear to Swimwear," 38–52.

39. David Carr interviewed by Carl Compton (1987 or later), 13, HCOHP; Lencek and Bosker, *The Beach*, 83–84, 106, 133–138, 189–194, 211–222, 248–256.

40. Roberts, "Pretty Women," 133–171, quote from 156; William Rivers, "Florida: The State with the Two-Way Stretch," *Harper's Magazine* (February 1955), 34; Elizabeth Bronwyn Boyd, "Southern Beauty," 74–106.

41. "Sidelights on Beauty Revue," *GDN* (23 May 1927); "Beauty Revue Vies with Colorful Old World Pageants," *GDN* (22 May 1927); "Largest Crowd in Galveston's History Witnesses Revue," *GDN* (23 May 1927).

42. "Virginia Beach Gets National Beauty Pageant," *VBN* (14 July 1939); "Beauty Contest Finals Tonight," *VBN* (25 August 1939); "Crowning of 'Miss Virginia Beach' to Be Highlight of Third Annual Sand Festival," *VBSN* (10 July 1954).

43. On the history of beauty pageants, see Latham, "Packaging Woman," 149–167; Henry Pang, "Miss America," 687–696; Watson and Martin, "Miss America Pageant," 105–126.

44. "Hot News in Florida," *PCNH* (30 January 1936); "'Miss Hospitality' Will Be Chosen and Crowned by Gov. Wright Tonight," *BDH* (8 June 1949); "Pascagoula Girl Chosen and Crowned 'Miss Hospitality' in Climax to State Program," *BDH* (9 June 1949); "Miss Northwest Florida," *PCNH* (7 July 1954).

45. Merz, *Great American Band Wagon*, 147, 149; "Gulfport Feasts Its Eyes as Beauties Appear in Pageant," *BDH* (21 December 1925); "Finals for the Beauty Queen," *PCNH* (4 July 1947).

46. "Tourist Attraction," *PCNH* (27 June 1961). For examples, see "Rain?—Not Here," *VBN* (3 June 1938); "Virginia Beach Mer'maids," *VBN* (16 June 1939).

47. Crown Theatre ad, *BDH* (19 April 1920); "The Headlines Say," *VBN* (7 June 1935).

48. William Rivers, "City Full of Promoters," *PCNH* (22 August 1954); "Eat at the Sign of the Bathing Girl," *PCNH* (1 October 1935); Smiths' "Inc.," *PCNH* (18 April 1952); Nicole Cox, "Selling Seduction," 186–209.

49. "Travel Agents Find It's the Missus Who Enjoys 'Showing Off' in Travel," *PCNH* (27 June 1939).

50. "The Gayety Burlesk Theatre," *MBSN* (1 July 1965); "Show Place of the Gulf Coast," *BDH* (5 May 1954); "Show Place of the Gulf Coast," *BDH* (18 May 1954); "Playland Park," *BDH* (28 May 1954); "Playland Park," *BDH* (16 July 1954). On the emergence of mixed-sex attendance at burlesque shows, see Aldridge, "American Burlesque,'" 565–575; Friedman, "Habitats of Sex-Crazed Perverts," 203–238; Stanonis, *Creating the Big Easy*, 132–136.

51. On public swimming pools and beaches, see Wiltse, *Contested Waters*, 87–120.

52. "Biloxi's Bathing Tonight's Topic," *BDH* (22 April 1920); "Objects to Biloxi Rules," *BDH* (26 April 1920); "Biloxi's First Bathing Arrest," *BDH* (24 May 1920).

53. "Bathhouses on Wheels," *VBN* (28 July 1939).

54. "Side Glances," *PCNH* (12 January 1939); "From the Grand Strand," *MBN* (16 December 1949); Rosemary Diaries (27 May 1953), STDC; Cooke, *One Man's America*, 113; "Beach Base Participates in 'Dancer V,'" *MBSN* (25 May 1972).

55. Edmond Lebreton, "Sorry, Girls, but There Are Not Enough Men to Go Around," *BDH* (23 May 1942); Ralph G. Martin, *Best Is None Too Good*, 25; Bailey, *Front Porch to Back Seat*, 68–76, 110–117; Bailey and Farber, *The First Strange Place*, 15–61; Buszek, *Pin-Up Grrrls*, 201–239; Lencek and Bosker, *The Beach*, 196–198.

56. Alicia Hart, "Have Glamor on Beach and Budget, Too," *BDH* (8 July 1954).

57. "Myrtle Beach Choice: Bathing Suit—or Jail," *Life* (23 June 1952), 33.

58. "Bikinis Move to Bedrooms," *Life* (11 April 1960), 105; "Nothing Itsy Bitsy about a Hit," *Life* (22 August 1960), 40; "The St. Tropez Way for the U.S.A.," *Life* (13 January 1961), 67; Lencek and Bosker, *The Beach*, 220–222.

59. "What Do French Beaches Have That American Beaches Don't Have?" ad, *Harper's Magazine* (June 1961), back cover; "So Now I Own a Net Bikini," *Life* (7 May 1965), 33; Sharon Hudson, "Mermaids Will Do Own Swim 'Thing,'" *PCNH* (23 August 1970).

60. "How to Stuff a Wild Bikini" ad, *MBSN* (22 June 1965); "The Girls on the Beach" ad, *MBSN* (7 October 1965); Groneman, *Nymphomania: A History*, 125–129; Meyerowitz, *How Sex Changed*, 194–204.

61. "Girls, Watch Your Dress," *GC* (18 October 1967); Ellen Caldwell, "Mini-Skirts Ogled on Many Shapes," *GC* (8 October 1969); Ellen Caldwell, "Administration Pushes New Code," *GC* (5 November 1969).

62. Emily Germanis, "Miss Hospitality Crowning Tonight," *BDH* (28 July 1973); "High Fashions Promote State," *MBSN* (27 July 1967). On the meaning of plastics as modernity after the Second World War, see Meikle, *American Plastic*, 183–241.

63. Paul O'Neil, "Nudity," *Life* (13 October 1967), 107; Hoffman, "Certain Amount of Prudishness," 708–732; Shaffer, "On the Environmental Nude," 126–139.

64. Doug Smith to Florence Wills (30 July 1975), American Civil Liberties Union of Florida Records, SASC; Benjamin Sweeting to Peter Raben (18 August 1975), American Civil Liberties Union of Florida Records, SASC.

65. Benjamin Sweeting to Florence Wills, (2 June 1975), American Civil Liberties Union of Florida Records, SASC; Peter Raben to John MacArthur (6 August 1975), American Civil Liberties Union of Florida Records, SASC.

66. Jim Wiles, "The Real Problem at Bear Cut," *Grove Gazette* (July 1976), 20, American Civil Liberties Union of Florida Records, SASC. Similar situations occurred in San Francisco during the sexual revolution of the 1960s and 1970s. On the undermining of open sexuality by serial killers and sexual predators, see Sides, *Erotic City*, 123–139.

67. Carol Agate, "OK, Men, Cover Your Chests—or Let Women Sunbathers Go Topless, Too," *Los Angeles Times* (31 May 1981).

68. Sue Grace to the Editor, "Just Grin and Let the Nudists Bare It," *Biloxi Sun Herald* (28 July 1998); John Wirth to Governor Bob Martinez (2 July 1990), American Civil Liberties Union of Florida Records, SASC.

69. Hollis Alger to Ellen Wright (3 December 1943), Hollis M. Alger Letters, STDC; Meeting of the Board of Directors of the Galveston Chamber of Commerce (14 May 1945), GCCR; Meeting of the Board of Directors of the Galveston Chamber of Commerce (8 June 1948), GCCR; Meeting of the Board of Directors of the Galveston Chamber of Commerce (7 May 1948), GCCR; Helen Smith, "Galveston Tops U.S. in Syphilis," *GDN* (4 June 1970).

70. Bunny Hampton, "Special Delivery," *MBSN* (29 May 1976). On the impact of the birth control pill and the sexual revolution, see Bailey, *Sex in the Heartland*, 105–215; Elaine Tyler May, *America and the Pill*, 71–92.

71. Marie Gilbert, *Myrtle Beach Back When*, 19; Mark Garner interviewed by Catherine Lewis and Randall Wells (20 November 1992), 7, HCOHP; Sigmund Abeles, My Yes-Tiddies, 24, 32, Sigmund Abeles Papers, SCL.

72. Susan Jetton, "Beach Dwellers Like Tourists, but . . . ," *Charlotte Observer* (28 June 1976), Myrtle Beach Scrapbook, Volume 2, Boone Archive Room, Chapin Memorial Library.

73. John Conder to W. W. Smoak (22 July 1926), William Wightman Smoak Papers, SCL; *Arcady: A National Playground*; James Elliott, "Family-Style Holidays at Virginia Beach," *New York Times* (3 June 1951); "The Sombrero . . . for Mexican Cuisine," *PCNH* (2 March 1982).

74. Virgil Newton to John Herbert (24 January 1956), Virgil Miller "Red" Newton Papers, SASC.

75. *Sun-Fun Magazine* (12 April 1956), SCL; *Grand Strand Tourist Guide* (1974), SCL.

76. "How Long Can America Stand Erosion of Moral Principle?" *PCNH* (22 July 1962); "Offers a Solution," Milledge Leach to Editor, *PCNH* (1 August 1967); Zaretsky, *No Direction Home*, 4. The centrality of family to beach vacations can be evidenced by the idyllic design of Seaside, Florida. Just as Zaretsky argues that Ronald Reagan rode to the presidency on promises to restore American families, Seaside developer Robert Davis envisioned a quaint coastal town free of suburban sprawl. See Harvey Jackson, "Developing the Panhandle," 71–87.

77. "Good Publicity," *MBSOBN* (20 March 1957); Reverend Kenneth Haynes interviewed by William Henderson (5 November 1999), Community Bridges Oral History Project, COHCH. On the rise of the Christian right and the rhetoric of family values, see Dowland, "Family Values," 606–631; Ribuffo, "Family Policy Past as Prologue," 311–337; Watt, "Private Hopes of American Fundamentalists," 155–175.

78. "'Virginia Beach' on Air," Ruth Beach to Editor, *VBSN* (4 November 1954); "Iowa Housewife Selected Mrs. Myrtle Beach Guest," *MBSOBN* (29 May 1957).

79. "Gulfport Makes Ready for Golden Jubilee Observation," *BDH* (24 July 1948); "Fete Couples in Gulfport Celebration," *BDH* (26 July 1948).

80. Archie Benton interviewed by Catherine Lewis (21 May 1993), HCOHP; *Sunny Day Guide*, 46, SCL.

81. Ezra Mishan, "A Modest Proposal," *Harper's Magazine* (July 1972), 55; "Beach Contest Demeaning to Women Who Participate," *GC* (23 April 1990).

82. "Desert Revival for Altar?" *Atlanta Constitution* (20 July 1904); "She's Mother, Grandmother, and Prostitute," *MBSN* (10 April 1974).

83. Cole, *Redneck Riviera*, 2.

Chapter 5. Wet Lands

1. Allison, *Moonshine Memories*, 359–360.

2. Duhamel, *American the Menace*, 74.

3. Florida State Temperance pamphlet (n.d., c. 1904), Napoleon Bonaparte Broward Papers, SASC. On the movement for Prohibition in the South, see Grantham, *Southern Progressivism*, 160–177; Link, *Paradox of Southern Progressivism*, 31–57, 96–112; Joe Coker, *Liquor*, 37–122; Ownby, *Subduing Satan*, 41–55, 170–173; Ann-Marie Szymanski, "Beyond Parochialism," 107–136.

4. Rorabaugh, *The Alcoholic Republic*, 8–9, 54–56; Wilbur Miller, *Revenuers and Moonshiners*, 4–8, 170–184.

5. "Whiskey Buried on Gulfport Beach," *BDH* (5 April 1920); "Drys Push Drive against Alleged Bootleggers," *BDH* (22 August 1927); E. J. Cain interviewed by Law-

rence Evans (14 October 1938), Life Histories—Alabama, Federal Writers' Project, SHC. On smuggling operations, see McComb, *Galveston: A History*, 159–162; James Carter, "Florida and Rumrunning," 47–56; Sanders, "Delivering Demon Rum," 92–113.

6. "The Harrison Anti-Narcotic Federal Law," *Princess Anne Times* (9 July 1915); "Smith, Tired Out, Begins Vacation," *Atlanta Constitution* (18 November 1928); Matthew Ryan interviewed by William Hubbell assisted by Chester Morgan (1976), COHCH; Tom Yon, "On Soldier Bonus, Prohibition, and Other Subjects," *Congressional Record* (15 June 1932).

7. On saloon culture before Prohibition, see Stanonis, *Creating the Big Easy*, 107–111, 124–138, 174–175; Powers, *Faces along the Bar*, 48–71.

8. Haddock to Robert Dosh (12 January 1929), Robert "Bert" Dosh Papers, SASC.

9. Lerner, *Dry Manhattan*, 98–147; Kenneth Rose, *American Women*, 67–89; Murphy, "Bootlegging Mothers," 174–194. On the cultural rebellion against Prohibition and the freedom allowed by the automobile, see Stanonis, *Creating the Big Easy*, 54–57, 124–130; Seiler, *Republic of Drivers*, 29–68.

10. Charley "Uncle Bud" Ryland interviewed by Jack Kytle (21 September 1938), Life Histories—Alabama, Federal Writers' Project, SHC; "Veteran, 106, Bags Deer," *New York Times* (21 November 1954).

11. Ray Thompson, "Know Your Coast: Biloxi's Historic Blue Monday," *BDH* (4 October 1957). On the history and controversy of blue laws, see Wallenstein, *Blue Laws and Black Codes*, 36–59; McCrossen, *Holy Day, Holiday*, 105–110, 143–145; Lucas, "The Unholy Experiment," 163–175; Raucher, "Sunday Business," 13–34; Leon Miller, "Majority Wanted Barabbas Too," 3–40, 57–65.

12. C. Von Tinglestadt to Editor, *BDH* (8 July 1921); Conscientious Citizen to Editor, *BDH* (14 July 1921); George Coad, "Gulf Coast Turns to 'Sinful' Pursuits," *New York Times* (25 August 1929); Ray Thompson, "Know Your Coast: When Sunday Movies Were Illegal in Gulfport," *BDH* (5 January 1958).

13. "Showdown Impending over Sunday Movies," *BDH* (18 April 1942); McCrossen, *Holy Day, Holiday*, 106.

14. Wallenstein, *Blue Laws and Black Codes*, 57; "Sunday Law Changes Get Endorsement," *MBSN* (8 February 1962); Raucher, "Sunday Business," 24–27.

15. Although each state adopted a regulatory board, the names of such agencies varied by state and county and occasionally changed over time. For clarity, "ABC" is used for all alcohol control boards since this was the most common name adopted.

16. "Virginia Sells Liquor," *New York Times* (16 May 1934); "Rehabilitation of the Bootlegger," *VBN* (23 August 1940).

17. "Hilliard Leaves ABC's Employ; Staff Here Cut," *VBN* (23 November 1934).

18. "Deadline Is Set on Beer Signs," *VBN* (4 February 1938); "Liquor Stores Repaint Fronts," *MBN* (21 July 1939); "Whiskey Stores Can Descreen," *BDH* (11 June 1968).

19. Committee Appointed on Clean Up and General Repair of City, Minutes of the Board of Directors of the Galveston Chamber of Commerce (6 September 1946), GTHC; "Four Biloxians State Opinions on Liquor Bill," *BDH* (1 March 1960); "Does Our Community Need Liquor?" *MBSN* (3 November 1966). For insight into post–

Second World War debates about alcohol, see Marshall Morgan, "Tennessee Preachers and the Demon Rum," *Harper's Magazine* (February 1954), 44–51; Peck, *The Prohibition Hangover*, 20–24.

20. Cooper J. Darby interviewed by Mike Garvey (19 May 1976), COHCH; Wilson Evans II interviewed by Orley Caudill (11 June 1981), COHCH; William Hubbell interviewed by Orley Caudill (21 August 1975), COHCH; "Let's Give Our Police a Break," *VBN* (24 February 1950).

21. "What Price Honor?" *VBN* (28 July 1950).

22. Interview of Edgar W. (Jack) Jones (n.d., c. 1961), C. Farris Bryant Papers, SASC; Interview of James Hooten (n.d., c. 1961), C. Farris Bryant Papers, SASC.

23. Interview of Edgar W. (Jack) Jones (n.d., c. 1961), C. Farris Bryant Papers, SASC; Interview of James Hooten (n.d., c. 1961), C. Farris Bryant Papers, SASC; Elmer Emrich to William Jamison (7 July 1961), RE: Panama City Investigation, C. Farris Bryant Papers, SASC.

24. R. H. Comfort to Thomas Lee (11 October 1961), C. Farris Bryant Papers, SASC; "B-Girl Law Charges Thrown Out by Judge," Pensacola newspaper clipping (26 October 1961), C. Farris Bryant Papers, SASC.

25. Andrew Stanley interviewed by C. Bergen Berry (April 1991), HCOHP; "Been Fishin' since Before I Could Walk" (n.d.), These Are Our Lives, WPA, Mississippi Department of Archives and History; Jim Kelly interviewed by R. Wayne Pyle (28 February 1979), COHCH.

26. "Florida Ranks at Bottom of Regional 'Shine List," *Jacksonville Florida Times-Union* (31 December 1955); "Bootlegging Vote Can Win an Election," *MBSOBN* (4 May 1960); "34 Shine Stills Destroyed in Calhoun County," *PCNH* (22 July 1962).

27. "Governor Tells Patrol to Halt Liquor Trucking," *BDH* (2 May 1956); Elmer Emrich to William Jamison (18 July 1961), RE: Panama City Investigation, C. Farris Bryant Papers, SASC; Catherine Lewis interviewed by Randall Wells (13 October 1993), HCOHP.

28. Humes, *Mississippi Mud*, 105–137. For more on Phenix City, see "A Sawdust Trail Brings New Days," *Life* (4 October 1954), 49; Margaret Ann Barnes, *Tragedy and Triumph of Phenix City*.

29. "Police Destroy Still Operating in Town Limits," *VBN* (10 November 1939); "Smash Still, Arrest Two Men," *BDH* (29 March 1960); "Norfolkian Is Arrested in Raid on Whisky Still," *VBSN* (6 December 1962).

30. Round Table Discussion IV: Park Rules and Regulations, Tenth Annual Meeting Minutes, Association of Southeastern State Park Directors (6–9 November 1951), National Association of State Park Directors, Forest History Society; "Why Not?" Pat Christy to Editor, *VBSN* (14 January 1960); "State Hotel Group Takes Stand on Local Option," *VBSN* (18 January 1962); United States Brewers Association ad, *PCNH* (31 July 1947); United States Brewers Association ad, *VBSN* (13 February 1964).

31. Larry Boulier, "Everyone Is Responsible," *MBSOBN* (27 February 1957).

32. "A Symbol of Hypocrisy," *MBSOBN* (3 February 1960); "Chamber Members Favor Liquor Referendum," *MBSN* (13 October 1966); "Re: Liquor by the Drink Leg-

islation," Minutes of the Board of Directors of the Galveston Chamber of Commerce (14 March 1967), GTHC.

33. "Why Not Local Option?" *VBSN* (11 February 1960).

34. "Local Groups Take Action in Endorsing Legislation for 'Local Option' on Sale of Alcoholic Drink," *VBSN* (28 January 1960); "Local Option Is Favored by State Restaurtnt [*sic*] Groups," *VBSN* (4 February 1960); "A Sensible By-the-Drink Plan," *VBSN* (28 January 1960); "Downing, Liquor, Bonds, Win Beach Easily," *VBS* (7 November 1968).

35. "Brown-Bag Rules Given," *MBSN* (27 July 1967); "Tourism Cited for Mini-Bottle," *MBSN* (1 February 1973).

36. "Beach Street Beat," *MBSN* (30 June 1973).

37. Schlitz ad, *BDH* (6 April 1934); "Bootleg Whiskey Drinkers May Be Flirting with Death Warns Official of Alcohol Unit," *VBSN* (12 January 1961); "Moonshine Operation Profitable and Deadly," *PCH* (6 August 1962).

38. "Four Biloxians State Opinions on Liquor Bill," *BDH* (1 March 1960).

39. "Wet and Dry," *New York Times* (1 May 1960); "Prohibition Is Over in Mississippi Today," *New York Times* (1 July 1966); "Louisiana House Committee Passes Liquor Sale Bill," *BDH* (14 June 1960).

40. Mrs. Charles Bergeron to Editor, *BDH* (5 March 1960); "Sheriff Seizes Liquor Bought in New Orleans," *BDH* (14 March 1960); "The Bootleggers Are Happy," *BDH* (16 March 1960).

41. "Wet and Dry," *New York Times* (1 May 1960); "Legal Liquor in Mississippi," *Down South* (September-October 1966), 16; Peck, *The Prohibition Hangover*, 21; Terry Wooten, "Legality Brings Demise of Mississippi 'Joints,'" *PCNH* (2 July 1967).

42. "The Road Behind" (1958), John Herbert Peck Papers, SASC; Edgar Cole to Bertha Cole (5 December 1909), Elsie H. Booker Collection, SHC.

43. Lears, *Something for Nothing*, 112–121, quote from 114; Isaac, *Transformation of Virginia*, 98–103; Ownby, *Subduing Satan*, 69–87, 116–118; Adam Ellick, "A Ban on Cockfighting, but Tradition Lives On," *New York Times* (6 July 2008).

44. Mrs. W. J. Ward to Anna Roosevelt (31 March 1939), cited in Green, *Looking for the New Deal*, 191; Kofoed, *The Florida Story*, 86–122, quote from 86; Remarks of Reubin Askew to an Anti-Casino Gambling Luncheon (3 February 1978), Reubin O'Donovan Askew Speeches, SASC.

45. Paul Eliot Green to Mary (14 March 1918), Paul Eliot Green Papers, SHC; George Coad, "Gulf Coast Turns to 'Sinful' Pursuits," *New York Times* (25 August 1929); Anthony Costantini to Harry Engler (18 June 1942), Anthony Costantini Letter, STDC; Hollis M. Alger to Ellen Wright (30 June 1943), Hollis M. Alger Letters, STDC.

46. "Gambling—Past, Present and Future," *PCNH* (15 March 1939).

47. "Pin-Ball Operators File Pleas of Guilty to Gambling Charges," *VBN* (9 June 1939); "Are We Getting What We Pay For?" *VBN* (9 June 1939).

48. "City Commission on Trial," *GDN* (21 November 1939); "Gymer Silent on Rumored Return of Gaming Equipment," *GDN* (2 December 1939); "Shutdown Is Said Agreed Upon by Gaming Interests," *GDN* (8 December 1939); "Five Charged as Police Seize Gaming Equipment," *GDN* (27 December 1939).

49. A. S. Mann to Richard Keating and Duke Newcome (15 July 1963), C. Farris Bryant Papers, SASC; William Jamison to Jimmy Kynes (12 March 1963), C. Farris Bryant Papers, SASC. For an excellent description of politics, corruption, and tourism in a southern county, specifically of Georgia's McIntosh County where Sheriff Tom Poppell exploited passing tourists headed to Florida, see Melissa Fay Greene, *Praying for Sheetrock*.

50. My Trip Diary (11 March 1939), STDC; "Games of Chance Given Set Back by Latest Action," *VBN* (26 August 1938); Interview of William Hubbell by Orley Caudill (25 August 1975), COHCH; Anonymous to Richard Keating and Duke Newcome (24 June 1963), C. Farris Bryant Papers, SASC.

51. "Gambling—Two Kinds," *PCNH* (16 January 1939); "Gaming in 'Private Clubs' Permissible," *BDH* (21 July 1960).

52. "High Cost of Gambling," *VBN* (7 July 1939).

53. Grenville Mellen interviewed by Orley Caudill (23 January 1974), COHCH; "North Carolina Again Leads," *VBN* (14 April 1939). On the issue of gambling during the Depression, see Gragg, "Selling 'Sin City,'" 83–106; Haller, "Changing Structure of American Gambling," 87–114; Moody, "Nevada's Legalization of Casino Gambling," 79–100; McComb, *Galveston: A History*, 161–166; Stanonis, *Creating the Big Easy*, 77–80.

54. Trillin, *U.S. Journal*, 100.

55. John Popham, "Gambling Called Heaviest in Biloxi," *New York Times* (23 October 1951); "Biloxi's Hand Is Called at Last," *Life* (5 November 1951), 38.

56. R. W. Chambers to William Jamison (19 June 1962), C. Farris Bryant Papers, SASC.

57. V. M. Newton to Dean Carl Ackerman (24 January 1951), Virgil Miller Newton Papers, SASC; "What Has Happened Since Kefauver," *Life* (1 October 1951), 22.

58. "Dear Mr. Governor," *VBN* (11 August 1950). On the hearings, see Jeanine Derr, "Biggest Show on Earth," 19–37; Lisby, "Early Television on Public Watch," 236–242.

59. President to T. D. Woodbury (26 October 1951), Society of American Foresters, Forest History Society.

60. "Bay Voters Spurn Dog Track," *Panama City News* (11 August 1954); Ebro ad (19 April 1968), *The Weekender* supplement, *PCH* (19 April 1968).

61. "League for Political Decency Maps Platform," *VBN* (31 March 1950); "Virginia Beach Voters Return Administration Candidates to Offices in Tuesday's Election," *VBN* (16 June 1950); "Judge Kellam Calls Special Grand Jury to Investigate Charges of Lawlessness," *VBN* (30 June 1950); "State and Local Police Stage Widespread Raids; Clubs Called 'Common Nuisances,'" *VBN* (21 July 1950); "Needed Divorce," *VBN* (22 September 1950).

62. "Scandal Whiffed in Garden Spot," *VBN* (7 September 1951); "Two of 19 Indicted by Grand Jury in June Found Guilty by P.A. Circuit Court Jury," *VBN* (13 October 1950).

63. "The Odor at Virginia Beach," *VBN* (20 October 1950); "Why Vote 100% H-A-S-H?" *VBN* (3 August 1951); "Preaching or Practicing," *VBN* (25 June 1953).

64. M. Bulgerin to the Galveston Chamber of Commerce (n.d., c. 1955), Galveston Chamber of Commerce, Rosenberg Library.

65. Larry Boulier, "Larry Boulier Asks a Wee Bit of Time to Join Him in Thoughts Regarding the Forthcoming City Election," *MBSN* (9 September 1965).

66. "Galveston May Be 'Open,' but not 'Wide Open,'" *BDH* (7 June 1956); "Wide-Open Galveston Mocks Texas Laws," *Life* (15 August 1955), 26.

67. Proceedings of Meeting of Galveston Chamber of Commerce (23 September 1955), GTHC.

68. Minutes of Galveston Chamber of Commerce Meeting (20 September 1955), GTHC; "Texas: V for Vice," *Time* (25 May 1959); "Re: Publicity," Minutes of the Board of Directors of the Galveston Chamber of Commerce (21 May 1959), GTHC.

69. Anthony Lewis, "High Court Ruling Helps Poor Man to Freedom," *New York Times* (6 August 1963). On *Gideon v. Wainwright* (1963), see Anthony Lewis, *Gideon's Trumpet*.

70. On federal intervention in the South and reapportionment, see Bodenhamer, *Fair Trial*, 92–128; Douglas Smith, "Into the Political Thicket," 263–285; Howison, "Not a Cotton Picker's Dream," 680–693; Maniha, "Structural Supports," 315–343; Moore and Kelling, "To Serve and Protect," 49–65.

71. Petigny, "Spread of Permissive Religion," 399–422.

72. "Is Bingo Truly Legal in Florida Now?" *PCH* (5 July 1967).

73. John Monk, "Tourists Miss Their Bingo," *MBSN* (22 May 1977); Delind, "Bingo," 149–156; Kim King, "Gambling for God," 3–7.

74. Concerned Citizen to Editor, *BDH* (15 July 1973); "Police Observe Bingo, but Make No Arrests," *BDH* (21 July 1973); Odette Durocher to Editor, *BDH* (22 July 1973); John Monk, "Tourists Miss Their Bingo," *MBSN* (22 May 1977).

75. John Monk, "Area Quietly Is Largest County Fair," *MBSN* (23 June 1977); "Open for Business," *MBSN* (4 June 1977); "Bingo Game Open Today," *MBSN* (3 June 1977).

76. Schaap, "Growth of Native American Gaming," 365–389.

77. "Official: Ban Would Bleed Budget," *Biloxi Sun Herald* (31 July 1998); Cohen, *Chasing the Red, White, and Blue*, 155–156.

78. Paul Kleiber to Editor, *GDN* (5 July 1972); Simon, *Boardwalk of Dreams*, 194–216.

79. Lulu Ames to Jessie Daniel Ames (1 April 1929), Jessie Daniel Ames Papers, SHC.

80. Ruth Taylor, "Who Is Delinquent?" *VBN* (14 April 1944); "Air-Rifles and Brick Bats," *VBN* (5 May 1944); James Gilbert, *Cycle of Outrage*, 3–41, 63–76.

81. "Supervisors to Ask Additional Secondary Road Mileage; Hear Complaint of 'Hell Raising,'" *VBN* (30 June 1950); Fred Singleton to Editor, *VBSN* (13 June 1957); "Car Sleeping Should Be Curbed," *VBSN* (13 June 1957).

82. "Warns of Liquor Sales to Minors," *PCNH* (24 April 1952); "Dealers Who Sell Drinks to Minors Campaign Targets," *Panama City News* (22 July 1954); "Beverage Supervisor Pledges Strict Holiday Enforcement," *PCH* (21 March 1958); "Grand Jury Calls Attention to Sale of Liquor to Minors," *BDH* (8 December 1956); David Poling, "Where Has Church Failed on the Drinking Problem?" *BDH* (1 June 1968).

83. "Students on Coast," *BDH* (7 April 1928); Robert and Gladys Walker interviewed by Sadie Hornsby (n.d.), Life Histories—Georgia, Federal Writers' Project, SHC; Laurie, "Spring Break," 10–11.

84. "College Boys Have Last Fling in Miami," *Life* (30 April 1951), 113; Dwayne Walls, "For Teens, Living at Beach," *Charlotte Observer* (23 May 1965); "Nothing Can Beat the Facts," *VBSN* (26 July 1962); Stephanie Pace, "PACEing the Strand," *MBSN* (8 April 1972).

85. "Alabama Judge Warns Students on Misbehaving in Panama City," *PCH* (1 March 1958); "Mayor of Beach Resort Affirms Ban on Beer," *PCNH* (9 March 1958); Warren Williams, "Invasion Ending; Alabama Won It," *GC* (21 March 1973); "Hordes of Sun-Hungry Teenagers," *PCNH* (14 March 1982); "Pot Smoking Youths Told 'to Hit the Road,'" *PCNH* (12 March 1982).

86. Ministerial Association Representatives Requests [*sic*] Chamber's Assistance Re Prostitution, Etc., Minutes of the Board of Directors of the Galveston Chamber of Commerce (10 April 1956), GCCR.

87. Quality Courts Motel (19 September 1964), Federal Bureau of Investigation St. Augustine Surveillance Files, SASC; Gail Shackelford to Editor, *MBSN* (8 May 1973); Belasco, *Americans on the Road*, 129–174.

88. "Students Pour into Daytona," *PCH* (12 April 1968); Mormino, *Land of Sunshine*, 124–125, 316–322; Laurie, "Spring Break," 11–18.

89. "Howling Mob Battles Police," *Panama City News* (19 June 1961); "Virginia Beach Revelers Fight Police," *New York Times* (6 July 1976).

90. Eldridge Thompson, "Rock, Bottle-Throwing Incident Mars Ocean Drive Easter Eve," *MBSN* (30 March 1967); "N. Beach Is Orderly Despite a Near-Riot," *MBSN* (2 April 1970); John Monk, "Motel Owners Criticize Police," *MBSN* (16 April 1974); John Monk, "Arrests Cloud Easter Weekend," *MBSN* (15 April 1974).

91. "Civic Center Takes on Nightclub Air," *VBSN* (14 May 1963); "Let's Promise More Teen-age Recreation," *VBSN* (27 June 1963).

92. "What They Need Is a Place to Go," *Life* (19 August 1966), 39; Doris Patrick, "View of Virginia Beach," *VBSN* (14 May 1964); "Beach Teen Club a Fresh, New Approach," *VBSN* (21 May 1964); "Beach War Opens Again with Adults vs. Boppers," *VBSN* (20 July 1967).

93. "'The Purple Haze' Disappears Weekly," *VBS* (18 April 1968); "Coffee & Mushrooms at Lonnie's," *GC* (9 February 1971); Jimmy Tharpe, "Controversial Beach Salon to Open Again," *PCNH* (10 July 1976).

94. Joseph Lowenthal, "Ex-User Discusses 'Pot,'" *VBSN* (22 February 1968); "'Nice Kids' in Virginia Beach Smoke Marijuana Too," *VBS* (29 August 1968); John Hogg to Editor, *VBS* (9 April 1970); Les Lehigh, "LSD Slipping but Homegrown Pot Increasing," *VBS* (18 July 1970); "26% of Ball Students Claim Marijuana Use," *GDN* (5 June 1970).

95. Stephanie Pace, "PACEing the Strand," *MBSN* (23 October 1971); Cooper Terry to Editor, *MBSN* (21 August 1971).

96. Dirk Langlotz, "Police Should Give Tourists 'Break,'" *GC* (9 April 1987); "Driving Drunks Off the Road," *Changing Times* (July 1982), 53; "Louisiana Court Upholds Drinking Age of 21," *New York Times* (3 July 1996). Louisiana legislators in 1987 made it illegal to sell alcohol to those under 21, but allowed those 18–21 to buy or consume alcohol. The law against sellers was rarely enforced. The loophole was closed in 1996.

97. "The Nonrepresented Voters," *BDH* (9 March 1954); "Our Disfranchised Citizens," *VBSN* (21 April 1964); Pat Brooks, "How Much in Sales Taxes Does Myrtle Beach Supply? It's a Deep, Dark Secret," *MBSN* (11 September 1969).

98. "Bootlegging Vote Can Win an Election," *MBSOBN* (4 May 1960); Remarks of Governor Reubin Askew to the 42nd Annual Conference of the Florida Peace Officers Association (15 July 1971), Reubin O'Donovan Askew Speeches, SASC.

99. Connolly, "By Eminent Domain," 448.

Epilogue

1. Ed Kerr, "Southerners Who Set the Woods on Fire," *Harper's Magazine* (July 1958), 29, 33.

2. Morgan, *Distance to the Moon*, 105.

BIBLIOGRAPHY

Archival Sources

Chapin Memorial Library, Boone Archive Room
    Myrtle Beach Scrapbook, Volume 2
Coastal Carolina University, Kimbel Library, Waccamaw Room
    Horry County Oral History Project
Forest History Society
    National Association of State Park Directors
    Society of American Foresters
Loyola University New Orleans, J. Edgar and Louise S. Monroe Library, Special Collections and Archives, Stanonis Travel Diary Collection
    Ann Diary
    Anna P. Kelly Diary
    Anthony Costantini Letter
    Beirne Brues, Diary of a Trip to Southernmost Florida
    Brinker Family Diary-Scrapbook
    Claire Grant Cook Scrapbook
    Edith K. Miller Diary
    Edward Newton Reser Letters
    H. M. Abbot Diary-Scrapbook
    Hazel Timms Diary
    Hollis M. Alger Letters
    Jeanelle Landstrom Family Diary
    Leather Worker Union Diary (1902)
    Maude Lierch Diaries
    Mrs Claire Grant Cook Scrapbook
    My Trip Diary (1939)
    My Trip Diary (1950)
    Our First Trip to Florida Scrapbook (1954)
    Our Trip to Florida Diary (1938)
    Part 1 of First Trip to Florida Diary (1961)
    Rosemary Diaries
    S. M. Simister Diary-Scrapbook
    Spiral Memo Diary (1949)
    Trip'O'Log Diary (1927)

William O. Golloway Diaries
Ye Old Family Scrap Book (1949)
Mississippi Department of Archives and History
WPA Interviews
Rosenberg Library, Galveston and Texas History Center
Alma Simmang Simpson Papers
Brantly Harris Papers
Galveston Chamber of Commerce Records
Galveston Convention and Tourist Bureau
John D. Blagden Letter
Louise F. Bache Report
Nellie Watson Letter
Walter E. Grover Article
The Historic New Orleans Collection, Williams Research Center, Archives and
Manuscripts Division
1947 Hurricane Scrapbook
Davis Family Papers
Dufour and Woolfley Families Papers
Letter of Angela Moynan
Tulane University, Amistad Research Center
Alexander Tureaud Papers
Mary McLeod-Bethune Papers
Tulane University, Howard-Tilton Memorial Library, Special Collections, Louisiana
Research Collection
Harold Newton Lee Papers
University of Florida, Smathers Libraries, Special and Area Studies Collections
American Civil Liberties Union of Florida Records
Beautiful DeFuniak Springs (pamphlet c. 1915)
C. Farris Bryant Papers
The End of the Rainbow Valparaiso Reality Company, c. 1923
Federal Bureau of Investigation St. Augustine Surveillance Files
Florida National Organization of Women Records
James Edmundson Ingraham Papers
James Edwards Ledger
John Herbert Peck Papers
Millard Caldwell Papers
Napoleon Bonaparte Broward Papers
Noegel Family Collection
Reubin O'Donovan Askew Speeches
Robert N. "Bert" Dosh Papers
Sierra Club of Florida Chapter Records
Thomas Yon Papers
Two Trains Daily Via L&N (pamphlet c. 1915)
Virgil Miller "Red" Newton Papers

University of New Orleans, Earl K. Long Library, Louisiana and Special Collections
New Orleans Association of Commerce Minutes
New Orleans Association of Commerce News Bulletin
University of North Carolina, Southern Historical Collection
Charles Barrington Simrall Papers
Elsie H. Booker Collection
Federal Writers' Project
Genevieve Pearce Moore Diary
Howard Washington Raper Papers
Jessie Daniel Ames Papers
John Thomas Woodside Autobiography
Paul Eliot Green Papers
University of South Carolina, South Caroliniana Library
Arcady: A National Playground Where the Leaders of Contemporary Life May Sustain Their Capacity for Work by Bringing to Its Utmost the Art of Rest and Recreation. New York: Arcady Executives, 1929
C. A. Donehoo Papers
Grand Strand Tourist Guide
James W. Gauker Papers
Ocean Pines Motor Court pamphlet (c. 1940)
Sigmund Abeles Papers
Sun Fun Magazine
Sunny Day Guide, Virginia Beach: Surfside East, Summer 1987
William Wightman Smoak Papers
University of Southern Mississippi, Center for Oral History and Cultural Heritage
Community Bridges Oral History Project
Virginia Historical Society
Isabel Louise Ball Baker Papers
James River Elementary School Oral History Project
Sarah Evelyn Baylor Blackford Diary

Periodicals

American Lumberman
Atlanta Constitution
Barrier Islands Newsletter
Biloxi Daily Herald
Biloxi Herald
Biloxi Sun Herald
Baltimore American
Boston Journal
Changing Times
Chicago Daily Inter Ocean
Christian Advocate

Christian Science Monitor
Confederate Veteran
Congressional Record
Coastal Carolinian
Crisis
Down South
The Gulf States Magazine
Gull's Cry
Galveston Daily News
Grove Gazette
Harpers' Magazine
Jacksonville Florida Times-Union
Jet
Life
Los Angeles Times
Louisiana Weekly
Myrtle Beach Daily News
Myrtle Beach Sun
Myrtle Beach Sun-News
New England Journal of Medicine
New Era: A Magazine of Progress for Northwest Florida
New York Evangelist
New York Herald
New York Observer and Chronicle
New York Times
Ocean Beach News
Outlook
Panama City Herald
Panama City News
Panama City News-Herald
Princess Anne Times
The Rotarian
Time
Virginia Beach News
Virginia Beach Sun
Virginia Beach Sun-News
Who: The Magazine about People

Published Primary Sources

Abbott, Karl. *Open for the Season*. Garden City, N.J.: Doubleday, 1950.
Allison, Thomas. *Moonshine Memories*. Montgomery, Ala.: NewSouth Books, 2001.
Amory, Cleveland. *The Last Resorts*. New York: Harper & Brothers, 1952.

Anderson, Sherwood. *Letters of Sherwood Anderson*. Edited by Howard Mumford Jones. Boston: Little, Brown, 1953.

Bachelder, John. *Popular Resorts, and How to Reach Them*. Boston: John B. Bachelder Publisher, 1875.

Bechet, Sidney. *Treat It Gentle: An Autobiography*. Cambridge, Mass.: Da Capo Press, 1960, 2002.

Bissell, Richard. *How Many Miles to Galena? Or Baked, Hashed Brown or French Fried?* Boston: Little, Brown, 1968.

Burman, Ben Lucien. *It's a Big Country: America off the Highways*. New York: Reynal, 1956.

Carter, W. Horace. *Virus of Fear*. Tabor City, N.C.: W. Horace Carter, 1991.

Chicago Commission on Race Relations, *The Negro in Chicago: A Study of Race Relations and a Race Riot*. Chicago: University of Chicago Press, 1922.

Cohen, David. *Chasing the Red, White, and Blue*. New York: Picador, 2001.

Cole, Richard. *The Redneck Riviera*. Mt. Pleasant, S.C.: Corinthian Books, 2002.

Cooke, Alistair. *One Man's America*. New York: Alfred Knopf, 1952.

Dos Passos, John. *State of the Nation*. Boston: Houghton Mifflin, 1944.

Duhamel, Georges. *American the Menace: Scenes from the Life of the Future*. Translated by Charles Miner Thompson. Boston: Houghton Mifflin, 1931.

Faris, John. *Seeing the Sunny South*. Philadelphia: J. B. Lippincott, 1921.

Ford, Norman. *Where to Retire on a Small Income*. 7th ed. New York: Harian Publishers, 1955.

———. *Where to Retire on a Small Income*. 19th ed. Greenlawn, N.Y.: Harian Publishers, 1975.

Grant, Madison. *The Passing of the Great Race: Or, The Racial Basis for European History*. 4th rev. ed. New York: Charles Scribner's Sons, 1936.

Green, Elna, ed. *Looking for the New Deal: Florida Women's Letters during the Great Depression*. Columbia: University of South Carolina Press, 2007.

Greene, Casey Edward, and Shelly Henley Kelly, ed. *Through a Night of Horrors: Voices from the 1900 Galveston Storm*. College Station: Texas A&M University Press, 2000.

Hart, Albert Bushnell. *The Southern South*. New York: D. Appleton, 1910.

Holmes, Marion. *Six in a Ford*. Portland, Maine: Falmouth Publishing, 1951.

Ilf, Ilya, and Eugene Petrov. *Little Golden America: Two Famous Soviet Humorists Survey These United States*. Translated by Charles Malamuth. New York: Farrar & Rinehart, 1937.

Inlet Beach on the Gulf of Mexico. DeFuniak Springs, Fla.: McCaskill Investment Company, c. 1920s.

Jackson, Charles Tenney. *The Fountain of Youth*. New York: Outling Publishing, 1914.

Kofoed, Jack. *The Florida Story*. Garden City, N.J.: Doubleday, 1960.

Leisureguide: The Grand Strand. Miami: Leisureguides Incorporated, 1977.

Low, A. Maurice. *America at Home*. London: George Newnes, 1908.

Martin, Ralph G. *The Best Is None Too Good*. New York: Farrar, Straus & Company, 1948.

Mason, Gilbert. *Beaches, Blood, and Ballots: A Black Doctor's Civil Rights Struggle.* Jackson: University Press of Mississippi, 2000.

Mauldin, Bill. *Back Home.* New York: William Sloane, 1947.

Merrick, Caroline. *Old Times in Dixie Land: A Southern Matron's Memories.* New York: Grafton Press, 1901.

Merz, Charles. *The Great American Band Wagon.* New York: Literary Guild of America, 1928.

Mississippi: The WPA Guide to the Magnolia State. Jackson: University Press of Mississippi, 1938, 2009.

Muir, John. *A Thousand-Mile Walk to the Gulf.* Edited by William Frederic Badé. Boston: Houghton Mifflin, 1916.

Muirhead, James Fullarton. *The Land of Contrasts: A Briton's View of His American Kin.* Boston: Lamson, Wolffe & Company, 1898.

Munday, Billy. *The Black Shadow and the Red Death.* New York: Broadway Publishing, 1914.

Murdock, Will. *Banana Republic: A Year in the Heart of Myrtle Beach.* Charleston, S.C.: Frontline Press, 2003.

Myers, Minnie Walter. *Romance and Realism of the Southern Gulf Coast.* Cincinnati: Robert Clarke Company, 1898.

Nesterowicz, Stefan. *Travel Notes.* Translated by Marion Moore Coleman. Cheshire, Conn.: Cherry Hill Books, 1970. Originally published as Notatki z podrozy po Ameryce Polnocnej. Toledo, Ohio: Parvski, 1909.

O'Rell, Max, and Jack Allyn. *Jonathan and His Continent: Rambles through American Society.* New York: Cassell & Company, 1889.

Phillips, Kevin. *The Emerging Republican Majority.* New Rochelle, N.Y.: Arlington House, 1969.

Pindell, Terry. *Making Tracks: An American Rail Odyssey.* New York: Grove Weidenfeld, 1990.

Poe, Edgar Allan. *Tales.* London: Wiley & Putnam, 1845.

Points, Betty Lou. *America the Beautiful.* New York: Greenwich Book Publishers, 1957.

Pyle, Ernie. *Ernie's America: The Best of Ernie Pyle's 1930s Travel Dispatches.* Edited by David Nicols. New York: Random House, 1989.

———. *Home Country.* New York: William Sloane, 1947.

Reeder, Rollin. *Project Myrtle: Fun, Sun and Health Education.* USC College of Health and Physical Education, 1975.

Rose, Chris. *1 Dead in Attic: After Katrina.* New York: Simon & Schuster, 2005, 2007.

Royall, Anne. *Mrs. Royall's Southern Tour, or Second Series of the Black Book.* Washington, D.C., 1830.

Schweid, Richard. *Catfish and the Delta: Confederate Fish Farming in the Mississippi Delta.* Berkeley, Calif.: Ten Speed Press, 1992.

State Farm Road Atlas. Bloomington, Ill.: Rand McNally, 1951.

Texas: A Guide to the Lone Star State. Rev. ed. New York: Hastings House, 1940, 1969.

Thompson, Dino. *Greek Boy: Growing Up Southern, a Myrtle Beach Memoir.* Myrtle Beach: Snug Press, 2002.

Thompson, Hunter. *The Proud Highway: Saga of a Desperate Southern Gentleman, 1955–1967*. London: Bloomsbury Publishing, 1997.

Trethewey, Natasha. *Beyond Katrina: A Mediation on the Mississippi Gulf Coast*. Athens: University of Georgia Press, 2010.

Trillin, Calvin. *U.S. Journal*. New York: E. P. Dutton, 1971.

Ward, Robert De C. "The Acclimatization of the White Race in the Tropics." *New England Journal of Medicine* 201 (26 September 1929): 617–627.

Webster, Noah. *A Dictionary of the English Language*. Edited by Chauncey Goodrich. 10th ed. London: George Routledge & Sons, 1866.

West, James. *Plainville, U.S.A.* New York: Columbia University Press, 1945.

The WPA Guide to Florida. New York: Pantheon Books, 1939, 1984.

Yelverton, Thérèse. *Teresina in America*. London: Richard Bentley & Son, 1875.

Young, Ernest. *North American Excursion*. London: Edward Arnold & Company, 1947.

Electronic Primary Resources

The Great American History Machine. College Park: Academic Software Development Group, University of Maryland, 1991.

Secondary Sources

Abbott, Carl. *Boosters and Businessmen: Popular Economic Thought and Urban Growth in the Antebellum Middle West*. Westport, Conn.: Greenwood, 1981.

———. *The New Urban America: Growth and Politics in Sunbelt Cities*. Chapel Hill: University of North Carolina, 1987.

Adam, Thomas. *Buying Respectability: Philanthropy and Urban Society in Transitional Perspective, 1840s to 1930s*. Bloomington: Indiana University Press, 2009.

Adams, Jessica. *Wounds of Returning: Race, Memory, and Property on the Postslavery Plantation*. Chapel Hill: University of North Carolina Press, 2007.

Albanese, Catherine. *Nature Religion in America: From the Algonkian Indians to the New Age*. Chicago: University of Chicago Press, 1990.

Aldridge, A. Owen. "American Burlesque at Home and Abroad: Together with the Etymology of 'Go-Go Girl,'" *Journal of Popular Culture* 5 (December 1971): 565–575.

Alexander, Charles. "Prophet of American Racism: Madison Grant and the Nordic Myth." *Phylon* 23 (1962): 73–90.

Alexander, Mary Ellen. *Rosalie and Radishes: A History of Long Beach, Mississippi*. Gulfport, Miss.: Dixie Press, 1980.

Allnutt, Brian. "The Negro Excursions: Recreational Outings among Philadelphia African Americans, 1876–1926." *Pennsylvania Magazine of History and Biography* 129 (January 2005): 73–104.

Alperin, Lynn. *History of the Gulf Intracoastal Waterway*. U.S. Army Engineer Resource Support Center, January 1983.

Anderson, R. Bentley. *Black, White, and Catholic: New Orleans Interracialism, 1947–1956*. Nashville, Tenn.: Vanderbilt University Press, 2005.

———. "Black, White and Catholic: Southern Jesuits Confront the Race Question, 1952." *Catholic Historical Review* 91 (July 2005): 484–505.

Andrews, Gregg. "Black Working-Class Political Activism and Biracial Unionism: Galveston Longshoremen in Jim Crow Texas, 1919–1921." *Journal of Southern History* 74 (August 2008): 627–668.

Armstead, Myra. *"Lord, Please Don't Take Me in August": African Americans in Newport and Saratoga Springs, 1870–1930*. Urbana: University of Illinois Press, 1999.

Arnesen, Eric. *Waterfront Workers of New Orleans: Race, Class, and Politics, 1863–1923*. Urbana: University of Illinois Press, 1991.

———. "What's on the Black Worker's Mind: African-American Workers and the Union Tradition." *Gulf Coast Historical Review* 10 (Fall 1994): 5–18.

Aron, Cindy. *Working at Play: A History of Vacations in the United States*. New York: Oxford University Press, 1999.

Arsenault, Raymond. "The End of the Long Hot Summer: The Air Conditioner and Southern Culture." *Journal of Southern History* 50 (November 1984): 597–628.

Ash, Stephen. *When the Yankees Came: Conflict and Chaos in the Occupied South, 1861–1865*. Chapel Hill: University of North Carolina Press, 1995.

Avila, Eric. *Popular Culture in the Age of White Flight in Suburban Los Angeles*. Berkeley: University of California Press, 2004.

Ayers, Edward. *The Promise of the New South: Life after Reconstruction*. New York: Oxford University Press, 1992.

Bailey, Beth. *From Front Porch to Back Seat: Courtship in Twentieth-Century America*. Baltimore, Md.: John Hopkins University Press, 1988.

———. *Sex in the Heartland*. Cambridge, Mass.: Harvard University Press, 1999.

Bailey, Beth, and David Farber. *The First Strange Place: Race and Sex in World War II Hawaii*. Baltimore, Md.: John Hopkins University Press, 1992.

Bankston, Carl, III. "New People in the New South: An Overview of Southern Immigration." *Southern Cultures* 13 (Winter 2007): 22–44.

Barnes, Catherine. *Journey from Jim Crow: The Desegregation of Southern Transit*. New York: Columbia University Press, 1983.

Barnes, Margaret Anne. *The Tragedy and the Triumph of Phenix City, Alabama*. Macon, Ga.: Mercer University Press, 1999.

Barry, Kathleen. *Femininity in Flight: A History of Flight Attendants*. Durham, N.C.: Duke University Press, 2007.

Bednarek, Janet R. Daly. "City Planning and Municipal Airports: 1927–1940." *Planning Perspectives* 15 (October 2000): 349–375.

Belasco, Warren. *Americans on the Road: From Autocamp to Motel, 1910–1945*. Cambridge, Mass.: MIT Press, 1979.

Bell, Andrew McIlwaine. *Mosquito Soldiers: Malaria, Yellow Fever, and the Course of the American Civil War*. Baton Rouge: Louisiana State University Press, 2010.

Bennett, James. *Religion and the Rise of Jim Crow in New Orleans*. Princeton, N.J.: Princeton University Press, 2005.

Biddle, Jeff. "Explaining the Spread of Residential Air Conditioning, 1955–1980." *Explorations in Economic History* 45 (September 2008): 402–423.

Bodenhamer, David. *Fair Trial: Rights of the Accused in American History*. New York: Oxford University Press, 1992.

Borstelmann, Thomas. *The Cold War and the Color Line: American Race Relations in the Global Arena*. Cambridge, Mass.: Harvard University Press, 2001.

Boyd, Elizabeth Bronwyn. "Southern Beauty: Performing Femininity in an American Region" PhD diss., University of Texas, 2000.

Bragaw, Donald. "Loss of Identity on Pensacola's Past: A Creole Footnote." *Florida Historical Quarterly* 50 (April 1972): 414–418.

Braukman, Stacy. "'Nothing Else Matters but Sex': Cold War Narratives of Deviance and the Search for Lesbian Teachers in Florida, 1959–1963." *Feminist Studies* 27 (2001): 553–575.

Brown, Ben. "Free Men and Free Pigs: Closing the Southern Range and the American Property Tradition." *Radical History Review* 108 (Fall 2010): 117–137.

Brownell, B. A. "Introduction." In *Searching for the Sunbelt: Historical Perspectives on a Region*, edited by Raymond Mohl. Knoxville: University of Tennessee Press, 1990.

Bushman, Donald, and William Stanley. "State Senate Reapportionment in the Southeast." *Annals of the American Geographers* 61 (December 1971): 654–670.

Buszek, Maria Elena. *Pin-Up Grrrls: Feminism, Sexuality, Popular Culture*. Durham, N.C.: Duke University Press, 2006.

Butler, J. Michael. "The Mississippi State Sovereignty Commission and Beach Integration, 1959–1963: A Cotton-Patch Gestapo?" *Journal of Southern History* 68 (February 2002): 107–148.

Cahn, Susan. *Sexual Reckonings: Southern Girls in a Troubling Age*. Cambridge, Mass.: Harvard University Press, 2007.

Carlton, David, and Peter Coclanis. *The South, the Nation, and the World: Perspectives on Southern Economic Development*. Charlottesville: University of Virginia Press, 2003.

Carrigan, William, and Clive Webb. "Muerto por Unos Deconocidos (Killed by Persons Unknown)." In *Beyond Black & White: Race, Ethnicity and Gender in the U.S. South and Southwest*, edited by Stephanie Cole and Alison Parker, 35–60. College Station: Texas A&M University Press, 2004.

Carter, James, III. "Florida and Rumrunning during National Prohibition." *Florida Historical Quarterly* 48 (July 1969): 47–56.

Chamberlain, Charles. *Victory at Home: Manpower and Race in the American South during World War II*. Athens: University of Georgia Press, 2003.

Clark, Patricia. *The Spirit of the Times: Amusements in Nineteenth-Century Baltimore, Norfolk, and Richmond*. Charlottesville: University Press of Virginia, 1989.

Cobb, James. "World War II and the Mind of the Modern South." In *Remaking Dixie: The Impact of World War II on the American South*, edited by Neil McMillen, 3–20. Jackson: University Press of Mississippi, 1997.

Coburn, David. *Racial Change and Community Crisis: St. Augustine, Florida, 1877–1980*. Gainesville: University of Florida Press, 1991.

Cocks, Catherine. *Doing the Town: The Rise of Urban Tourism in the United States, 1850–1915*. Berkeley: University of California Press, 2001.

———. *Tropical Whites: The Rise of the Tourist South in the Americas*. Philadelphia: University of Pennsylvania Press, 2013.

Coker, Joe. *Liquor in the Land of the Lost Cause: Southern White Evangelicals and the Prohibition Movement*. Lexington: University Press of Kentucky, 2007.

Conkin, Paul. *A Revolution Down on the Farm: The Transformation of American Agriculture since 1929*. Lexington: University Press of Kentucky, 2008.

Connolly, Nathan D. B. "By Eminent Domain: Race and Capital in the Building of an American South Florida." PhD diss., University of Michigan, 2008.

———. "Colored, Caribbean, and Condemned: Miami's Overtown District and the Cultural Expense of Progress, 1940–1970." *Caribbean Studies* 34 (January-June 2006): 3–60.

Cooper, Christopher, and H. Gibbs Knotts. "Declining Dixie: Regional Identification in the Modern American South." *Social Forces* 88 (March 2010): 1083–1101.

Cooper, Gail. *Air-Conditioning America: Engineers and the Controlled Environment, 1900–1960*. Baltimore, Md.: John Hopkins University Press, 1998.

Costa, Dora. "The Evolution of Retirement: Summary of a Research Project." *American Economic Review* 88 (May 1998): 232–236.

Cox, Karen, ed. *Destination Dixie: Tourism and Southern History*. Gainesville: University Press of Florida, 2012.

———. *Dreaming of Dixie: How the South Was Created in American Popular Culture*. Chapel Hill: University of North Carolina Press, 2011.

Cox, Nicole. "Selling Seduction: Women and Feminine Nature in 1920s Florida Advertising." *Florida Historical Quarterly* 89 (Fall 2010): 186–209.

Craft, Erik. "Private Weather Organizations and the Founding of the United States Weather Bureau." *Journal of Economic History* 59 (December 1999): 1063–1071.

Cunningham, Patricia. "From Underwear to Swimwear: Branding at Atlas and B.V.D. in the 1930s." *Journal of American Culture* 32 (March 2009): 38–52.

Davis, Jack. *Race against Time: Culture and Separation in Natchez since 1930*. Baton Rouge: Louisiana State University, 2001.

Dawdy, Shannon Lee. *Building the Devil's Empire: French Colonial New Orleans*. Chicago: University of Chicago Press, 2008.

Dean, Cornelia. *Against the Tide: The Battle for America's Beaches*. New York: Columbia University Press, 1999.

Delind, Laura. "Bingo: Some Whys and Wherefores of a Popular Pastime." *Journal of Popular Culture* 18 (Fall 1984): 149–156.

Derr, Jeanine. "'The Biggest Show on Earth': The Kefauver Crime Committee Hearings." *Maryland Historian* 17 (December 1968): 19–37.

Dochuk, Darren. *From Bible Belt to Sunbelt: Plain Folk Religion, Grassroots Politics, and the Rise of Evangelical Conservatism*. New York: W. W. Norton, 2011.

Doorley, Michael. "Irish Catholics and French Creoles: Ethnic Struggles within the Catholic Church in New Orleans, 1835–1920." *Catholic Historical Review* 87 (January 2001): 34–55.

Dorr, Lisa Lindquist. "The Perils of the Back Seat: Date Rape, Race and Gender in 1950s America." *Gender and History* 20 (April 2008): 27–47.

Dowland, Seth. "'Family Values' and the Formation of the Christian Right Agenda." *Church History* 78 (September 2009): 606–631.

Dudziak, Mary. *Cold War Civil Rights: Race and the Image of American Democracy.* Princeton, N.J.: Princeton University Press, 2000.

Durrenberger, E. Paul. *It's All Politics: South Alabama's Seafood Industry.* Urbana: University of Illinois Press, 1992.

Ellis, Ann. "The Greek Community in Atlanta, 1900–1923." *Georgia Historical Quarterly* 58 (Winter 1974): 400–408.

Endy, Christopher. *Cold War Holidays: American Tourism in France.* Chapel Hill: University of North Carolina Press, 2004.

Fitzgerald, Michael. *Urban Emancipation: Popular Politics in Reconstruction Mobile, 1860–1890.* Baton Rouge: Louisiana State University Press, 2002.

Flink, James. *The Automobile Age.* Cambridge, Mass.: MIT Press, 1988.

Floyd, Blanche. *The History of the First United Methodist Church, Myrtle Beach, South Carolina, 1938–1988.* Myrtle Beach: Kwik Printing, 1988.

Foley, Neil. "Partly Colored or Other White: Mexican Americans and Their Problem with the Color Line." In *Beyond Black & White: Race, Ethnicity and Gender in the U.S. South and Southwest,* edited by Stephanie Cole and Alison Parker, 123–144. College Station: Texas A&M University Press, 2004.

———. *The White Scourge: Mexicans, Blacks and Poor Whites in Texas Cotton Culture.* Berkeley: University of California Press, 1997.

Fox Gotham, Kevin. "Urban Space, Restrictive Covenants and the Origins of Racial Residential Segregation in a U.S. City, 1900–1950." *International Journal of Urban and Regional Research* 24 (September 2000): 616–633.

Francaviglia, Richard. "Main Street U.S.A.: A Comparison/Contrast of Streetscapes in Disneyland and Walt Disney World." *Journal of Popular Culture* 15 (June 1981): 141–156.

Freidel, Frank. "Boosters, Intellectuals, and the American City." In *The Historian and the City,* edited by Oscar Handlin and John Burchard, 115–120. Cambridge, Mass.: MIT Press, 1963, 1977.

Freund, David. *Colored Property: State Policy and White Racial Politics in Suburban America.* Chicago: University of Chicago Press, 2007.

Friedman, Andrea. "'The Habitats of Sex-Crazed Perverts': Campaigns against Burlesque in Depression-Era New York City." *Journal of the History of Sexuality* 7 (October 1996): 203–238.

Gaston, Paul. *The New South Creed: A Study in Southern Mythmaking.* Baton Rouge: Louisiana State University Press, 1970.

Gatta, John. *Making Nature Sacred: Literature, Religion, and Environment in America from the Puritans to the Present.* New York: Oxford University Press, 2004.

Gilbert, James. *A Cycle of Outrages: America's Reaction to the Juvenile Delinquent in the 1950s.* New York: Oxford University Press, 1986.

Gilbert, Marie. *Myrtle Beach Back When.* Laurinburg, N.C.: St. Andrews Press, 1989.

Gilmore, Glenda Elizabeth. *Gender and Jim Crow: Women and the Politics of White Supremacy in North Carolina, 1896–1920.* Chapel Hill: University of North Carolina, 1996.

Goldfield, David. "From the Editor: Searching for the Sunbelt." *OAH Magazine of History* 13 (October 2003): 3–4.

Gould, Virginia. "In Defense of Their Creole Culture: The Free Creoles of Color of New Orleans, Mobile, and Pensacola." *Gulf Coast Historical Review* 9 (Fall 1993): 27–42.

Gragg, Larry. "Selling 'Sin City': Successfully Promoting Las Vegas during the Great Depression, 1935–1941." *Nevada Historical Society Quarterly* 49 (June 2006): 83–106.

Grantham, Dewey. *Southern Progressivism: The Reconciliation of Progress and Tradition.* Knoxville: University of Tennessee Press, 1983.

Greene, Jack. *Pursuits of Happiness: The Social Development of Early Modern British Colonies and the Formation of American Culture.* Chapel Hill: University of North Carolina Press, 1988.

Greene, Julie. "Spaniards on the Silver Roll: Labor Troubles and Liminality in the Panama Canal Zone, 1904–1914." *International Labor and Working-Class History* 66 (Fall 2004): 78–98.

Greene, Melissa Fay. *Praying for Sheetrock: A Work of Nonfiction.* Reading, Mass.: Addison-Wesley Publishing, 1991.

Gregory, James. *The Southern Diaspora: How the Great Migrations of Black White Southerners Transformed America.* Chapel Hill: University of North Carolina Press, 2005.

Groneman, Carol. *Nymphomania: A History.* New York: W. W. Norton, 2000.

Grossman, James R. *Land of Hope: Chicago, Black Southerners, and the Great Migration.* Chicago: University of Chicago Press, 1991.

Gualtieri, Sarah. "Strange Fruit? Syrian Immigrants, Extralegal Violence and Racial Formation in the Jim Crow South." *Arab Studies Quarterly* 26 (Summer 2004): 63–85.

Hahn, Steven. *The Roots of Southern Populism: Yeoman Farmers and the Transformation of Georgia Upcountry, 1850–1890.* New York: Oxford University Press, 1983.

Haller, Mark. "The Changing Structure of American Gambling in the Twentieth Century." *Journal of Social Issues* 35 (Summer 1979): 87–114.

Hansen, Devon. "Shades of Change: Suntanning and the Twentieth-Century American Dream." PhD diss., Boston University, 2007.

Hardwick, Susan Wiley. *Mythic Galveston: Reinventing America's Third Coast.* Baltimore, Md.: John Hopkins University Press, 2002.

Harmon, Sharon. "The Founding of St. Joseph's Parish: The Catholic Church and Race Relations in Pensacola, Florida, 1865–1900." *Gulf Coast Historical Review* 13 (Spring 1997): 98–119.

Harris, Neil. "Urban Tourism and the Commercial City." In *Inventing Times Square: Commerce and Culture at the Crossroads of the World,* edited by William Taylor, 66–82. Baltimore, Md.: Johns Hopkins University Press, 1996.

Harvey, David. *The Urban Experience.* Oxford: Basil Blackwell, 1989.

Hawes, Joseph. "The Signal Corps and Its Weather Service, 1870–1890." *Military Affairs* 30 (Summer 1966): 68–76.

Haynes, Robert. *A Night for Violence: The Houston Riot of 1917*. Baton Rouge: Louisiana State University Press, 1976.

Hoffman, Brian. "'A Certain Amount of Prudishness': Nudist Magazines and the Liberalization of American Obesity Law, 1947–58." *Gender and History* 22 (November 2010): 708–732.

Horne, Gerald. "Race from Power: U.S. Foreign Policy and the General Crisis of White Supremacy." In *Window on Freedom: Race, Civil Rights, and Foreign Affairs, 1945–1988*, ed. Brenda Gayle Plummer, 45–66. Chapel Hill: University of North Carolina Press, 2003.

Hoover, Calvin, and B. U. Ratchford. *Economic Resources and Policies of the South*. New York: Macmillan, 1951.

Hourigan, Richard, III. "Welcome to South Carolina: Sex, Race, and the Rise of Tourism in Myrtle Beach, 1900–1975." PhD diss., University of Alabama, 2009.

Howison, Jeffrey. "'This Is Not a Cotton Picker's Dream': Reapportionment, Conservative Ideology, and the Urban-Rural Divide." *Journal of Urban History* 37 (September 2011): 680–693.

Huber, Patrick. "A Short History of 'Redneck': The Fashioning of a Southern White Masculine Identity." *Southern Cultures* 1 (Spring 1995): 145–166.

Hugill, Peter. "Good Roads and the Automobile in the United States, 1880–1929." *Geographic Review* 72 (July 1982): 327–349.

Humes, Edward. *Mississippi Mud: A True Story from a Corner of the Deep South*. New York: Simon & Schuster, 1994.

Humphreys, Margaret. *Yellow Fever and the South*. Baltimore, Md.: John Hopkins University Press, 1999.

Ingham, John. "Building Businesses, Creating Communities: Residential Segregation and the Growth of African American Business in Southern Cities, 1880–1915." *Business History Review* 77 (Winter 2003): 639–665.

Isaac, Rhys. *The Transformation of Virginia, 1740–1790*. Chapel Hill: University of North Carolina Press, 1982.

Jackson, Harvey H., III. "Developing the Panhandle: Seagrove Beach, Seaside, Watercolor, and the Florida Tourist Tradition." In *Southern Journeys: Tourism, History and Culture in the Modern South, edited by Richard Starnes*, 71–87. Tuscaloosa: University of Alabama Press, 2003.

———. "The Florida Room: From 'Redneck Riviera' to 'Emerald Coast': A Personal History of a Piece of the Florida Panhandle." *Florida Historical Quarterly* (Winter 2003): 316–322.

———. *The Rise and Decline of the Redneck Riviera: An Insider's History of the Florida-Alabama Coast*. Athens: University of Georgia Press, 2011.

———. "The Rise and Decline of the Redneck Riviera: The Northern Rim of the Gulf Coast since World War II." *Southern Cultures* 16 (Spring 2010): 7–30.

Jackson, Kenneth. *Crabgrass Frontier: The Suburbanization of the United States*. New York: Oxford University Press, 1985.

Jacobson, Matthew Frye. *Barbarian Virtues: The United States Encounters Foreign Peoples at Home and Abroad, 1876–1917*. New York: Hill & Wang, 2000.

———. *Roots Too: White Ethnic Revival in Post–Civil Rights America*. Cambridge, Mass.: Harvard University Press, 2006.

Johnson, Arthur. "The Early Texas Oil Industry: Pipelines and the Birth of an Integrated Oil Industry, 1901–1911." *Journal of Southern History* 32 (November 1966): 516–528.

Johnson, David. "Disney World as Structure and Symbol: Re-Creation of the American Experience." *Journal of Popular Culture* 15 (June 1981): 157–165.

Johnson, Howard. "Bahamian Labor Migration to Florida in the Late Nineteenth and Early Twentieth Centuries." *International Migration Review* 22 (Spring 1988): 84–103.

Jordan-Bychkov, Terry. "The Creole Coast: Homeland to Substrate." In *Homelands: A Geography of Culture and Place across America*, edited by R. L. Nostrand and L. E. Estaville, 73–82. Baltimore: Johns Hopkins University Press, 2001.

Jung, Moon-Ho. *Coolies and Cane: Race, Labor, and Sugar in the Age of Emancipation*. Baltimore, Md.: John Hopkins University Press, 2006.

Kahrl, Andrew. *The Land Was Ours: African American Beaches from Jim Crow to the Sunbelt South*. Cambridge, Mass.: Harvard University Press, 2012.

———. "Sunbelt by the Sea: Governing Race and Nature in a Twentieth-Century Coastal Metropolis." *Journal of Urban History* 38 (March 2012): 488–508.

Karsner, Douglass. "Aviation and Airports." *Journal of Urban History* 23 (May 1997): 406–436.

Kaufman, Wallace, and Orrin Pilkey, Jr. *The Beaches Are Moving: The Drowning of America's Shoreline*. Durham, N.C.: Duke University Press, 1983.

Kein, Sybil, ed. *Creole: The History and Legacy of Louisiana's Free People of Color*. Baton Rouge: Louisiana State University Press, 2000.

Keith, Jeanette. *Country People in the New South: Tennessee's Upper Cumberland*. Chapel Hill: University of North Carolina Press, 1995.

Kennedy, David. *Over Here: The First World War and American Society*. 25th anniversary edition. New York: Oxford University Press, 2004.

Kieckhefer, Richard. *Theology in Stone: Church Architecture from Byzantium to Berkeley*. New York: Oxford University Press, 2004.

King, J. Crawford, Jr. "The Closing of the Southern Range: An Exploratory Study." *Journal of Southern History* 48 (February 1982): 53–70.

King, Kim. "Gambling for God: Charity and Self-Interest in the Bingo Parlor." PhD diss., University of North Carolina at Chapel Hill, 1985.

King, P. Nicole. *Sombreros and Motorcycles in a Newer South: The Politics of Aesthetics in South Carolina's Tourism Industry*. Jackson: University Press of Mississippi, 2012.

Kirby, Jack Temple. *Media-Made Dixie: The South in the American Imagination*. Rev. ed. Athens: University of Georgia Press, 2004.

Knight, Henry. *Tropic of Hopes: California, Florida, and the Selling of American Paradise, 1869–1929*. Gainesville: University Press of Florida, 2013.

Landers, Jane. *Black Society in Spanish Florida*. Urbana: University of Illinois Press, 1999.

Lassiter, Matthew. "De Jure/De Facto Segregation: The Long Shadow of a National Myth." In *The Myth of Southern Exceptionalism*, edited by Matthew Lassiter and Joseph Crespino, 25–48. New York: Oxford University Press, 2010.

Latham, Angela. "Packaging Woman: The Concurrent Rise of Beauty Pageants, Public Bathing, and Other Performances of Female 'Nudity.'" *Journal of Popular Culture* 29 (1995): 149–167.

Laurie, John. "'Spring Break': The Economic, Socio-Cultural and Public Governance Impacts of College Students on Spring Break Host Locations." PhD diss., University of New Orleans, 2008.

Lears, Jackson. *Something for Nothing: Luck in America*. New York: Viking, 2003.

Ledesma, Irene. "Natural Disasters and Community Survival in Texas and Louisiana in the Gilded Age." *Gulf Coast Historical Review* 10 (1994): 72–84.

Lencek, Lena, and Gideon Bosker. *The Beach: The History of Paradise on Earth*. New York: Penguin, 1998.

Lerner, Michael. *Dry Manhattan: Prohibition in New York City*. Cambridge, Mass.: Harvard University Press, 2007.

Lesseig, Corey. "'Out of the Mud': The Good Roads Crusade and Social Change in Twentieth-Century Mississippi." *Journal of Mississippi History* 60 (March 1998): 50–72.

Lewis, Anthony. *Gideon's Trumpet*. New York: Vintage, 1989.

Lewis, Catherine Heniford. *Horry County, South Carolina, 1730–1993*. Columbia: University of South Carolina Press, 1998.

Lewis, Earl. *In Their Own Interests: Race, Class, and Power in Twentieth-Century Norfolk Virginia*. Berkeley: University of California Press, 1991.

Lewis, Tom. *Divided Highways: Building the Interstate Highways, Transforming American Life*. New York: Viking, 1997.

Lichtenstein, Alex. "Good Roads and Chain Gangs in the Progressive South: 'The Negro Convict Is a Slave.'" *Journal of Southern History* 59 (February 1993): 85–110.

Link, William A. *The Paradox of Southern Progressivism, 1880–1930: The Fred W. Morrison Series in Southern Studies*. Chapel Hill: University of North Carolina Press, 1992.

Lisby, Gregory. "Early Television on Public Watch: Kefauver and His Crime Investigation." *Journalism Quarterly* 62 (Summer 1985): 236–242.

Loftin, Bernadette. "A Woman Liberated: Lillian C. West, Editor." *Florida Historical Quarterly* 52 (April 1974): 396–410.

Love, Eric. *Race over Empire: Racism and U.S. Imperialism*. Chapel Hill: University of North Carolina Press, 2004.

Lucas, John. "The Unholy Experiment: Professional Baseball's Struggle against Pennsylvania Sunday Blue Laws, 1926–1934." *Pennsylvania History* 38 (Spring 1971): 163–175.

Maniha, John. "Structural Supports for the Development of Professionalism among Police Administrators." *Pacific Sociology Review* 16 (July 1973): 315–343.

Martin, C. Brendan. "To Keep the Spirit of Mountain Culture Alive: Tourism and Historical Memory in the Southern Highlands." In *Where These Memories Grow: History, Memory, and Southern Identity, edited by* W. Fitzhugh Brundage, 249–270. Chapel Hill: University of North Carolina Press, 2000.

Marty, Martin. *Modern American Religion*. Vol. 1, *The Irony of It All, 1893–1919*. Chicago: University of Chicago Press, 1986.

———. *Modern American Religion*. Vol. 3, *Under God, Indivisible, 1941–1960*. Chicago: University of Chicago Press, 1996.

Maurer, Noel, and Carlos Yu. "What T. R. Took: The Economic Impact of the Panama Canal, 1903–1937." *Journal of Economic History* 68 (September 2008): 686–721.

May, Elaine Tyler. *America and the Pill: A History of Promise, Peril, and Liberation*. New York: Basic Books, 2010.

May, Kirse. *Golden State, Golden Youth: The California Image in Popular Culture, 1955–1966*. Chapel Hill: University of North Carolina Press, 2002.

McComb, David. *Galveston: A History*. Austin: University of Texas Press, 2010.

———. "Galveston as a Tourist City." *Southwestern Historical Quarterly* 100 (January 1997): 331–360.

McCrossen, Alexis. *Holy Day, Holiday: The American Sunday*. Ithaca, N.Y.: Cornell University Press, 2000.

McCullough, David. *The Path between the Seas: The Creation of the Panama Canal, 1870–1914*. New York: Simon & Schuster, 1977.

McDonough, Michael. "Selling Sarasota: Architecture and Propaganda in the 1920s Boom Town." *Journal of Decorative and Propaganda Arts* 23 (1998): 10–31.

McElya, Micki. *Clinging to Mammy: The Faithful Slave in Twentieth-Century America*. Cambridge, Mass.: Harvard University Press, 2007.

McGreevy, John. *Parish Boundaries: The Catholic Encounter with Race in the Twentieth-Century Urban North*. Chicago: University of Chicago Press, 1996.

McIntyre, Rebecca. *Souvenirs of the Old South: Northern Tourism and Southern Mythology*. Gainesville: University Press of Florida, 2011.

McMillen, Neil. *Dark Journey: Black Mississippians in the Age of Jim Crow*. Urbana: University of Illinois Press, 1989.

McWilliams, James. *American Pests: The Losing War on Insects from Colonial Times to DDT*. New York: Columbia University Press, 2008.

Meikle, Jeffrey. *American Plastic: A Cultural History*. New Brunswick, N.J.: Rutgers University Press, 1995.

Melosi, Martin. *Garbage in the Cities: Refuse, Reform, and the Environment, 1880–1980*. College Station: Texas A&M Press, 1981.

———. *The Sanitary City: Urban Infrastructure in America from Colonial Times to the Present*. Baltimore, Md.: Johns Hopkins University Press, 2000.

Meyer, William. *Americans and Their Weather*. New York: Oxford University Press, 2000.

Meyerowitz, Joanne. *How Sex Changed: A History of Transsexuality in the United States*. Cambridge, Mass.: Harvard University Press, 2002.

Miller, Leon. "But the Majority Wanted Barabbas Too: The Blue Law Battle in Arkansas in the 1920's." MA thesis, University of Arkansas, 1980.

Miller, Wilbur. *Revenuers and Moonshiners: Enforcing Federal Liquor Law in the Mountain South, 1865–1900*. Chapel Hill: University of North Carolina Press, 1991.

Mohl, Raymond. "Black Immigrants: Bahamians in Early Twentieth-Century Miami." *Florida Historical Quarterly* 65 (January 1987): 217–297.

Monmonier, Mark. *Coastlines: How Mapmakers Frame the World and Chart Environmental Change*. Chicago: University of Chicago Press, 2008.

Moody, Eric. "Nevada's Legalization of Casino Gambling in 1931: Purely a Business Proposition." *Nevada Historical Society Quarterly* 37 (June 1994): 79–100.

Moore, Mark, and George Kelling. "'To Serve and Protect': Learning from Police History." *Public Interest* 70 (Winter 1983): 49–65.

Moreno, Tom, Modeste Hargis, and William Coker. "Tom Moreno: A Pensacola Creole." *Florida Historical Quarterly* 67 (January 1989): 329–339.

Morgan, James. *The Distance to the Moon: A Road Trip into the American Dream.* New York: Riverhead, 1999.

Mormino, Gary. *Land of Sunshine, State of Dreams: A Social History of Modern Florida.* Gainesville: University Press of Florida, 2005.

Murphy, Mary. "Bootlegging Mothers and Drinking Daughters: Gender and Prohibition in Butte, Montana." *American Quarterly* 46 (June 1994): 174–194.

Neary, Timothy. "Black Belt Catholic Space: African-American Parishes in Interwar Chicago." *U.S. Catholic Historian* 18 (Fall 2000): 76–91.

Nelson, Megan Kate. "The Landscape of Disease: Swamps and Medical Discourse in the American Southeast, 1800–1880." *Mississippi Quarterly* 55 (Fall 2002): 535–567.

Newman, Mark. "Desegregation in the Catholic Diocese of Richmond, 1945–1973." *Virginia Magazine of History and Biography* 117 (2009): 356–387.

Nickerson, Michelle, and Darren Dochuk, eds. *Sunbelt Rising: The Politics of Space, Race, Place, and Region.* Philadelphia: University of Pennsylvania Press, 2011.

Noll, Steven, and David Tegeder. *Ditch of Dreams: The Cross Florida Barge Canal and the Struggle for Florida's Future.* Gainesville: University Press of Florida, 2009.

Nuwer, Deanne Stephens. "'The Biloxi Fishermen Are Killing the Goose That Laid the Golden Egg': The Seafood Strike of 1932." *Journal of Mississippi History* 66 (Winter 2004): 325–352.

Ownby, Ted. *Subduing Satan: Religion, Recreation, and Manhood in the Rural South, 1865–1920.* Chapel Hill: University of North Carolina Press, 1990.

Padgett, Charles. "'Without Hysteria or Unnecessary Disturbance': Desegregation at Spring Hill College, Mobile, Alabama, 1948–1954." *History of Education Quarterly* 41 (Summer 2001): 167–189.

Painter, Nell. *Exodusters: Black Migration to Kansas after Reconstruction.* New York: W. W. Norton, 1992.

Pang, Henry. "Miss America: An American Ideal, 1921–1969." *Journal of Popular Culture* 2 (March 1969): 687–696.

Patterson, Gordon. *The Mosquito Crusades: A History of the American Anti-Mosquito Movement.* New Brunswick, N.J.: Rutgers University Press, 2009.

Peck, Garrett. *The Prohibition Hangover: Alcohol in America from Demon Rum to Cult Cabernet.* New Brunswick, N.J.: Rutgers University Press, 2009.

Peiss, Kathy. *Cheap Amusements: Working Women and Leisure in Turn-of-the-Century New York.* Philadelphia: Temple University Press, 1986.

Pelt, Peggy. "Wainwright Shipyard: The Impact of a World War II War Industry on Panama City, Florida." PhD diss., Florida State University, 1994.

Peterson, Jon. "The City Beautiful Movement." *Journal of Urban History* 2 (August 1976): 415–435.

Petigny, Alan. "The Spread of Permissive Religion." *Canadian Review of American Studies* 39 (Winter 2009): 399–422.

Phelts, Marsha Dean. *An American Beach for African Americans.* Gainesville: University Press of Florida, 1997.

Pilkey, Orrin, and Katherine Dixon. *The Corps and the Shore.* Washington, D.C.: Island Press, 1996.

Pitman, Bambra. "Culture, Caste, and Conflict in New Orleans Catholicism: Archbishop Francis Janssens and the Color Line." *Louisiana History* 49 (September 2008): 423–462.

Poliakoff, Eli. "Charleston's Longshoreman: Organized Labor in the Anti-Union Palmetto State." *South Carolina Historical Magazine* 103 (July 2002): 247–264.

Powers, Madelon. *Faces along the Bar: Lore and Order in the Workingman's Saloon, 1870–1920.* Chicago: University of Chicago Press, 1998.

Preston, Howard. *Dirt Roads to Dixie: Accessibility and Modernization in the South, 1885–1935.* Knoxville: University of Tennessee Press, 1991.

Priest, Tyler. "Extraction not Creation: The History of Offshore Petroleum in the Gulf of Mexico." *Enterprise and Society* 8 (June 2007): 227–267.

Pruett, Katherine, and John Fair. "Promoting a New South: Immigration, Racism, and 'Alabama on Wheels.'" *Agricultural History* 66 (Winter 1992): 19–41.

Rabinowitz, Howard. *Race Relations in the Urban South, 1865–1890.* Urbana: University of Illinois Press, 1978, 1980.

Rathje, William, and Cullen Murphy. *Rubbish: The Archeology of Garbage.* New York: Harper Collins, 1992.

Raucher, Alan. "Sunday Business and the Decline of Sunday Closing Laws: A Historical Overview." *Journal of Church and State* 36 (Winter 1994): 13–34.

Reiser, Andrew. *The Chautauqua Movement: Protestants, Progressives, and the Culture of Modern Liberalism, 1874–1920.* New York: Columbia University Press, 2003.

Renda, Mary. *Taking Haiti: Military Occupation and the Culture of U.S. Imperialism, 1915–1940.* Chapel Hill: University of North Carolina Press, 2001.

Revels, Tracy. *Sunshine Paradise: A History of Florida Tourism.* Gainesville: University Press of Florida, 2011.

Ribuffo, Leo. "Family Policy Past as Prologue: Jimmy Carter, the White House Conference on Families, and the Mobilization of the New Christian Right." *Review of Policy Research* 23 (March 2006): 311–337.

Rice, Bradley Robert. *Progressive Cities: The Commission Government Movement in America, 1901–1920.* Austin: University of Texas Press, 1977.

Richter, Amy. *Home on the Rails: Women, the Railroad, and the Rise of Public Domesticity.* Chapel Hill: University of North Carolina Press, 2005.

Roberts, Kathleen Blain. "Pretty Women: Female Beauty in the Jim Crow South." PhD diss., University of North Carolina, 2005.

Rorabaugh, W. J. *The Alcoholic Republic: An American Tradition.* New York: Oxford University Press, 1979.

Rose, Chanelle. "Neither Southern nor Northern: Miami, Florida, and the Black

Freedom Struggle in America's Tourist Paradise, 1896–1968." PhD diss., University of Miami, 2007.

Rose, Kenneth. *American Women and the Repeal of Prohibition*. New York: New York University Press, 1996.

Rove, Anne. *The Idea of Florida in the American Literary Imagination*. Baton Rouge: Louisiana State University Press, 1986.

Rucker, Brian. "Satsumaland! A History of Citrus Culture in West Florida." *Gulf Coast Historical Review* 12 (Fall 1996): 60–77.

Rugh, Susan Sessions. *Are We There Yet? The Golden Age of American Family Vacations*. Lawrence: University Press of Kansas, 2008.

Rushing, Wanda. *Memphis and the Paradox of Place: Globalization in the American South*. Chapel Hill: University of North Carolina Press, 2009.

Sanders, Randy. "Delivering Demon Rum: Prohibition Era Rumrunning in the Gulf of Mexico." *Gulf Coast Historical Review* 12 (Fall 1996): 92–113.

Scarpaci, Jean Ann. "Immigrants in the New South: Italians in Louisiana's Sugar Parishes, 1880–1910." *Labor History* 16 (Spring 1975): 163–183.

Schaap, James. "The Growth of the Native American Gaming Industry: What Has the Past Provided and What Does the Future Hold?" *American Indian Quarterly* 34 (Summer 2010): 365–389.

Schulman, Bruce. *From Cotton Belt to Sunbelt: Federal Policy, Economic Development, and the Transformation of the South, 1938–1980*. New York: Oxford University Press, 1991.

Sculle, Keith. *Fast Food: Roadside Restaurants in the Automobile Age*. Baltimore, Md.: John Hopkins University Press, 1999.

Scott, John. "Yellow Fever Strikes Bay St. Louis: The Epidemic of 1897." *Journal of Mississippi History* 63 (June 2001): 119–128.

Scott, Rebecca. *Degrees of Freedom: Louisiana and Cuba after Slavery*. Cambridge, Mass.: Harvard University Press, 2005.

Sears, John. *Sacred Places: American Tourist Attractions in the Nineteenth Century*. New York: Oxford University Press, 1989.

Seiler, Cotton. *Republic of Drivers: A Cultural History of Automobility in America*. Chicago: University of Chicago Press, 2008.

Settje, David. *Faith and War: How Christians Debated the Cold and Vietnam Wars*. New York: New York University Press, 2011.

Shaffer, Marguerite. "On the Environmental Nude." *Environmental History* 13 (January 2008): 126–139.

Shebby, Lee. "Travelling the Sunshine State: The Growth of Tourism in South Dakota, 1914–1939." *South Dakota History* 19 (Summer 1989): 194–223.

Shermer, Elizabeth Tandy. *Sunbelt Capitalism: Phoenix and the Transformation of American Politics*. Philadelphia: University of Pennsylvania Press, 2013.

Short, Joanna. "Confederate Veteran Pensions, Occupation, and Men's Retirement in the New South." *Social Science History* 30 (Spring 2006): 75–101.

Shulman, Bruce. *From Cotton Belt to Sunbelt: Federal Policy, Economic Development, and the Transformation of the South, 1938–1980*. New York: Oxford University Press, 1991.

Sides, Josh. *Erotic City: Sexual Revolutions and the Making of Modern San Francisco.* New York: Oxford University Press, 2009.

Simon, Bryant. *Boardwalk of Dreams: Atlantic City and the Fate of Urban America.* New York: Oxford University Press, 2004.

Smith, Douglas. "Into the Political Thicket: Reapportionment and the Rise of Suburban Power." In *The Myth of Southern Exceptionalism*, edited by Matthew Lassiter and Joseph Crespino, 263–285. New York: Oxford University Press, 2010.

Smith, Mark. *Camille, 1969: Histories of a Hurricane.* Athens: University of Georgia Press, 2011.

Smith, Ryan. *Gothic Arches, Latin Crosses: Anti-Catholicism and American Church Designs in the Nineteenth Century.* Chapel Hill: University of North Carolina, 2006.

Souther, Jonathan M. "Twixt Ocean and Pines: The Seaside Resort at Virginia Beach." MA thesis, University of Richmond, 1996.

Spears, Jennifer. *Race, Sex, and Social Order in Early New Orleans.* Baltimore, Md.: John Hopkins University Press, 2009.

Stanonis, Anthony. *Creating the Big Easy: New Orleans and the Emergence of Modern Tourism, 1918–1945.* Athens: University of Georgia Press, 2006.

———, ed. *Dixie Emporium: Tourism, Foodways, and Consumer Culture in the American South.* Athens: University of Georgia Press, 2008.

Starnes, Richard. "Creating a 'Variety Vacationland': Tourism Development in North Carolina, 1930–1990." In *Southern Journeys: Tourism, History, and Culture in the Modern South*, edited by Richard Starnes, 138–153. Tuscaloosa: University of Alabama Press, 2003.

———. *Creating the Land of the Sky: Tourism and Society in Western North Carolina.* Tuscaloosa: University of Alabama Press, 2005.

———, ed. *Southern Journeys: Tourism, History, and Culture in the Modern South.* Tuscaloosa: University of Alabama Press, 2003.

Stathakis, Paula Maria. "Almost White: Greek and Lebanese-Syrian Immigrants in North and South Carolina, 1900–1940." PhD diss., University of South Carolina, 1996.

Stillman, Clara G. "Florida: The Desert and the Rose." In *These United States: Portraits of America from the 1920s*, edited by Daniel H. Borus, 87–93. Ithaca, N.Y.: Cornell University Press, 1992.

Stokes, Barbara. *Myrtle Beach: A History, 1900–1980.* Columbia: University of South Carolina Press, 2007.

Szczygiel, Bonj. "'City Beautiful' Revisited." *Journal of Urban History* 29 (January 2003): 107–133.

Szymanski, Ann-Marie. "Beyond Parochialism: Southern Progressivism, Prohibition, and State-Building." *Journal of Southern History* 69 (February 2003): 107–136.

Thomas, Mary Martha. *Riveting and Rationing in Dixie: Alabama Women and the Second World War.* Tuscaloosa: University of Alabama Press, 2002.

Turner, Elizabeth Hayes. *Women, Culture, and Community: Religion and Reform in Galveston, 1880–1920.* New York: Oxford University Press, 1997.

Turner, Patricia. *Ceramic Uncles and Celluloid Mammies: Black Images and Their Influence on Culture.* Charlottesville: University of Virginia Press, 2002.

Tuttle, William. *Race Riot: Chicago in the Red Summer of 1919*. Urbana: University of Illinois Press, 1970, 1996.

Wallenstein, Peter. *Blue Laws and Black Codes: Conflict, Courts, and Change in Twentieth-Century Virginia*. Charlottesville: University of Virginia Press, 2004.

Ward, Jason Morgan. "'No Jap Crow': Japanese Americans Encounter the World War II South." *Journal of Southern History* 73 (February 2007): 75–104.

Warner, Margaret. "Hunting the Yellow Fever Germ: The Principle and Practice of Etiological Proof in Late Nineteenth-Century America." *Bulletin of History of Medicine* 59 (Fall 1985): 361–382.

Watson, Elwood, and Darcy Martin. "The Miss America Pageant: Pluralism, Femininity, and Cinderella All in One." *Journal of Popular Culture* 34 (2000): 105–126.

Watt, David Harrington. "The Private Hopes of American Fundamentalists and Evangelicals, 1925–1975." *Religion and American Culture* 1 (Summer 1991): 155–175.

Weeks, Jim. *Gettysburg: Memory, Market, and an American Shrine*. Princeton, N.J.: Princeton University Press, 2003.

Weitz, Seth. "Bourbon, Pork Chops, and Red Peppers: Political Immortality in Florida, 1945–1968." PhD diss., Florida State University, 2007.

Wilson, Anthony. *Shadow and Shelter: The Swamp in Southern Culture*. Jackson: University Press of Mississippi, 2006.

Wilson, William. *The City Beautiful Movement*. Baltimore, Md.: Johns Hopkins University Press, 1994.

Wiltse, Jeff. *Contested Waters: A Social History of Swimming Pools in America*. Chapel Hill: University of North Carolina Press, 2007.

Wiser, Vivian. "Weather, USDA, and the Farmer." *Agricultural History* 63 (Spring 1989): 51–61.

Wolcott, Victoria. *Race, Riots, and Roller Coasters: The Struggle over Segregated Recreation in America*. Philadelphia: University of Pennsylvania Press, 2012.

———. "Recreation and Race in the Postwar City: Buffalo's 1956 Crystal Beach Riot." *Journal of American History* 93 (June 2006): 63–90.

Wood, Peter. *Black Majority: Negroes in Colonial South Carolina from 1670 through the Stono Rebellion*. New York: Alfred Knopf, 1974.

Woodward, C. Vann. *Origins of the New South, 1877–1913*. Baton Rouge: Louisiana State University Press, 1951, 1971.

Wright, Gavin. *Old South, New South: Revolutions in the Southern Economy since the Civil War*. Baton Rouge: Louisiana State University Press, 1986, 1996.

Yanner, Keith, and Steven Ybarrola. "'He Didn't Have No Cross': Tombs and Graves as Racial Boundary Tactics on a Louisiana Barrier." *Oral History Review* 30 (Summer-Fall 2003): 1–28.

Yuhl, Stephanie. *A Golden Haze of Memory: The Making of Historic Charleston*. Chapel Hill: University of North Carolina Press, 2005.

Zaretsky, Natasha. *No Direction Home: The American Family and the Fear of National Decline, 1968–1980*. Chapel Hill: University of North Carolina Press, 2007.

Zebrowski, Ernest, and Judith Howard. *Category 5: The Story of Camille*. Ann Arbor: University of Michigan Press, 2005.

INDEX

Clough, George Roy, 201, 202, 203
Clower, Olive, 34
Coad, George, 181, 194
Coastal Barrier Resource Act (1982), 75
Coastal Carolina University, 55
Coastal Engineering Research Center, 75
Coast Alliance, 93
Coastal Zone Management Act (1972), 75
Coastweek, 93
cocaine, 214
cockfighting, 193
Cocks, Catherine, 118
Cole, Edgar, 193
Cole, Nat King, 138
Cole, Richard, 175, 176
Coleman, James, 187
Coleman, Robert, 210
Collie, Sue, 190
Collins, Benjamin, 13
Colvin, Alton, 79
Colwell, Margret, 213
Comfort, R. H., 186
commercial fishing, 102
commercialism, 73
Community Relations Council (Myrtle Beach, S.C.), 113
Compton, Carl, 149
Conches, 103
Conder, John, 32
Cone, Fred, 194
Coney Island (N.Y.), 3, 76
"Confederacy, The" (Virginia Beach, Va., drama), 37
Connie (hurricane), 84
Connolly, Nathan D. B., 10, 96, 216
construction booms, 34, 75, 93, 143
Continental Trailways, 56
convention centers, 24, 39–40
conventions, 34–35, 39–40, 88, 103, 130, 134, 136
Conway and Seashore Railroad, 14
Cook, Claire, 46
Cook, Tom, 79
Cooke, Alistair, 162

Coolman, Karen, 152
corruption, 106, 117, 198, 200; police, 137, 215–16; politics, 178, 180, 184, 189, 204; tourism, 16, 178, 202
Costantini, Anthony, 65
Cotton Carnival (Galveston, Tex.), 11
cotton industry, 12–13, 17, 23, 33, 97
Council of Garden Clubs of Princess Anne County and Virginia Beach, 87
Couric, Gertha, 103
Cox, S. D., 32
Creole Coast, 97
Creoles, 98–99, 100, 128
Crews, A. B., 24
crime rates, 184, 206
Cross Florida Barge Canal, 21
Crown Theatre (Biloxi, Miss.), 158
Cuba, 58, 102
Cucinitti, Lonnie, 213
cultural conservatism, 116, 141, 147, 152, 177, 183
Culverhouse, Sollie, 185
Cummings, John, 84

Daffin, Jimmy, 41
Daffin, M. J. "Doc," 136, 137, 138, 185–86
Damon, David, 90
Daniels, Rufus, 136
Darby, Cooper, 12, 184
Darby, William, 171
Darley, Mike, 49
Darsey, Barbara, 100
Davis, Clayton, 201
Davis, Hortense, 72
Davis, Jefferson, 27, 37
Davis, Varina, 60, 61
Dawson, Sam, 22
Day, Daniel, 43
Daytona Beach, Fla., 14, 141, 211
Daytona Normal and Industrial College (Bethune-Cookman College), 142
debt peonage, 97
Dedeaux, Curtis, 192, 197
DeFuniak Springs, Fla., 143, 144

Deliverance House (Myrtle Beach, S.C.),
147
Delta Drug Company, 120
Democratic Party, 128, 199
demographic changes, 26, 29, 182, 204–5,
222n1
dengue fever, 64
Destin, Fla., 54, 80
Diane (hurricane), 84
dichlorodiphenyltrichloroethane (DDT),
15, 66–67, 218
Disneyland, 40
Disney World, 40
Dixie Mafia, 187
Dixie Sherman Hotel (Panama City,
Fla.), 13
Dodds, George, 70
dogfighting, 187
dog racing, 193, 200
Dominican Republic, 58
Donehoo, C. A., 124
Dorsey, Jimmy, 78
Dosh, Robert "Bert," 71
Dos Passos, John, 48
Downing, Thomas, 90
Drinkwater, Edward, 14
drunk driving, 214, 215
Duhamel, Georges, 178
dunes, 34, 65, 80, 82
Dunnagan, Claude, 162
Durocher, Odette, 205

Eastern Airlines, 21
economic exploitation, 109, 113
Edge, Walter, 74
Edgewater Gulf Hotel (Biloxi, Miss.), 29,
35, 55, 125, 180
Edwards, James, 205
Edwards, John, 1, 2
Egerton, Richard, 39
Eglin Air Force Base (Fla.), 49, 50, 181
Eighteenth Amendment, 178, 179
Eight Flags (Miss.), 40
Eiseman, Meyer, 32

Eisenhower, Dwight D., 20
electric lights (municipal), 26, 28, 32, 35
Elliott, James, 170
Eloise (hurricane), 79, 80
Emrich, Elmer, 137
environmentalism, 67, 75, 93
Episcopalians, 145, 147
evacuations, 45, 59, 61, 76
Evans, Arthur, 29, 30
Evans, Orin, 62
Evans, Wilson, II, 102, 128, 129–30, 184
exotic dancing, 159–60, 162, 187

family values, 170–74, 213, 248n76. *See
also* cultural conservatism
Farlow, Allison, 42
farming, 14, 55, 110, 114, 129
Farnsworth, W. L., 84
Federal Highway Act (1921), 18
Federal Writers' Project, 103
Federation of Civic Leagues (New
Orleans, La.), 120, 123
fencing laws, 56, 230n111
Fernandina Beach, Fla., 20, 57, 59
films, 38, 119, 134, 137, 151, 155, 158–59,
172, 181
Fiorelli, Michael, 31
fire departments, 26, 35
Firth, J. Malcolm, 87
Fisher, Dorinda, 205
Flagg, Henry, 168
Flagler, Henry, 2, 10, 141
Flood Control Act (1936), 74
flood insurance, 75, 81
Florida, 1, 11, 13, 17, 21–22, 33; American
Beach, 129, 138; Daytona Beach, 14,
141, 211; DeFuniak Springs, 143, 144;
Destin, 54, 80; Fernandina Beach,
20, 57, 59; Fort Lauderdale, 75, 125,
209, 211; Fort Walton Beach, 49, 54,
80, 152–53, 157; hurricanes, 70, 85;
Jacksonville, 2, 3, 61–62, 97, 105, 136;
Long Beach, 28, 209; Miami, 27, 78, 84,
92, 134, 157; Panhandle, 20, 27, 56, 65;

Florida (*continued*)
  Pensacola Beach, 2, 3, 65, 97, 98, 100;
  Saint Petersburg, 22, 159; Seaside, 218,
  248n76; St. Augustine, 2, 97–100, 102,
  111, 125, 130, 133–34; Tampa, 10, 102,
  199; tourism economy, 22, 23, 31. *See
  also* alcohol sales: Florida; gambling:
  Florida; Panama City
Florida East Coast Railroad, 141
Florida Motel and Hotel Association, 134
Florida Peace Officers Association, 216
Florida State Board of Health, 62
Florida Supreme Court, 26, 198
Floyd, A. B., 206
Floyd, Blanche, 148
Ford, Norman, 54
foreign tourists, 51–52, 53
forest fires, 217
Fort Benning (Ga.), 188
Fort Lauderdale, Fla., 75, 125, 209, 211
Fort Morgan State Park (Ala.), 88
Fort Moultrie (S.C.), 1
Fortner, Henry, 82
Fort Story (Va.), 46, 47, 49
Fort Walton Beach, 49, 54, 80, 152–53, 157
Foster, June, 138
Fountain, Armand, 180
Freidel, Frank, 9
French Government Tourist Office, 164
Friedberg, Gerald, 135
Frontier City (Virginia Beach, Va.), 40
Frontierland (Panama City, Fla.), 144
Fynn, David, 215

Gable, Clark, 167
Galveston, Tex., 2, 8–11, 20, 22, 28; civil
  rights movement, 97–98, 100, 105,
  126–28, 136; hurricanes, 67–68, 69,
  70–71, 80, 87, 94; religion, 145, 148,
  149–50
Galveston Chamber of Commerce, 26, 39,
  66, 73, 189; civil rights movement, 125,
  129, 136; litter problem, 87–88, 89, 90
Galveston Ministerial Association, 201

Galveston Plan, 69
Galvez Hotel (Galveston, Tex.), 11, 35
Gamble, James, 142
gambling, 15–16, 137, 177–78, 188, 194,
  204–6; Florida, 185–86, 193–94,
  195–96, 197–200; Mississippi, 184, 196,
  197, 198, 205–6; South Carolina, 194,
  205; Texas, 195, 203, 207, 210; Virginia,
  185, 194, 196, 197, 200–201
gambling taxes, 193, 194, 197
Gardner, Charles, 77
Garner, Mark, 80, 108, 113, 134–35, 169
Garrick, Myrtle, 164
gasoline taxes, 44, 56, 71, 76, 79
Gatewood, William, 82
Gauker, James, 140, 162
Gay, Clarence, 85
Gayety Burlesk Theatre (Myrtle Beach,
  S.C.), 160
gay rights movement, 166, 173
Geigy Chemical Company, 66
gender roles, 171, 180
General Federation of Women's Clubs, 154
General Survey Act (1824), 74
Georgia, 5, 57, 109, 110, 136
Geraris, Gus, 104
Gibbons v. Ogden, 74
Gibson, Jurow, 187
Gideon, Clarence Earl, 203
Gideon v. Wainwright, 203
Gilbert, Earl, 200
Gilbert, Marie, 169
Gillich, Mike, 187
Golden Nugget Bingo Hall (Biloxi,
  Miss.), 205
Goldfield, David, 7, 8
golfing, 17, 31, 81, 86, 120, 148, 170, 175
Golloway, William, 89
Gonzales, Maria, 100
Goodman, Bill, 54
Goodrich, Floyd, 195
Goodwyn, Larry, 134
Gore, Lynnie, 80
Gould, Virginia, 98

Gournas, Peter, 104
Grace, Sue, 168
Grady, Henry, 6–7
Graham, Billy, 149
Graham, Bob, 82
Grant, Madison, 58, 119
Graves, Bibb, 145
Gray, Barney, 83
Grayson, George, 18
Great Depression, 33, 34, 64
Greater Myrtle Beach Chamber of
    Commerce, 182, 189
Great Society, 81, 113
Green, Marila, 76
Green, Paul, 111, 194
Greystone Hotel (Montgomery, Ala.), 103
Griffin, Marvin, 109
Griffitts, Thomas, 64
Grover, Les, 212
Grover, Walter, 142
Gualtieri, Sarah, 104
Guice, Daniel, 132
Guiteras, Juan, 59
Gulf and Ship Island Railroad, 12, 63
Gulf Coast Community College, 55, 164
Gulf Coast Development Company, 13
Gulf Coast Military Academy, 54
Gulf Islands National Seashore, 36
Gulf Park College, 54, 55, 207
Gulfport Chamber of Commerce, 38
Gulfport Post of the American Legion, 36
Gymer, George, 195

Haiti, 58
Hansen, Devon, 118
Hardie and Ellis Realty Company, 35
Hardy, James Chappel, 54
Hardy, William Henry, 12
Hare, Edward, 175
Harley Davidson Biker Rally (Myrtle
    Beach, S.C.), 37
Harlow, Jean, 119
Harris, Brantly, 127
Harris, John, 85

Harrison, Albertis, 38, 39
Harrison, Benjamin, 14
Harrison, Byron "Pat," 64
Harrison County Advertising Advisory
    Commission (Miss.), 30
Harrison County Civic Action
    Committee (Miss.), 131
Harry Fitzpatrick and Company, 32
Hart, Albert, 117
Hart, Alicia, 120, 163
Harvey, David, 16
Hatcher, L. E., 195
Hawaii, 58
Hayes, Eleonora, 106
Haynes, Kenneth, 173
Hays, Will, 35
Hazel (hurricane), 80, 81, 84
Helgren, Richard, 40
heroin, 214
hippies, 166, 214
Hodges, Charles, 205
Hodges, Mark, 93, 94
Hogg, John, 214
Holland, E. P., 63
Holmes, Marion, 28
Hooten, James, 185, 186
Hoover, Calvin, 7
Horry County School Board (S.C.), 136
horse racing, 193, 197
horses, 83
hospitality, 3–4, 38, 62, 157
Hotel and Motel Industry of Palm Beach
    County, 28
Hotel Dixie-Sherman (Panama City,
    Fla.), 112
Hotel Peabody (Memphis, Tenn.), 103
hotel tax, 41, 86
Hotel Warner (Virginia Beach, Va.), 48
Houston, Tex., 90, 92, 126
Howard, Harry, 59
Howell, Henry, 190
Hubbell, William, 118, 184, 196
Hucks, Collin, 46
Hudson, Larry, 105

25, 129, 138; civil rights movement, 114, 134–36; growth, 7, 13–14, 19–20, 24–26; Harlem community, 113, 114; hurricanes, 81, 83–84, 85; litter problem, 88, 89; off-season, 28, 45; Pavilion, 150; religion, 145, 147, 148–49, 150; timber industry, 13, 14

Myrtle Beach Air Force Base, 24, 48

Myrtle Beach Chamber of Commerce, 22, 25, 31, 38

Myrtle Beach City Council, 85

Myrtle Beach Farms Company, 14

Myrtle Beach High School, 214

Myrtle Beach Municipal Airport, 48

Myrtle Beach Police Department, 214

Myrtle Beach Sales Company, 32

Myrtle Beach State Park, 51, 135

Nall, A. H., 88, 188

Natchez, Miss., 8, 9, 37

Nathan, David, 203

National Academy of Sciences, 90

National Association for the Advancement of Colored People (NAACP), 121, 131, 132, 133–35, 137–38

National Association of State Park Directors, 88

National Guard, 76, 192

National Hotel (Galveston, Tex.), 38

National Interstate and Defense Highways Act (1956), 20

National Organization for Women, 152, 153

National Weather Service, 81, 83–84

Native Americans, 206

Nelms, Julia, 53

Nesbitt, Bob, 128

Nesterowicz, Stefan, 101

Newcomb College, 209

New Deal, 20, 64

New Jersey, 62, 65, 78

Newman, Isaiah DeQuincey, 135

New Orleans, La., 8, 12, 19–20, 27, 36, 59–60, 98, 102, 207; civil rights movement, 105, 120–24; hurricanes, 70, 71, 76; Little Woods/Lincoln Beach, 121, 123, 129, 138; Pontchartrain Beach, 138, 139; Seabrook Beach, 120–21, 123; yellow fever outbreak, 62, 64

New Orleans and Northeastern Railroad, 12

Newport News, Va., 92, 104

Newton, Virgil "Red," 171

Niagara Falls (N.Y.), 95

Nineteenth Amendment, 207

Nix, Catherine, 165

Nixon, Richard M., 21, 81

Noegel, Pearl, 5

Norfolk, Va., 14, 15, 97, 105, 111

Norfolk and Virginia Beach Railroad and Improvement Company, 14

Norfolk Naval Base (Va.), 50

North Carolina, 3, 14, 21, 23, 74, 78, 84, 104, 134–35; alcohol sales, 182, 186, 191

North Myrtle Beach, S.C., 25, 212

Northwestern Life Insurance Company, 197

Norton, Bob, 169

nuclear waste, 90

nudism, 165–67, 168, 175

Oceana Naval Air Station (Va.), 47

Ocean Forest Hotel (Myrtle Beach, S.C.), 14, 35, 39, 103

Ocean Pines Motor Court (Myrtle Beach, S.C.), 124

Ocean Springs, Miss., 59, 71

O'Daniel, W. Lee, 195

oil industry, 75, 91–93

Okeechobee hurricane, 94

Oklahoma, 192

Old Dominion University, 54

Old Spanish Trail, 71

Oleander Festival (Galveston, Tex.), 37, 86

O'Neil, Paul, 166

Operation Friendly Hand (Myrtle Beach, S.C.), 113

Operation Surf (Miss.), 131
organized crime, 187–88, 199, 200
Our Mother of Sorrows (Biloxi, Miss.), 100
Owens, Lee, 96
Owens, Roscoe, 137, 185
oysters, 90, 101

Pace, Stephanie, 26, 46, 152, 209
Packer Corporation, 22
Pageant of Pulchritude (Galveston, Tex.), 156
Panama, 58
Panama Canal, 11, 12, 13, 20
Panama City, Fla., 6, 9, 35, 55; beach erosion, 79, 80, 82; civil rights movement, 136, 137–38; environmental issues, 80, 91; growth, 13, 25, 26, 94; military presence, 47, 49, 54, 105; religion, 145, 149, 150, 151; tourist economy, 21, 28, 30–31, 33, 40–43, 112, 144; vice, 185–87, 195–96, 200, 207, 209–13
Panama City Chamber of Commerce, 25, 30
Pan American World Airways, 51
Paris green, 66
Parker, Al, 196
Parker, James Moore (Mrs.), 132
parking lots, 8, 122
Parks, Marshall, 14
Pascagoula, Miss., 27, 71
Pass Christian, Miss., 27, 70–71, 72
paternalism, 127, 143
Patricia Manor (Myrtle Beach, S.C.), 124
Patrick, Doris, 213
patriotism, 130, 149, 211
Patterson, Albert, 188
pavilions, 11, 35, 150
Peck, John Herbert, 193
Pensacola and Atlantic Railroad, 143
pensions, 3, 54, 179
Perrine, John, 28
Perry, John, 13

Petticoat Junction (Panama City, Fla.), 40
Phenix City, Ala., 187, 188, 201
philanthropy, 142, 143
Philippines, 58
Phillips, Elizabeth, 114
Phillips, Kevin, 7, 221n1
Phillips, Ruby, 78
picketing, 137
Piedmont Airlines, 21
piers, 35–36, 51, 79, 126–28, 168
Pilkey, Orrin, 9
Pindell, Terry, 19
Pirate Band, 45
Pirateland Amusement Park (Myrtle Beach, S.C.), 40, 144, 172
Pitts, Lavelle, 210
Plant, Henry, 2, 10
plantations, 8, 99, 107, 110–12, 142, 207
Playland Park (Miss.), 160
Playtown, U. S. A. (Virginia Beach, Va.), 38
Pleasure Pier (Galveston, Tex.), 36, 126–28, 151, 168
Plessy, Homer, 98
Poe, Edgar Allan, 1
Points, Betty Lou, 51
police departments, 15, 26, 35, 45, 73, 153
polio, 90
pollution, 15, 53, 75, 89, 91, 93
Ponce de Leon Hotel (Saint Augustine, Fla.), 2, 35
Pontchartrain, Lake, 12
Pork Chop Gang, 26
Port Arthur, Tex., 127
poverty, 3, 5, 16, 23, 98, 99
Prendergast, Janice, 43
Presbyterians, 145, 147, 174
Price, Joseph, 59
Priest, Tyler, 92
Princess Anne Hotel (Virginia Beach, Va.), 14, 15
Prine, Ila, 115
Progressive Era, 2
Prohibition, 180, 184, 187, 192, 197

Roudenbush, Jake, 79, 80
Royall, Anne, 116
Ruddick, Maurice, 109
Rugh, Susan Sessions, 144
Rumble, Harry, 201
Ryland, Charley, 181

Saint Louis Cathedral (New Orleans, La.), 70
Saint Louis Hotel (New Orleans, La.), 70
Saint Petersburg, Fla., 22, 159
sales taxes, 24, 41, 44, 97, 133, 215
Salt Marsh Mosquito Survey of the South Atlantic and Gulf States, 64
Sandbox (Virginia Beach, Va.), 213
Sand Festival (Virginia Beach, Va.), 77, 173
Sandusky, Tommy, 27
sanitariums, 3
sanitation, 2, 35, 63
Sawada, Kosaku, 115
Scarborough, Fred, 188
Scarborough, Oliver, 188
Schweid, Richard, 4
Scott, Samuel, 53
scrapbooks, 10
Scruggs, Cyrus, 198
Seacoast Telephone Company, 171
seafood industry, 101
Sea Horse Inn (Virginia Beach, Va.), 112
sea oats, 82
Searight, Loyce, 100
Sea Shore Camp Ground, 95
Sea Side Inn (Myrtle Beach, S.C.), 14
Sea Side Inn (New Orleans, La.), 121
Seawall Amusement Company (Galveston, Tex.), 11
seawalls, 69–73, 76, 78–79, 85, 120, 218
segregation/desegregation, 7, 81, 96, 99, 100
Sehrt, Clem, 192
Sennett, Mack, 158
Sennett's Bathing Beauties, 158
Senyk, Joan, 152, 153

service economies, 16
sewage systems, 26, 28, 35, 61, 73, 89–90, 113–14
sexuality: community standards, 155, 162, 164, 174, 247n66; marketing, 15, 159, 177; tourism, 140, 150–52, 168, 171–72
Seymour, Sherry, 59, 61
Shackelford, Gail, 210, 211
sharecropping, 97, 101, 107, 129, 143
Shea, John, 217
Shepard, Alan, 38, 40
Sherman, Walter Colquitt, 13
Shermer, Elizabeth Tandy, 8
Shields, Harmon, 79
shipbuilding industry, 13
Ship Island (Miss.), 36, 167–68
sickle cell anemia, 58
Sierra Club, 75, 93
Simpson, Alma Simmang, 68, 69, 118, 154
Simpson, C. I., 63
Simpson, Robert, 77
Sims, Dale, 151
Singleton, Fred, 208
sit-ins, 133, 137
Skrmetta, Pete, 36
Skyline Drive, 48
slavery, 1, 57, 58, 97, 103
Slow Toke Saloon (Panama City, Fla.), 213
Smith, Al, 180
Smith, Doug, 166
Smith, Helen, 169
Smith, Mark, 81
Smoak, W. W., 107, 170
smuggling, 179, 186, 192, 198
Society for American Foresters, 200
Sollee, W. C. B., 61
South Carolina, 1, 5, 20, 88, 170; Charleston, 8, 36, 97, 116, 136; gambling, 194, 205; immigrants, 104, 107; North Myrtle Beach, 25, 212; Surfside Beach, 63, 174; tourism economy, 23, 42. See also alcohol sales: South Carolina

POLITICS AND CULTURE IN THE TWENTIETH-CENTURY SOUTH

A Common Thread: Labor, Politics, and Capital Mobility in the Textile Industry
by Beth English

"Everybody Was Black Down There": Race and Industrial Change in the Alabama Coalfields
by Robert H. Woodrum

Race, Reason, and Massive Resistance: The Diary of David J. Mays, 1954–1959
edited by James R. Sweeney

The Unemployed People's Movement: Leftists, Liberals, and Labor in Georgia, 1929–1941
by James J. Lorence

Liberalism, Black Power, and the Making of American Politics, 1965–1980
by Devin Fergus

Guten Tag, Y'all: Globalization and the South Carolina Piedmont, 1950–2000
by Marko Maunula

The Culture of Property: Race, Class, and Housing Landscapes in Atlanta, 1880–1950
by LeeAnn Lands

Marching in Step: Masculinity, Citizenship, and The Citadel in Post–World War II America
by Alexander Macaulay

Rabble Rousers: The American Far Right in the Civil Rights Era
by Clive Webb

Who Gets a Childhood: Race and Juvenile Justice in Twentieth-Century Texas
by William S. Bush

Alabama Getaway: The Political Imaginary and the Heart of Dixie
by Allen Tullos

The Problem South: Region, Empire, and the New Liberal State, 1880–1930
by Natalie J. Ring

Cold War Dixie: Militarization and Modernization in the American South
by Kari Frederickson

Faith in Bikinis: Politics and Leisure in the Coastal South since the Civil War
by Anthony J. Stanonis